The Paradox of Tar Heel Politics

The Paradox of

The Personalities, Elections, and Events That Shaped Modern North Carolina **ROB CHRISTENSEN**

Tar Heel Politics

THE UNIVERSITY OF NORTH CAROLINA PRESS Chapel Hill

This book was published with the assistance of the Thornton H. Brooks Fund of the University of North Carolina Press.

Set in Arnhem, The Sans, and Poplar types
By Tseng Information Systems, Inc.
Manufactured in the United States of America

The paper in this book meets the guidelines for permanence and durability of the Committee on Production Guidelines for Book Longevity of the Council on Library Resources.

Library of Congress Cataloging-in-Publication Data
Christensen, Rob.
The paradox of Tar Heel politics : the personalities, elections, and events that shaped modern North Carolina / Rob Christensen.
    p. cm.
Includes bibliographical references and index.
ISBN 978-0-8078-3189-2 (cloth : alk. paper)
1. North Carolina—Politics and government—1865–1950. 2. North Carolina—Politics and government—1951– 3. Political culture—North Carolina. I. Title.
F260.C57 2008
975.6'043—dc22   2007042126

cloth   12 11 10 09 08   5 4 3 2 1

For Margot

Contents

Illustrations

Acknowledgments

You don't spend nearly a decade working on a book without a lot of help. I would like to thank the editors at the *News and Observer* for their encouragement and support in general; I am particularly grateful to Melanie Sill for providing me the time to research the book. David Perry, the veteran editor-in-chief of UNC Press, had the patience to help a new author shape his book. The advice and encouragement of Michael Weisel, a budding historian, was invaluable at a time when I was struggling. The critical reading by the wise and all-knowing John Sanders has improved my manuscript in countless ways, although he, of course, is in no way responsible for the book's shortcomings or errors.

I am indebted to the giants of southern political writing, particularly C. Vann Woodward, George B. Tindall, and V. O. Key. I also relied heavily on the work of such talented contemporary historians as Jeffrey Crow, Julian Pleasants, Tim Tyson, and David Cecelski.

North Carolina politics have been charted by an extraordinary group of journalists, and I have stolen liberally from them, including W. J. Cash, Gerald Johnson, Jonathan Daniels, William Snider, Ernest Furgurson, Tom Wicker, Ferrel Guillory, Claude Sitton, Howard Covington, Marion Ellis, and my colleague John Drescher, to name just a few.

The staffs of the Wilson Library at UNC–Chapel Hill, the Perkins Library at Duke, the D. H. Hill Library at N.C. State, and the Library of Congress in Washington, D.C., were always helpful. I would particularly like to thank Bob Anthony, the curator of the North Carolina Collection. A special thanks also should go to the crack research staff at the *News and Observer*.

Lastly, I would especially like to thank my wife Margot, who was a graceful history widow for nearly a decade. I could not possibly have written this book without her encouragement and support.

The Paradox of Tar Heel Politics

*History is past politics and
politics is present history.*
—*Sir John Seeley*

Introduction

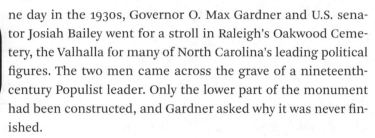

ne day in the 1930s, Governor O. Max Gardner and U.S. senator Josiah Bailey went for a stroll in Raleigh's Oakwood Ceme-
tery, the Valhalla for many of North Carolina's leading political
figures. The two men came across the grave of a nineteenth-
century Populist leader. Only the lower part of the monument
had been constructed, and Gardner asked why it was never finished.

"Because the money gave out," Bailey replied. "That is the
way life is. One minute a man's name is on every tongue and all
are anxious to do him honor, and then suddenly he is cut down.
At first people praise his memory and then in a little while he is
forgotten."

"That," Gardner said, "is what the erosion of time often does
to a man's fame."

Gardner and Bailey are barely remembered today, even
though they helped shape North Carolina politics in the twentieth century.

Gardner, a high-living textile tycoon, is considered the architect of modern state government and a central figure in the
formation of the state's sensibility regarding politics. Gardner
was an advocate of business progressivism, the animating force
in twentieth-century Tar Heel politics. Politics was largely controlled by big business. The state lit the cigars for corporate executives but was hostile to organized labor; it generously spent
money on roads and universities but was stingy when it came
to the poor. State leaders sought a measure of fairness toward
its black citizens, as long as it didn't threaten the system of segregation. It was a business progressivism that was in tune with
North Carolina's growing urban middle class of lawyers, power-
company executives, bankers, textile-plant owners, newspaper
publishers and editors, and others.

Bailey, a former editor of the *Biblical Recorder*, represented a
more unvarnished brand of conservatism that grew out of the

tobacco and cotton fields, the hard pews of fundamentalist churches, and what one astute observer called "a dark and unfathomable abyss of race feeling." Bailey's brand of conservatism called for less government, the enforcement of traditional values of morality, and a strict racial line.

But conservatives and probusiness moderates such as Bailey and Gardner have never been able to rule the state unchallenged. The unfinished Oakwood grave marker the two men mused over belonged to Leonidas Polk, a national Populist leader who set in motion the most powerful pitchfork uprising in the South in the 1890s—one that sent the conservatives and their business allies packing.

North Carolina has always had a strain of cornbread populism—an unwillingness to give Wall Street, the big banks, or the big insurance companies free rein. So North Carolina elected populists such as Marion Butler, Robert Reynolds, and John Edwards to the U.S. Senate and they put Daniel Russell and Kerr Scott in the governor's mansion.

The strains of business progressivism, conservatism, and populism are often comingled, so that thousands of people voted for both a conservative such as Senator Jesse Helms and a business progressive such as Governor Jim Hunt. Many people's politics don't fit into nice little pigeonholes.

National observers are often confounded by North Carolina's puzzling politics. What kind of state is North Carolina? Was it the state that repeatedly sent Jesse Helms, Josiah Bailey, Sam Ervin, and a parade of other conservatives to Washington, or was it a state that elected a stream of center-left Democrats such as Jim Hunt, John Edwards, and Terry Sanford? North Carolina is, of course, both states, which is why it has been described as a political paradox. It is a state shaped by both fundamentalist churches and great universities, by poor yeomen farmers and industrialists, by an urge to move into the national mainstream and a reverence for the traditions, both good and bad, of the Old South.

Long before it became fashionable to talk about America's political polarization, North Carolina was a boiling political cauldron. Throughout the twentieth century, the state frequently oscillated between its progressive impulses and its broad conservative streak, sometimes swinging back and forth in ugly, violent spasms.

At its core, North Carolina, like the rest of the South, is conservative leaning. You don't have to climb very far up most family trees to find a small farmer—surely the most individualistic and self-reliant of souls. The state is, as Senator Elizabeth Dole recently noted, the buckle of the Bible Belt, and if one wants to rise in higher office, one must take North Carolinians' deep religiosity into account. A state bristling with so many military bases, and one where hunting is still a young man's rite of passage, is bound to respect the uniform. Old attitudes toward race still have a powerful echo.

But all that is true of most of the South. What sets North Carolina apart is its progressive streak. The state's voters are willing to elect liberals who they think will look after the average man—as long as he does not transgress southern racial customs.

North Carolina led the great southern educational revival in the early twentieth century and was often in the forefront of education initiatives in later years. The state pushed through so many reforms and raised so many taxes that it was nicknamed the "Wisconsin of the South" in the 1920s. In 1950 North Carolina was briefly represented in the Senate by the South's leading liberal, Frank Porter Graham. In the early 1960s, while Alabama's George Wallace was standing in the schoolhouse door, North Carolina's Terry Sanford was quietly setting the stage for racial integration. North Carolina was such a leader in the South in higher education, the arts, and economic development that it was labeled the "Dixie Dynamo" in the 1960s.

On the question of race, North Carolina had a southern-rim-state mentality. North Carolina was the only state in the country to elect an African American to Congress between 1898 and 1928. By midcentury, North Carolina was regarded as the least repressive state in the South for blacks. The national sit-in movement began in North Carolina, in part because the state had so many historically black colleges. In the 1990s Harvey Gantt ran the most competitive Senate race of any African American in the South in the twentieth century, drawing more votes than President Bill Clinton in the state in 1996.

But there were also sharp limits to North Carolina's progressivism. The Populists of the 1890s were turned out of office in an orgy of intimidation, voter fraud, and violence. The Democrats maintained control through white supremacy that disfranchised black voters. The labor movement was crushed with bullets and billy clubs. Efforts to bring a liberal "New Deal" government to Raleigh were beaten back by powerful machine politics. The state produced some of the leading strategists of segregationist Dixie. In 1950 Frank Graham was defeated in a virulent race and red-baiting campaign. In the 1960s North Carolina had the largest Ku Klux Klan membership in the South. Jesse Helms headed what may have been the South's most powerful political machine since that of Louisiana governor Huey Long, helping give rise to the Reagan Revolution.

For these and other reasons, North Carolina has been home to some of the nation's roughest political range wars during the past century.

Various observers have attempted to describe North Carolina's politics. Midcentury political scientists or journalists such as V. O. Key or John Gunther portrayed North Carolina as a progressive garden in a reactionary cotton field. By the 1970s revisionism had set in, with political observers such as Merle Black, William Chafe, and Walter DeVries describing the state as a progressive paradox, arguing that the state's conservative instincts outweigh its national progressive reputation. A more recent generation of historians, such as Timothy Tyson, David Cecelski, and Glenda Gilmore, have focused on the latent racism and the untold stories of the struggles of African Americans. Paul Luebke has divided the state into modernists and traditionalists—those like Helms who are tied to conservative churches, tobacco, and long-held values, and modernizers such as Hunt who are connected with big industry and want an active government to nurture economic growth. All of these theories say something true about the state. The story of North Carolina's politics is nuanced, multilayered, and at times contradictory.

North Carolina history is sometimes presented as a soothing narrative. North Carolina is a politically moderate state, run by reasonable, business-oriented leaders that have worked together to help a poor state pull itself up by its bootstraps. North Carolina, so the narrative goes, has avoided the demagogues of other southern states, such as South Carolina's Cole Blease, Mississippi's Theodore Bilbo, and Georgia's Eugene Talmadge.

But the truth is far more complicated. North Carolina has taken center stage in the great political debates of the twentieth century—the place of black people in society, the role of organized labor, urban versus rural culture, class antagonisms, industrialism, the role of government in helping the disadvantaged, the national response to fascism and communism, women's rights, the role of religion in public life, racial quotas, homosexuality, and abortion, to name a few.

I have written about North Carolina politics for thirty-five years for the *Raleigh News and Observer*, the state capital newspaper, and at times I have felt deserving of extra combat pay. I witnessed a district Republican convention that turned into a brawl. I have been denounced by name by Jesse Helms in huge, sweet-smelling tobacco warehouses as an example of what is wrong with America. The state GOP convention once passed a resolution throwing out the *News and Observer*. As I was being led out, dozens of people stood on their chairs shaking their fists amid shouts of "Throw the bastard out!" As I left the hall, the presiding officer, Barry McCarty, thundered: "The cancer has been surgically removed." I once spent a day visiting country stores with Lieutenant Governor Jimmy Green, a mossback Conservative Democrat, who for his amusement would make me sweat while he chronicled my journalistic sins to groups of hard-looking men. But such mistreatment is child's play compared to what other North Carolinians have experienced over the years.

So, like Max Gardner and Josiah Bailey, let's wander through North Carolina's political graveyard to see what we can find.

Prologue

The modern era of North Carolina politics began on November 8, 1898, with an election so violent, raw, and corrupt that it could have been held in one of the tin-pot dictatorships of Latin America.

Republican governor Daniel Russell, a 300-pound aristocratic planter, barely survived a lynch mob when his train pulled into the southeastern North Carolina towns of Maxton and Hamlet. "Lynch him. Lynch the fat son of a bitch," voices from the mob cried as they rushed the train. North Carolina avoided what would have been one of the ugliest moments in American history only because the governor was hidden in a baggage compartment.[1]

A shaken Russell, age fifty-three, shortly thereafter contemplated resigning as governor. "The irritations incident to being a Republican and living in the South are getting too rank to be borne," Russell wrote to a friend.[2]

The election of 1898 was electioneering as war—a form of gun-barrel politics where politicians rode into town accompanied by hundreds of horsemen wearing red shirts and armed with Winchester rifles. It was an election that saw the government of North Carolina's largest city overthrown by a coup d'etat. The losers were not merely thrown out of office but threatened with a hangman's noose. There was such a breakdown of law and order that Republican leaders begged President William McKinley to send in federal troops—a generation after Reconstruction.

The 1898 election saw the white power structure—the Democratic Party, the business community, and the major newspapers—overthrow a biracial Populist coalition that briefly held power in the 1890s as a result of anger over big business's control of politics in Raleigh and Washington. The election would set the pattern for much of the twentieth century. It would cement Democratic control, disfranchise black voters, and consign the Republicans to a mainly regional party in the Mountains and foothills. It would also serve as the political proving ground for tactics that would be used repeatedly by conservative whites to hold power.

Life at Turn of the Century

At the turn of the century, North Carolina was a poor, rural state of 1.8 million people—1.2 million whites and 624,469 blacks. North Carolina had one foot in an earlier era—marked by the timeless rhythms of rural life, veneration of the Lost Cause, and a nineteenth-century view of race relations—and one foot in the New South of textile mills, electric streetlights, and go-getting boosterism.

Unlike neighboring Virginia and South Carolina, the state was not as dominated by a flourishing planter aristocracy. North Carolina may have had slaves, but its slave culture was not as pronounced as in the Deep South. Corn liquor drunk out of a jug, not mint juleps sipped from elegant silver cups, was customary. Small farmers, whose lives were not radically different from those of their grandparents, dominated the state. Among southern states, North Carolina was bested only by the Mississippi Delta and the Ozarks of Arkansas as the most rural place in the South.[3]

It was the muscle of men and mules, not machinery, that allowed farmers, many of them sharecroppers, to coax crops of cotton, tobacco, corn, sweet potatoes, soybeans, and peanuts out of the ground. Self-sufficient farm families made their own hominy grits, slaughtered their own meat, made their own lye soap, milked their own cows, churned their own butter, gathered their own eggs, preserved their own fruits and vegetables, and often made their own clothes. Life was hard and frequently isolated. Roads were primitive. Socializing was conducted at church picnics, funerals, hog killings, and corn shuckings. A trip to a nearby town was a special event. About one-third of the white farmers and two-thirds of the black farmers were sharecroppers who did not work their own land.

For many people, farm life was subsistence living. A study of 351 black and white farm families in Chatham County found pervasive, grinding poverty. Most tenants lived in unpainted frame houses at least thirty years old, many of which had large holes in the roof and floor. None had running water, and only eight houses had an outdoor privy. The children were taught in six old, weather-stained, one-teacher schools by teenage girls, none of whom had a college degree. North Carolina had the worst schools and the highest illiteracy rate in the South.[4]

Despite such backwardness, North Carolina was beginning to industrialize. So many cotton mills sprang up in the rolling Piedmont section in the middle of the state that North Carolina was being called the "Massachusetts of the South." By 1900 there were 177 textile mills in North Carolina—most located in small, company-owned mill towns. In the previous ten years, North Carolina had jumped from tenth to third in the nation in the number of cotton mills.[5] In Durham, James B. "Buck" Duke emerged as one of the country's great robber barons on his way toward dominating the world tobacco market with his American Tobacco Company.[6]

North Carolina had only six towns with more than 10,000 people, with Wilmington, the largest, boasting a population of 20,055 in 1900. In the towns, people enjoyed such modern conveniences as electric streetcars, telephones, and electric lights. It was an age when, for $20, one could buy a Thomas Edison "Improved Gramophone." *Horseless Age* magazine announced that Henry Ford of Detroit was selling gasoline-operated vehicles. Men were already experimenting in the building of airplanes, although the Wright Brothers' flight at Kitty Hawk was still seven years away.

Daniel Russell and the Rise of the Fusionists

Even during the Civil War, North Carolina had been a state divided. It had only reluctantly joined the Confederacy, although once committed it lost more men than any southern state.

With the end of Reconstruction and the withdrawal of the occupying federal troops after 1876, the Democrats regained control of the state. But the Democrats' grip was always tenuous. North Carolina was the most politically competitive state in the South during the last half of the nineteenth century, with a strong and active Republican Party dominated by white ex-Unionists in the Mountains and foothills. Nearly one-half of the party's votes came from blacks, mainly located in the old slaveholding lands of the east.[7] The Democrats never won more than 54 percent of the vote in races for governor between 1880 and 1896.[8] Making North Carolina's politics even more volatile was the growth of one of the most active Populist Party movements in the South.

No state except for Texas had more farms than North Carolina in that era. And in the 1890s, farmers were experiencing hardships that would only be surpassed by the Great Depression of the 1930s. When cotton prices collapsed, many farmers blamed Wall Street and the big railroads that controlled the cost of shipping farm products to market. They also blamed big business's allies in Raleigh.

"There is something radically wrong in our industrial system," wrote Leonidas Polk, the state's first agriculture commissioner and a Populist leader. "There is a screw loose. The wheels have dropped out of balance. The railroads have never been so prosperous and yet agriculture languishes. The banks have never done a better or more profitable business, and yet agriculture languishes. Manufacturing enterprises never made more money or were in more flourishing condition, and yet agriculture languishes. Towns and cities flourish and boom and grow and boom, and yet agriculture languishes."[9]

The ruling Democrats were generally conservative and closely aligned with the state's industrialists and the railroads, which financed their elections and provided them with free rail passes. Public officials and party leaders held railroad stock and served as railroad lobbyists and attorneys. The most powerful man in the state capital, it was said, was Colonel A. B. Andrews, the vice president of the Southern Railway.

The Democrats opposed efforts by farmers, liberals, and reformers to regulate railroad rates, restrict working hours, and expand public education. They quashed local self-government rule—thereby blocking the election of blacks—by requiring the legislature to appoint justices of the peace who in turn named county commissioners.

In 1894 North Carolina underwent a pitchfork revolution, overthrowing two decades of Conservative Democratic rule. The revolution was carried out by a biracial coalition of Republicans and Populists. The Republicans— hill country ex-unionists and blacks—combined forces with small white farmers, who were so fed up with the Conservative Democrats that they joined the Populist Party. Theirs was an uneasy, shaky alliance forged out of desperation, and it held together only a few years. Still, these so-called Fusionists crafted one of the most daring and radical experiments in southern political history.

In 1894 the pitchfork crowd swept the state. The Fusion ticket elected seven of the state's nine congressmen and a majority of both houses of the legislature. In the days before voters directly chose senators, the General Assembly elected Populist Marion Butler and Republican Jeter Pritchard of Asheville to the U.S. Senate. Pritchard was the only Republican elected to the Senate from the South between the 1880s and the election of John Tower of Texas in 1961. Butler, a Sampson County lawyer and newspaper publisher, was the only member of the Populist Party ever elected to the Senate from the South.

The Fusion-dominated legislature in 1895 instituted a series of progressive reforms. They passed a 6 percent interest ceiling on loans, raised taxes on railroads and other businesses, and increased spending on public schools and colleges. North Carolina's election laws were made the fairest in the South. With voter registration open to all and with election officials making sure of an honest count, 85 percent of the registered voters went to the polls in 1896. Local self-government was restored.

In 1896 the Fusionists completed their revolt by electing Daniel Russell as governor. To be a white Republican in the nineteenth-century South was to court ostracism. But Russell, a wealthy planter who railed against the rich and powerful, was a maverick. He was a member of a slaveholding family who believed that blacks should have equal rights. He was a Republican when most respectable white men in eastern North Carolina were Democrats. Native whites who joined the GOP were derisively referred to as scalawags. In some ways, Russell was bigger than life—and not just because of his massive frame, wide-brimmed planter's hat, heavy cane, and deep voice. He possessed a brilliant intellect, a pugnacious temperament, and a contrary streak as wide as the Cape Fear River.

Russell joined the Republican Party shortly after it was organized in North Carolina following the Civil War. The Republican Party enjoyed a brief period of power following the war, when Congress imposed military rule on ten southern states, including North Carolina. During the period of Radical Reconstruction, Republicans controlled the governor's office from 1868 until 1876. At age twenty-two Russell was elected a superior court judge, and at thirty-three he was elected to Congress. There he served one term as a member of the National Greenback Labor Party, a splinter party that blamed the country's economic ills on moneylenders, bankers, and bondholders.

In 1896 Russell became the state's first Republican governor in twenty years, swept into office with a legislature composed of seventy-two Republicans, sixty-four Populists, one Silverite, and thirty-three Democrats. The Fusionists captured all but one of the state's congressional seats.

Taking office in January 1897, Russell called his election a victory for "the weak and oppressed" over the "entrenched battlements of prevailing privilege and lawless power." He put forth a progressive agenda calling for higher taxes to improve the public schools and the university, creation of reform schools for youthful criminals, and a more efficient court system. Russell railed against the "railroad kings, bank barons, and money princes." When A. B. Andrews sent an emissary to offer the governor a federal judgeship if he dropped his efforts to nullify the state's sweetheart railroad deal,

Russell threatened to shoot him if he ever returned. "This is one time they [the trusts] have not got the governor," Russell said.[10]

But from the day he took office, Russell was a marked man. Noting his inaugural ball, the *News and Observer*, a Democratic Party mouthpiece, ran an editorial cartoon depicting a cigar-smoking Russell watching blacks dancing at the ball. The black cartoon character said: "I ain't gwine to cook no mo."[11]

George White and the Rise of Blacks

Life for African Americans in the last decades of the nineteenth century was better in many ways than it would be for their children. Call it the forgotten generation. Under the customs of segregation, blacks and whites attended separate schools and churches. But the rules of segregation had not hardened into law as they would in the twentieth century, and northerners would be surprised to see blacks eating in restaurants and serving on juries. Nowhere else in the South did African Americans hold as much political power as they did in North Carolina.

Few men better exemplified the possibilities for blacks in late nineteenth-century North Carolina than George H. White. Born in rural Bladen County of a free mulatto father and a mother who may have been a slave, White succeeded in nearly everything he tried—law, education, banking, real estate development, and politics. Educated at prestigious Howard University in Washington, D.C., White was a school principal and attorney before entering politics.

A six-foot, 200-pound man with a booming voice, White began his career in Republican politics in 1880, winning election to the state legislature and then serving as solicitor or district attorney from the New Bern area. As the only black prosecutor in the country, White demanded to be addressed as "Mister" rather than by his first name, as most blacks were then addressed.

White's move to Tarboro enabled him to run for Congress in a district that was nicknamed the "Black Second," one of the few places in the country where an African American had a chance of winning. The district was created in 1872 by the Democrats, who packed it with as many black Republican voters as they could to help elect Democrats to Congress in surrounding districts. All four of the black congressmen that North Carolina sent to Washington during the late 1800s were elected from this district, the most of any district in the South. The district, which was 70 percent black, also elected more than fifty African Americans to the state legislature, as well

Congressman George H. White
(Courtesy of the North Carolina Collection, Wilson Library, UNC–Chapel Hill)

as numerous mayors, town commissioners, registers of deeds, sheriffs, and clerks of court.

During his four years in Congress (1897–1901), White was the only African American representative, and he saw himself as the spokesman for 10 million black Americans. He tried to reduce congressional representation in southern states that disfranchised black voters. He introduced the first bill to make lynching a federal crime. Like other politicians of his day, White rewarded his political supporters, mainly black Republicans, with political patronage appointments. During his first six months in office, White appointed twenty-nine black postmasters in such towns as Littleton, Rocky Mount, Halifax, Windsor, Wilson, and Weldon. In some rural areas, the postmasters located their offices in their homes, forcing whites to visit black neighborhoods.

There was a surge in black elected officials after the Fusion legislature returned control of local government to voters. In no other state were there so many black officeholders. Suddenly there were hundreds of black county commissioners, justices of the peace, magistrates, county coroners, surveyors, constables, and policemen all across eastern North Carolina's Black Belt. In 1897 there were eleven blacks in the 170-member legislature.[12]

The White Supremacy Campaign

Whites living in eastern North Carolina could assume this was only the beginning of black political influence. The great migration of African Americans from the South to the North had not begun. Black voters were in a position to strongly influence politics in thirty-eight counties. In 1900 blacks outnumbered whites in eighteen eastern counties and composed more than 40 percent of the population in twenty more counties. For many whites, the idea of black equality was unthinkable. Among those troubled by the rise in black political influence was Charles Brantley Aycock.[13]

In the golden age of political speech making—an age when public debates were spectacles that sometimes lasted five hours—Aycock was the most celebrated political orator in North Carolina. If listeners wanted an emotional experience, Aycock gave it to them with stories of Confederate heroes and the dark days of Reconstruction. Aycock grew up immersed in politics. He listened late into the night to the stories of politicians visiting his father, Benjamin, a farmer and local politician. By age nine, he was entertaining local crowds by reciting political speeches, mimicking manners and gestures of the politicians.

Aycock can be considered the poster boy for North Carolina's schizophrenic politics. He is mainly remembered today as a progressive leader for education. But at the turn of the century, Aycock rose to power as the voice for white supremacy. Other progressive voices of that era, such as President Woodrow Wilson and Raleigh newspaper editor Josephus Daniels, mixed progressive reforms with racist tactics or policies—a combination that is difficult to comprehend today, when many people equate liberalism with racial justice.

Aycock was a product of his time and place, but unlike Russell he rarely questioned the basic assumptions of most whites. Born in 1859, he was the youngest of ten children, including three boys who served in the Confederate army. His father owned thirteen slaves and later, as a state legislator, opposed black suffrage. All his life, Aycock was an advocate of "Anglo-Saxonism," a popular intellectual fad of the day that combined white supremacy with the glorification of all things English. It was a Rudyard Kiplingesque age of European colonialism around the world, and many believed it was the "white man's burden" to rule over people of color whether in Africa, Asia, or the United States.

In the American South, racial views were hardening. The first generation of free blacks since slavery had come of age, and there was increased competition for jobs and housing between whites and blacks in the urbanizing South. The economic depression of the 1890s—as hard times often do—added to racial friction. The federal government withdrew as a protector of blacks, and the Republican administration of William McKinley seemed more interested in creating a new American empire from the possessions seized from Spain during the Spanish-American War than reopening old sectional wounds. The U.S. Supreme Court's decision in *Plessy v. Ferguson* in 1896 made its famous "separate-but-equal" doctrine the law of the land, opening the door for states to replace a haphazard system of segregation by custom with the rigid formal segregation of Jim Crow. Two years later the Supreme Court upheld Mississippi's literacy test and poll tax requirements for voting. Northern attitudes about southern blacks were also changing in the era of imperialism. "If the stronger and cleverer race," said an editorial in the Boston-based *Atlantic Monthly*, "is free to impose its will upon 'new-caught, sullen peoples' on the other side of the globe, why not in South Carolina and Mississippi?"[14]

As the Democrats battled to retain political control and racial temperatures rose, political violence increased across the South. This was the heyday for lynching, which reached its peak in 1892 when 235 people were lynched in the country—155 of them blacks. The elections of 1894 in Ala-

Governor Charles Brantley Aycock
(Courtesy of the North Carolina Collection, Wilson Library, UNC–Chapel Hill)

bama, Georgia, and Louisiana were the most violent since the Klan-ridden days of Reconstruction. In Louisiana's election of 1896, the militia was called out three times to try to control the beatings, killings, and intimidation tactics of roving bands of armed Democratic "regulators."[15]

To regain control of North Carolina in 1898, the Democrats turned to their most talented organizer, Furnifold Simmons, a forty-four-year-old New Bern attorney and former congressman. The Democrats' goal was to retake the General Assembly. Once the legislature was back in Democratic hands, the Democrats could regain control of the election machinery, end local control of local government, and bar African Americans from voting, thereby depriving the Republican Party of nearly one-half of its votes. Simmons's plan for the Democrats was simple: a wedge must be driven between the mainly rural white Populists supporting the Fusionist ticket and the black Republicans. "Our state," Simmons said, "is the only community in the world, with a majority of white voters, where the officers to administer the government are the choice of Negroes, and not of whites. This condition has been brought about by an unfortunate division among the white people, and it is likely to continue until that division is removed, and unity again prevails among them as it did prior to 1892."[16]

To finance the white supremacy campaign, Simmons and his allies raised money from bankers, railroad executives, lawyers, and manufacturers, promising them that the Democratic Party would not raise corporation taxes if they regained power. Simmons and company also promised denominational colleges that they would not support increased appropriations for the University of North Carolina at Chapel Hill (UNC)—a secret deal that later shocked UNC supporters.

In the 1890s, campaigns were still conducted mainly at political rallies that were part serious debate and part entertainment, and which often lasted for hours. So there was a premium placed on powerful orators. The Democrats' leading stump speaker was Aycock. At mass rallies, Aycock preached against "Russellism, Fusionism, and Black Domination." Aycock and other Democrats accused the Russell administration of being scandal-ridden and said the Democratic Party represented reform and good government. But his main target was blacks holding office, blacks committing crimes, black juries freeing black defendants, and black men attacking and insulting white women.[17]

The white supremacists were handed one of their most effective campaign issues by Alexander Manly, the editor of the *Wilmington Daily Record*. Manly, a light-skinned black man, was the descendant—probably the grandson—of former North Carolina governor Charles Manly (1849–51) and a slave woman. In August Manly wrote an inflammatory editorial that became a rallying cry for the white supremacists. The editorial was written in response to a speech delivered a year earlier by Rebecca Latimer Felton of Georgia, who had urged white men to "lynch a thousand times a week if necessary" to protect white women from black rapists. Manly wrote that Felton's comments would be worth considering if indeed there was widespread rape of white women by black men. But not every white woman who cried rape was telling the truth, Manly wrote. And in fact, black men were "sufficiently attractive for white girls of culture and refinement to fall in love with them, as is well known to all." He added that there have been many instances of white men who seduced or raped black women. "Tell your men that it is no worse for a black man to be intimate with a white woman than for a white man to be intimate with a colored woman," Manly wrote.[18]

Manly touched the rawest of nerves, exploring deeply held sexual taboos at a time when the white supremacy campaign was beginning to build to a pitch. There was talk in Wilmington of burning the newspaper and running Manly out of town. But Simmons, knowing a useful campaign issue when he saw one, advised local white supremacists to hold their fire until after the election.

Serving as the propaganda arm of the white supremacy campaign were the state's Democratic newspapers, most notably the *News and Observer* of Raleigh. The paper was edited by Josephus Daniels, then thirty-six, a former schoolmate and friend of Aycock and a member of the Democratic Party's inner ruling circle. The *News and Observer* circulated through much of eastern North Carolina, the section of the state with the largest black population, where white racial fears were the strongest. "The *News and Observer* was the printed voice of the campaign," Daniels wrote in his 1941 memoirs. "The *News and Observer* was relied upon to carry the Democratic message and to be the militant voice of white supremacy, and it did not fail in what was expected, sometimes going to extremes in its partisanship."[19]

Nearly every day from mid-August until the election, the Raleigh newspaper ran editorial cartoons featuring a white supremacy message at the top of the front page. They depicted such scenes as a white man being crushed under a foot of the "Negro." They pictured a black administrator supervising white girls at a state institution for the blind. There were white women appearing before a black deputy clerk of court, and white road workers toiling under the supervision of a black overseer. Simmons, who said the cartoonist's salary was paid with Democratic Party funds, reprinted the cartoons and distributed thousands of them in the western part of the state where the *News and Observer* did not circulate. By the end of the campaign, the *News and Observer* was frequently running front-page stories—often with a black border to gain extra attention—of the latest rumor of a black outrage. The incidents ranged from a crime committed by a black person to rumors that African Americans from across the South were planning to migrate to North Carolina to create "a sovereign Negro state."

A prime target of the Democratic papers was George White. White's every move and utterance was put under a microscope by the Democratic press. His words were often distorted and taken out of context and every incident blown up. A week before the election, the *News and Observer* ran a front-page story alleging that the congressman's wife, Cora White, a schoolteacher educated at Oberlin College, received an express package containing rifles. It also said that White's daughter was circulating a petition "asking all colored people to refuse to work for white people."[20]

If the Democrats were going to seize power, they needed to intimidate the tens of thousands of registered black voters. The Red Shirts, as members of the vigilante organization called themselves, mainly roamed the counties bordering South Carolina, attending rallies and disrupting meetings of Republicans, Populists, and blacks. The Red Shirts first appeared in South Carolina during Reconstruction. They materialized in North Carolina after South Carolina senator Benjamin "Pitchfork Ben" Tillman, one of the South's leading racial demagogues, made a campaign swing through the state.[21]

The Red Shirts became an intimidating campaign prop, often accompanying Democratic speakers when they came into town. Daniels remembered the "terrifying spectacle" of seeing Red Shirts accompany Tillman to a rally in Pembroke.

> If you have never seen three hundred red-shirted men towards sunset with the sky red and the red shirts seeming to blend with the sky, you cannot conceive the impression it makes. It looked like the whole world was carmine. I then understood why red-shirted men riding through the country, even if they said nothing and shot off no pistols, could carry terror to the Negroes in their quarters. . . . They usually rode horses and had weapons, and their appearance was the signal for the Negroes to get out of the way, so that when the Red Shirt brigade passed through the Negro end of town, it was as uninhabited as if it had been a graveyard.[22]

In the closing weeks of the campaign, the Democrats imported the race-baiting Tillman. In Sanford, 2,500 people showed up to hear Tillman say they should rub the black pitch from the Tar Heel State. In Burlington, twenty cotton mills were closed and 142 lambs and pigs were killed for a rally that reportedly drew 7,000. In Rockingham, 4,000 people showed up at a rally, and in Roxboro, 2,000. In Charlotte, 1,000 mounted Red Shirts accompanied Tillman, who told the crowd that Manly "ought now to be food for cat-fish in the bottom of the Cape Fear River, instead of going around above ground."[23]

Two days before the election, the *News and Observer* published an unsigned front-page poem called "THE WHITES SHALL RULE."

The whites shall rule the land or die
The purpose grows in hearts of steel
With burning cheek and flashing eye
We wait what waiting may reveal.
But, come what may the whites must hold
What white men's patriot valor bought;
Our grandsire's ashes not yet cold,
Hallow the soil for which they fought.[24]

Simmons gathered hundreds of photographs of black elected officials and either published them in pro-Democratic papers or mailed them across the state. It was the sort of expensive, saturation political advertising campaign that would later become familiar in the TV age. On November 3, a few days before the election, Simmons mailed out 100,000 copies of a letter rallying Democratic forces—the 1898 equivalent of a last-minute television advertising blitz:

NEGRO CONGRESSMEN, NEGRO SOLICITORS, NEGRO REVENUE OFFICERS, NEGRO COLLECTORS OF CUSTOMS, NEGROES in charge of white institutions, NEGROES in charge of white schools, NEGROES holding inquests over white dead. NEGROES controlling the finances of great cities, NEGROES in control of the sanitation and police of cities, NEGRO CONSTABLES arresting white women and white men, NEGRO MAGISTRATES trying white women and white men, white convicts chained to NEGRO CONVICTS, and forced to social equality with them. The battle has been fought, the victory is within our reach. North Carolina is a WHITE MAN'S State and WHITE MEN will rule it, and they will crush the party of Negro domination beneath a majority so overwhelming that no other party will ever again dare to attempt to establish Negro rule here.[25]

Seeking the protection of the federal government, George White met with President William McKinley in September to warn him of the "unholy war that Democrats are making on the color line."[26] On October 21, Republican senator Jeter Pritchard sent two confidential letters asking federal authorities to intervene to prevent a race war. One letter, sent to McKinley, was the subject of a special cabinet meeting held three days later. But U.S. attorney general John Griggs said the McKinley administration could only send federal troops to North Carolina if requested by the governor or if there was interference with the U.S. mail. Griggs dispatched a deputy attorney general to North Carolina to monitor events.

From the beginning of the election, Governor Russell harbored few illusions about the campaign the Democrats were preparing to unleash or what it would mean. He believed the election of a Democratic legislature would mean the end of the Populist Party, the disfranchisement of many voters, and the impeachment of Fusionist public officials. Democrats described the election of 1898 as "a revolution" and compared it with the Spanish-American War. "In 1898 North Carolina people were engaged in two wars, each waged with such a fury as to make it sometimes difficult . . . to tell which was the bloodier, the war against Spain or the war to drive the Fusionists from power," wrote Daniels.[27]

As the election drew nearer, the air was filled with threats of political disorder and assassinations against Republican and Populist leaders. On October 26, Russell issued an executive proclamation ordering "all ill disposed" persons of every party to "desist from all unlawful practices and turbulent conduct." The governor said there was reason to believe that in several counties along the southern border there was a threat of being "invaded by certain armed and lawless men from another state. That several political meetings in Richmond and Halifax Counties have been broken up and dispersed by armed men, using threats, intimidation. And in some cases property has been actually destroyed and citizens fired on from ambush. That several citizens have been taken from their homes at night and whipped."[28]

There were so many personal threats made against Russell that the governor kept a loaded pistol handy. Russell was "that infamous malignant blot upon the state," wrote Rebecca Cameron to her cousin, former congressman Alfred Waddell, a Democratic leader. "I do most earnestly trust,

Governor Daniel Russell
(Courtesy of the North Carolina Collection, Wilson Library, UNC–Chapel Hill)

if it come to blows, that he [Russell] will chamber the first ball fired in that mass of val[v]ular tissue which does duty for a heart in the gubernatorial carcass."[29] In a speech in Wilmington, Waddell took up the same theme against the man who had once unseated him from Congress.

> I do not hesitate to thus publicly declare, that if a race conflict occurs in North Carolina, the very first men that ought to be held to account are the white leaders of the Negroes who will be chiefly responsible for it. To begin at the top of the list, I scorn to leave any doubt as to who I mean by this phase, I mean the governor of this state who is the engineer of all the deviltry. He has been here several times lately to counsel with his "savages," and they watched with pride his Falstaffian figure which "lards the lean earth as he walks along" perspiring and conspiring for the degradation of the white people of this city and of the state whose best interests he has solemnly sworn to protect.

Waddell called for the people of North Carolina to do their duty so that "even the greasey spot will disappear from the executive chair next winter. . . . There are people who regard politics as a mere game to be played by self constituted leaders for the stakes of office. As with all gamblers, sometimes the players become desperate, and the game becomes dangerous."[30]

The governor's friends warned Russell that if he traveled home to Wilmington to vote, he might be lynched. Russell brushed them off, saying he would not allow threats to stop him. Russell traveled to Wilmington without incident. But on his return trip, Russell's train stopped at Maxton, where he was met by Cameron Morrison, a Red Shirt leader and future governor, who forced him to hide in the baggage compartment, protecting him from mobs there and in Hamlet. Russell's family would credit Morrison with saving the governor's life.

Months of race-baiting, propaganda, and night riding did its work. On election day, North Carolina's voters delivered the Democrats a landslide victory. The Democrats won 134 of the 170 seats in the General Assembly as well as five congressional seats. The great experiment in Fusion politics was finished.

Bloody Wilmington

In no place in North Carolina was the racial temperature any higher than in Wilmington, the state's largest and most important city at the turn of the century. Blacks outnumbered whites 11,324 to 8,731. It was regarded as one of the best cities for African Americans in the South, with a substantial black middle class that shared in the city's political power. The reforms of the Fusionist legislature had returned local control to Wilmington, ending fifteen years of Democratic-controlled government. The new mayor and six of Wilmington's ten aldermen, including two blacks, were Fusionists. Blacks worked on the police force, in the fire department, and as mail carriers. There was a black justice of the peace, deputy clerk of court, coroner, and superintendent of streets.

The rabble-rousing leader of the white supremacist forces in Wilmington was Waddell, a former Confederate cavalry officer who served four terms in Congress before Russell—the man whose life he threatened—defeated him in 1878. In the fall of 1898, the gray-bearded Waddell addressed a meeting of about fifty leading white citizens, telling them that rather than waiting for the next municipal election in 1899, the Fusionist Wilmington government should be overthrown and white supremacy restored immediately. "We will never surrender to a ragged raffle of Negroes, even if we have to choke the Cape Fear River with carcasses," Waddell said.[31]

In the days leading up to the election, there were a series of marches and "white man's rallies" in Wilmington. Paramilitary units were formed that included veterans of the recent Spanish-American War. White groups purchased a new rapid-firing Gatling gun, a precursor to the machine gun, for $1,200.[32] Newspapermen from across the country gathered in Wilmington in the days before the election in anticipation of the impending "revolution."

Two days after the election, a group of about 500 heavily armed white men gathered at the courthouse and began marching toward Alexander Manly's newspaper office. By the time they reached the office, the crowd had grown to about 2,000. The mob ransacked the newspaper office, poured kerosene over the floor, and set it ablaze. Manly had already fled the city days earlier, after receiving a warning from a prominent white man that he was about to be lynched, according to an account written by his widow, Carrie Manly, in 1954.

Returning to the armory, the white mob came across a group of twenty-five black men, some of them armed. A police officer moved between the two groups and urged the blacks to disperse. What happened next is not clear, but a shot rang out and a white man fell wounded in the arm. There was a fusillade of gunfire, and when it was over six black men had fallen, two killed instantly. A running gun battle broke out throughout the city. At the sound of a fire bell, the white vigilantes quickly moved into the black section with weapons of mass destruction—a Gatling gun drawn by two horses and two one-pound Hotchkiss cannons drawn on wagons.

The sporadic gunfire soon turned into a manhunt in the black neighborhoods. They sought out Daniel Wright, a black politician, whom the whites accused of shooting the first white man to fall. They surrounded his house, demanding his surrender. He opened fire from the attic, wounding two members of the white mob. Wright was captured, made to run a gauntlet, and was cut down in a hail of bullets.

How many people died in the ensuing violence will probably never be known. The *New York Times* reported the deaths of nine black men. The *News and Observer* reported eleven dead black men. Waddell said about twenty blacks were killed. The coroner reported impaneling fourteen coroner's juries. But a state study published in 2006 said "other evidence indicates that the total number of deaths was as high as sixty."[33] Panic spread throughout Wilmington's black community, and at least 500 blacks fled the city to the nearby woods and swamps in fear of their lives.

The same day, Democrats engineered what must surely be one of the few coups d'etat in American history. The Fusionist leaders of Wilmington's city government were not on the ballot. But the Democratic insurrectionists were not about to wait until the 1899 municipal election to change the leadership. The Democrats sent a delegation to city hall demanding the resignation of Mayor Silas Wright, the aldermen, and the police force. Wright at first hesitated, but when between 100 and 200 armed men showed up in city hall, he and the aldermen resigned and a new city council was sworn into office with Waddell as mayor.

The next morning, with the help of soldiers with fixed bayonets, prominent Republicans were rounded up without arrest warrants. Six black Republicans were marched to the train station and put on a "north bound train and placed in a special car with a guard under orders to carry them beyond the limits of the state."[34] That afternoon, a large crowd of Democrats gathered to banish some white Republicans, yelling "white niggers" and other epithets.

The forced exile of the Republican leaders was followed by a voluntary exodus of 2,100 black residents from Wilmington, including many members of the black middle class. Within two years, Wilmington was transformed from a city with a small black majority to a city with a slight white majority. Wilmington would never recover its position as North Carolina's leading city.[35]

Russell was so disheartened by events that he considered resigning.

"My troubles have come because I have been honest and unpurchaseable and have tried to help the common people," Russell confided to his friend Benjamin Duke, the Durham tobacco tycoon and a Republican. He said he feared he could not return to his home in Wilmington. Pressure was put on Murchison National Bank to foreclose the mortgage that the bank held on Russell's home. A milk dealer took out a newspaper advertisement, saying: "Don't drink Russell's milk or you'll turn black." "The devils are breaking up our business and it looks like we will be driven from our home," Russell wrote. Russell asked Duke if he might have a position for him in New York with the American Tobacco Company.[36]

In Washington, McKinley met with his cabinet to discuss the violence in Wilmington. Secretary of War Russell Alger called the events "a disgrace to the state and the country" and said he would have sent troops to North Carolina if Russell had made the request. McKinley expressed deep concern about the violence but chose not to interfere. McKinley felt any action by the federal government would only aggravate the race conflict. Attorney General Griggs demanded the U.S. attorney for the Eastern District of North Carolina conduct an investigation and prosecute the culprits. But the local federal prosecutor said the case was too weak, with "no information reliable from any witnesses except from newspaper reports."[37]

Aycock defended the mob violence as a justified act to preserve the peace. "This was not an act of rowdy or lawless men," Aycock said in a speech in 1900. "It was the act of merchants, of manufacturers, of railroad men—an act in which every man worthy of the name joined."[38] In fact, business leaders had bankrolled the Democratic campaign in an effort to oust a Populist government they viewed as a threat. As the *Charlotte Observer*, a probusiness Democratic newspaper, editorialized: "The businessmen of the state are largely responsible for the victory. Not before in years have the bank men, the mill men, and the businessmen in general—the backbone of the property interests of the state—taken such sincere interest. They worked from start to finish, and furthermore they spent large bits of money in behalf of the cause."[39]

It was a pattern repeated throughout the twentieth century—business money put into the hands of political operatives who used race to keep the farmers and textile workers from supporting Populist movements. The campaign of 1898 was not just a war over white supremacy; it was also the triumph of industrial interests over the farmers.

After the Democrats retook the legislature, they rewarded business by abolishing the Railroad Commission and replacing it with a tamer North

Carolina Corporation Commission and staffing it with three probusiness Democrats. The Democrats did not let the street violence and deaths in Wilmington mar their "good will jubilee" held later in the month in Raleigh to celebrate their political victory. There were speeches, bands, fireworks, and buildings festooned with bunting and red, white, and blue lights. The three-hour torchlight parade included 150 horsemen, carriages, bicyclists, and other men carrying pitchforks, brooms, and banners, and they passed under a specially constructed white victory arch—decorated with gaily colored bunting and thousands of small flags. At night, thousands of barrels of tar were set on fire to light the city. "To one standing on the arch in front of the city hall, it looked not unlike a great, dark-flowing river on which a million lights floated," the *News and Observer* reported. "Tar barrels blazed, rockets hurtled across the sky, horns blew, bells rang and men yelled like mad."[40]

The parade ended with speeches in Nash Square, with editor Daniels presiding. (A statue of Daniels now stands in Nash Square.) While the speaking was going on, a small group of men marched to the state Blind Institution and chiseled off the name James Young from the cornerstone. Young, the black director of the institution, had been a Democratic target during the campaign. Soon the Democrats would wipe the names of most African Americans off the voting registry lists and essentially remove black men from North Carolina politics.

The Whites Shall Rule

Despite the Red Shirt campaign, there were those in the African American community who believed—or maybe just held out hope—that North Carolina would not follow the Deep South states in disfranchising black voters. But those who thought North Carolina was somehow different from the rest of the South, somehow immune to raw racial appeals, or less committed to the ideology of white supremacy were to be disappointed again and again during the next century.

Throughout the campaign of 1898, Democratic forces had denied that they planned to purge black voters, calling it "the most stupid lie of the campaign." But disfranchisement was a critical component of their plan to regain political control of the state. The Democrats had convinced enough white voters to cast their ballots for Democrats in 1898, but they could not be sure they could do the same in future elections.

North Carolina Democrats did not have to look far for a model of how to accomplish permanent political control. Mississippi (1890), South Carolina

(1895), and Louisiana (1898) had already disfranchised their black voters, and the rest of the South would soon follow. At the request of Simmons, several prominent Democratic attorneys drew up a suffrage amendment patterned after Louisiana's law. The North Carolina amendment would require all voters to be newly registered, to pass a literacy test, and to write a section of the state constitution. There was a large gap between the ability of whites and blacks to read. At the time, 53 percent of all blacks were illiterate, while 19 percent of whites could not read or write. To make sure whites would not be disfranchised, the amendment granted an exemption to the literacy test for any person or his descendant who was registered to vote before January 1, 1867—the so-called grandfather clause. Since blacks lost the right to vote in 1836, the grandfather clause permitted illiterate whites to vote. The grandfather clause would lapse in 1908, giving the state time to teach white boys to read. A poll tax was also levied, making it difficult for blacks with subsistence-level incomes to vote. The amendment would go into effect July 1, 1902.[41]

The scattered voices against the bill came from the few remaining black Republican lawmakers. When Representative Isaac Smith, a black Republican from Craven County, made the case for continued black voting rights, his remarks were repeatedly interrupted by broad laughter from his white Democratic colleagues. "He [the black man] regards the ballot as the one thing in life worth having above all others," Smith said. "And now it is sad that he's about to have it taken away. It comes down hard on this weak race. We have been slaves once and we know what it means to be free. To me, this is the most serious thing on earth. I ask you most kindly to consider well what you are about to do. Take away from the colored man this privilege, and he will never again consider you his friend."[42]

Before packed galleries in the Capitol, the suffrage amendment passed by an 81-to-27 margin in the House and by a 42-to-6 margin in the Senate the next day. Rather than calling a constitutional convention like other southern states, the Democratic leaders were confident enough in their own political power to place the amendment before the voters in the form of a referendum. They scheduled the referendum in August to prevent it from being influenced by the November presidential elections.

The Democrats moved to quickly take control of the election machinery, consolidating power in the state elections board. Under the Fusionist reforms, county boards of elections had been given broad authority to oversee elections. The General Assembly reasserted legislative control of county government, ending the self-rule that had enabled blacks to win local offices in eastern North Carolina.

With the brutal 1898 election still fresh in their memories, the Republican and Populist leaders had a clear picture of the kind of referendum campaign the Democrats were planning. "Their plan does not mean argument or discussion," wrote state auditor Hal Ayer, a Populist. "It means riot, slander, abuse, physical violence and general anarchy. Their plan now is to Red-Shirt every town in the state, and to terrorize voters through the means of such characters as can be hired to wear red shirts, drink mean whiskey and raise [a] commotion generally."[43]

The Democratic ticket, headed by Aycock, the Democratic gubernatorial candidate, barnstormed the state together, campaigning for both their election and the suffrage amendment. Aycock's tour was like a traveling political carnival—or military maneuvers. In town after town, he was met by processions with brass bands, floats with pretty girls dressed in white to symbolize the purity of white women, and contingents of mounted Red Shirts. Also part of the road show was the Gatling gun that had been purchased by white supremacists in Wilmington in 1898—machine gun as political totem. Before the tour was over, the Democrats estimated they had traveled 4,000 miles by train and 1,000 miles by horse and buggy, speaking to 75,000 people.

"There is no use mincing matters," Simmons said in opening the tour in Burlington before a crowd of 2,000. "This amendment discriminates against the Negro in favor of the white man. We intended that it should so discriminate and I am here today to defend that discrimination. This is a white man's state. We have raised the white flag here. Who will haul it down? The Negro can't do it, and the white man that does, spot him. Write on his brow, traitor—traitor to country, and race; to wife and child, aye to father and mother. Let him be an outcast upon the face of the earth."[44]

Some thoughtful men, such as journalist Walter Hines Page, a Cary native and future U.S. ambassador to Great Britain during World War I, were privately contemptuous of the campaign. Publicly, Page called for moderation and deplored the violence. "The political expression of this crusade was a disfranchising amendment," Page wrote in *Autobiography of a Southerner* in 1906. "But the oratorical expression of it became a cry of race hatred. Men whose faithful servants were Negroes; Negroes who had shined their shoes in the morning and cooked their breakfasts and dressed their children and groomed their horses and driven them to their offices;

Negroes who were the faithful servants and constant attendants on their families—such men spent the day declaring the imminent danger of Negro 'equality' and 'domination.'"

The suffrage amendment—stripping the vote from one-third of all North Carolinians—passed by a 59 percent to 41 percent margin. Only 31 of 97 counties voted against it, and those were mainly in the Mountain and Piedmont sections of the state, where there were relatively few black voters. Only the campaign of terror and widespread voter fraud could explain the election results. Every one of the eighteen counties with black majorities voted to strip African Americans of their right to vote. In New Hanover County, where the Wilmington mayor said any blacks trying to vote should be killed, the amendment was ratified by a 2,967-to-2 margin. "The stench," said Butler, "is awful." The Populist senator would later say North Carolina was no more covered by the U.S. Constitution than was the Philippines, where American troops were attempting to put down an insurrection.[45] Aycock won by an even larger margin and the Democrats swept nearly every major state office.

"It's a glorious victory that we have won and the very extent of it frightens me," Aycock said after receiving a telegram of his election as governor and the passage of the suffrage amendment.[46]

Blacks' Good-bye to Congress

Black North Carolinians faced a new world, stripped of political power and diminished by new laws dictating where they could sit on the train, or eat in a restaurant, or get a drink of water. "Let the Negro race of North Carolina not grow discouraged," wrote J. W. Smith, editor of the *Star of Zion*. "God is still on the throne; and if we will draw nigh to him, he will draw nigh to us and make all things work together for good to them that love the Lord. . . . Every race of people that amounts to anything today came up through severe conflict and much oppression. As black people we have seen darker days than we see today."[47]

In August 1900, shortly after the disfranchisement amendment passed, George White announced he would not seek a third term to the U.S. House. He cited three reasons for his decision. Even if he won the most votes, the Democrats would not validate his election; he did not have the money to wage an expensive campaign; and, finally, the political attacks on him had wrecked his wife's health and he was afraid another campaign would kill her. Cora Lena White died in 1905 at age forty after suffering from poor health for years. White blamed his wife's death on the white supremacy campaigns.[48]

Delivering a farewell address in Congress in January 1901, White said black people were advancing

> in the face of lynching, burning at the stake, with the humiliation of Jim Crow cars, the disenfranchisement of our male citizens, slander and degradation of our women, with the factories closed against us. . . . With all these odds against us, we are forging our way ahead, slowly, perhaps, but surely. . . . These parting words are in behalf of an outraged, heart-broken, bruised, and bleeding, but God-fearing people, faithful, industrious, loyal people-rising people, full of potential force. The only apology that I have to make for the earnestness with which I have spoken is that I am pleading for the life, the liberty, the future happiness, and manhood suffrage of one-eighth of the entire population of the United States.

White concluded: "This Mr. Chairman is perhaps the Negroes' temporary farewell to the American Congress; but let me say, Phoenix-like he will rise up some day and come again." There was loud applause, and then debate resumed on the agriculture appropriations bill.[49]

No African American served in Congress again until Oscar Stanton De Priest, a Republican from Chicago, took office on April 15, 1929.

The Rise of the Democrats

While blacks, Republicans, and Populists disappeared from North Carolina's political scene, a new generation of white Democratic leaders arose. Furnifold Simmons served in the U.S. Senate for thirty years, becoming chairman of the powerful Senate Finance Committee and the state's political boss. Josephus Daniels became North Carolina's most politically powerful newspaper editor and served as secretary of the navy under Woodrow Wilson and as U.S. ambassador to Mexico under President Franklin Roosevelt. Claude Kitchin, who replaced George White in Congress, became House majority leader during the Wilson administration. Five of the men heavily involved in the white supremacy campaigns became governors of North Carolina: Aycock (1901–5), Robert Glenn (1905–9), William Walton Kitchin (1909–13), Locke Craig (1913–17), and Cameron Morrison (1921–25). Monuments were built to them and they became storied figures, with their words of wisdom still etched in stone in the state government buildings in downtown Raleigh.

Looking back through the rearview mirror of a century, the Democrats who engineered the political revolution around 1900 may seem to us to be reactionaries. But in fact, their politics is not easy to categorize. Many of them viewed themselves as part of the Progressive Movement. Some of the Democrats who championed white supremacy also pushed for improving public education and child labor laws. While some became defenders of big business, others railed against the power of the railroads and the oil and tobacco trusts. If the state was to advance, Democrats said, black people had to be removed from the political arena.

What happened in North Carolina in 1900 seemed inevitable. All across the South in the 1890s and during the first decade of the twentieth century, black people were disfranchised, the informal customs of segregation became hardened into law, and the Democratic Party became the dominant force for decades. It was a bloody age. A white supremacist campaign in Georgia in 1906 resulted in four days of antiblack rioting in Atlanta. In 1900 white mobs rioted against blacks in New Orleans for three days. There were brutal antiblack riots in such northern cities as New York City, Akron, Ohio, and Springfield, Illinois, as well. "Rioting in the North," wrote historian John Hope Franklin, "was as vicious and almost as prevalent as in the South."[50]

But only North Carolina went through a violent political revolution. What made the state different? Primarily this: in no other southern state had the Republicans and Populists gained control of the political machinery. In order to reclaim power, the Democrats felt they had to rekindle racial passions and resort to violence, intimidation, and fraud. Were such radical measures necessary for the Democrats to unseat the Fusionists? Given the decline of the Populists across the country, and given the fragile nature of the coalition between poor white farmers and blacks, it seems likely that the Democrats eventually would have regained power. By choosing to whip up racial hatred, the Democrats unleashed demons that were difficult to contain. In Wilmington, they took control of North Carolina's largest city at the point of a gun barrel—an action that seems almost inconceivable within the American experience. If they had waited until 1899 for the municipal elections, the Democrats—who by then controlled the election machinery—likely could have regained power without bloodshed.

Aycock, who became one of North Carolina's most beloved governors, was to maintain throughout his life that the Democrats had saved the state from anarchy. The closest Aycock apparently ever came to expressing public regret was during a speech to the state Democratic convention in 1904, when he said: "I knew that our own passions had been aroused and that we were in danger of going too far."

Some contemporaries, such as Walter Hines Page, considered all the talk of black violence to be little more than political propaganda. "The plain fact was the Negro did not threaten the white man," Page wrote in 1906. "Life was going on as peacefully as at any time in the history of the state. The Negroes did not even take a very active part in politics; and when they did they were defeated, by fair means or foul; and they lost interest in this form of activity."[51]

But some thought that the white supremacy campaigns had been inevitable. Writing his memoirs in 1937, superior court judge Robert W. Winston, a former law partner of Aycock and brother of Francis D. Winston, an organizer of the white supremacy campaign, reflected on the Democratic efforts: "It cost bloodshed and rioting—the usual price of white supremacy, whether in Ethiopia or Egypt, in South Africa or in the Southern states."[52]

chapter 1 **The Simmons Machine**

The new era of North Carolina politics formally began on a crisp, clear January day in 1901 amid 1,500 tromping soldiers in broad-brimmed hats and leggings, blaring bands, and a sea of flags and bunting. Stepping off a special train that took him from his home in Goldsboro to his new residence in Raleigh was Charles Brantley Aycock, a forty-one-year-old attorney and the newly elected governor. A carriage pulled by four plumed white horses carried Aycock and his family from the station to the Capitol. Crowds lined Martin and Fayetteville Streets to catch a sight of the new governor, with cheering men doffing their hats and women waving their handkerchiefs as he passed by. Atop a bunting-draped platform on the east side of the Capitol, Aycock took the oath of office. An old man held up a white supremacy banner and a young boy held a white rooster, the symbol of the Democratic Party. Small boys sat on the second-floor balcony, their legs dangling over the edge. A band played "Dixie."

This was no ordinary inauguration, but the fruits of what Aycock called a "revolution." North Carolina had been "redeemed" for the Democratic Party and for whites—just as it had been in 1877 when federal troops withdrew, ending the period of Reconstruction. The populists were for all practical purposes dead. The Republicans were to be vanquished from power for generations. Blacks were no longer a factor. And white Democrats were beginning seventy-two years of uninterrupted rule in North Carolina. The political mold was cast for most of the twentieth century.

Aycock was the man of the hour. But the man behind the new governor was Furnifold McLendel Simmons, a forty-seven-year-old New Bern attorney who for the next thirty years would be a U.S. senator and a political figure so powerful that the state's Democratic organization would become known as the Simmons Machine. Simmons not only held the seat longer than any North Carolinian had ever held it before, but he also exerted a powerful political influence back home. Only once in his thirty years of influence was his choice for governor defeated, and Simmons corrected that "error" by politically destroying the man who had the temerity to buck his machine. The list of his political lieutenants who he helped put in the governor's mansion is a long one: Aycock, Robert Glenn, Locke Craige, Cameron Morrison, and Angus McLean. Even O. Max Gardner, who would later found his own political dynasty, could not get elected governor until he made his peace with the old man.

Simmons controlled state politics with a potent organization that extended into every rural crossroads and mill village. He had a keen sense of what motivated voters, often engaging in raw racial demagoguery. And according to his contemporaries, he and his political operatives had few qualms about stealing an election if necessary. "The record of Simmons's career makes one of the saltiest chapters in the history of American politics," wrote journalist W. J. Cash.[1]

The bridle of one-party rule had been forcefully put on the state. The question of race, as far as the Democratic leadership was concerned, was a settled question: African Americans were to be second-class citizens. But North Carolina's dueling impulses were also evident during the early decades of the century. The Simmons Machine was a ruthless, antireform organization that loved to thump the Bible in public but had few reservations about stealing an election behind closed doors. It reflected the social conservatism of the countryside: North Carolina should be run for the benefit of whites only, women shouldn't bother their little heads over voting, liquor was the devil's tool, and Catholics couldn't be trusted with power.

But at the same time, the Simmons Machine oversaw an era of business progressivism, as North Carolina began moving away from agriculture and toward textile, furniture, and cigarette factories that would make the state the most industrialized in the South. There was a major push for the improvement of the public schools, the creation of one of the nation's largest road-building programs, and the rise of the University of North Carolina as the premier public university in the South.

While the Democratic Party may have reached a consensus on white supremacy, there were still major debates between party conservatives and progressives on several issues: the right of women to vote, prohibition, cleaner and fairer elections, the teaching of evolution in schools, the amount of money that should be spent to educate black children, and the degree to which government policies should tilt toward big business. And there would be factional and personality disputes as well, as various Demo-

Senator Furnifold Simmons
(Courtesy of the North Carolina Collection, Wilson Library, UNC–Chapel Hill)

cratic leaders bristled at the idea of taking orders from the tough party boss.

Simmons was a product of the landed gentry of eastern North Carolina, the second of five children who grew up on a Jones County plantation near the coastal town of New Bern. The plantation had been in the family for generations and covered more than 1,000 acres and worked more than 100 slaves. Educated at what later would become Duke University, Simmons returned home to his father's plantation, married, and two years later moved to New Bern to begin practicing law and dabbling in politics.

The political disadvantages of being a white Democrat in the state's Black Belt soon were driven home to Simmons. The young lawyer was twice defeated in legislative races, losing to black candidates. On his third try for political office, Simmons was elected to Congress in 1886 at age thirty-four—thirteen years after his first political race. Simmons won the election when African American voters split between two black candidates—a development that was likely helped along by his politically influential father-in-law, who is said to have helped finance both black candidates.[2]

Although he later became the architect of the white supremacy campaigns, Simmons courted black voters as ardently as any white Democrat in the late twentieth century. For two years, he represented in Congress the district known as the Black Second. He obtained money for a post office in a black community, made sure blacks were hired for federal public works projects, and introduced a bill to establish a commission "to inquire into the progress of the colored race." But Simmons's experiment with biracial politics failed him in 1888, when he was unseated by a black Republican school principal. The loss humiliated Simmons, who forty years later in a radio address boasted that even though he once had lost to a black man, he "had fixed it so that forever hereafter no Negro could beat any white man for an office in North Carolina."[3]

Simmons rose in politics as a talented and ruthless organizer and tactician. As state Democratic Party chairman, he oversaw a party sweep in the 1892 elections and as a reward accepted a federal patronage appointment as internal revenue collector for eastern North Carolina. His success prompted the Democrats to call on him again to run the white supremacy campaigns of 1898 and 1900. Simmons always regarded the removal of black voters as his greatest accomplishment. When his father was murdered by a black trespasser in 1903, Simmons would hint darkly that his father was "assassinated by a Negro who was perhaps seeking vengeance for what I had done."

It was clear the spoils of the white supremacy campaigns would go to Simmons and Aycock, the strategist and the public face of the Democratic revolution. But the two men had different ideas about their political futures. Aycock wanted to be a senator, and he argued that Simmons's administrative skills better suited him for governor. But Simmons insisted that the Senate seat was his and that Aycock be governor. The move enabled Simmons to hold power for thirty years as the Democratic Party boss.

Simmons was a short man with a long mustache who often wore rumpled clothes. Only his cold, hard, slanting eyes set him apart. He was an adequate public speaker but not a gifted one in an age of oratory. He usually let his supporters make the speeches, while he operated behind the scenes. "He was such a little man to have so much power—quiet, shrewd, and with a sense of humor which sometimes popped out like a pixie's over his cigar," wrote Raleigh newspaperman Jonathan Daniels. "If I ever saw a realist he seemed like one. What he had was the combination of crude and shrewd political power." Daniels said Simmons had as much power as any Tammany Hall boss in New York City.[4]

He was the political boss in an age of mostly uneducated voters who often lived in relative isolation, whether in the farm country of the east, the mill villages of the Piedmont, or the hollows of the Mountains. North Carolina was last in the United States in the number of library books and had one of the lowest newspaper readerships in the country. It was a narrow world before the Internet or TV, and only toward the end of Simmons's reign would radio and automobiles become widely available.[5]

Travel by candidates over poor, muddy roads was difficult, so most people never met those they were voting for. But when they did meet the candidates, it was often a memorable experience. "Election campaigns were red hot and brought to the rural districts a flavor and excitement that were relished and savored for months thereafter," wrote journalist Burke Davis. "The staple doctrines consisted of 'keeping the nigger in his place,' guarding the hearthstone from priests and the Pope, drinking bootleg and voting dry, railing at Wall Street, and tipping one's hat to the Methodist panjandrums."[6]

Newspapers often were mere partisan megaphones rather than independent sources of reliable information. So networks of political supporters—county courthouse rings, local businessmen, county and precinct chairmen—had considerable influence in both persuading voters and getting them to the polls.

In an age before civil-service regulations, Simmons relied heavily on the

U.S. Postal Service for political patronage. Under a Democratic president, he appointed many of the estimated 3,000 postmasters, railway postal clerks, postal inspectors, and rural letter carriers and helped decide postal delivery routes. Postal employees were often a source of political views in their communities, and many could be counted upon to help their patron at election time. As the Democratic political boss, Simmons also influenced the hiring of other federal workers, such as census takers, marshals and deputy marshals, tax collectors and deputy tax collectors, and, in the customs houses, collectors, storekeepers, and gaugers. In Raleigh there was also plenty of political patronage: state printers, fertilizer inspectors, magistrates, and other jobs in prisons, asylums, and elsewhere. Simmons also paid close attention to constituent services, helping provide flowering shrubs from the botanical gardens, ordering the government to help stock fish ponds, providing baseball tickets, and distributing free garden seeds.

But at the heart of the Democratic Party's power was its role as protector of the white power in the South. And at the top of the machine was Simmons, the man they called the "great chieftain of white supremacy." "The Simmons Machine reached to the headwaters of every Little Buffalo and Sandy Run in North Carolina; into every alley of every factory town," wrote Cash. "It carefully planted as axiomatic in the people's mind the belief that its overthrow meant inevitable subjection to their ex lackeys. He was the symbol of white supremacy. Topple him, it toppled."[7]

Jim Crow

In few other eras in American history has there been a more vivid demonstration of the importance of political power than in the South in the twentieth century. The literacy test radically changed the political equation in North Carolina. In 1896 there were 126,000 black North Carolinians registered to vote. By 1902 there were 6,100. The Republican vote was decimated all across the eastern counties. In 1896, 58 percent of the New Hanover County voters cast their ballots for the Republican candidate for governor. By 1904 the GOP vote was 4.2 percent. In Warren County, the Republican vote went from 64 percent to 10 percent. Democracy was in retreat. Fewer people were now voting. In 1896, 330,997 North Carolinians cast their ballot for governor. By 1904 only 208,615 people did so.[8]

If African Americans had been able to vote, white politicians would have ignored them at their own peril. But stripped of their vote, blacks helplessly watched as Democratic white-controlled legislatures and local governments passed a series of Jim Crow laws creating a cradle-to-grave system of segregation. The laws started with separate railroad cars, but it soon spread to separate hospitals, parks, water fountains, restaurant entrances, seating sections in buses, and movie theaters. Even cemeteries were segregated. Law forbade white children, who had been nursed by black women, to use school textbooks used by black children.

In 1915 the state Senate narrowly defeated a constitutional amendment to implement a plan, proposed by Clarence Poe, the editor of the Raleigh-based *Progressive Farmer* magazine, to create separate agriculture districts for blacks and whites. The idea was modeled after the black townships of South Africa. North Carolina's most famous author of that period was Thomas Dixon of Shelby, whose best-known novel, *The Clansman: An Historical Romance of the Ku Klux Klan*, was published in 1905 and became a best seller. A decade later the book, which glamorized the Klan, was made into the movie *The Birth of a Nation*, which helped make Hollywood the nation's film capital.

Jobs once open to black men, such as barbers and carpenters, dried up. In Greensboro in 1870, 30 percent of blacks were employed in skilled occupations. By 1910 only 8 percent were. In 1884, 16 percent of the city's black labor force worked in factories. Not a single black was listed as a factory worker in 1910.[9]

World War I saw thousands of black North Carolinians serve in the armed services, while others headed north to work in war-related industries. But instead of their situation improving, there was a violent white backlash across the country, with race riots in Chicago and other cities, a rise in lynchings, and a revival of the Ku Klux Klan. Governor Thomas Bickett, regarded as a moderate on race relations in his day, told the General Assembly in 1920 that if any of the 25,000 black North Carolinians who had migrated north wanted to return to the state, they would be welcome. "But if, during their residence in Chicago, any of these Negroes have become tainted or intoxicated with dreams of social equality or of political dominion, it would be well for them to remain where they are, for in the South such things are forever impossible."[10]

North Carolina's brand of racial segregation was a milder version than was found elsewhere in the South. North Carolina was an Upper South state, where racial fears were not as strong as in the Deep South. There was more of a sense of civility in the state—fewer lynchings, less racist rhetoric from politicians. There were five state-supported colleges for blacks—the most in the South. Prodded by the threat of federal lawsuits, North Carolina was among the first southern states to create graduate programs at black colleges and to begin closing the huge gap between the pay of white and black public schoolteachers. Outside observers saw in North Carolina a forward-looking state that was more open to the aspirations of its black citizens.

But black North Carolinians often saw something else. And if black North Carolinians could not use the ballot, they could—and did—vote with their feet.

Black people started moving north after emancipation. But the stream of black people became a river following World War I. By train, automobiles, and buses they headed to New York, New Jersey, Pennsylvania, Washington, D.C., and West Virginia. Between 1910 and 1930, an estimated 57,000 black North Carolinians headed north. The migration slowed during the Depression of the 1930s and then accelerated during the 1940s, as blacks sought work in northern defense-related industries during World War II. Between 1930 and 1950, an estimated 222,000 black North Carolinians packed their bags.[11] The great migration profoundly reshaped North Carolina's demographics. In 1880 black people composed 38 percent of North Carolina's population. By 1950 it was down to 27 percent, and by 2000 it was 22 percent.[12]

Progressivism—For Whites Only

As Simmons headed to Washington, North Carolina was in the early stages of the Progressive Era—part of a national reaction to the Gilded Age of robber barons, powerful railroads, and big-business monopolies. On the national scene, the era produced populists such as William Jennings Bryan and progressives such as Republican Teddy Roosevelt and Democrat Woodrow Wilson. This was the era of corporate trust-busting, muckraking, and governmental reform. In the cotton fields and small towns of the South, there was still a deep suspicion of Wall Street.

The Democratic Party was now the undisputed master of North Carolina politics. But it was a much broader party than it had been prior to the counterrevolution. It included not only the Conservative Democrats of the pre-1898 revolution, but it also had absorbed the old Populist Party. During the century's first two decades, North Carolina's Democratic politics became a tug-of-war between its historically conservative impulses and a progressive mood of reform; between the interests of farmers and those of the rising industrialist class; and between the Simmons Machine and party insurgents. The lines were not always clear. There were shifting alliances and factions shaped by different issues as well as by personal ambitions.

Tar Heel progressives pushed, with varying degrees of success, for child-labor laws, regulation of railroad freight costs, primary elections, direct election of senators, voter initiative referendums and recall, secret ballots, and improved public health. The era saw an explosive growth in government, and North Carolina led the way. Across the country, state revenues increased by 300 percent between 1903 and 1922. In the South, revenues increased by 400 percent during that period. In North Carolina, government revenues increased 600 percent, the most of any state. In 1921 the legislature abandoned the property tax and turned to the progressive income tax to finance state government.

Few areas of North Carolina life needed more progress than education. At the turn of the century, schools in the South were the worst in the nation. And North Carolina's public schools were the worst in the South. North Carolina spent 50 cents per pupil per capita for education, tying Alabama as the lowest in the South. The national average was $2.84. The average length of the school term in North Carolina was 70.8 days, the lowest in the South. The national average was 144.6 days. The illiteracy rate among white North Carolinians (19.4 percent) was the second highest in the South and four times the national average of 4.6 percent.[13]

Teaching was a part-time job. Schools were often rude one-room buildings where children sat on crude homemade wooden benches and the teacher had a chair, but no desk. When the winter winds blew through the cracks in the walls, even the rusted woodstoves often could not keep the schoolrooms warm. There were no public high schools in rural areas, and no school libraries anywhere. The schools were financed by local property taxes. The legislature in 1899 appropriated $100,000 to help improve the schools—the first state appropriation for schools in thirty years.

But the first decade of the twentieth century saw an educational awakening across the South, with North Carolina leading the way. The education crusade, in part, grew out of the white supremacy campaign. The main device to exclude blacks from voting was the literacy test, which was not required for whites because of a grandfather clause. But the clause would expire in 1908, and the Democrats promised to make sure all white boys could read and write by then. "Our motive was political as well as humanitarian," Simmons later recalled. "We must educate our youth. This [suffrage] amendment and this promise in its behalf were the real beginning of our educational renaissance."[14]

Aycock had been in office a little more than three months when a private train pulled into Winston-Salem bearing a group of northern philanthropists, including John D. Rockefeller Jr. At the Conference for Southern Education, political leaders and educators, northern philanthropists, and ministers set in motion a campaign to improve public education in Dixie. The crusade swept the South—Tennessee and Virginia in 1903, Georgia in 1904, Alabama, South Carolina, and Mississippi in 1905, Louisiana in 1906, Kentucky and Arkansas in 1908, and Florida in 1909. "Starting from further behind than almost any other state," historian C. Van Woodward wrote, "North Carolina began her movement earlier, and by the time the regional crusade was under way her leaders were in a commanding position."[15]

The pivotal figure was Aycock—the voice of white supremacy who became the voice of educational reform; the man who helped engineer the Jim Crow laws but who was regarded by his contemporaries as a leading progressive voice. Aycock's lifelong interest in education was awakened as a boy in rural Wayne County when his mother, Serena, was asked to sign a land deed. "I cannot write my name," Serena confessed. "I will have to make my mark." "I then and there made a vow," Aycock later recalled, "that every man and woman in North Carolina should have a chance to read and write."[16]

Aycock taught in the Wayne County schools at age sixteen and later, as a lawyer, led an effort to raise local school taxes and worked part-time for two years as the county school superintendent. As governor, Aycock used his bully pulpit. Speaking at rallies across the state, Aycock urged audiences to raise local taxes to build new schoolhouses, employ trained teachers, and consolidate the large number of small school districts. He urged parents to send their children to school. During the summer of 1902, Aycock organized a group of speakers that held more than 350 rallies in seventy-eight of the state's ninety-seven counties.

Leading a Bible Belt state, Aycock imbued his reform politics with an almost religious fervor—a tactic followed by his progressive admirers, such as Governors Kerr Scott and Jim Hunt. "God give us patience and strength that we may work to build up schools that shall be as lights shining throughout the land—ten, fifty, a thousand candle-power," Aycock told a southern education conference in Athens, Georgia, in 1902. "Behind this movement for the education of the children of our land there stands the One who said, 'Let there be light.'"[17]

Aycock used different methods of persuasion, including trying to shame people into building better schools. "Thank God for South Carolina," Aycock said. "She keeps North Carolina from the foot of the column of illiteracy."[18] Aycock ridiculed fathers who sat around whittling while their children worked in mills rather than going to school. "Oh, I wish there wasn't a white pine stick in the universe," Aycock said. "We have spent 50,000 years in North Carolina whittling white pine sticks."[19]

By the end of Aycock's four-year term, there were 690 new schoolhouses erected, including 599 for whites and 91 for blacks. Enrollment for both races rose dramatically. Perhaps most remarkably, the number of school districts levying school taxes increased from 30 in 1900 to 229 in 1904.[20]

While Aycock provided the vital spark of leadership, the education push extended well beyond his administration. There were few rural high schools until the legislature in 1907 passed a rural high school law. Within a year, 160 new rural high schools opened. A state constitutional amendment was approved in 1918 that extended the school year from four months to six months.

All across the South, the "educational awakening" had brought major improvements. But nowhere were the results as impressive as in North Carolina, where the state's spending on public schools rose 1,200 percent. By 1920, North Carolina had surpassed most of the other southern states in public school spending, although it was still spending only half the national average.[21]

While it was an era heavily influenced by the Progressive Movement, it was, in the words of historian Woodward, "progressivism for white men only."[22] If the political rationale for the education crusade was to make sure white boys could pass the literacy test and vote, some Democrats asked, why educate blacks? Some argued that a poor state like North Carolina could not afford to educate both whites and blacks. Others said educating African Americans would only ruin a good field hand and make black people too assertive, so that they would no longer "know their place." "We want the Negro to remain here, just about as he is—with mighty little change," said an editorial in the *Windsor Ledger* in Bertie County, a Black Belt county. "We want them to become better cooks, better servants, better wash women, better workmen in farm and field and shop. We will cheerfully pay taxes to give him that sort of schooling. But that is not what the Negro wants."[23]

Shortly after Aycock took office, several bills were introduced in the General Assembly to divide school funding based on the amount each race paid in taxes. Aycock calculated that if only black taxpayers financed black schools, the abysmal average of $1.13 spent on each black child in 1902 would fall to 57 cents per child. One bill, a constitutional amendment dividing school funding by the race of the taxpayer, passed the Senate Judiciary Committee unanimously and was sent to the floor on March 1, 1901. But a day later, the bill was sent back to committee, never again to see the light of day. According to the accounts of contemporaries, the bill was killed as a result of an extraordinary private threat from Aycock, who had been governor for less then two months. Aycock, who had no veto power, privately told members of the legislature he would view passage of the bill as a violation of his campaign pledge, and if the measure passed he would resign as governor.[24]

Legislative leaders backed down, but the debate over the funding of black schools raged throughout Aycock's four years as governor. At the state Democratic Convention in 1904, Aycock defeated a move, which had broad support, to split school funding based on taxes paid by the races.

In what some of his contemporaries thought was his finest moment, Aycock argued that the state constitution required the education of black children as well as white. To not do so would cause North Carolina to be condemned by fair-minded people across the country. And Aycock said whites had always seen it as their duty to look after the education of blacks, even in the days of slavery. He said the times called for "statesmanship and not passion or prejudice."

An electrified Democratic convention endorsed Aycock's position and rejected resolutions calling for a division of school funds based on race. The issue continued to be raised but never as seriously as in 1904. It was the first step away from the virulent racism of the white supremacy campaigns. Despite the defeat of the racial division of school funding, the gap between the funding of black and white public schools in North Carolina actually grew. For every $1 spent on a black child in North Carolina in 1915, $3.22 was spent on a white child. But through the period of segregation, North Carolina did better by its black students than any other southern state.[25]

Simmons Is Challenged

As the state's political boss for three decades, Simmons periodically had to crush challenges to his power. Simmons faced growing criticism from the Democratic Party's progressive/populist wing that increasingly viewed him as the conservative tool of the state's industrial interests. Although a product of the old plantation economy of the east, Simmons forged close ties with the rising industrialists of the Piedmont—the state's textile, timber, tobacco, railroad, and power-company leaders. As a result, the Simmons Machine rarely lacked for political cash. Democratic progressives were angry over Simmons's support for higher tariffs sought by various North Carolina industries, such as the influential lumber industry. Tariffs were a powerful issue of the early twentieth century, with probusiness Republicans supporting protectionist policies and Democrats and progressive Republicans opposing higher tariffs. Simmons had also angered some Democrats by leading the successful effort to abolish the sale of alcoholic beverages in 1908, eleven years before national prohibition.

By 1912, the more rural, more progressive wing of the Democratic Party was in full revolt. Among those who challenged Simmons in the Democratic primary that year was Aycock, his old political ally.

After his term as governor ended in January 1905, Aycock practiced law in Goldsboro and Raleigh and served as an elder statesman in the state Democratic Party. Aycock initially supported Simmons, but by the end of the decade Aycock was becoming increasingly disenchanted with his old ally's protariff, probusiness record in the Senate.

But Aycock was in poor health, plagued by heart problems. The campaigning for the Senate, his legal practice, and other speaking engagements took their toll. Aycock was in Birmingham in April 1912, in the middle of delivering an education speech, when he collapsed and died at age fifty-two.

Even after Aycock's death, Simmons still faced a serious challenge from Governor William W. Kitchin. A popular six-term congressman from Roxboro and a member of a powerful political family, Kitchin was elected governor in 1908—the only time the Simmons Machine lost control of the governor's mansion during its thirty-year reign. Kitchin won the gubernatorial nomination on the sixty-first ballot in a marathon Democratic convention in Charlotte that raged nonstop over four days and four nights.

Simmons was replaced as state party chairman. His political foe now controlled the state's election machinery as well as state government patronage powers. Four years later, Kitchin tried to unseat Simmons.

A shrewd campaigner, Simmons sought to dispel talk that he had grown rich as the political spokesman for the railroad and lumber trusts. Five weeks before the primary, Simmons boarded a train in Washington, D.C., to travel to Charlotte for a rare campaign speech. When he reached his hotel, Simmons realized he had left his valise on the train and would have to wear his old, wrinkled suit.

"These hands are clean," Simmons said holding up his hands. "Not a dishonest penny in private or public life has ever touched them. I have not done a single thing since I have been a member of the Senate that if known to all my constituents would bring to my cheeks the blush of shame."

He then stepped from behind the table and threw his arms aloft.

"Do I look like rich man?"

"No! You don't look like much of anything," one man shouted.[26]

In the era before television or radio advertising, Simmons distributed 100,000 copies of his speech across the state, which he believed had a decisive influence on the election. Simmons easily vanquished his political adversaries, winning with 57 percent of the vote. Kitchin came in second with 32 percent, while a third candidate, N.C. Supreme Court justice Walter Clark, was third with 11 percent.

Simmons had crushed a popular sitting governor and the only man who had successfully challenged his political control of the state. He had reclaimed control of the party. Kitchin's once-promising political career was now in the dustbin. The outcome of 1912 was clear: Simmons would continue as the state's political boss for another generation. "Power was used to advance power," wrote journalist W. J. Cash. "Every Democratic politician came to be embraced within the machine; any attempt to operate outside it began to be political suicide. It named governors, passed on all appointments, framed all legislative programs. Simmons was merciless in destroying those who opposed him. To those who served him well he gave commensurate rewards."[27]

Simmons was about to enjoy his period of greatest influence on the national scene. Along with Simmons's reelection, 1912 saw Democrat Woodrow Wilson elected president and the Democrats capture control of Congress. Despite being portrayed as a pseudo-Republican in his 1912 reelection campaign, Simmons became a reliable Wilson ally. At the request of Wilson, he coauthored the Underwood-Simmons Tariff Act of 1913, which reduced duties an average of 30 percent—the largest reduction since the Civil War. The tariff act included the creation of the federal income tax.

As a member of the Senate Commerce Committee from 1906 until 1930, Simmons championed many public works projects, particularly improvements to the state's waterways and harbors. Simmons was among the chief backers of the creation of the Atlantic Intracoastal Waterway. During World War I, Simmons used his influence to help North Carolina land three military bases, including what would become the huge army facility at Fort Bragg. He was Senate Finance Committee chairman from 1913 to 1919 and the ranking Democrat on the committee for his remaining decade in the Senate. Simmons was a hard-working, studious senator who mastered complicated issues and whose idea of light reading was perusing tariff schedules. He participated significantly in crafting legislation involving the postal service, roads, forest reserves, agriculture, and other programs.

A New Dynasty Comes Knocking

The 1920s were Simmons's last years in power, and the old man scrambled to keep his political grip as memories of his Red Shirt days faded and the state rapidly industrialized. It would take all of Simmons's schemes—crooked elections, race-baiting, and anti-immigrant politics— to hang on.

In 1920 the Simmons Machine was challenged by Lieutenant Governor O. Max Gardner, a charismatic lawyer and textile manufacturer from Shelby, who would eventually succeed Simmons as North Carolina's political kingmaker. Gardner was part of a new generation in North Carolina politics, one that had not participated in the white supremacy campaigns, did not dwell on the Civil War and Reconstruction, and did not rely on crude race-baiting to win office.

Simmons referred to Gardner as a "brash and romantic young man" and regarded him as an interloper when he announced for governor. The machine candidate for governor in 1920 was Cameron Morrison. A tough, tobacco-chewing politician originally from Richmond County, Morrison had been a leader of the Red Shirt organization who was credited with saving Daniel Russell, the state's last Republican governor, from being lynched in 1898. As a member of the North Carolina Senate, Morrison had helped push through a constitutional amendment disfranchising black voters. For Morrison, reform was a detested word, and as a machine politician he had helped kill many of the reform proposals pushed by progressive Democrats. "We don't have to go to Nebraska, Wisconsin or New Jersey to learn our democracy," Morrison said, referring to three states where the Progressive Movement was particularly strong.[28]

At age fifty, Morrison was in line to be rewarded for his service to Simmons. But there was a problem. While Gardner vigorously campaigned across the state, Morrison couldn't be convinced to leave his house. Morrison's wife died in November 1919, and Morrison remained in seclusion for three months, spending much of the time in his bed. Only after Simmons threatened to dump him did Morrison shake off his depression and hit the campaign trail. But by that time Gardner had built up a substantial lead in the Democratic primary. Simmons roused his hatchet man from a monumental drunk and ordered him to make sure the machine remained in control in Raleigh.[29]

A. D. Watts, or "Aus" as he was known, was Simmons's political alter ego. Simmons had made Watts his secretary, where he controlled federal political patronage in the state. Later the senator secured for Watts, a native of

Statesville, an appointment as collector of internal revenue for the state's western district. "With me," Watts once remarked, "the voice of the Democratic Executive Committee is the voice of God." And of course the voice of the Democratic Executive Committee was Simmons.[30]

Watts needed a wedge issue to use against Gardner, and he found it with the women's suffrage movement. The movement started late in North Carolina, with the first organization formed in 1894 in Asheville. For many white men, the idea of a woman casting a ballot was little more than a joke. When a bill was first introduced in the General Assembly in 1897 to give women the vote, the measure was sent to the committee on insane asylums, where it died.

But pressure to allow women to vote had been gradually building during the first two decades of the century from both women and male progressives. Bills to allow women to vote in municipal or presidential elections died in the 1917 legislature. Other suffrage bills died in 1915 and 1919. When Congress passed the Nineteenth Amendment to the U.S. Constitution giving women the right to vote, only one member of North Carolina's congressional delegation voted for it. Simmons, of course, was an opponent.

In the summer of 1920, a special session of the General Assembly was called to consider ratification of the women's suffrage amendment. At the time, 35 of the necessary 36 states had ratified the amendment, and women's rights advocates in North Carolina hoped the Tar Heel State would cast the decisive vote. Some of the political indicators were good. The North Carolina Republican Party endorsed the suffrage amendment in 1918. In April 1920 the state Democratic Party adopted the suffrage amendment as part of its platform, with Gardner as a leading advocate of suffrage and Morrison leading the opposition. But the legislature, buffeted by intense lobbying by both sides, rejected the suffrage amendment. The opposition to women's suffrage was more than just the result of traditional views about a woman's place in society. As in much of the South, the suffrage movement in North Carolina became entangled in the politics of race. Many Conservative Democrats, including Simmons, worried that if women gained the right to vote, large numbers of literate black women would soon be voting, thereby breaching the color line of politics. Democratic leaders were concerned that if the federal Constitution could be amended to allow women to vote, it could also be amended to permit African Americans to vote. They also feared that the enforcement clause of the Nineteenth Amendment would establish federal control of elections and jeopardize white supremacy and the doctrine of states' rights. Congressman Yates Webb of Shelby, Gardner's uncle, said he believed it would "enfranchise 110,000 Negro women of North Carolina for the sake of letting a few active agitating white women in spots throughout North Carolina have the right to vote." Governor Thomas Bickett (1917–21) said that a "Negro man could be controlled but nothing could frighten a Negro woman."[31]

The Simmons Machine fanned the fears about women and race. In Oxford, Morrison compared women's suffrage to socialism. In Wilson, he called upon white women to stand together to prevent black women from voting. In Wilmington, Morrison warned of the return of the days of black rule of the 1890s. Handbills were distributed in heavily black counties of eastern North Carolina depicting Gardner advancing arm and arm with a black woman. "To the Democratic Voters of Martin County," read one pro-Morrison circular. "The Susan B. Anthony Woman's Suffrage Amendment confers the right to vote on the Negro women as well as the white women. Those who favor woman [sic] suffrage vote for Gardner. Those who are opposed to woman suffrage vote for Morrison."[32]

The attacks worked, and Gardner's lead had all but evaporated by the June 5th primary. Controlling the election machinery, the Simmons organization made sure the rest disappeared. The vote count took an extraordinary eleven days as the absentee ballots trickled in from the machine-controlled Mountain counties, where there was a rich tradition of election fraud. With each day of counting, Gardner's initial lead shrunk before finally disappearing. When the vote counting stopped, Morrison defeated Gardner by a mere 87 votes. Morrison won 49,070 votes; Gardner won 48,983 votes, with former Congressman Robert Page collecting 30,180 votes.

It was, in all likelihood, a stolen election. "Watts and others, living and dead, stated after the 1920 primary that I led in the first race," Gardner recalled. "I know beyond all question and from their own admission that they deliberately stole nominations from me in 1920. . . . Watts always said that he did me a good service in stealing 10,000 votes from me, and I was too young to be governor at that time and that eight years of maturing judgment made me a much better governor than I would have been in the first instance. Of course, his compliment was rotten and I made up my mind that if I ever became governor that I was going to fight for a secret ballot and an honest count." Morrison won the primary runoff by 10,000 votes.[33]

Business Progressivism

Party progressives did not expect much from Morrison, viewing him as an antireform political henchman for the Democratic Machine. But to their surprise, Morrison became an activist governor unlike anything North Carolina had ever seen.

The 1920s underscored North Carolina's progressive paradox like no other decade. There was a revival of the Ku Klux Klan, as white racial views hardened following World War I. There was a rise of religious fundamentalism, with its suspicion of Catholicism and the teaching of evolution. But alongside the social conservatism was a wave of business progressivism that saw North Carolina begin an unprecedented expansion of roads, colleges, and other programs that was the envy of the South.

North Carolina's economic boom of the 1920s would have been unimaginable just a generation earlier. North Carolina was still a largely poor, rural state whose residents earned less than half the national average. By 1920, however, North Carolina followed only Texas as the most-industrialized southern state, with more than 600 manufacturing plants. Manufacturing replaced farming as the state's chief source of wealth. All across the gently rolling terrain of the Piedmont could be heard the sounds of thousands of spindles producing more cotton textiles than any other state. The state boasted of the world's largest towel mill in the world in Kannapolis, the largest denim mill in Greensboro, the largest damask mill in Roanoke Rapids, the largest men's underwear factory in Winston-Salem, and the largest hosiery mill in Durham, and Gastonia had become the world's largest producer of combined yarn.

The United States had become a nation of smokers, and North Carolina was glad to help folks light up such Tar Heel brands as Camels, Chesterfields, and Lucky Strikes. Smoking had become chic, and the newspapers and magazines were filled with advertising endorsements from famous athletes and movie stars. Not only did the state's farmers grow the most brightleaf tobacco, but its manufacturing plants also produced the most cigarettes, perfuming the manufacturing towns of Winston-Salem, Durham, and Reidsville with the sweet smell of tobacco. While many farmers were struggling, the cigarette business was creating a new class of the super rich, including the Duke, Reynolds, and Gray families, who would use their fortunes to build great mansions, develop major universities such as Duke University in Durham and Wake Forest University in Winston-Salem, and set up great philanthropic enterprises.

In the foothills of the Appalachian Mountains, near the plentiful hardwood forests, manufacturing plants were producing more wooden furniture than any other place in the country. Sofas, chairs, tables, and beds produced in Thomasville, Lexington, Statesville, Lenoir, and Hickory adorned the homes of the nation's growing middle class. In 1921 the Southern Furniture Exposition Building was erected in High Point, making that city the southern furniture capital and annually attracting thousands of commercial buyers from around the country.

There were plenty of other signs that North Carolina was discarding its old nineteenth-century image as the "Rip Van Winkle State." Wachovia Bank in Winston-Salem was the largest bank between Washington, D.C., and Atlanta. Greensboro had so many insurance companies that it had become known as the "Hartford of the South." Asheville had exploded in a frenzy of real estate development, and its famous Grove Park Inn had become a resort that attracted the likes of Henry Ford and Thomas Edison. Charlotte's business community was showing the hustle that would eventually make it the state's leading center of commerce. North Carolina saw its per capita income grow at triple the national rate during the 1920s.

Morrison may have been an antireform, machine politician, but he was also the voice of Charlotte's business community. Progress was the watchword all across the South, as community leaders of all political stripes were in the mood to spend money for schools, roads, and other public improvements. It was an era of what historian George B. Tindall called "business progressivism." This was not the liberal progressivism of the turn-of-the-century era associated with Teddy Roosevelt and Woodrow Wilson. This was the go-getting boosterism of novelist Sinclair Lewis's fictional character George Babbitt. Even the *Southern Textile Bulletin* of Charlotte, the voice for the conservative textile industry, published an editorial with the headline: "Expenditures Produce Prosperity." Business leaders backed increased public spending if they thought it would help commerce, pushing for better roads to ship their products or classrooms to educate the children of their executives.

Taking office, Morrison called upon the forces of "progressive democracy" to "war for righteousness with the reactionary and unprogressive forces of our state." At the top Morrison's list was a road bond issue of $50 million that was designed to create a road network connecting all the county seats. To put that sum in perspective, that same year, Congress appropriated $75 million to begin construction of a national highway system.

The rest of the South was astonished at the size of the bond proposal. Senator Carter Glass of Virginia remarked to University of Virginia president Edwin Alderman, a North Carolina native, that the state was "crazy" for undertaking such a large debt. "Maybe as you say, North Carolina is going to the poorhouse," Alderman replied. "But it is riding there cheerfully and gaily on the best roads in the South." With black Model T's replacing horses and buggies—the number of automobiles grew from 2,400 in 1910 to 140,860 in 1921 and 464,373 in 1928—the state could not build roads fast enough. The legislature followed up with bond issues of $15 million in 1923, $20 million in 1925, and $30 million in 1927. By the end of the 1920s, only the state of New York had a larger bonded indebtedness than North Carolina.[34]

North Carolina's highway system drew gaping road officials from as far away as Australia and Japan. Italian dictator Benito Mussolini, famous for making the trains run on time, dispatched an engineer to North Carolina, where he spent nearly a week studying how the state kept the automobile traffic moving. Envious of North Carolina's road building, Louisiana governor Huey Long raided North Carolina, luring away twenty-one of the state's road-building experts with higher salaries.[35]

Morrison also backed a $20 million university bond issue, which passed with the help of vigorous campaigning by up-and-coming political figures such as UNC professor Frank Porter Graham and textile executive Luther Hodges (a future U.S. senator and North Carolina governor, respectively). The money provided the new classrooms and dormitories necessary for a modern university.

Between 1918 and 1929, the university's faculty grew from 78 to 225 and annual state appropriation went from $270,000 to $1.3 million. As the state poured money into Chapel Hill, the university was transformed from a provincial college to a renowned university. In 1922 UNC became only the second school in the South to join the prestigious Association of American Universities.

"No one factor fully explains this spectacular flowering of Chapel Hill," wrote journalist William Snider. "Stimulating, creative people were assembled in an inspiring place at a special time of challenge and growth in North Carolina." Recognizing UNC's newfound eminence in 1930, Governor O. Max Gardner said "the election of a president of this university is of more importance to North Carolinians than the election of any governor or any senator at any time."[36]

While critics would sometimes complain that North Carolina had a Cadillac university system and a Chevrolet public school system, the budget for secondary and elementary public schools nearly doubled under Morrison. The state's bonded indebtedness grew from $12 million to $107 million

Governor Cameron Morrison
(Courtesy of the North Carolina Collection, Wilson Library, UNC–Chapel Hill)

during his four years as governor. It was during the 1920s, wrote historian Tindall, that North Carolina won its reputation as the "Wisconsin of the South" at a time when Wisconsin was synonymous with progressivism.[37]

With a modernized tax system—personal and corporate income taxes replaced state property taxes—taxes rose in North Carolina more rapidly than in any state except Delaware between 1913 and 1930. Between 1915 and 1925, state expenditures grew by 847 percent, the largest rate of increase in the country and triple the national average.[38] "We have learned how to make money in North Carolina and how to spend it for the glory of God and the uplift of humanity," Morrison told a teacher's conference in 1921.[39]

Despite the large increases in expenditures, North Carolina still had a relatively conservative, lean government because it was spending comparatively little at the beginning of the century. By 1927, North Carolina was still ranked forty-fifth in state government spending, with only three states spending less per person.[40]

While Morrison was the toast of the growing urban middle class as he pushed forward with new roads, he never strayed far from the state's deeply ingrained social conservatism. He winked at the growth in the 1920s of the Ku Klux Klan, whose membership rolls grew to an estimated 50,000 North Carolinians. He preached against the evils of demon rum and came down hard on the side of fundamentalists in the great "monkey-versus-man" debate. As chairman of the State Board of Education, he banned two biology textbooks in 1924 that discussed the theory of evolution. "I don't want my daughter or anybody's daughter to have to study a book that prints pictures of a monkey and a man on the same page," Morrison said. This prompted the tart-tongued William Oscar Saunders of the *Elizabeth City Independent* to weigh in with a story headlined: "REFUSES TO STAND UP ALONGSIDE MONKEY—GOVERNOR MORRISON ISN'T GOING TO INVITE CHANCE OF SOMEONE SEEING RESEMBLANCE."[41]

The 1920s saw a revival of fundamentalism in North Carolina and elsewhere. For many pious people, the Jazz Age was deeply unsettling—with its secularism, hip flasks, flappers with bobbed hair, long cigarettes and short skirts, and automobiles giving young couples new freedom to drive off and do who knows what. By the middle of the decade, fundamentalists had launched a major political effort in North Carolina to ban the teaching of evolution in North Carolina schools. After victories in Tennessee, Mississippi, and Arkansas, the antievolution movement focused on North Carolina. If North Carolina could be convinced to pass antievolution legislation, the movement was set to take its battle to Congress. Preachers, revivalists, and political figures such as former presidential candidate William Jennings Bryan fanned the flames in North Carolina, with evolution decried from the pulpits, revival tents, and tobacco warehouses as the devil's work. "The day is not distant when you will be in the grip of the Red Terror and your children will be taught free love by the damnable theory of evolution," warned revivalist Baxter McLendon.[42]

But in a decisive battle in 1925, antievolution legislation was killed in the North Carolina House by a 64 to 46 vote. Helping defeat the measure was intensive lobbying by Harry Woodburn Chase, president of UNC, and William Louis Poteat, president of Wake Forest College, both of whom incurred the wrath of many for their stands. Among the more notable opponents was a twenty-eight-year-old N.C. House member from Morganton named Sam Ervin Jr., a future U.S. senator. Ervin argued that the antievolution legislation would limit free speech and free thought. The only good feature of the bill, Ervin said, was that "it will gratify the monkeys to know they are absolved from all responsibility for the conduct of the human race. . . . The passage of this resolution would be an insult to the Bible. It would be an insult to the people of North Carolina. I don't believe the Christian religion's endurance depends upon the passage of some weak-kneed resolution of the General Assembly of North Carolina. It is too big, too strong for that."[43]

The evolution battle continued in political campaigns and in the legislature until 1927, but it never again came close to passage. Although most North Carolinians probably viewed Charles Darwin's theories with considerable skepticism, the state's rejection of antievolution legislation strengthened its growing image as the South's most progressive state.

The Fall of the Simmons Machine

By the late 1920s, Simmons was an old, frail-looking, emaciated man, and fewer people could remember the days when he had been called the "great white chieftain." His chief operative, Aus Watts, had been ruined by scandal. As a reward for his political chores, Morrison appointed Watts the state's first revenue commissioner in 1921. Few were surprised when Watts, a man of questionable morals, was arrested in 1923 by two Raleigh police detectives and a uniformed officer, who burst into his Fayetteville Street apartment and found a black woman under his bed. Watts was charged with abetting prostitution. "I've been caught," he told reporters the next day. "I'm ruined. I'll not lie. I'll take my medicine."[44] Watts resigned as revenue commissioner and returned home to Statesville, where he was hospitalized. When he died four years later, most of the state Democratic leadership attended his funeral.

If Watts had still been around, he might have saved Simmons from making a fatal political error in 1928, when he bolted from the Democratic Party in the presidential race and helped carry the state for Republican presidential candidate Herbert Hoover. Many southern Democrats were alarmed by the presidential candidacy of New York governor Al Smith. Since the Civil War, the Democratic Party had largely been a regional southern party, with only two Democrats winning the White House—Grover Cleveland and Woodrow Wilson. For many southerners, Smith represented a new "alien" wing of the Democratic Party, one composed of big-city machines, northeastern ethnics, Roman Catholics, and those who wanted to end prohibition. North Carolina had the smallest foreign-born population in the country in 1920—0.3 percent compared to 13 percent nationally.[45]

Simmons had long been suspicious of what he called the "scum" immigrating to the United States from southern and eastern Europe. In 1906 Simmons pushed an amendment through the U.S. Senate creating a national literacy test for voting. The measure was defeated in the House, which Simmons blamed on lobbying by the steamship and railroad companies that benefited from immigration. Still, it was a shock when Simmons broke with his party and endorsed Hoover.

"I am not a prejudiced man," Simmons said in a three-hour campaign speech delivered on statewide radio in October 1928. "My action in this matter is based upon my conscientious conviction. Feeling as I do, it is utterly impossible for me—I would rather die, I would rather have my right arm cut off, I would rather have my tongue cleave to the roof of my mouth, than to vote for Alfred E. Smith for President of the United States. In God's name, do not place upon the untarnished brow of the Democratic Party the brand of Liquor, Alienism, and Plutocracy."[46]

While few Tar Heel Democrats were enthusiastic about Smith, Gardner, the Democratic nominee for governor in 1928, and other top Democrats tried to keep the state in line for Smith. They worried that mass defections to Hoover would hurt other Democrats on the ticket. Gardner and others conducted a radio campaign on behalf of Smith. Torchlight parades were held across the state, including one in Laurinburg in which an eleven-year-old Terry Sanford carried a sign reading: "Me and Ma is for Al."

But selling Smith in the Bible Belt was a difficult chore. Everywhere North Carolina Democrats felt under siege—a feeling they experienced later in the century when they were saddled with such unpopular Democratic presidential candidates as George McGovern, Walter Mondale, and Michael Dukakis. "They called him a liquor head and a Catholic, and that is all you had to say down in that country," recalled Thad Eure, who was elected to the legislature in 1928 and who later went on to a legendary career as North Carolina's secretary of state.[47]

Simmons unsheathed his most reliable political weapon—race-baiting. Simmons said white Catholic nuns were already teaching black children and the Catholic Church everywhere accorded blacks "such equality in church relations as is not extended to them by other religious organizations." The senator printed at least 500,000 posters showing Ferdinand Q. Morton, a black civil service commissioner in New York, dictating to his white secretary. "Does Party regularity mean more to you than the purity of the White Race?" read the poster.[48]

North Carolina was one of seven states in the Solid South that went Republican in the presidential contest. Hoover carried the state over Smith by a 55 percent to 45 percent margin, the only time between 1872 and 1968 North Carolina voted for a Republican president. Hoover provided long-enough coattails to elect two North Carolina Republicans to Congress and forty-seven GOP members to the 170-member North Carolina General Assembly—both twentieth-century records at the time.

But it was to be a Pyrrhic victory for Simmons. The old political boss may have helped elect Hoover, but he had alienated not only the rising Gardner organization but also many Old Guard Democrats who had once served as his political lieutenants.

The Democratic Party began pulling the plug on the Simmons Machine and on Simmons, who at seventy-four was now the oldest man in the U.S. Senate. Gardner, the newly elected governor, appointed a State Board of Elections composed of Simmons's enemies. For the first time in two decades, the senator did not control the election machinery. In a move widely seen as a slap at Simmons, the General Assembly in 1929 adopted a secret ballot and restricted the use of absentee ballots—both moves that Simmons opposed and that limited his opportunities to manipulate the vote totals. The legislature also passed a bill requiring primary candidates to sign pledges agreeing to support the party nominee in the fall.

Other factors also worked against Simmons. Many southern voters were outraged when Hoover invited the wife of the first black congressman elected in the twentieth century—Republican representative Oscar De Priest of Chicago—to a White House tea. "A great blow to the social stability of the South," was how North Carolina senator Lee Overman described the tea.[49]

But even more important was the Wall Street crash of 1929 and the beginning of the Great Depression. Simmons had not only switched sides, but he also had helped put a man in the White House whom many Democrats now blamed for the textile mills and furniture factories either closing or cutting back hours across the state. "You might have stood as good a chance as ever, had it not been for Hoover's miserable failure," J. W. Heatherly wrote to Simmons. "The Democrats are terribly sore on you because you supported Hoover."[50]

Simmons's opponent was Josiah Bailey, a Raleigh attorney, who was a former Simmons strategist. Bailey broke with the Simmons Machine, saying he was offended by all the vote stealing. He had sought the Democratic nomination for governor in 1924 without Simmons's approval, and the old political boss had crushed him. But with Simmons's power on the wane, Bailey was ready to pounce again in 1930.

Simmons hoped to energize what in the latter part of the twentieth century might be called the Moral Majority—the churches and the antiliquor and temperance vote. He counted on people remembering his long service to the Democratic Party and not his one defection. Simmons declared he was "a better Democrat than ever" and said he planned to be "buried in a Democratic coffin."

Simmons's allies sought to link Bailey to liquor and bars and even spread rumors that the former editor of the *Biblical Recorder* was on the Vatican payroll with a salary of $10,000 per month. But even among his core constituency, Simmons faced problems. Many of the antiliquor voters were women, and Bailey reminded them that Simmons had opposed giving women the very votes that he was now asking that they cast for him. The Simmons Machine knew it was in trouble. Frank Hampton, who had taken over from the disgraced Watts as his chief political operative, complained that the campaign was a "mess." "Ungrateful skunks and sons of bitches who have eaten bread from the senator's table," Hampton wrote to a friend, "are fighting him all over the state and trying to bring a great career to a close in humiliation and defeat and break his heart and throw him out in his old age."[51]

For nearly fifty years in politics, Simmons had successfully played the race card, and he was not about to change tactics at this late date. Simmons's political operatives distributed 50,000 copies of a circular accusing

Bailey of opposing segregation and the disfranchisement of blacks around the turn of the century. Another anonymous circular bore the headline: "Tammany and North Carolina Negroes Would Defeat Simmons."

For Simmons it was too little, too late. The state was changing. North Carolina, which was 10 percent urban when Simmons was elected, was now 26 percent urban.[52] Playwright Paul Green won the Pulitzer Prize in 1927 for *In Abraham's Bosom*, a play about race relations in the South, and Thomas Wolfe had published his acclaimed novel, *Look Homeward, Angel*, in 1929. Liberal Frank Porter Graham would be named president of the University of North Carolina two days after Simmons's defeat. North Carolina's newspapers—the mouthpieces for white supremacy at the turn of the century— were now judged the most liberal in the South. A year earlier, the American Historical Association had held its annual meeting in Durham. Robert D. W. Connor, a UNC historian, had declared that the South had "shaken itself free from its heritage of war and Reconstruction. Its self-confidence restored, its political stability assured, its prosperity regained, its social problems on the way to solution."[53]

Bailey defeated Simmons in a landslide, taking 61 percent of the vote to Simmons's 39 percent. Only six of the forty-nine Republicans elected to the General Assembly two years earlier survived the 1930 election. Simmons could not believe the Democratic voters had rejected him. Democratic politics had been his personal fiefdom for the entire century. So the old man began searching for other explanations. It was New York liquor money that had done him in. The national Democratic Party was gunning for him. The election was stolen. The complaints sparked a Senate investigation; but after holding two days of hearings in North Carolina, U.S. senator Gerald Nye, a progressive Republican from Nebraska and chairman of the Senatorial Campaign Committee, found no evidence of irregularity.

A fifty-year political career had ended. More than any other man, Simmons had put his personal stamp on twentieth-century North Carolina politics. He helped shape an era of Democratic one-party rule. Although he held power in the twentieth century, Simmons was essentially a nineteenth-century man. He saw no contradiction in a democracy affording second-class citizenship to African Americans or women. He took it for granted that white men should rule. "Yet was he not speaking the language and reflecting the attitudes of his generation?" Duke University historian Richard L. Watson Jr. asked. "How many of his political contemporaries approached these problems differently?"[54]

Simmons ruled for thirty years by using a political tactic employed across the South: preventing working people from gaining power by driving a wedge between blacks and whites. No matter how low the white dirt farmer or mill hand may have been on the social rung, he was still higher than any black person.

But Simmons also illustrated the contradictions in North Carolina politics. Despite his racism, Simmons was the state's political boss during a time of great progress in the schools, the roads, and the universities that helped North Carolina earn the reputation as the South's most progressive state.

Simmons could be politically ruthless, relying on the violence and intimidation of the Red Shirts to grab power and allowing his political operatives to steal votes to stay in power. And he routinely appealed to people's worst instincts, pitting one group against another. But he was personally honest, and when he retired he was comfortable but by no means rich. In fact, state government was relatively clean during the era ruled by the Simmons Machine. "The only things Democrats steal—so it is said—are votes, and generally in recent years that has been a stealing among themselves," journalist Jonathan Daniels observed.[55]

Simmons was never a beloved figure like Aycock, and today he is nearly forgotten. There are no monuments to him. Many of his political views became an embarrassment to the Democratic Party as the twentieth century progressed. But North Carolina has never before nor since known a political boss as powerful as Furnifold Simmons.

"I have little fear regarding the final judgment of posterity," Simmons wrote at the conclusion of his memoirs. "Doctor, I wish you to examine my record thoroughly and to feel free to write the truth. You may wait until I have passed on if you desire."[56]

With his defeat, the political center of gravity in North Carolina shifted west from New Bern to Shelby for the next generation.

chapter 2 **The Shelby Dynasty**

f one picked up the September 11, 1932, edition of the *News and Observer*, one could easily come away with the impression that society was coming apart. The Raleigh newspaper reported that in Goldsboro 15,000 watched a "Hoover Cart Rodeo." The 300 cannibalized automobiles displayed were powered by North Carolina mules rather than Detroit engines because people could no longer afford gas or tires. Each contestant received a three-pound bag of grits and a free pass to see the Marx Brothers classic film *Horse Feathers*.

In High Point, textile-mill strikers clashed with highway patrolmen, with the strikers throwing rocks and the troopers responding with tear gas. In Greensboro the Socialist Party of North Carolina held its first state convention. In Chapel Hill, Governor O. Max Gardner introduced Roscoe Pound, the dean of the Harvard University Law School, who soothed his audience by saying that democracy was still safe. "I don't believe we need a Mussolini or any other kind of dictator," Pound said.

Just as the hard times on the farm in the 1890s had produced a pitchfork revolt against the Conservative Democrats and business leaders who controlled the state, so did the Great Depression of the 1930s. Labor unions struggled to gain a foothold in the growing number of textile mills. Robert Rice "Bob" Reynolds—a junior-league Huey Long—clowned his way to the U.S. Senate. And it took all of the power of the state's political establishment and large bags of cash from the business community to prevent another populist takeover of Raleigh.

The takeover might have succeeded if North Carolina's political boss in the 1930s, O. Max Gardner, a textile millionaire and a lawyer, had not been such a masterful politician. Gardner's political organization, which became known as the Shelby Dynasty, controlled state politics from 1928 to 1948. He helped put several men in the governor's office, including his brother-in-law. And he could remove people from office as well, forcing out a U.S. senator who had become an embarrassment to the state.

Gardner was a charismatic figure who dominated a room. He was 6' 1" and powerfully built, with a deep, commanding voice, good looks, and an easy manner that allowed him to trade quips with President Franklin Roosevelt or the boys at the Shelby drugstore. He was a snappy dresser who favored double-breasted suits and a bow tie and who sometimes spent his weekends at the playgrounds of the rich. Gardner had a first-rate mind, a ready wit, and a gift for making people like and trust him. "He became what people said was Power," wrote Jonathan Daniels. "He has both brains and charm. He is a big, good-looking man . . . hearty and witty. He has an honest, if sometimes sentimental, affection for the poor, and easy and increasing fellowship with the rich."[1]

The Path to Power

Gardner was born on March 22, 1882, in Shelby, a small town located west of Charlotte. The son of a country doctor, Gardner was left penniless when both of his parents died. He attended North Carolina State College in Raleigh (now known as North Carolina State University) on a scholarship and with the financial help of a sister. Almost from the time he arrived in Raleigh, Gardner was a big man on campus. He was captain of the football team and made All-Southern tackle in 1902. He was the class president, a champion debater, and the commencement speaker, and after graduation he spent an additional two years on campus teaching organic chemistry. As a law student at the University of North Carolina at Chapel Hill, Gardner gave boxing lessons, ran a boarding house, and was elected captain of the Carolina football squad at a time when player eligibility rules were more lax. At his request, his coach excused him from playing against his old teammates at N.C. State.

Returning home to Shelby, he opened a law practice and married into the local political dynasty. Fay Lamar Webb was the daughter of superior court judge James L. Webb, who had held public office for fifty years as mayor, state senator, and president pro tem of the state Senate without ever having been defeated. Her uncle was Congressman E. Yates Webb. Gardner eventually moved into Webbley, an elegant neoclassical mansion built in 1852, which was owned by his father-in-law.

Gardner began a rapid climb in politics, winning election to the North Carolina Senate at age twenty-eight and becoming lieutenant governor at age thirty-three. But when the thirty-seven-year-old Gardner ran for governor in 1920, he was defeated in the Democratic primary by the powerful Simmons Machine in what was probably a stolen election. Rather than seeking revenge, Gardner sued for peace with Simmons, the aging political boss. Gardner agreed not to run for governor in 1924, observing the state's tradition of rotating the governor's office between the eastern and western sections of the state. Instead, he swung his political organization behind Robeson County businessman Angus McLean, Simmons's handpicked choice for governor. In turn, Simmons agreed to back Gardner for governor in 1928.

During his eight years in the political wilderness, Gardner bided his time, building his legal practice and investing in various business interests. He became one of the largest cotton growers in Cleveland County. Intrigued by the new fabric rayon, Gardner formed in 1925 the Cleveland Cloth Mills, which included a mill village to house its workers. In 1928 Gardner waltzed into the governor's mansion, promising to push a reform agenda.

The Depression

"Everybody blue about stock market breaking so terrifically," wrote First Lady Faye Gardner in her diary, after the market crashed in October 29, 1929, nine months after her husband took office.[2]

Even before the crash, there were signs of economic trouble in North Carolina. The state had gone on a spending spree in the 1920s and was now deeply in debt. After borrowing heavily to build roads and other projects, state and local government debt had risen from $77 million in 1920 to $560 million in 1929 ($6.5 billion in 2006 dollars). The agricultural economy had been in a funk, with many farmers struggling to hang on, while many gave up the rural way of life for the mill town. Even in the booming 1920s, North Carolina had been dubbed "a poor man's paradise," with the state ranking forty-first in per capita income.

But that was nothing compared to what was to come. North Carolina's countryside was soon a scene of despair—and North Carolina had more farmers than any state except Texas and Mississippi in 1930.[3] The gross farm income in the state dropped from $310.5 million in 1929 to $144.3 million in 1932. Cotton prices plummeted from 16.8 cents per pound to 6 cents per pound; tobacco fell from 18.5 cents per pound to 12 cents. The number of bank failures in an age before federal deposit insurance—215 Tar Heel banks closed between 1929 and 1933—could not begin to tell the heartbreak as families saw their savings wiped out. From his office, Gardner could see the lines of desperate depositors lining up outside a bank on Fayetteville Street. "All depressed about rumors of Commercial Bank here closing tomorrow," Faye Gardner wrote in her diary in December 1931. "To bed at 12, but not much sleep. Times are tragic. . . . Another rainy day. Max and I headachy after a sleepless night. The bank closed as predicted—thousands lost their all. Runs being made on two other banks. City in turmoil."[4]

President Herbert Hoover had promised a chicken in every pot. But now the most impoverished were living off wild blackberries, huckleberries, dandelions, and pokeweed greens. Thieves stole from smokehouses and milk bottles began disappearing from porches. Armies of the poor took to the roads in search of work or food. Malnutrition was blamed for thousands of deaths. In Fayetteville, thirty unemployed cotton workers went to the sheriff's office asking for food. The men had gotten up before dawn to beat their neighbors to blackberry patches to feed their families. "We don't want to do anything wrong," their leader told the sheriff, "because we are law abiding people, but we are desperate, and we are liable to do anything before we see our wives and children starve." The sheriff found them food.[5]

"I lie awake at night wondering how I let my ambitions lead me into the governorship at a time like this," wrote Gardner in a rare moment of self-pity.[6]

The governor was not immune from the economic meltdown. He lost $800,000 (or about $9.4 million in 2006 dollars) in the stock market, leaving him with his textile mill as his major remaining asset. And even the mill looked shaky.[7]

Not immediately realizing the extent of the hard times, Gardner first reacted to the Depression with modest remedies. He lobbied the textile manufacturers to cut back on production in an effort to boost prices. In a series of pre-Rooseveltian fireside chats on the radio, Gardner encouraged people to keep garden plots, a cow, and some chickens so if they did not have any money at least they would not starve.

Gardner also used the bully pulpit to buck up the spirits of fellow Tar Heels. "If by some magic we in North Carolina could regain our faith in ourselves and each other, in our institutions and agencies of public and private service," Gardner said, "the whole face of the state would be transformed within 60 days. We should remember that there has been no change in the basic character of our people. We are the same people we have always been and North Carolina possesses everything she ever possessed except money. And some day we can make money again if we do not turn yellow and quit. We must carry on in North Carolina."[8]

But more radical measures were needed. Much of the cost of government was financed by local property taxes, which became a crushing burden for farmers losing money on their cotton crop and for laid-off textile workers. With people not paying their taxes, local governments were going belly up. Thirty-nine counties and seventy-eight towns in North Carolina had declared bankruptcy by December 1932. All across the state, tax-relief associations formed and demanded that the state reduce the property-tax burden.

In June 1930 Gardner slipped off to Washington, D.C., to the Brookings Institution, the widely respected liberal-leaning think tank, to arrange for Henry Seidmann, the institution's director of government research, to conduct a four-month study of North Carolina state government. On December 29th, Gardner released the Brookings report, which recommended the sweeping reorganization and centralization of state government as a way both to reduce costs and to provide tax relief for beleaguered property owners. The Brookings report called for the state to take over from the counties the financing of the secondary and elementary schools and the construction and maintenance of most highways. It proposed the creation of a central-purchasing agency and a study of the consolidation of the three main state-supported college campuses—the University of North Carolina in Chapel Hill, State College in Raleigh, and the North Carolina College for Women in Greensboro—into a single system. It proposed shrinking the number of state agencies from ninety-two to fourteen and the reduction of the state's elective executive offices from thirteen to three. The report also recommended the consolidation of some counties.

Local property taxes could be slashed, Gardner said, because counties would no longer be responsible for roads, convicts, or schools. The state would pay for the upkeep of the roads by raising the tax on gasoline. It was an ambitious plan of retrenchment, reorganization, and reform that the desperate economic conditions made possible.

The governor's first hurdle was to push through the General Assembly the transfer of the road system from the counties to the state. Gardner had to overcome the opposition of 150 local road boards, taking away power from 600 leaders, many of whom were powerful courthouse politicians or leading local businessmen. And he had to deal with the opposition of other

Governor O. Max Gardner at the telegraph key in the Executive Mansion
(Courtesy of the North Carolina Collection, Wilson Library, UNC–Chapel Hill)

vested interests, such as road-machinery salesmen and road contractors who were tied to the local politicians. The governor countered by going over the heads of the politicians and making a statewide radio address, during which he urged citizens to write or send wires to their legislators. "The only clients I represent," Gardner told a radio audience, "are the 3,000,000 citizens of North Carolina."[9]

Gardner wooed the lawmakers at receptions at the Executive Mansion, worked his extensive press contacts, and imported two ex-governors—Virginia's Harry Byrd and New York's Al Smith—to address the legislature on the merits of the plan. The passage of the highway bill broke the logjam. Soon the legislature was adopting other parts of the plan, including consolidation of the university system and the creation of a state banking commission, a state division of personnel, and a local government commission. On July 1, 1931, the state took over 45,000 miles of county roads and took responsibility for 4,000 county convicts. To head the new university system, Gardner supported a popular, although controversial, college professor and former UNC schoolmate named Frank Porter Graham.

Gardner was less enthusiastic about taking over responsibility for financing the public schools, because he thought the imposition of a sales tax—the most likely source of financing—would hurt the poor. The legislature passed the school takeover bill in 1931 but left it to the 1933 legislature and Gardner's successor as governor, J. C. B. Ehringhaus, to pass a three-cent sales tax.

Any momentary joy Gardner may have felt over his legislative victories was tempered by the daily struggle to keep state government financially afloat during the Depression. State appropriations were cut by 20 percent in 1931, slashed again in 1932, and cut by 32 percent in 1933. The lucky state employees who kept their jobs found their paychecks cut again and again. A schoolteacher earning $1,000 per year in 1932 found her pay cut to $672 in 1933. Others were laid off. Highway construction ground to a halt.[10]

With his hat in hand, Gardner made trips to New York City to gain extensions on state's bonds or short-term loans. Gardner relied on North Carolina businessmen such as Charles Cannon and John W. Hanes to use their Wall Street connections to help keep the state financially afloat.

Despite the constant struggles, North Carolina's state government navigated the Depression better than most states and avoided having to pay its workers and teachers in script. Gardner's performance drew favorable national attention. Gardner addressed both the Virginia and Kentucky legislatures to talk about how North Carolina handled the Depression.[11]

Labor Battles

While Gardner won wide praise for reorganizing state government, his handling of the labor movement was far more controversial. The need for industrialization was almost a civic religion. North Carolina was still a very poor state, with residents earning only 47 percent of the national average when Gardner took office in 1929. What North Carolina was offering the northern textile tycoons was cheap labor, and the state's business and political leadership was determined to keep its workers from organizing.[12]

North Carolina underwent an industrial revolution in the early decades of the twentieth century. It was a subtle revolution, however, because the state lacked the outward symbols of industrialization—the belching smokestacks, fiery furnaces, and giant ports of the North. Instead, North Carolina had a more genteel industrialization, spread out in small mill towns. Instead of row houses, there were small detached houses, often with gardens in the back.

Unlike northern states, North Carolina did not rely on floods of foreign immigrants to work in its textile, furniture, and tobacco factories. Thousands of sharecroppers and other farmers, finding they could no longer scratch out a living from the land, abandoned the countryside to work in the mills springing up along the fall line of the Piedmont near sources of water power. By 1930, North Carolina was the industrial giant of the South, leading the region in total value added by manufacturing.[13]

North Carolina towns from the Coastal Plain to the Mountains vied with one another to attract new textile mills. People clamored for the jobs because no matter how many hours they worked or how meager the pay, life was easier than on their hardscrabble farms. "Even under the manufacturer's avarice and his thumb, the first workers saw more cash in a month then they had seen on the farm in a year," wrote Jonathan Daniels. "Industrialization with all its evils was an escape. What it did in the South was to put the degradation of the rural poverty of the South in one place where it could be seen. It was not worse there than on the hill farms. If it had been, not all the labor agents in the world could have kept the stream moving which filled the villages in times when villages, by modern standards, were much worse."[14]

Working in a textile mill was more than just a job; it was a way of life. The mill hand's family often lived in a village built by the mill owner. A worker bought his goods at the company store and worshipped in the company-built church, where the minister could usually be counted on to preach on the beneficence of the mill owner. Initially, the mill workforces were dominated by women and children, who often worked from sunup to sundown, just as they did on the farm. But by 1900, men began to outnumber women in the mills.

The South attracted the textile industry from New England with its promise of low wages, and it often required the husband, wife, and children working for a family to make ends meet. In 1920 the National Industrial Conference computed that the "minimum American standard" of living in Charlotte was $1,438 per year (or about $14,595 in 2007 dollars). In 1921 the average textile wage in North Carolina was $624 per year ($7,076 in 2007 dollars).[15] In the eyes of progressive reformers, the number of children, especially young girls, working in the mills was a scandal. Children under age fourteen legally could work a forty-eight-hour week in North Carolina if they had completed four years of schooling. And an estimated three-quarters of the spinners in Tar Heel plants were girls under fourteen.

Textile workers were often looked down upon as "poor white trash" or "lintheads" (because of the cotton lint that stuck to their heads after a day in the mill). Working around machinery in the card room was often dangerous, sometimes leading to mangled hands and arms. An injured worker no longer able to perform his or her work would sometimes simply be laid off. The long hours working amid the clouds of lint and the whirring spindles took their toll in respiratory diseases and people aging and dying before their years. The textile industry opposed any action to combat byssinosis until the 1970s. Writer and social critic W. J. Cash painted a bleak portrait of the textile worker. "A dead-white skin, a sunken chest, and stooping shoulders were the earmarks of the breed," Cash wrote in his classic book, *The Mind of the South*. "Chinless faces, microcephalic foreheads, rabbit teeth, goggling dead-fish eyes, rickety limbs, and stunted bodies abounded. The women were characteristically stringy-haired and limp of breast at twenty, and shrunken hags at thirty or forty. And the incidence of tuberculosis, or insanity and epilepsy, and above all, of pellagra, the curious vitamin-deficiency disease which is nearly peculiar to the South, was increasing."[16]

The first generation off the farms in the nineteenth century more readily accepted the conditions they found. They often were friendly with the mill owner. And changing mill jobs was easy. But as the 1920s approached, the second generation was less compliant. Many of the mills were taken over by large corporations that brought in efficiency experts to speed up production and lower costs.

After the textile industry went into an economic tailspin in late 1920, there was a round of wage cuts and new requirements that fewer workers tend more spindles—a practice called "stretch-outs" by workers. This time, the mill owners did not mind if their factories were closed for a time because of the industry downturn, and they waited for the strikers to run out of food and money.

Gardner was a mill owner and industry ally, but he was no mere mouthpiece for big business: he took pride in the quality of his mill village. But he was also a personal injury lawyer, often suing corporations on behalf of injured workers. Early in his administration, Gardner pushed through the legislature a workman's compensation act, so that the cost of injuries would not be borne only by the worker.

Gardner had been governor only three months in 1929 when the 1,800 workers at Loray Mills, the largest mill in Gaston County, went on strike. Worker discontent had been building as a result of the decision by the mill's Rhode Island owners to bring in a new superintendent to make the plant more efficient. Ordered to cut costs, the superintendent increased the workload, cut wages by 20 percent, and reduced the workforce from 3,500 to 2,200. Months of unrest, including several brief walkouts, had preceded the strike. During one walkout, Loray workers paraded a coffin down Gastonia's main street. At intervals, a man impersonating the superintendent rose out of the coffin and asked, "How many men are carrying this thing?"

"Eight!" the group shouted.

"Lay off two," the effigy responded. "Six can do the work."[17]

The 1929 strike was spearheaded by the communist-led National Textile Workers Union. Its chief organizer was a New England communist named Fred Beal who wanted to make Gastonia a "citadel of the class struggle." Gaston County was the third-largest textile county in the country, calling itself the "South's City of Spindles." There were more than 570 mills within a 100-mile radius around Gastonia's town center. Loray Mill was the largest textile plant in the county.

By the time the Loray Mill workers went on strike, Gastonia was a tinderbox. Besides the businessmen's traditional antipathy to labor unions, the communist involvement had turned much of the community against the organizing effort. Antiunion newspaper advertisements warned against world revolution, atheism, racial mixing, and free love.

Workers demanded a $20-per-week minimum salary ($237 in 2007 dollars), equal pay for women and children, abolition of the stretch-out, and union recognition. The strike soon spread to nearby Gaston County mills. The company responded by evicting families from mill-owned housing, and a group of armed masked men demolished the union headquarters. After several scuffles between strikers and strikebreakers, Gardner acceded to a request by Loray Mill's management to send 250 National Guardsmen to Gastonia to help keep order and, of course, to break the strike. After two weeks with no resolution, Gardner sent the National Guard home. The mill owners responded by organizing their own "Committee of 100," many of whose members were made deputy sheriffs. Many workers returned to the mill as community pressure built against the strike. When the remaining 200 strikers were evicted from their mill-owned homes, they set up a tent city and vowed to protect their community.

On June 7, Gastonia police chief O. F. Aderholt and four officers entered the union headquarters without a warrant and tried to disarm and arrest one of the guards. Exactly what happened may never be certain, but shots rang out, wounding the officers and killing the chief. Fifteen of the union men were indicted for conspiracy leading to murder, even though most of them were not even present at the shooting. In a sensational, heavily publicized trial in Charlotte, a mistrial was declared after one of the jurors went mad at the sight of a bloodstained dummy of Chief Aderholt that was used as a prop by the prosecution. The mistrial sparked outrage in Gaston County, and union foes turned to vigilantism. A mob formed a caravan of more than 100 automobiles that roamed through Gaston County, wrecking union property and terrorizing organizers.

Several days later, vigilantes fired in broad daylight into a truck of workers heading toward a union meeting, killing Ella May Wiggins, a local strike leader in nearby Bessemer City. Wiggins, twenty-nine, was the mother of nine children—four of whom were deceased. After her husband had deserted her, she supported her family earning nine dollars a week at the American Mill. Wiggins, the secretary of the union, kept up morale among the strikers living in the tent city with her mountain ballads. As the dirt was shoveled onto her grave, a coworker sang one of her songs, called "Mill Mother's Lament."

> We leave our home in the morning,
> We kiss our children good-by.
> While we slave for the bosses,
> Our children scream and cry.
> And when we draw our money

Our grocery bills to pay,
Not a cent to spend for clothing
Not a cent to lay away.[18]

With public sentiment against the unions, staging a fair trial was difficult. There were fifty witnesses to the murder in broad daylight of Wiggins.
Five antiunion Loray Mill workers were indicted for her murder, but each
won jury acquittal. But sixteen union members charged with second-degree
murder of the Gastonia police chief were found guilty during their second
trial after only an hour's deliberation, receiving sentences ranging from
five to twenty years. Beal, the chief organizer, and three others jumped bail
and fled to the Soviet Union to avoid imprisonment. After growing disillu-
sioned with the Soviet Union, Beal returned in 1933 to the United States and
surrendered himself. He was paroled in 1942 on the basis that he had not
received a fair trial. The case became a cause in national left-wing circles,
and the strike inspired six novels.

A month after the killing of Wiggins in October 1929, the struggling
North Carolina labor movement produced new martyrs. This time it was
not communists but the anticommunist American Federation of Labor
(AFL) that was trying to organize the Baldwin and Clinchfield mills in the
Mountain town of Marion. Some 650 workers walked off the job following
several months of labor disputes involving stretch-outs and the firing of
union leaders. In the early morning hours of October 2, while workers were
trying to persuade the day-shift crew to stay off the job, McDowell County
deputy sheriffs began shooting, killing six and seriously wounding twenty-
five others. All were shot in the back.[19]

The sheriff, twelve deputies, and two mill officials were arrested and
charged with murder. But a jury would not convict them. A union organizer
and three strikers were, however, sent to prison for their role in trying to
evict a strikebreaker who had moved into the home of a striker. Today in
the state AFL-CIO headquarters in Raleigh there is a plaque memorializing
the martyrs killed in Marion.

In nearly every instance, North Carolina communities were aligned
against the labor unions and the strikers. Police force was used to quell
the strikes, and toughs were hired by the mill owners and deputized by
local authorities. Ministers and newspapers railed against the unions.
North Carolina's textile mills were one-fifth to one-third smaller than those
in New England or in England, making it easier for management to control the workers. For many mill hands fresh off the farm, the idea of labor

unions was an alien, big-city concept that they did not trust. And the radicalism of some of the labor organizers only reinforced that view. Gastonia, wrote Cash, had the effect of fixing "solidly in the minds of the great mass of Southerners the equation: labor unions & strikers + Communists & atheism & social equality with the Negro—and so to join to the formidable list of Southern sentiments already drawn up against the strikers the great central one of racial feeling and purpose."[20]

The violence did not quell the labor movement. There were strikes in Pineville, Lexington, Bessemer City, Leaksville, Charlotte, Durham, Fayetteville, Gibsonville, and Raleigh. The labor violence attracted unfavorable national attention, just at the time when the state was becoming a regional leader in educational improvements and road construction and was building the University of North Carolina into a great center of learning. Even during this period of union bashing, significant voices in North Carolina called for better treatment of textile workers. An open letter written by UNC professor Frank Porter Graham and signed by 390 North Carolina citizens called for a study of conditions in the textile industry, a reduction of the workweek, elimination of child labor, and the right of "individual laborers to organize or not organize."[21]

Liberals such as Nell Battle Lewis, a *News and Observer* columnist, raged at Gardner for siding with mill owners. "Judging by events of recent months," Lewis wrote, "I take it that the State of North Carolina is at war against a great group of its own people already discriminated against in the laws of the State. On whatever apparently reasonable pretext State troops are called out in our industrial disputes, the practical effect is to range the armed force of the State against the workers and in defense of the mill owners."[22]

By the end of his four-year term, Gardner grew more sophisticated in his handling of labor disputes. He was more likely to send in mediators to negotiate than to send the National Guard to break a strike. On occasion, he brought both sides to the mansion for separate jawboning sessions.

During Gardner's final year as governor in July 1932, there was a massive strike in the greater Greensboro area, where workers were angered over wage cuts and layoffs. So-called flying squadrons of strikers went from mill to mill in High Point, Jamestown, Kernersville, Lexington, and Thomasville, urging workers to leave their workplaces, cutting off electricity, and in some cases bodily carrying workers out of the plants. By the end of the day, about 15,000 workers in 150 plants walked off the job. In High Point that evening, 10,000 workers gathered on the streets in a festive mood as authorities nervously watched. Ignoring calls by mill owners to deploy the National Guard, Gardner drove to High Point, where he dismissed the contingent of 100 highway patrolmen and met separately with the mill owners and the labor leaders, helping negotiate an agreement.

Even Gardner's critics, such as Nell Lewis, gave him credit for becoming more subtle in his dealings with labor. "Both Gastonia and Marion have been dark blots on the Gardner Administration, but they are considerably redeemed by the governor's recent action at High Point, where there was no violence, no bloodshed and where a reasonable compromise was reached," wrote Lewis. "The governor is quoted as saying: 'The method by which this dispute was settled ought to become a precedent for the adjustment of future labor disagreements.' Would that he had arrived at that eminently sensible conclusion in 1929. Maybe if he had Alderholdt, Ella May Wiggins and the six workers at Marion, or some of them, would be alive today. But we are learning, slowly learning."[23]

In the end, the labor movement found North Carolina fallow ground. By 1939 only 4.2 percent of the nonagricultural workforce was unionized, the second-lowest percentage in the nation.[24] North Carolina's industrial wages lagged near the bottom—a function of both the lack of unionization and the dominance of the low-paying textile industry. As late as the 1950s, North Carolina governors were using state power to break strikes. A proposal by Governor Jim Hunt in 1977 to create a North Carolina labor education center at N.C. Central University in Durham—to conduct courses on collective bargaining, grievance procedures, occupational safety, and other issues—was blocked by business interests. A group of Klansmen and neo-Nazis were acquitted of the 1979 murder of five communists involved in labor organizing, even though they were gunned down in broad daylight at a Greensboro anti-Klan rally as the TV cameras rolled. The plight of North Carolina's textile workers and their efforts to organize were immortalized in the 1979 movie *Norma Rae*, for which actress Sally Field won an Oscar. North Carolina was the least-unionized state in the country in 2004, with only 2.7 percent of its workforce belonging to a union. In Mississippi, by comparison, 4.8 percent of its workers were union members.[25]

The crushing of the labor movement in the 1920s meant that unlike in many northern and midwestern industrial states, there would be little check on the political power of the business community in North Carolina. The General Assembly continues to give business most of what it wants. And with rare exceptions, North Carolina still elects governors with close ties to the state's big banks, textile mills, tobacco companies, and utilities—even though North Carolina is among the most blue-collar states in the country.

The Creation of the Shelby Dynasty

Despite the Depression and labor unrest, Gardner enjoyed his time as governor. The sociable Gardners entertained so frequently in the Executive Mansion that aside from breakfast, it is estimated that he and wife Faye ate only thirty-six meals alone during their four years in office. Their dinner guests included New York governor Franklin Roosevelt, ambassador and arts patron Harry Guggenheim, Virginia governor Harry Byrd, aviator Charles Lindbergh, World War I flying ace Eddie Rickenbacker, former New York governor Al Smith, and *Time* magazine founder Henry Luce and his wife, Clare Boothe Luce. He could be salty and enjoyed bantering with bellhops, taxi drivers, store clerks, and farmhands. "He took a youthful delight in living," said his aide Edwin Gill, a future state treasurer. "And this fresh spirit was contagious and caused others to revert to the days of their youth, to laugh, to enjoy the sheer thrill of being alive."[26]

Sometimes, on out-of-state trips, Gardner took along Thad Eure, the N.C. House of Representatives principal clerk, and passed him off as "Colonel Eure" to Roosevelt and other political heavyweights. Eure said such displays were typical of Gardner, who liked grand entrances into towns with a police escort and sirens blaring. In one instance, Gardner entered an eastern North Carolina town where he was met by a lone police motorcycle. That prompted Gardner to remark to his driver: "Don't you reckon they got more than one motorcycle in this damn town?"[27]

Gardner was a natural-born campaigner. He once described the process of running for governor as kissing the tails of everybody in North Carolina with the understanding that when he was elected they would all have to kiss his.[28]

Gardner now possessed a powerful political organization. He worked to rebuild the Democratic Party after the disastrous 1928 election, melding together the old Simmons Machine with his own. The governor was determined that his reorganization of state government would not be sabotaged by his political foes.

Although the Democrats were in complete control of the state, North Carolina was sharply divided politically in the 1930s. The division had a strong urban/rural flavor. The Gardner organization had the support of bankers, textile-mill owners, utility-company executives, tobacco executives, and the courthouse organizations of the Piedmont and the Mountains.

The opposing faction centered on the tobacco farmers and shopkeepers of eastern North Carolina. The pitchfork brigade eyed with suspicion the centralization of power in state government brought about by Gardner, opposed the levying of a sales tax, and thought the Shelby Dynasty was excessively tied to the state's powerful industrial interests. There was a whiff of agrarian revolt to their politics, as well—the remnants of the Populist Movement of the 1890s. They supported such insurgents as Richard Fountain, Ralph McDonald, and Kerr Scott for governor and Bob Reynolds for the U.S. Senate in the 1930s and 1940s. This populism would later sometimes take a more conservative form: Jesse Helms, although a business ally, won the support of some of the pitchfork crowd by promising to rattle the cages of the Washington bureaucrats and the United Nations.

"The Democratic Party in North Carolina, even before we had got what we call a two-party system, was always a two-party system," recalled newspaperman Jonathan Daniels. "We had the conservative and the Democratic wings of the party. And they were just as clearly two political parties almost as the Democrats and the Republicans."[29]

Despite his control of the machinery, Gardner was worried about a populist revolt from desperate Depression-era voters. "I am convinced that were it not for the known fact that we are in the process of preparing the people for an opportunity to express their convictions concerning their government in November, we would today be in the midst of a violent social and political revolution," Gardner wrote to a conservative friend before the 1932 elections. "If I were Roosevelt, I would become more liberal. I would march with the crowd, because I tell you the masses are marching and if we are to save this nation it has got to be saved by the liberal interpretations of the sentiments now ruling in the hearts of men. I am satisfied that we are in the day of a new deal and that many of our preconceived ideas and formulas are going to be thrown into the discard."[30]

Gardner's two goals in 1932 were to elect J. C. B. Ehringhaus governor and Cameron Morrison to the U.S. Senate. Gardner plucked Ehringhaus, a fifty-year-old Elizabeth City attorney and former legislator, out of political retirement to be his successor. Ehringhaus campaigned on Gardner's record and on the need to balance the budget during the economic crisis. Ehringhaus was narrowly elected in a primary runoff, despite charges by Lieutenant Governor Richard Fountain that he was a tool of "powerful companies" that would shift the tax burden to the "little man" from the corporations.

But Gardner failed in his effort to elect Morrison to the Senate. Since leaving the governor's mansion in 1925, Morrison had settled into the life of a country squire. During the last year of his administration, Morrison married Virginia Watts, the widow of Durham financier George Washington Watts, who had inherited a $9 million tobacco fortune ($104 million in 2006 dollars). Morrison had also courted millionaire George Vanderbilt's widow, but he was turned down—or so the story goes—when he tried to spit tobacco juice out of her limousine window that was so clean he thought it was open.

In 1925 Morrison purchased 160 acres to create an estate in Charlotte he called Morrocroft and settled into life as a gentleman farmer. With his newfound wealth, Morrison became one of the state Democratic Party's biggest financiers. In 1930 Gardner appointed him to fill the vacancy left by the death of Senator Lee Overman of Salisbury. The appointment of the man who had once stolen a governor's race from him helped Gardner meld together the old Simmons Machine with the Shelby Dynasty. "You Gardners are the best sports I ever knew," Morrison said after being informed of his appointment.[31]

Morrison proved to be a good sport himself. The same month Gardner appointed Morrison to the Senate, the governor faced a personal financial crisis when Shelby's First National Bank, like many banks across the country, was on the brink of failing. Cleveland Cloth, Gardner's textile mill, had a large sum of money deposited in the bank. The governor, who was one of the bank's directors, faced the prospect of either "going bust" if he kept his money in the bank or causing the bank to fail if he withdrew his company's money. In desperation, Gardner turned to Morrison, who put up enough of his wife's money to rescue the bank. "Cam came to the rescue," First Lady Faye Gardner wrote in her diary.[32]

Few political observers expected Morrison to have any trouble holding on to the Senate seat in 1932. Folksy, tobacco chewing, deep-pocketed, and with a voice described as "waves breaking around a lighthouse," Morrison confidently predicted he would carry 99 of 100 counties in the primary. Still, there were three challengers to Morrison, most notably Bob Reynolds. "In my party everyone that can't get any other job or political office is running against me," Morrison quipped. "They ought to run for president. It would do 'em about as much good and get 'em just as much publicity."[33]

Our Bob

There was no reason why Morrison should have taken Reynolds seriously. The forty-seven-year-old Asheville lawyer had run for higher office three times, losing races for Congress, lieutenant governor, and the U.S. Senate. He cultivated a reputation as a playboy who had been married four times—and he wasn't yet finished. But if there was ever a time when people were ready to gamble on a populist demagogue, 1932 was such a time.

Reynolds could have been North Carolina's Huey Long. But he was more interested in chasing women than starting a revolution.

Born in 1884 into an old Buncombe County family, Reynolds had long ago learned the art of "bunk"—a term derived from a windy nineteenth-century congressman from Buncombe County. Reynolds worked as a patent-medicine salesman in Chicago, acted in vaudeville, ran a skating rink in New Orleans, and had traveled around the world writing travel books, making films, and seeking adventure. And everywhere he traveled, the handsome, charming Reynolds sweet-talked beautiful women.

The first Mrs. Reynolds was an attractive, wealthy New Orleans debutante named Fannie Menge Jackson who died as a result of childbirth, leaving him the equivalent of $3.7 million in today's dollars. The second Mrs. Reynolds was a seventeen-year-old Georgia beauty named Mary Bland whom he divorced after three years. The third Mrs. Reynolds was twenty-three-year-old Denise D'Arcy, a pretty French woman whom he divorced after a year. The fourth Mrs. Reynolds was Eva Grady, a Ziegfeld Follies showgirl who died of tuberculosis after three years of marriage.

When he wasn't wooing women or globe hopping, Reynolds dabbled in politics. His father had been a clerk of court, and one of his uncles had been a sheriff and another a police chief. At age twenty-six, Reynolds began his political career with a successful campaign for district solicitor (prosecuting attorney). With a gift for gab and the slick moves of a patent-medicine salesman, Reynolds campaigned through the mountains, riding on an old flea-bitten, one-eyed nag. He campaigned with a wink and a nod. "I don't want this job just to serve you, although I reckon I can do that just as well as anybody," Reynolds said. "I want it for the money. I'm a young lawyer and I need experience. I want to get it at your expense."[34]

In 1923 the restless Reynolds, who had a lifelong wanderlust, once again took to the road. Signing up with a film company, Reynolds fitted out a Ford truck with a bed and kitchen and traveled across France, Holland, Germany, Switzerland, Italy, Spain, Algiers, Djibouti, China, and Japan. He was arrested in Italy for taking illegal pictures and was robbed near Hong Kong by Chinese pirates. While traveling, Reynolds launched an unlikely campaign for the Democratic nomination for lieutenant governor. Meeting North Carolinians at various exotic locales, he urged them to write their

Senator Robert Reynolds (Photograph by Burnie Batchelor;
courtesy of the *Raleigh News and Observer* and the Batchelor family)

friends back home and asked them to vote for him. He mailed thousands of postcards from the Taj Mahal, the Pyramids, or Westminster Abbey to what he called his "God-fearing, tater-raisin', baby-havin'" constituents. "Having a grand time; wish you were here. May not be back in time for elections, but vote for me just the same."[35]

This proved not to be a winning strategy. But, encouraged that he could draw a respectable number of votes while globe hopping, Reynolds tried campaigning at home. In 1928 he unsuccessfully challenged Senator Overman. But four years later, the millionaire Morrison was a perfect foil for Reynolds in Depression-ridden North Carolina.

Reynolds left Asheville in the guise of a poverty-stricken man of the people. He donned a ragged suit and worn shoes and drove a broken-down Tin Lizzie. Before entering a town, Reynolds often emptied his radiator so that when he arrived steam would be pouring from under the hood. Feigning poverty, Reynolds asked the crowd for gas money to help him get to the next town, or borrowed an automobile, or asked for a place to stay since he could not afford a hotel. He would take a couple of dollar bills out of his pocket and wave it to the crowd, calling on God to witness that it was all the money he had in the world. So phony were his pleas of poverty, Reynolds never bothered to cash hundreds of the small campaign checks he was given although he framed some as campaign souvenirs.[36]

It was Reynolds, the common man, versus Morrison, the plutocrat. As campaign props, the former patent-medicine salesman used a menu from Washington's Mayflower Hotel, where the senator stayed, and a jar of caviar. "What do you think he eats?" Reynolds asked. "He does not eat cabbage nor turnips nor ham and eggs, not fatback like you and I do. My friends, think of it. Senator Morrison eats caviar. What the hell's caviar? This here jar ain't a jar of squirrel shot," Reynolds said, producing a jar. "It's fish eggs. Friends, it pains me to tell you that Cam Morrison eats fish eggs and Red Russian fish eggs at that and they cost two dollars. Now fellow citizens, let me ask you. Do you want a senator who ain't too high and mighty to eat good old North Carolina hen eggs or don't you?"[37]

Playing on voter's religious biases, Reynolds claimed Morrison ate "eggs Benedictine. They's regular hen eggs alright, but they's cooked up by special Benedictine monks that they keep there in the hotel just for that purpose." He said Morrison had rolls of money larger than toilet paper rolls and donned a tuxedo for dinner.[38]

Reynolds blamed big business for the Depression. He called for redistribution of the wealth, repeal of national Prohibition, and an end to immigration. And he said Morrison was in the pockets of the Duke Power Company. "Your government is ruled not by the president of the United States," Reynolds asserted, "but by the invisible and heretofore invincible power of Wall Street, the investment bankers who have brought on us the destruction we experience at this hour."[39]

With his showmanship, good looks, and gift for gab, Reynolds cut quite a figure on the campaign trail. He was courteous, friendly, and funny, and people could sense that he genuinely liked them. When he was courting his future wives, Reynolds sometimes suggested that he was part of the fabulously wealthy Reynolds tobacco family. But on the campaign trail, the candidate denied any such connections.

"Folks you know this isn't true," he said in Edenton. "If I were the son of R. J. Reynolds I wouldn't be running around North Carolina in an old rickety Ford. I would buy me a big beautiful car as long as from here to that table like Cam Morrison's. I would have me a chauffeur wearing livery like an admiral's and a footman. Cam's got a footman. When he drives up to the Mayflower [Hotel] in Washington, the footman opens the door and stands there with a rug on his arm. When Cam steps out, the footman gives it a twirl—like this—and Cam goes walking in like this."[40] His pantomime of the footman laying out the red carpet and his mimicking of Morrison's stride and voice left his audiences roaring with laughter. "Old Cam can't get his tootsies dirty," Reynolds said.

Morrison first dismissed Reynolds as a political sideshow. But as Reynolds caught on, Morrison went on the offensive. The senator said Reynolds was only feigning poverty and that before he became a candidate, "Our Bob" had been driving a Cadillac and using a private plane. Not only was Reynolds driving a Cadillac, Morrison said, but Reynolds's car also was ten inches longer than his own. Reynolds replied that it was not his Cadillac—the car and the mountain estate belonged to his mother and were held in trust for his children. The airplane belonged to a local dentist, he said.[41]

Morrison took to the radio airwaves to explain to voters that he was no aristocrat—merely a humble country boy who married well late in life. "When I ran for governor they said I was too poor to live in the governor's mansion. And now because during the latter part of my administration, God gave me for a wife a noble Christian woman, now my opponents say I am too rich to be trusted," Morrison said in a radio speech in Raleigh. "It isn't a case of the husband of a wealthy woman wanting to buy a place. I battered myself up when I was poor. It is a question of whether I am going to lose my place because I married a noble woman who has some money."[42]

But for Morrison it was too little, too late. Reynolds led the primary with 43 percent, followed by 39 percent for Morrison and 18 percent for two other candidates. Raleigh newspaper columnist Nell Battle Lewis created an imaginary scene of Morrison contemplating the election returns.

> Through richly furnished chambers paced a distracted figure, spitting tobacco juice at random and bellowing like a wounded bull.
>
> "Ah'm ruined. Ya-a-as, mah country men, Ah'm ruined. Ah jes' can't beat it. Mah heart is broken. Oh Sarah, they've broken my heart. Mah own people, a-trying ter ruin me, repudiatin' their Guv'nor, the greates' Guv'nor they've had sence the Civil War—disownin' an' malignin' an' forsaken' an' humilatin' their devoted public servant who never had another thought outside th' welfare of Grandole N'th Carolina, a-votin' against th' statesman that gave 'em th' wonderful Program of Progress an' wants ter protect th' Home an' the' Church an' all the fundamentals of this Grea-a-a-t Christian Democracy—a votin' against me in favor of a dripping wet that wants to bring back th' vile saloon an' that ain't never done nuthin' fer the' state a-tall."[43]

Reynolds was the first statewide politician to call for repeal of Prohibition. Reynolds called Prohibition "a calamitous dose of political hypocrisy which has been fed to us for 13 years from a tarnished spoon of morality" that helped only gangsters while spreading disrespect for the law.[44]

For Morrison, whom writer W. J. Cash described as "the arch paladin of the dry South," this was political heresy. Morrison "believed in Prohibition innocently and without hypocrisy, as something commanded by God through his holy men, identified with the South, and enacted into law in his state and in Congress by the Democratic Party," Cash wrote.[45] So identified with Prohibition was Morrison, his campaign manager taught a German Bullfinch to whistle "How Dry I Am."[46]

In the runoff election, Morrison attempted to turn the liquor issue against Reynolds. "Here I have been working in and for the Democratic Party for 40 years and this showman comes along and gets the people all excited over the prospect of getting them drunk; and these young boys just coming up want to beat me because I am against liquor," Morrison said in Dunn. "It's about the hardest proposition I ever encountered."

Morrison was hurt when the national Democratic Party endorsed repeal of Prohibition just two days before the runoff election. Morrison pleaded with voters to forget Reynolds's picture of him as a plutocrat and remember him as their longtime friend. "I'm the same old Cam I always was," Morrison said. "They are jest telling more lies on me than usual."[47]

Reynolds trounced one of North Carolina's most famous politicians in the runoff by an astounding 65 to 35 percent — at the time the widest margin ever in a Democratic primary. Reynolds won even though Morrison was backed by the state's Democratic Machine and endorsed by the major newspapers.

In a letter to his friend, Franklin Roosevelt, who was then campaigning for president, Gardner tried to explain what was happening. "It is a mistake to say that these currents of thought are wholly the creations of demagogues. They spring naturally from the oppressed and bewildered minds of men. It is not enough to call these movements mob psychology. They are really the mass thinking of a people who have either been forgotten or deceived. Demagogues do not create movements. They merely ride upon them."[48]

Later in the century, voters could remedy the nomination of a demagogue by one party in the fall. But in 1932, North Carolina was still a one-party state, and Reynolds won the general election by more than a 2 to 1 margin.

Super Lobbyist in Washington

As Gardner was leaving the governor's office, his friend Roosevelt was moving into the White House. The two men were elected governor in 1928 and had struck up a friendship. They corresponded and attended a football game together in Atlanta, and Roosevelt was an overnight guest in the Executive Mansion in Raleigh.

During the 1932 presidential campaign, Gardner stumped for Roosevelt and was at FDR's side during a whistle-stop tour across the state. By the end of the campaign, there were rumors that Gardner was in line for a cabinet post. But Gardner had other plans. While continuing to oversee his mill in Shelby, Gardner moved to Washington, D.C., where he leveraged his friendship with FDR and his wide political connections to become one of the most powerful lawyer-lobbyists of the New Deal. Gardner spent his remaining fourteen years in Washington, moving in the highest political and social circles. But he continued to dominate North Carolina politics, helping elect his friends and relatives as governor.

Unlike many business leaders, Gardner came to Washington as an enthusiastic New Dealer. In Gardner's view, radical changes were needed not only to lift the country out of the Depression, but also to save capitalism. "The one hope for the immediate present is Roosevelt, and if he does not come through with something big and radical in my judgment we are lost," Gardner wrote a friend.[49]

In the whirlwind first 100 days of the New Deal, Gardner worked with a committee of industrialists to help draft Roosevelt's National Industrial Recovery Act, which established the National Recovery Administration (NRA). The NRA's cotton-textile code was able to do what the industry had been unable to accomplish voluntarily—end cutthroat competition and overproduction by placing production curbs on individual cotton mills. In return, the textile manufacturers agreed to end child labor, institute a forty-hour workweek and a minimum wage, and accept in theory the principle of collective bargaining.

When FDR went on the radio for a fireside chat to sell the NRA to the American people, Gardner helped write the speech. Gardner sought to convince his friends and business associates of the need for the textile industry to change. "I am more and more convinced that the men and women who work in the mills ought to have some larger share in the profits of the industry, and I am in no sense a socialist," Gardner wrote to his business partner in North Carolina.[50] Gardner paid his own workers in Shelby above-average wages, prompting complaints from other mill owners in the area. But Gardner fought union efforts to organize his workforce, leading to a strike in 1934 over allegations that union leaders at his plant had been fired in retaliation for their organizing efforts. The strike was settled, but Gardner did not recognize the union.

Setting up a law practice in Washington, Gardner started as the legal counsel for the Cotton Textile Institute, a trade group for cotton manufacturers. Soon his client list grew to include the Rayon Producers Group, United States Lines, Coca-Cola, Pan American Airways, the Hearst Corporation, and the Aviation Corporation. A columnist reported—apparently correctly—that Gardner was earning the princely sum of $100,000 per year, or the equivalent of $1.5 million in 2006 dollars.

The White House doors were always open to Gardner. He wrote speeches for key New Deal officials. The Gardners were social friends of FDR and occasionally dined with the president. Faye Gardner helped Eleanor Roosevelt plan White House garden teas and other social functions. As a Christmas present for FDR in 1942, Gardner gave the president a pair of pajamas made of nylon parachute cloth woven at his Shelby mill. Gardner wanted to emphasize the value of synthetics research to help offset the Japanese monopoly on silk, the traditional material for parachutes. FDR sent Gardner a note saying: "I hope when I wear them [the pajamas] that I do not start counting ten and jump."[51]

While many of North Carolina's leading businessmen quickly turned against the liberal New Deal, Gardner remained an ardent backer—an important channel between FDR and the conservative business community. He expressed approval of the president's willingness to "stand up to the plate and bat the hell out of the reactionaries."[52]

Gardner's views on race were advanced for a white southerner of his day. While Gardner did not criticize segregation, he sought to ameliorate the worst aspects of it. As governor, Gardner was sharply criticized when he was photographed in 1929 with a white boy and a black girl who were essay winners in the "Live-at-Home" contest, a program designed to encourage people to become self-sufficient by growing more of their own food. When he was warned that he was handing his foes political ammunition, Gardner said he would make use of the picture himself in any future political campaign. When Depression-era legislative budget cutters proposed merging the state's two major black public colleges—what would become N.C. A&T State University in Greensboro and N.C. Central University in Durham—Gardner killed the plan.

In later years, Gardner encouraged the registration of blacks at the mill precinct near his factory in Shelby, so that by the 1940s there were 500 African Americans voting in that precinct. He praised his son Ralph for organizing a black Boy Scout troop. He donated land to Shelby for use as a park for blacks. He told the mayor of Shelby near the end of World War II that it was a waste of money to build a new school for blacks because racial segregation could not last much longer. And he said privately what no southern politician could say publicly. "I have no doubt, as you know, that the young Negroes of today will be the voters of tomorrow," Gardner wrote to his son in 1940. "In the next 20 years the Negroes will not be denied the franchise by fictitious political figments."[53]

Gardner also served on the board of directors of the Rosenwald Fund, a foundation started by the founder of Sears and Roebuck, which funneled $25 million to build schools for blacks in the South, including hundreds of schools in North Carolina. On his way from Washington to one Rosenwald Fund board meeting in Chicago, he rode the train with First Lady Eleanor Roosevelt, a fellow board member and an early advocate for black civil rights, engaging in long discussions about postwar race relations. Nervous that Gardner was getting too out in front of his contemporaries on such an explosive issue, Faye Gardner convinced her husband, who was beginning to experience health problems, to resign from the board.

During most of their years in Washington, the Gardners lived in apartment 770 of the Mayflower Hotel on Connecticut Avenue—a hotel that served as home for many of the leading figures in the nation's capital. The hotel was something of a Democratic stronghold, with the Democratic National Committee headquarters on the second floor. The Gardners quickly became part of Washington's high society, their names regularly appearing in the social columns of the city's newspapers. If leading socialite Pearl Mesta threw one of her soirees, chances were that the Gardners were present. The Gardners were a fixture at Embassy Row parties. His regular guests at the Mayflower included Senator Walter George of Georgia, syndicated political columnist Drew Pearson, New Deal insiders such as Tom Corcoran and Harry Hopkins, Chief Justice Fred Vinson, Vice President John Nance Garner, and a young congressional aide named Lyndon Johnson. Comedian Jack Benny was a guest at one party.

After becoming deputy treasury secretary, Gardner often ended his parties by offering his most prominent guest a newly minted silver dollar. "I will give you this dollar on two conditions," Gardner said. "One that you keep it forever, so that you will never be broke. The other that you go home—right now."[54]

The Gardners were chauffeured around Washington by a black North Carolinian named Roosevelt—named after Teddy, not FDR. Gardner and friends rarely missed a Kentucky Derby, sometimes renting a Pullman Car to travel to Churchill Downs in style. There were weekends in Sommerville, the New Jersey mansion of tobacco heiress Doris Duke, or duck shooting at Ichauway, the Georgia plantation of Coca-Cola Company chairman Robert Woodruff. There were outings off Cape Cod on the yacht of textile magnate Russell Leonard. The Gardners attended the gala premiere of the movie *Gone With the Wind* in Atlanta.

The ex–college football star retained his love of sports, whether winning money off the national Republican Party chairman at Washington's Burning Tree Country Club or enjoying a ringside seat in Madison Square Garden to watch the Joe Louis–Max Baer fight. He rarely missed a Washington Redskins game. Redskins owner George Preston Marshall credited Gardner with helping save the National Football League when Congress was preparing to shut down the stadiums during World War II. Arguing that Americans needed a diversion even in time of war, Gardner took a number of congressional leaders to a Redskins game so they could see that 40 percent of the spectators were in military uniform.

In supporting the New Deal, Gardner was in tune with most North Carolinians. Roosevelt's strongest support was in the South. Roosevelt's programs to rescue agriculture, including tobacco, were particularly popular among southerners. Southern members of Congress played a pivotal role in helping enact Roosevelt's programs into law. Among the North Carolinians who helped Roosevelt was "Muley Bob" Doughton. As chairman of the House Ways and Means Committee, the Mountain Democrat helped push through a number of key New Deal programs, including the Social Security Act of 1935, despite complaints from Republicans who called it socialism.

But following Roosevelt's reelection in 1936, cracks began to appear in Roosevelt's solid southern support. Many southerners were wary of Roosevelt's ties to organized labor and feared that he was shifting the party more toward northern liberalism. While Gardner continued to publicly back the New Deal, privately he was becoming more skeptical of some of FDR's proposals. He quietly opposed Roosevelt's so-called court-packing plan, in which the president proposed to expand the U.S. Supreme Court in order to prevent the conservative justices from overturning some of his programs.

Gardner played a high-wire political game, remaining a New Deal insider while at the same time surreptitiously helping conservative antiadministration Democratic friends win reelection. During the 1938 elections, Roosevelt tried to purge two anti–New Deal senators from the South—Walter George of Georgia and "Cotton" Ed Smith of South Carolina. Gardner took a so-called vacation at the mountain resort of Highlands, near the Georgia–North Carolina border. From Highlands, Gardner helped direct George's reelection effort. Whether Roosevelt ever learned of Gardner's efforts to thwart him is not clear. He also used his political organization to keep Josiah Bailey of North Carolina in the Senate.[55]

Roosevelt was very popular in North Carolina, winning the state with 69.6 percent, 72.4 percent, 77 percent, and 69.1 percent during his four elections. But conservatives such as Bailey were troubled by Roosevelt's liberalism.

Bailey, who unseated Simmons in 1930, became one of the leading anti–New Deal Democrats in the Senate. He won reelection in 1936 by giving lip service to Roosevelt—at Gardner's suggestion. But by December 1937, Bailey and many other southern Democrats were in full revolt. Bailey was the principal drafter of a ten-point Conservative Manifesto, which denounced the strikes, demanded lower federal wages, defended states' rights, and warned of the dangers of creating a permanent welfare class. Nearly 2 million copies of the manifesto were distributed across the country. "The manifesto," wrote historian David Kennedy, "constituted a kind of founding charter for modern American conservatism. It was among the first systematic expressions of an anti-government political philosophy that had deep roots in American political culture but only an inchoate existence before the New Deal."[56]

Dynasty Maker

Even as an influential lawyer-lobbyist in Washington, Gardner was still the most powerful political personality in North Carolina politics during the 1930s and 1940s. From his suite in the Mayflower Hotel, he read his mail subscriptions to North Carolina's daily newspapers. He maintained close contact with political leaders by telephone and through the mail. As the state's Democratic National Committeeman, along with Bailey, Gardner dispensed federal political patronage. Bailey boasted in 1936 that he had helped 4,000 North Carolinians find jobs with government agencies.[57]

Keeping a political organization with a markedly probusiness tilt in power at home during the desperate days of the Depression was a constant struggle. In 1932 Ehringhaus barely won election as governor. And in 1936 the Gardner Machine received an even bigger scare from a most unlikely source—a thirty-three-year-old liberal college professor from Illinois.

The Shelby Dynasty was not very popular in 1936. In trying to keep state government afloat during the Depression, Ehringhaus made some politically difficult decisions. He cut the state budget by nearly one-third. He imposed a three-cent sales tax to largely finance the schools. But Ehringhaus kept the schools open during the Depression and actually extended the school year to eight months. And while other states were forced to close schools, North Carolina's teachers and other state employees continued to receive steady paychecks.

In finding a successor for Ehringhaus in 1936, Gardner did not have to look far. He chose his brother-in-law, Clyde Hoey, a prominent Shelby lawyer and former congressman who was best man in Gardner's wedding. Hoey looked like a southern politician out of a comic strip—favoring old-fashioned, swallow-tailed English walking coats, a stiff, high-winged collar, a fresh carnation or rose in his lapel, and sometimes striped trousers and high-top shoes. During the day he wore a gray coat, switching to a more formal black one in the evening. He wore this formal outfit even when pitching for a team of state officials at their annual baseball game with the

Senator Josiah Bailey
(Courtesy of the *Raleigh News and Observer*)

Catholic clergy. The son of an impoverished Cleveland County Confederate war veteran, Hoey was apprenticed as a newspaper printer at age twelve. He started the *Cleveland Star* at age sixteen and was elected to the N.C. House at age twenty.

Hoey, whose white hair flowed over his collar in the back, was famous for issuing forth an endless storehouse of blarney and flowery speech about southern virtues. He once admitted after a speech, delivered in his stentorian voice: "I didn't have anything to say. So I turned it on and let it run until I thought they had enough, and then cut it off."[58] One of the most popular political figures in midcentury North Carolina, Hoey as governor walked at 11 A.M. every morning from his office in the Capitol to a soda fountain on Fayetteville Street to get a Coca-Cola, bowing to all the ladies on the way. Hoey's Sunday school lessons at the Edenton Street Methodist Church were broadcast on statewide radio. At the same time, Hoey had a reputation as a womanizer.

Behind the Senator Foghorn–style bluster was a first-rate mind. When tobacco tycoon and textile magnates wanted a top lawyer, they hired Hoey. "He is more conservative than I am, and I regard him as the best lawyer in North Carolina," Gardner told a friend. "I wield a meat ax while he operates with a rapier."[59]

Hoey might have wielded a rapier—and the Gardner organization. But in 1936 he faced a political David with a slingshot in a liberal New Dealer named Ralph McDonald. None of the Democratic powers took McDonald seriously at first, regarding him as little more than a gadfly. They were more concerned with a third gubernatorial candidate, Lieutenant Governor A. H. "Sandy" Graham, who tried to make Gardner the main issue in the campaign: "Shall all the policies and all the principal personnel of the Ehringhaus administration be perpetuated for another four years under the direction of Max Gardner, the highly paid, super lobbyist who represents special interests in Washington and runs North Carolina by long distance telephone?"[60]

But it was McDonald—with his gift for political phrase making—who caught the imagination of Depression-era North Carolina. In no other governor's race in North Carolina during the twentieth century were conservative/liberal economic fault lines so clearly delineated. A native of Illinois, McDonald was reared in Arkansas, worked in the Fayetteville, N.C., public school system, and rose to become head of the psychology and education department at Salem College in Winston-Salem. Interested in school

Governor Clyde Hoey speaking into a radio microphone.
(Courtesy of the *Raleigh News and Observer*)

finance, McDonald was elected to the General Assembly in 1934 and discovered a potent political issue in the sales tax.

Attacking the sales tax as a regressive measure that would hurt the poor, McDonald proposed instead that taxes be raised on stocks, corporations, entertainment, and big stores. With his slogan, "Let's Have a New Deal in North Carolina," McDonald criticized the state's political establishment, which "while boasting of their loyalty to President Roosevelt are actually seeking to destroy the policies of the New Deal at every turn."

"While Roosevelt has saved business by restoring purchasing power," McDonald said, "this North Carolina combine has imposed a blatant reduction on purchasing power by levying a sales tax. While Roosevelt has sponsored a program of security and freedom for the masses, in North Carolina the aged, the helpless, and the unemployed have been abandoned to the caprices of fate."[61]

Nor did McDonald have any reluctance to appeal to class differences. "The purpose of the New Deal in North Carolina is to tear down these fences built around wealth by machine politicians and lobbyists who would tax the little man nearly out of existence to protect their own selfish interests," he said in Monroe.[62]

As the campaign wore on, it became clear that McDonald was tapping into a deep vein of public discontent about the sales tax and the Depression. McDonald's donning of the New Deal mantle came at a time when Roosevelt was extraordinarily popular in North Carolina and in the South. "I think I'd have voted Roosevelt to be dictator," said Raymond Goodmon, who would later become Richmond County sheriff.[63]

With the Depression and the pitched labor battles, many North Carolinians were open to appeals to social class. Mill owners "claim they're not making money," complained one Gastonia worker. "Well if they are not making money, I ask you, how can they afford to build these fine mansions to live in? How can every member of the family own his or her own car? How can they afford to make trips to foreign countries? How can they afford to send their children to college and obtain the best education when the poor mill worker can't make enough money to buy milk for his under-nourished children and can't buy books to send them to school and the mothers must watch the flour sack like a hawk watching a chicken to get hold of them to make little under-garments for her children?"[64]

Any doubt that the pitchfork brigade was closing in on the Shelby Dynasty was erased at a mass rally held a little more than a week before the primary at Raleigh's Memorial Auditorium. More than 3,500 people jammed into the auditorium to hoot and holler as McDonald ridiculed the Gardner Machine, scourged corporate wealth, and praised President Roosevelt. It was said to have been the largest indoor rally ever held for a North Carolina political candidate at that time.

Nobody drew the class lines any sharper than Thomas W. Ruffin, a Raleigh attorney and one of the rally's speakers. "I can see the dawn of a new day breaking in North Carolina," Ruffin said. "A day when it will not take a stick of dynamite to get into the governor's office. A day when the latchstring will be on the outside of the door. A day when the muddy feet of the laboring man will be as welcome on the carpets that cover the floor of the governor's office as the patent leather shoes and gray spats of the corporate president. A day when the smell of fertilizer on the farmer's pants will be more welcome than the fragrant aroma of a 50-cent cigar in the mouth of a fawning politician."[65]

After initially ignoring McDonald, the Shelby crowd counterattacked. Hoey said McDonald's policies of taxing the wealthy would "drive industry and wealth out of the state, decrease employment and so bankrupt the state that it would be necessary to put a heavy tax on land to pull ourselves out of the hole. . . . You can't build a great state on hate. You can't divide people into classes and groups and have a great state."[66] (Apparently Hoey had forgotten the white supremacy campaigns.)

Such populist attacks, Hoey believed, would not sell in North Carolina. "I feel justified in saying that the common sense of North Carolina has proven strong enough to withstand an attack of the same sort of political disease which befell Louisiana under [Huey] Long, Georgia under [Eugene] Talmadge . . . and a number of other states where government, public education and business generally have been set back 10 years or more because the people believed wild promises and elected to office the demagogues who made them," he said in Charlotte.[67]

The June primary results were a cold shower for the Gardner organization. Hoey led the primary by a 38 percent to 37 percent margin, with only 4,458 votes separating the two candidates. The McDonald camp was convinced the election was stolen from them by courthouse rings in the Mountains that were aligned with the Shelby Dynasty—a charge that persons familiar with politics of that era found quite believable.

If the first primary was tough, the Hoey-McDonald runoff of 1936 was the ugliest election since the last time the Red Shirts had mounted up. It was a sharply drawn ideological battle, class warfare, and a brutal struggle for power. The primary divided families and sparked fistfights.

Angered over what he believed to have been widespread ballot cheating, McDonald switched strategies. He began talking less about repealing the sales tax and began making more personal attacks on Hoey and Gardner. McDonald called Hoey a "power company lobbyist whom Mr. Gardner had picked out to rule his provincial domain in North Carolina while he, Gardner, draws his $100,000 fee for representing special interests in Washington."[68]

Hoey called McDonald a "rank outsider" and implied he was a political crackpot. But that was just the beginning, as the candidates tramped across the state trading charges and counter charges.

MCDONALD IN DUNN: "I have frequently thought what a coincidence it is that a man with so much hooey should be named Hoey."

HOEY IN THOMASVILLE: "All that he [McDonald] exposed was himself as an insufferable egotist and a common character assassin."

MCDONALD IN SCOTLAND NECK: "North Carolina cannot afford to have a man for governor who has been bought and paid for with power company money."

HOEY IN RAEFORD: "McDonald said that I had slandered him. In the first place, that's hardly possible."

MCDONALD IN NEW BERN: "There are three forms of adjectives: Good, better, best; bad, worse, worst. Gardner, Ehringhaus, Hoey."

HOEY IN GREENSBORO: "He [McDonald] is the great public enemy in North Carolina."

MCDONALD IN RALEIGH: "They have circulated a report throughout Eastern North Carolina that if I am elected governor, I will put Negro and white children together. They went so far as to say I went to such schools in Illinois. Those statements are deliberate and malicious lies conceived in the perverted minds of crooked politicians."[69]

Not that there weren't lighter moments. McDonald challenged voters to look under Hoey's long-tailed coat to see what he was hiding under there. So Hoey invited anyone from the audience to check his pockets—an invitation that apparently no one ever accepted. "If you see any money in there I'd like to know it," Hoey said, "for I've been badly in need of some for the last few days."

A worried Gardner swung into action, effectively taking control of the Hoey campaign for the runoff and demonstrating the full power of the machine—with its courthouse connections, its patronage, and its entrée into the state's corporate boardrooms. Gardner began calling the corporate offices across the state, leaning on the executives to contribute money to stamp out the left-wing insurgency. "I am putting pressure on everywhere," Gardner wrote to a friend, "and we are going to organize for a crushing victory . . . to settle for some time to come rebellion and revolution."[70]

How much money poured into Hoey's campaign will probably never be known because of the lax campaign-finance reporting laws of the era. But Gardner put in $50,000 (about $730,000 in 2007 dollars) of his own money. Wachovia Bank president Robert Hanes threw another $25,000 (about $365,000 in 2007 dollars) into Hoey's kitty.[71]

The Shelby organization could also rely on state employees kicking back part of their salaries into the Democratic Party coffers. The state Democratic chairman set quotas for each department in state government.[72] Hoey's political message was reshaped as Gardner nudged him to the political left; soon Hoey was proclaiming himself an enthusiastic supporter of FDR and the New Deal.

The Shelby Dynasty also used the patronage powers of the federal New Deal to make sure there would not be a similar New Deal in North Carolina. The New Deal federal relief programs, principally the Works Project Administration (WPA) and the Civilian Conservation Corps, employed 225,000 North Carolinians during the 1930s and early 1940s. The army of workers built roads, bridges, and airports and cleared parkland at a cost of $172 million. Their projects ranged from Mount Mitchell State Park to Raleigh Memorial Auditorium, from the Blue Ridge Parkway to the migratory bird refuge at Swan Quarter. And while the federal workers were supposed to be politically neutral, they could be a powerful tool in the hands of a practiced politician like Gardner.

(Among those working in New Deal programs was a young Duke University law student named Richard Nixon, who earned $30 per month working in the school library as part of the National Youth Administration [NYA], a liberal program suggested by Eleanor Roosevelt. Another NYA worker was Jesse Helms, a Wake Forest College student, who made $18.75 per month doing sports publicity. At UNC, Terry Sanford had an NYA job working in the dining room of Swain Hall.)

George Coan, the state WPA director, received an invitation to spend a weekend at Gardner's Washington home. Coan, a former mayor of Winston-

Salem and a Democratic-patronage appointee, said the ex-governor told him he wanted him to mobilize the 2,500 WPA supervisors in the state to work for Hoey and to help convince the 45,000 WPA workers to vote for his brother-in-law.

In return for helping elect Hoey, Coan demanded a job in the Hoey administration as chairman of the state Highway and Public Works Commission—a demand that Gardner agreed to on the spot without checking with Hoey. (Coan never got the appointment.) Gardner said he would send an emissary to Raleigh with details of a plan. A week later, Coan said, a Gardner lieutenant showed up at his office and tossed a paper bag on his desk containing $25,000 (about $365,000 in 2007 dollars) to be used to help turn out the vote of WPA workers.[73]

During the final day, the candidates let loose their final salvoes. At a rally in Greensboro, Hoey said: "I do not say McDonald is a Socialist because all the Socialists and Communists in North Carolina who vote in the Democratic primary are supporting him, because I believe in being fair although McDonald has been fair about nothing."[74]

At a rally in Winston-Salem, McDonald skewered the Shelby Dynasty.

O. Max Gardner, the number one lobbyist of the United States, came back to North Carolina in a last desperate effort to make his brother-in-law, Clyde Hoey, the number one lobbyist in North Carolina, governor. Are we going to let him do it? No, we are going make this July 4, 1936 a real Independence Day. We are going to bury that Gardner-Ehringhaus-Hoey Machine so deep under honest votes tomorrow that the day will go down in history as the date on which the free and uncontrolled citizenship of North Carolina arose and with a mighty avalanche of ballots decreed that ring rule, the royal succession, this government by lobbyists for privilege is forever ended.[75]

In the end, the Shelby Dynasty crushed the liberal antimachine insurgency by a 55 percent to 45 percent margin. McDonald could not overcome the flood of business money. As political scientist V. O. Key wrote, "The weight of the whole financial community [was] thrown against him. In North Carolina, as everywhere else, money talks in politics."

A grateful Hoey readily acknowledged that his brother-in-law had saved his political skin. "Words are wholly inadequate to express my gratitude," Hoey wrote. "No one had ever heretofore, performed a service like this for me, and nothing comparable to it in any way and I could not imagine anyone ever doing for another, what you have done for me."[76] Senator Harry

FOR GOVERNOR

RALPH McDONALD

One of the best informed men in North Carolina on matters of State Government.

The man who in 1936 received more votes (214,414) than any candidate for the nomination for Governor before or since.

The Democrat who deserves the nomination now because of his good sportsmanship in a close defeat, his loyal support of the Party in State and Nation, and because of the liberal program of State Government for which he stands.

A true and tried friend of Public Education.

The only candidate for Governor who has consistently fought for the farmers, the working men, the teachers, the low-paid State employees, and the childhood of the State.

The only candidate for Governor who proposes to repeal the "emergency temporary" sales tax without resort to a state tax on land.

Every man, woman and child he meets becomes his friend.

Cover page of pamphlet: "For Governor, Ralph McDonald" (Courtesy of the North Carolina Collection, Wilson Library, UNC–Chapel Hill)

Byrd, the political boss of Virginia, wrote to Gardner: "Heroic measures were necessary and you rose to the occasion in magnificent style."[77]

The Shelby Dynasty and the Byrd Machine in Virginia had few peers. "Virginia and North Carolina . . . fostered machines so autocratic and permanent that they were adjournments of the processes of popular government," wrote historian Francis Butler Simpkins. "However, the political juntas of these two states compensated for their cunning by furnishing the best governments south of the Potomac."[78]

The McDonald campaign charged that the Gardner organization had used its control of the election machinery to engage in some massive vote stealing, and there was enough circumstantial evidence to suggest they were right. In a runoff in which 480,000 votes were cast, the State Board of Elections mailed out a staggering 108,250 absentee ballots—the sort of ballots that could most easily be manipulated. The absentee ballots particularly flooded into the Mountain counties, which had a tradition of voter fraud and which were also political strongholds of the Shelby Dynasty. Swain County, which cast 2,004 votes in the first primary, was sent 1,500 absentee ballots for the runoff. In many Mountain counties, the number of absentee ballots sent was more than 50 percent the number of total votes cast in the first primary. According to Key, western North Carolina and southwest Virginia led the South in voter fraud using absentee ballots. Political workers would be given a supply of absentee ballots and, in "market basket" fashion, go in quest of votes. Notaries and justices of the people who were part of the Democratic Machine would approve the ballots without ever seeing the voter. One prominent state official estimated that in those years, control of the state machinery was worth 20 percent of the vote.[79] A 1944 study found that the statewide percentage of absentee ballots was 6.7 percent. But in hard-fought Mountain counties where the Democratic Machine held sway, such as Clay County, the percentage was as high as 26 percent.[80]

In a bout of conscience, the Democratic-controlled General Assembly voted in 1939 to restrict absentee balloting in the primaries—but to continue to allow it in the general election in case it was needed to keep Republicans out of office. Having been elected governor with the help of election fraud, Hoey declared that the state needed "to stop racketeering at the ballot boxes." In 1947 the legislature decided that vote stealing should be restricted in the general election as well.

Not only did Gardner install his brother-in-law in the Executive Mansion and reelect Bailey to the Senate, but the Gardner Machine also ousted two unfriendly statewide officials and elected newcomers handpicked by the organization—Thad Eure as secretary of state and Kerr Scott as agri-culture commissioner. (Eure would be secretary of state for fifty-two years, becoming a state landmark with his big red bow ties, his straw boaters in summer, and his booming declaration at Democratic rallies that he was "the oldest rat in the Democratic barn." He retired in January 1989 at age ninety.)

"Our forces are in complete control," Gardner wrote to his friend Wood-ruff, the chairman of Coca-Cola. "I am willing to put the state government of North Carolina under the so-called Gardner Dynasty up against the state government of any of our sister states on the basis of economy, efficiency and integrity. I honestly believe we have the best state government in the union, and there has never been a breath of scandal or corruption con-nected with the administration of the affairs of North Carolina as we have continued to go forward during the past thirty years."[81]

After the 1936 election, Gardner boasted that North Carolina was the only state in the country where conservative Democrats who faced compe-tition from the left had won. And he took credit for moving both Hoey and Bailey to the left. The liberal movement, Gardner wrote to a friend,

> will spend itself in time, but my thought is that we should go along with it, try to direct it as far as possible, yielding where yielding is wise and then finally at the proper time take a stand. But when we take a stand we will have advanced forward considerably beyond the front lines of our old intrenchment [sic]. I am very much afraid that we have abandoned for some time to come our old Democratic doctrine of levying taxes for the support of the government economically administered. It has never been contemplated by our party until this period that taxes should be levied in order to effectuate the distribution of wealth, and of course this program contravenes our entire conception and construction of the Constitution.[82]

The Shelby Dynasty's hold on Raleigh was politically secure for the next twelve years. In 1940 Melville Broughton, a Raleigh lawyer and a Gardner friend, was elected governor. In 1944 the machine-backed candidate for governor was Gregg Cherry. In the summer of 1943, Cherry and a group of his top supporters assembled on the front porch of Webbley, Gardner's Shelby mansion, to ask for his political blessing. Knowing Cherry's reputa-tion for being the best lawyer in Gastonia when sober and the second-best lawyer in Gastonia when drunk, Gardner elicited a promise from Cherry that he would not touch a drop of whiskey during the campaign.[83]

Even after Gardner's death, the remnants of his organization helped install William Umstead and Luther Hodges in the Executive Mansion in the 1950s and Sam J. Ervin and B. Everett Jordan in the Senate. "They had very, very carefully crafted a state organization of sheriffs, political leaders, and hacks all over the state," said Lauch Faircloth, a Clinton businessman and future U.S. senator who went up against the organization. "That was a Costa Nostra."[84]

Mr. Reynolds Goes to Washington

While Gardner pulled the political strings in Raleigh, there was not much he could do about Reynolds. Official Washington had awaited the arrival of the latest specimen of the Dixie Demagogues — a North Carolina "Kingfish" who many anticipated would rival Louisiana senator Huey Long.

Reynolds became a loyal supporter of the New Deal, backing FDR even on such controversial proposals as his plan to pack the U.S. Supreme Court with friendly judges. Reynolds maintained southern solidarity on racial issues, joining other southern senators in filibustering against antilynching legislation. Even a maverick populist such as Reynolds could not challenge the racial mores of the day. But unlike other southern demagogues, Reynolds never made racist appeals.

Reynolds clashed over patronage with Democratic powers Gardner and Bailey. According to Bailey, Reynolds proposed that the two senators collect 10 percent of the salaries of all their appointees — an idea the strait-laced Bailey, who detested Reynolds, called "deplorable and disgraceful."[85] When Reynolds tried to get one of his Asheville political cronies appointed as U.S. attorney for the western district, Roosevelt vetoed it. At a White House meeting, FDR told Reynolds he would not appoint his choice because it was well known the man kept a "fat whore" in Charlotte. "Well, Mr. President," Reynolds drawled, "she's not so fat." FDR roared with laughter and later appointed the Reynolds crony.[86]

A publicity hound, Reynolds was always finding ways to get his picture in the newspapers. He was photographed in Indian attire and in a Mexican charro suit, and he even took a fee for appearing in Lucky Strikes ads. But his most celebrated stunt occurred when sexy movie star Jean Harlow, the platinum blond bombshell, visited Capitol Hill in January 1937 and posed for a photograph with Reynolds. Although photographers egged Reynolds to kiss her, the senator at first demurred. Purred Harlow: "The trouble with this gentleman is that he doesn't seem to want to go through with it."

This spurred Reynolds to grab Harlow and give the actress a passionate kiss using what he would later call his best "Hollywood technique." The photograph made the newspapers across the country. *Life* magazine devoted a full page to the embrace. Far from being embarrassed by the publicity, Reynolds gloried in it. During campaign appearances back home, he curried favor with his female constituents by declaring the lips of North Carolina women, not those of Jean Harlow, to be the sweetest in the world. "And I ought to know," Reynolds said.[87]

Reynolds devoted his energies to touring the country, globe-trotting, and chasing women. Jonathan Daniels said Reynolds "plays the Southern gallant like a heavy-handed Hollywood actor playing a Southern part, he is sort of a poor man's peacock strutting and kissing where the boys in the filling stations would like to kiss and strut too."[88]

The state political leadership considered Reynolds, in the words of Winston-Salem banker Robert Hanes, "a clown, and a playboy and a wise cracker." But they were reluctant to challenge him in 1938. Although Reynolds was easily reelected, his political career would soon unravel.

Immediately after winning reelection in 1938, Reynolds began a six-week tour of Europe, where he met with numerous leaders. Speaking to reporters after returning home, Reynolds ignited a firestorm that eventually ended his political career. Reynolds said the United States must stop the "hate wave" against the European dictators. He praised the economic system and progress made in Germany and Italy. "What we should do is to open our eyes and find out what's going on in the world," Reynolds told reporters. "We sit over here and knock Hitler and knock Mussolini and everyone else who differs with us in how a government should be run."[89]

When he got back to the Senate, Reynolds said, "the dictators are doing what is best for their people. I say it is high time we found out how they are doing it, and why they are progressing so rapidly. Hitler has solved the unemployment problem. There is no unemployment in Italy. Hitler and Mussolini have a date with destiny; it's foolish to oppose them, so why not play ball with them?"[90]

Reynolds's comment drew sharp criticism. What was particularly devastating to his reputation was a nationally syndicated "Merry-Go-Round" column written by Drew Pearson and Robert S. Allen, in which they wrote that some of his colleagues had nicknamed him the "Tar Heel Fuhrer." "The wise-cracking Reynolds took a trip to Germany last summer and was wined, dined and flattered by moguls of the Goering-Goebbels clique," they wrote. "He came back singing their praises and acclaiming Hitler as a great man."

Despite the column, there was no evidence Reynolds met with any top German or Italian officials. But even before the trip, Reynolds was becoming increasingly isolationist in his views and anti-immigrant in his rhetoric. Reynolds's isolationist views ran against the tide of public opinion in North Carolina. As the war clouds gathered in Europe, no region of the country was more supportive of Great Britain and intervention than the South. Reynolds was the only southern senator who consistently voted with the isolationists, who were mainly midwestern Republicans.

Joining the Senate Foreign Relations Committee in January 1939, Reynolds became a sharp critic of Roosevelt's foreign policy. Reynolds denounced the American arms buildup. He opposed the Lend-Lease program, which allowed America to sell destroyers to England, calling Great Britain the "bloodiest aggressor the world has ever known." He said the Soviet Union under Stalin was far worse than Germany under Hitler. When Germany invaded Czechoslovakia, Reynolds sought to explain it away. When Hitler seized land, he did it "in the way that sometimes the boys in Texas and in North Carolina used to move a fence with the aid of a shotgun, instead of doing it legally by way of the surveyor. That is all Hitler did."[91]

Reynolds's isolationist views began to reveal a profascist tilt. In Washington, D.C., the senator set up an organization called the Vindicators Association. The stated purpose of the group was to keep America out of war, require all aliens to be registered and fingerprinted, stop all immigration for ten years, and deport all alien criminals and undesirables. The association claimed to have 118,000 members. Any American citizen could join, providing they were not black or Jewish. Members received a subscription to its magazine, a red, white, and blue feather to be worn in one's cap, and a button with the letter *V* and a picture of the U.S. Capitol and American flags in the background.

The magazine had an anti-Semitic message. Not only did it deny Jews membership, but it also frequently attacked the *Jewish Examiner*, claiming it wanted Jewish refugees from Germany to immigrate to the United States to take away jobs from Americans.[92] He urged his readers to set up groups in neighborhoods of seven members, called the "Circle of Seven," to discuss ways to preserve America—a small enough group to make it difficult for outsiders to infiltrate. The Vindicators had a program for boys aged ten to eighteen called the Border Patrol, in which they could earn a badge and a $20 reward for catching "alien crooks."

Reynolds began to develop a national following on the isolationist Right. In Boston he was greeted with "Reynolds for President" posters. "The

American people are not going to let their sons fight beside Communistic Russia, even for the so-called saving of democracy," Reynolds warned in Boston.[93]

Had Buncombe Bob become a closet Nazi? His biographer, Julian Pleasants, concluded the senator was a misguided nationalist who carelessly allowed himself to be used by extremists. "He was not an American fascist although he shared some of the ideas of fascism such as nationalism and race superiority," Pleasants wrote. "Reynolds had hoped to use his Vindicators organization and his anti-alien tirades to create publicity and thus promote his political career. He achieved, however, exactly the opposite result."[94]

The Fall of Our Bob

Criticism of Reynolds continued to mount. Joe Alsop, a columnist for the *Washington Star*, described Reynolds as "the most conspicuous mountebank-statesman of our day. He has the loudest voice, the lightest heart, and the lowest estimate of his sensibilities of any member of the Senate. He is not a very deep thinker, and his own significance has certainly escaped him. It is quite simply, that things can't be very bad in the United States if the people of a great state are willing to sacrifice their franchise for a joke."[95]

But it was no joke in 1941 when Senator Morris Sheppard of Texas died. Reynolds was elevated by the seniority system to the chairmanship of the Senate Military Affairs Committee, through which all bills pertaining to the military flowed. Newspapers across the country decried Reynolds's new role. The *Charlotte News* said that if Hitler had studied the Senate membership, "he could not have chosen a Military Affairs Committee chairman better suited to advance the Nazi cause than Robert Rice Reynolds."[96]

After Japan attacked the U.S. fleet at Pearl Harbor, Reynolds toned down his isolationist rhetoric. He generally supported the war effort. But while Reynolds remained chairman, the committee was really run by several administration supporters. Reynolds continued his maverick ways, however, opposing extension of the Selective Service law and entry of the United States into the United Nations. He decried the "pampering" of Japanese Americans held in internment camps.

In 1941 Reynolds's personal life was back in the headlines. The fifty-seven-year-old senator married Evalyn Walsh McLean, the twenty-year-old daughter of the publisher of the *Washington Post*. The McLeans were among the most socially prominent and richest families in Washington and owned two of the world's most famous gems, the Hope Diamond and the Star of India. McLean, a tall, attractive woman, had shocked her family when she declined to make her formal debut. She talked about wanting to work in a nightclub, but instead she decided to marry Reynolds, who she met at a party. She said they shared interests in nightclubs, parties, and flying. The press began to refer to Reynolds as "Hope Diamond Jr."[97]

Reynolds had long been an embarrassment to most Democratic Party leaders in North Carolina. But with World War II underway, it became imperative to replace Reynolds in the 1944 elections. Among those most anxious to dump Reynolds was Gardner. Gardner had known Reynolds since they played football together at UNC. As undergraduates they visited Europe together, working their way across the Atlantic on a cattle boat, and they had once had to use their fists to fight their way out of a Left Bank dance hall in Paris. But Gardner had had enough of Reynolds. "They say the Hope Diamond is the most valuable jewel in America, but it will not be valuable enough for Bob to pawn to retain his Senate seat," Gardner wrote to a friend. "If there is anything certain, it is the fact that he is going to be defeated."[98]

Although Gardner had consistently said he did not want to run for political office again, many Democratic leaders were now urging him to run for Reynolds's seat. And for awhile, Gardner was listening. "Every fiber of my nature rebels against the thought of this man sitting in judgment to pass on the issues of a trial whose verdict will color the channel of our civilization for the next hundred years," he said.[99]

But during a speech to a business group in Charlotte in April 1943, Gardner became drenched in sweat. A doctor found that his blood pressure had dangerously dropped. Worried about whether his health could stand the rigors of a campaign, Gardner announced he would not run for office. But he convinced his brother-in-law to run in his place.

Even the irrepressible Reynolds could now see he faced certain defeat. His isolationist views were highly unpopular. His antics were wearing thin. And after marrying an heiress, he could hardly campaign again as poor old Buncombe Bob. The senator announced he would not seek a third term, citing "the tremendous pressure of work" in Washington. Hoey easily won the Democratic primary, defeating Cameron Morrison, the man Reynolds had defeated to win his Senate seat.

Even though he did not seek reelection, Reynolds still maintained a following among fringe isolationists, who urged him to run for president as a third-party candidate in 1944. In June 1944 Reynolds organized a bipartisan political group called the American Nationalist Committee of Independent Voters, whose purpose, he said, was to stop the drift toward internationalism. But little came of it, and Reynolds quietly retired, first to Waldorf, Maryland, and then back to North Carolina.

But Reynolds missed the limelight, and six years after his retirement he considered challenging Hoey, the man who held his old Senate seat, in the 1950 Democratic primary. After weighing the situation, Reynolds decided he could not defeat the popular Hoey—who had a reputation as both a Bible-quoting Sunday-school teacher and a ladies' man. "I could never defeat Hoey," Reynolds wrote to his law partner. "I can't beat a man who goes around the state with a Bible in one hand and his pecker in the other."[100]

Reynolds, now sixty-five, challenged Democratic senator Frank Porter Graham, the former president of the University of North Carolina and one of the South's leading liberals. Reynolds entered a three-way primary in 1950 with Graham and Willis Smith. He called Graham "a well-meaning, dreamy-eyed reformer who wants to make over this nation and the whole world to suit his own ideals." Reynolds campaigned against immigration and socialized medicine, and for permitting each state to handle its own civil rights concerns. But Reynolds's day had passed. He was too old; he had no campaign funds or even a headquarters. Reynolds finished third in the primary with 9.3 percent of the vote, probably preventing Graham from winning the nomination in the first primary. He endorsed Smith in the runoff, helping him beat Graham.

Political theory was never one of Reynolds's strong suits. But Reynolds was a living link between the populism of the turn of the twentieth century, which blamed the nation's problems on Wall Street, bankers, and railroad magnates, and the populism of the latter part of the twentieth century, which targeted the United Nations, foreign aid, and health maintenance organizations.

Unlike other southern demagogues such as Huey Long, Reynolds is barely remembered today. Reynolds left few major legislative marks. He created no lasting political organization. But as Pleasants, his biographer, notes: "No man, save Huey Long, provided a better show for the people from 1933–1945 than Bob Reynolds."[101]

A Life Cut Short

As a high-powered, well-paid lobbyist, Gardner was rarely tempted to accept any of the federal appointments that were dangled in front of him. It took a personal tragedy to persuade Gardner to accept a government job.

In 1946 one of his sons, Decker, who was running the textile mill back in Shelby, committed suicide during a serious illness. Shaken by the death of his thirty-six-year-old son, Gardner considered leaving his Washington law practice and returning to Shelby. Instead, he took the advice of his friends and accepted an appointment from President Harry Truman to serve as undersecretary of the treasury in 1946. Gardner cut his ties to the Washington law firm that he founded. He sold his textile mill to the J. P. Stevens textile conglomerate for $3.1 million, or the equivalent of $32.2 million in 2007 dollars.

Gardner had developed a good relationship with Truman, who appreciated the North Carolinian's storytelling and genial personality. In 1946 Truman gave Gardner a choice plum: the coveted ambassadorship to the Court of St. James. Just hours before he was set to sail from New York to London on February 6, 1947, Gardner suffered a massive heart attack in the middle of the night. His wife called the house doctor, but there was nothing that could be done. A year after his death, the Shelby Dynasty came to an end.

From 1928 to 1948, the Shelby Dynasty ruled North Carolina politics. Gardner was one of the state's most gifted political figures. Forced to be innovative because of the Depression, Gardner reshaped state government. Before Gardner, the state's road system was controlled by hundreds of local political barons; after Gardner, the state was responsible for the highway system. Before Gardner, each county was its own jailer; after Gardner, there was a state prison system. Before Gardner, schools were financed entirely from local property taxes; after Gardner, the state paid for operation of the schools, including teacher salaries. Before Gardner, each of the three major state-supported universities was an individual duchy; after Gardner, there was a consolidated state university.

And there was more. Before Gardner, profligate cities, towns, and counties were free to borrow themselves into bankruptcy. After Gardner, the Local Government Commission policed their finances. Before Gardner, each state agency bought its own supplies and handled its own job applications. After Gardner, there was a state Division of Purchasing and Contract and a Division of Personnel.

Gardner was a political moderate who was willing to move to the left or the right as the times dictated. As a textile manufacturer and later as a top corporate lobbyist, Gardner was sympathetic to industry and was certainly no ally of organized labor. But in the boardrooms of North Carolina, Gardner was seen as a liberal businessman who was sympathetic to the New

Deal. And yet, Gardner was unwilling to see a "Little New Deal" recreated in Raleigh, and when his power was threatened from the left, he used all his political skills to crush the revolt.

When political scientist V. O. Key wrote that North Carolina was governed by "a progressive plutocracy," he had Gardner and the Shelby Dynasty in mind. "It has not been necessary for politicians in North Carolina to be, or to pretend to be, poor men," wrote Key in his 1949 classic *Southern Politics*. "It has not been necessary for them to cultivate rusticity to get votes. They have been unblushingly and unapologetically in favor of sound, conservative government. Progressive, forward-looking, yes, but always sound, always the kind of government liked by the big investor, the big employer.

"While investors and employers have been willing to be reasonable, they have aimed to keep control," Key wrote. "As a venerable North Carolinian put it: 'The big interests have known when to give way and when to play ball. They have been willing to be fair but not at the expense of their power.'"[102]

chapter 3 **Branchhead Boys**

There was a sense of mischief in the way Governor Kerr Scott so casually announced he was appointing the South's leading liberal to the U.S. Senate. Near the end of an academic awards banquet in Chapel Hill in March 1949, Scott dropped the bombshell.

"While I'm on my feet," Scott told the audience in Lenoir Hall, "I want to make an announcement. The next senator from North Carolina will be Dr. Frank Graham." There was a moment of stunned silence among the 700 University of North Carolina leaders. Then there was thunderous applause and cheers.[1]

Graham, the sixty-two-year-old UNC president, was among the most beloved figures in the state, and one of the most polarizing. For nineteen years, Graham had presided over the University of North Carolina's emergence as the South's leading public university, helping make Chapel Hill the region's intellectual center. A kind, friendly man, "Dr. Frank," as he was affectionately known to a generation of Tar Heels, seemed the living embodiment of the state's educational crown jewel.

The Graham appointment was the liberal high-water mark in twentieth-century North Carolina politics, involving a progressive governor and a liberal senator. "Now is the winter of our discontent made glorious summer by the two sons of Carolina, Scott and Graham," wrote Harry Golden, editor of the liberal *Carolina Israelite* in Charlotte.[2]

The moment in history would help give birth to the post–World War II progressive wing of the North Carolina Democratic Party, influencing several generations of Democratic leaders, including Terry Sanford, Jim Hunt, Erskine Bowles, and John Edwards. It was a brief era that helped push North Carolina more toward the mainstream of the national Democratic Party. The postwar liberalism was the product of many things: the changes wrought by World War II, the strand of populism running through North Carolina's political DNA, and the moderation of the existing political machine. It was, after all, O. Max Gardner who launched the career of Scott and helped elevate Graham to the UNC presidency.

But in such a politically competitive state, it was a moment that could not last. The rising national pressure for racial integration would cause North Carolinians to retreat to safer conservatism. As in the 1890s, a Progressive Movement would be thwarted by a conservative reaction in which the flag of white supremacy would once again be unfurled. The Graham elevation would tear the state apart and cause North Carolinians to once again gaze into the racial abyss.

"A fine appointment you made," said an anonymous letter to Scott. "Comrade Graham will serve us faithfully and we can depend on him for much valuable information. I am recommending you for the Red Star Medal." The letter was signed: "Your Friend, Joe S. [Stalin]."[3]

The Rise of Kerr Scott

To visit Kerr Scott's modest, white, two-story clapboard house today in the rolling Piedmont countryside of Haw River is to step back into a different era of North Carolina. It is not hard to envision a period of dusty, unpaved roads and one-room schoolhouses, a time when the countryside was unmarred by telephone and power lines or cell phone towers. The rhythms of country life on Scott's dairy farm would have been familiar to those of earlier generations. Plowing was still done by hooking up mules or horses. The arrival of the first tractor was a memorable experience. One grew and canned one's own vegetables, killed one's own chickens, and cranked one's own ice cream. A boy's first chaw of tobacco was a rite of passage, and the nearest neighbor was a mile away.

Nearly every Sunday morning, even when he was governor, Scott made a ritual of walking a dirt road to his brother Ralph's farm. From there the two would set off together on the two-mile walk to Hawfields Presbyterian Church, where they would discuss politics, farming, or the neighbors. The Scott family had attended the church almost since it was established in 1755. Kerr Scott's grandfather, Henderson Scott, owned a tannery and made shoes for the Confederate army. Kerr's father, Robert Scott, known as "Farmer Bob," was a state legislator and a leader in agriculture issues who had unsuccessfully sought the Democratic nomination for state agriculture commissioner in 1908.

Kerr Scott followed in his father's footsteps in farming, politics, and religion. "My Dad had a fondness for saying that a man could never really expect to go to heaven unless he was a Democrat, a Presbyterian and owned a Jersey cow," recalled his son, Bob Scott. "For a long time I kept a few Jerseys around just for a safeguard."[4]

Kerr Scott lived almost his entire life among his cows, except for his student years at N.C. State University, a stint in the army, and when he was governor and senator—and even then he returned to Haw River every chance he got. Scott borrowed $4,000 from his father and bought a 224-acre tract of farmland, some tools, and a few head of sheep and cattle. Marrying his childhood sweetheart, Mary Elizabeth White, Kerr built the two-story house where he and Miss Mary lived the rest of their lives. A few months after getting married, Kerr took a job as an Alamance County farm agent, a post he held for the next ten years to supplement his farm income. He traveled from farm to farm in a buggy—or on horseback in extremely bad weather—and later in his Model T automobile. Money left over was used to buy more land. His farm eventually covered 1,300 acres and included 300 Holsteins and Jersey cows and had fifteen tenants and farmhands working the land.

The Scotts were prosperous farmers. But for most North Carolina growers, life was hard. Three out of four Tar Heel residents still lived in the countryside in the 1930s—among the highest percentage in the nation. And the countryside was largely dark. Power companies first strung their lines in the more lucrative markets in the towns and cities, but they were slow to extend them to far-flung farms, which was costly. Almost everybody who lived in North Carolina's towns and cities had electricity. The percentage of North Carolina farms served by electricity in 1935 was 3.2 percent, compared to a national average of 10.9 percent for farmers.

A study of farmers in Iowa and North Carolina in the 1920s painted a stark picture. While 76 percent of Iowa households had washing machines, only 0.6 of North Carolina farm families did. While 45 percent of Iowa farms had running water, only 0.9 percent of North Carolina farm families had such a convenience. While 46 percent of Iowa farm families had indoor toilets, only 0.6 percent of North Caroline farm families did. And while 100 percent of Iowa farm families had telephones, only 9 percent of North Carolina farm families could call their neighbors.[5]

Without electricity, life on the farm involved backbreaking work. For the farmers it meant milking cows and lifting feed and cotton by hand. Without electricity, life was lived with kerosene lamps and the constant danger of igniting a barn. Wood was split by ax to feed the woodstoves that were dirty and hard to regulate, and water hand pumped from wells had to be hauled to the house. There were no refrigerators, so vegetables had to be canned soon after they were picked. Because there were no washing machines, women bent over tubs using homemade lye soap to scrub the dirt out of clothes on washboards until their knuckles were raw. Several big, heavy irons had to be heated on the woodstove. Without electricity, there were no radios or telephones, and reading was difficult by kerosene lamps. "The lack of electric power," wrote historian William Leuchtenburg, "divided the United States into two nations: the city dwellers and the country folk. Farmers, without the benefits of electrically powered machinery, toiled in a nineteenth-century world; farm wives, who enviously eyed pictures in the *Saturday Evening Post* of city women with washing machines, refrigerators, and vacuum cleaners, performed their backbreaking chores like peasant women in a pre-industrial age."[6]

About half of the farmers were tenants working on someone else's land. North Carolina had more people, 1.4 million, living on the farm than any state in the country. North Carolina's farms were the smallest in the nation.[7]

The Depression had made a hard life even worse. When president-elect Franklin D. Roosevelt called a nationwide meeting of farm leaders at Warm Springs, Georgia, in 1932 to discuss how to rescue agriculture from the disaster of the Depression, Scott was the only southerner in the group. Out of such meetings came a series of New Deal programs that slowed the tide of farm foreclosures, extended electricity to the countryside, and created production controls aimed at stabilizing prices for tobacco.

Politically connected through his activity in the state Grange, where he was grand master, Scott was appointed to several New Deal jobs, culminating in regional director of the newly created federal Farm Debt Adjustment Administration for seven states. Everywhere Scott traveled in Depression-era North Carolina, farmers were being thrown off their farms because they could no longer make mortgage payments. Nash County, a tobacco-growing area east of Raleigh, alone reported 3,500 foreclosures of its 5,280 farms in 1930.[8]

Scott's job was to arrange financing to help keep farmers from losing land that had often been in their families for generations. "Those were both heart-rending and happy days for me," Scott said. "Heart-rending because of the misery, want and hunger we saw on every side; happy because of the fear we were able to lift from the eyes of tens of thousands of men, women and children."[9]

Traveling across the dusty roads of the rural South during the Depression helped shape Scott's political philosophy. Government could be a benevolent force, he believed, providing a helping hand for people who were struggling.

In 1936 Scott got his break in politics when Max Gardner, the boss of the Democratic Machine, tapped him as his choice to be state agriculture commissioner. Gardner was in the process of ridding Raleigh of his political foes, and those included Agriculture Commissioner William A. Graham. Graham had been appointed in 1923 upon the death of his father, who had also been agriculture commissioner. Scott won the Democratic primary with 52 percent of the vote, ending what he called "the Graham dynasty in the Department of Agriculture."

Scott was a farmer-politician. In the days before interstate highways, Scott commuted the fifty miles each way daily between his office in Raleigh and his farm in Haw River on the two-lane N.C. 54. Before leaving at 7 A.M. each morning, Scott met with his farmhands to give them the day's instructions.

The 1948 Governor's Race

Something was stirring in the South after World War II. The war was a dynamic force for social change, sending country boys to Europe and the South Pacific, encouraging women to take factory jobs, and opening up new opportunities for blacks. Thousands took lucrative war industry jobs. And thousands more poured into the state for training in such bases as Fort Bragg, Camp Lejeune, Camp Davis, Camp Butner, and Seymour Johnson Air Base.

For the first time since the Great Depression, there was now plenty of money in the pockets of people and in the coffers of government. The Depression, and then the war, made it difficult for states to undertake many new projects, and there was an urgent demand for schools, roads, and other public services. Returning veterans seemed less satisfied with the status quo.

Liberal populists who promised to shake up the old courthouse crowd were winning across the South. In 1946 "Big Jim" Folsom was elected governor of Alabama, and in 1948 Earl K. Long was elected governor of Louisiana and Fuller Warren was elected governor of Florida. Postwar voters were also sending New Dealers to the Senate, including John Sparkman of Alabama, Estes Kefauver of Tennessee, and Lyndon Johnson of Texas. Nowhere in the South was the sense of progress any greater than in North Carolina. "The prevailing mood in North Carolina is not hard to sense: it is energetic and ambitious," wrote political scientist V. O. Key in 1949. "The citizens are determined and confident; they are on the move. The mood is at odds with much of the rest of the South—a tenor of attitude and action that has set the state apart from its neighbors. Many see in North Carolina a closer approximation to national norms, or national expectations of performance, than they find elsewhere in the South. It enjoys a reputation for progressive outlook and action in many phases of life, especially industrial development, education and race relations."[10]

Although Gardner died in 1947, his political organization still held sway—or so it was thought. Scott put out feelers to leaders of the Democratic organization about running for governor. But when Scott visited Robert Hanes, the Winston-Salem banker and Gardner friend, who was now the key figure in the reigning Democratic organization, he was informed it was not his turn to be governor although he might be considered in the future.[11]

The Shelby Dynasty's candidate for governor in 1948 was Charles M. Johnson, a Pender County native and a career state employee, whom Gardner had appointed state treasurer in 1932. Johnson, fifty-seven, a distinguished-looking, white-haired man, had built a formidable political organization that included much of the state's business and political leadership.

The independent-minded Scott took on the machine, running a populist campaign for governor. This was to be the farmers' last political hurrah. In 1948 there were 302,000 farms in North Carolina, nearly agriculture's high-water mark in the state. Tobacco, cultivated on small plots and aided by a New Deal price-control and production-control program, had allowed the small farmer to hang on longer in North Carolina than elsewhere.[12]

Scott promised better roads to pull the farm family out of the mud. He vowed to extend electricity and telephone service to the countryside, and he said he would work for better schools and health facilities. His targets were often utility companies, banks, and oil companies—the major economic institutions that the so-called Branchhead Boys, the many rural people living at the "head of the branch," thought ignored them.

Terry Sanford, a future governor, remembered Scott on the stump. "He would ask everyone in the audience: 'Who wants a telephone? Raise your hand.' Nearly everyone in the audience would raise their hand. 'How many people don't have electric lights?' Half of them would raise their hands."[13]

Scott criticized Johnson for allowing Wachovia, North Carolina's largest bank, to hold state money without paying any interest—calling it "lazy money." He said Johnson was a "machine politician" whose friendship with the banks was costing taxpayers "a million dollars a year."[14]

Johnson emphasized his "sound and progressive" record. He accused Scott of practicing wedge politics, attempting to "align the rural population against the city population, one class of citizens against another."[15]

Scott was far more dynamic and articulate—by turns witty and sarcastic—than the colorless Johnson. Johnson led the first Democratic primary, but just barely. He won 40 percent of the vote, followed by 38 percent for Scott and the rest going to four lesser candidates. But Scott overtook him in the runoff, winning 54 percent. Scott carried 65 of the 100 counties, running strongest in the rural eastern half of the state where there long had been a populist strain.

He also was able to win such cities as Raleigh, Durham, and Greensboro with the help of a growing number of black voters. Although only 14 percent of eligible blacks were registered to vote in North Carolina, a disproportionate number were located in the cities. Blacks were slowly becoming politically involved. In 1931 the Negro Voter's League was formed in Raleigh to push for voter registration. The Durham Committee on Negro Affairs was created in 1935, and by 1940 the group was sending questionnaires to candidates.[16]

In some ways, Scott had begun reconstituting the old coalition of the Populists in the 1890s—small white farmers and blacks. Like the earlier Populists, Scott would find it difficult to hold together a progressive coalition in the face of the divide-and-conquer racial tactics of conservatives.[17]

Governor

On January 6, 1949, Scott donned a morning coat—or what he called his "two-cow suit" ("I had to sell two cows to buy it," said the first farmer in the Executive Mansion since 1893[18])—and outlined to an inaugural crowd in Raleigh's Memorial Auditorium his "Go-Forward Program."

While praising past administrations for their conservative stewardship, Scott said it was time to begin spending again. "In amassing a hoard of tax dollars we accumulated a vast backlog of public service needs," Scott said. "We must conclude that we do not have a real surplus, but actually a deficit in public services. To Go Forward, we must wipe out this deficit."[19]

Regardless of who was governor in 1949, North Carolina would have likely sharply increased spending. Even so, Scott's Go-Forward Program represented the largest expansion of government services in a generation. He proposed a $200 million bond issue for paving a farm-to-market system of secondary roads (the equivalent of $1.7 billion in 2007 dollars). He backed $50 million in bonds for school construction. He also supported major increases in teacher salaries and spending for health programs. To help pay for getting the state "out of the mud"—improving the roads— Scott proposed a one-cent-per-gallon gasoline tax increase, the first tax hike since J. C. B. Ehringhaus convinced the legislature to adopt the state sales tax in 1933 in the middle of the Great Depression. "The people," Scott said, "are demanding that something be done to lift them out of the mud." And there was plenty of mud. Of the 64,000 miles of roads for which the state was responsible, only 7,000 had a hard surface in 1948. Even many of the paved roads had fallen into disrepair because the heavy military vehicles of World War II had been so hard on them.[20]

More than a half century later, Raymond Massey remembers how important it was to have his rural Wake County road paved and was still grateful to Scott. The roads were often so dusty that mothers had difficulty hanging out their clean wash in the days before clothes dryers. In the heat of summer, windows often had to be closed to prevent the dirt from getting into a non-air-conditioned house. During snows and other bad weather, getting children to school became nearly impossible. Massey remembers the schools being closed twenty-five days in 1947. The bad roads could also mean the difference between life and death. In the days before ambulance service and rural telephones in many communities, doctors had to be summoned in person, and impassable roads often meant delayed medical treatment. "People would die simply because the roads were so bad," Massey said.[21]

Breaking with the probusiness tradition of past governors, Scott called for repeal of the 1947 Anti–Closed Shop Act that would hamper union organizing. Scott, who received strong backing from organized labor during his campaign, is the only North Carolina governor to call for repeal of the so-called right-to-work law.

Talk of large increases in spending, a tax increase, and prounion policies caused an immediate backlash against the plowboy populist in the conservative-leaning General Assembly and the business community. But Scott was their match—a political figure with charisma, a penchant for playing hardball, and a willingness to go over their heads and appeal directly to the people.

Scott, age fifty-two, was a large man with black hair and bushy eyebrows. He was blunt, rugged, quick-witted, and plainspoken with a slow country drawl. A hearty eater who had weighed as much as 252 pounds, Scott had slimmed down to 188 pounds for the governor's race. (As a fourteen-year-old, he had once eaten thirteen apple pies during a contest at a wheat-

Governor Kerr Scott (center) confers with brother Ralph Scott and supporter
J. Leslie Atkins Jr. (Courtesy of the *Raleigh News and Observer*)

thrashing dinner.) He nearly always wore a trademark rose in his lapel. He often had a plug of tobacco in his mouth or one of the ten cigars he consumed daily.

Scott would gather his friends at Green's Grill in Garner for dinners of chitlins—the entrails of a hog—and sweet potatoes, hominy, collard greens, and cornbread. The dinners eventually became the Wake County Chitlin Club and continued to meet annually for decades. "Society matrons could never warm to the country drawl or the plug of Brown's Mule or such talk as 'totting fair' and 'hoeing out,'" wrote Raleigh reporter Simmons Fentress. "To the country club set, he always was something of an uncultured, slightly rude intruder. The congressman's wife still talks of the governor who cast a worried look about her living room, then asked for a cuspidor."[22]

Scott often approached the legislature with little tact, viewing them as the tools of business lobbyists. Nor was he timid about attacking lobbyists by name when he thought they were trying to sabotage his program. On one occasion, Scott told the N.C. Citizens Association, the state's chamber of commerce, that their magazine, *We the People*, should be renamed *We the People Against the People*. The joke going around Raleigh was if anyone ever accused Scott of having any tact, he would take something to get rid of it. "I decided a long time ago that if ever I had a conviction about something, I was going to come out with it," Scott said. "The only time to hem and haw and straddle the fence is when you haven't made your mind up."[23]

When his Go-Forward Program became stuck in the legislature in March, the proverb-quoting Scott went on a forty-station radio hookup to urge people to descend on Raleigh the next day to pressure the lawmakers. "While there are those who talk about dangerous spending," Scott said, "I think the time has come to give some thought to dangerous withholding. Your Bible tells you that, 'There is that scattereth, and yet increaseth; and there is that withholdeth more than is meet, but it tendeth to poverty.'"[24] In a Bible Belt state, North Carolina governors—from Charles Brantley Aycock to Jim Hunt—routinely have used religion to rally support for new spending proposals.

Scott ripped the petroleum industry for opposing his gas tax, calling their criticisms "the insolent attack of rich outside corporations. . . . So long as I am governor, this oil monopoly, headed out of New York, will not be allowed to push our people in the mud." To those who balked at his health-spending plans, Scott retorted: "How long shall we ignore the fact, for instance, that we are not giving our children at the school age all the physical protection we accord hogs in a pen?"

At his urging, 5,000 people descended on the State Capitol to pressure the legislature to support his program, including the road bond issue. In June 1949 Scott began his fourth campaign in a year—this time to convince the public to pass the bond issue referendums. With the aid of highway contractors and trucking companies, Scott led a swing-from-the-hip, probond campaign, making more than fifty speeches and seventeen radio talks. The road bond issue easily passed. As a result, more miles of roads were paved during Scott's administration than in all previous administrations combined. (Although critics often complained that Alamance County got more than its fair share of road money, Governor Scott Road near his farm remains unpaved in the twenty-first century.)

Scott also pressured the power companies to expand telephone and power lines into rural areas. "I've been burned up by the way we have had to go about getting electricity in the country," Scott said. "I want to say that we farm people would never have had electricity at all unless we had gone to Washington to force the utilities to give it to us."[25] Dedicating a Carolina Power & Light Company power plant in Lumberton in 1949, Scott generated his own electricity when he referred to CP&L chairman L. V. Sutton, with whom he was sharing the platform, as "Low Voltage" Sutton.

Unlike many southern populists, Scott declined to play the race card. Scott liked to tell the story of a campaign appearance at a country store in eastern North Carolina where he met with a local political leader. "There was this fellow sitting on the counter and he leaned over and said, 'Commissioner, how are you standing on the nigger issue?' I looked right at him and said, 'Mister, I want you to know one thing. I am a white Southern Presbyterian.' The fellow slapped his hand on his leg and said, 'That's all I needed to know.'"[26]

Scott appointed the first black, Dr. Harold L. Trigg of Raleigh, to serve on the State Board of Education. Although Scott still believed in racial segregation, he also sought more parity for financing between black and white schools and better salaries for black teachers and black state mental-health workers. "I'm firmly convinced that we've got to go ahead and meet the issue of the minority race," Scott told a dairy farmers group shortly after taking office. "They came here against their will, brought in chains."[27]

Scott was inclusive in other ways as well. Scott appointed Susie Sharp as North Carolina's first female superior court judge. Sharp later became the first woman chief justice of the North Carolina Supreme Court.

Scott attracted a wide circle of admirers, including Jesse Helms, then a young Raleigh radio reporter. "Our present governor, as far as I am concerned, is the first North Carolinian in my lifetime who has the vision and the ability to become President of the United States," Helms wrote to Scott. "And he may represent North Carolina's only chance for that honor in my life time. . . . This is the political era of the 'little man.' You have a way of getting along with that little man. Make the most of it."[28]

Although Helms's conservative, probusiness politics were far different from Scott's, Helms would adopt his shoot-from-the-hip style when he entered the U.S. Senate. But instead of railing against big business, Helms would criticize big government and the United Nations. Helms may have thought that Scott was White House material. But the two men would soon be on opposite sides of a political fight that would tear North Carolina apart.

Dr. Frank

When Frank Graham arrived in Chapel Hill in 1905, the University of North Carolina was an old school, but not yet a great one. Chapel Hill was a small, rustic college town located near Durham. Franklin Street, the main drag through town, was a dirt road. Graham settled into a room on the third floor of Old East, the first building erected at a public university in the United States, with a view of the Old Well, the university's relatively new symbol.

Graham came to Chapel Hill with connections. His cousin, Edward Kidder Graham, was a popular English professor and future university president. Frank Graham was the son of a progressive Charlotte public school superintendent and former UNC student. Frank grew up in a book-filled home, imbued with a strong sense of Presbyterian duty and surrounded by future teachers.

Despite a slight 5'6", 125-pound frame, Frank Graham became a big man on campus—the president of the senior class, the editor of the *Daily Tar Heel*, a cheerleader, the president of the YMCA, and a member of the baseball team. After graduation Graham studied law, and he taught in high school before enlisting in the Marines during World War I. After the war, Graham's intellectual journey took him to New York, Chicago, Washington, D.C., and London. He earned a master's degree in history from Columbia University, worked on a PhD at the University of Chicago, and spent a year at the Brookings Institution, a liberal Washington think tank. He also studied a year at the London School of Economics, where he met Fabian socialists and Labourites.

Graham returned to Chapel Hill, became the dean of students for a year, and began a career as a popular history professor, but he was not destined for a quiet, scholarly life. Graham was a rising star on campus—bright, energetic, and with gift for remembering names and relating to people. In 1921 he was named a field leader for an unprecedented $20 million university bond issue, a landmark measure that helped transform the UNC campus. Graham spent six months traveling across the state, campaigning for the bond issue and helping create a network that would serve him and the university well. When the university presidency became vacant in 1930, Governor Gardner convinced Graham to take the position. He became the first president of the consolidated university in 1932, when the state-supported campuses at Chapel Hill, Raleigh, and Greensboro were brought together into one system.

Chapel Hill held a special place in North Carolina's psyche in the first half of the twentieth century. In a state without large cities or big-league professional teams, Chapel Hill was both the state's intellectual and sports center. North Carolina in the 1920s, 1930s, and 1940s was too poor a state to finance a first-class public school system. But it could finance a first-rate university so that the bankers, textile-mill owners, and lawyers did not have to send their sons up north to be properly educated.

Dr. Frank embraced life at Chapel Hill. Strolling around the campus, Graham sometimes challenged students to an Indian wrestling bout. He loved playing horseshoes and twirling a drum major's baton. Most Sunday evenings, Graham and his wife, Marian, opened the parlor of the president's home—a white-columned house set behind a low stone wall on Franklin Street—to students for informal conversations. Graham would shake a student's hand and then hold on, clasping it in his, engaging in quiet, intense conversation.

People would often struggle to describe the Graham charisma. "Charm of personality was inadequate to describe it," William Snider, a Greensboro newspaperman, said. "Built into Graham was a certain ironclad goodness, not puritanical nor sanctimonious, which stirred men and women to strive to be better than they were. He was a rumple suited little man with crinkly, smiling eyes and a bottomless faith in God's love and man's potential."[29]

Graham spent much of the 1930s working to keep UNC financially afloat in the midst of the Depression. As UNC emerged as the leading intellectual center of the South, Graham fought a running battle to preserve academic freedom. Graham defended the University of North Carolina Press as it published cutting-edge research on the South—studies by sociologists Howard Odum, Rupert B. Vance, and others that sometimes made traditionalists uncomfortable. He also championed the right of the university community to hear controversial speakers, such as black poet Langston Hughes and British philosopher Bertrand Russell. He ended the Jewish quota for students enrolling in UNC's medical school, prompting the resignation of the dean. When a UNC English professor, E. E. Ericson, dined at a hotel that catered to blacks in Durham with James W. Ford, a black candidate for vice president on the Communist Party ticket, Graham blocked an effort by trustees to fire Ericson. "If Professor Ericson has to go on the charge of eating with another human being, then I will have to go first," Graham told the trustees.[30]

In his inaugural speech as president in 1931, Graham laid out his credo:

> Freedom of the university means the freedom of the scholar to report the truth honestly without interference by the university, the state or any interests whatsoever. Freedom of the university means the freedom to study not only the biological implications of the physical structure of the fish but also the human implications of the economic structure of society. It means freedom from the prejudices of section, race or creed; it means a free compassion of her sons for all people in need of justice and brotherhood. It means the freedom of the liberated spirit to understand sympathetically those who misunderstand freedom and would strike it down. It means the freedom for consideration of the plight of the unorganized and inarticulate peoples in an unorganized world in which powerful combinations and high-pressure lobbies work their special will on the general life. In the university should be found the free voice not only for the unvoiced millions but also for the unpopular and even hated minorities. No abuse of freedom should cause us to strike down freedom of speech or publication, the fresh resource of a free religion and a free state.[31]

Graham went beyond his role as defender of the university, venturing into the treacherous grounds of social activism. In 1929 he publicly appealed for fair treatment of the striking Gastonia textile workers. The next year he drafted an Industrial Bill of Rights designed to protect worker rights, which was signed by 300 college professors, attorneys, newspaper editors, and others. As a committed New Dealer during the left-leaning thirties, Graham readily lent his name to hundreds of liberal groups and causes—apparently with little thought about how it might affect his responsibilities as university president. When a former UNC student, who was secretary of the state Socialist Party, was arrested in High Point for his role in a 1934 textile strike, Graham outraged conservatives by sending a telegram offering to put up his bond.

In 1938 Graham became the first president of the Southern Conference for Human Welfare (1938–48), a liberal group composed of activists, union officials, journalists, politicians, and various reformers that sought to repeal the poll tax and attack other social injustices. At its inaugural meeting in Birmingham, the 1,200 delegates, both black and white, sat together until Bull Connor, the Birmingham police commissioner, threatened them with arrest if they did not segregate themselves. Eleanor Roosevelt initially sat with the black delegates, moving across the segregation line only after being asked by police.

In his Birmingham speech, Graham delivered his message of the social gospel, which included references to a spiritual sung by a black choir.

"Deep River, My Home is Over Jordan." In the overtones of that song in the South our colored peoples are on the march, "into the Promised Land." This is their home. White and black have joined hands here to go forward by way of interracial cooperation toward the Kingdom of God. With all the marks that have been placed against us in the South let us prove at this Southern Conference for Human Welfare that we stand for the more helpless minorities and the underprivileged. Let us demonstrate, in our stumbling and defective way, that we wish to go the Jesus way, the slow way of education and the revelation of the inner life. Let us show that this Conference stands for the Sermon on the Mount, the American Bill of Rights, and American democracy.[32]

Graham's leadership of the organization drew criticism not only because of its liberal, prointegration agenda, but also because the group included communists. Graham's friends repeatedly urged him to leave the organization lest he be tainted. But Graham said he would rather stay and combat the communist influence from within.

As his social activism increased, his critics became louder. Few were more vociferous than David Clark of Charlotte, the editor of the *Southern Textile Bulletin*. "The University of North Carolina is the only Southern institution at which there appears to have been a drive for converts or definite contacts with the Red Movement in the United States," Clark wrote in 1940. "In recent years the University of North Carolina has stood alone in the South as a haven for Reds and fifth columnists."[33]

There was a small communist group operating in Chapel Hill, headed by Junius Scales, a grandnephew of a former North Carolina governor and a Greensboro native who published a procommunist periodical. Graham saw them as a few radicals and cranks rather than as part of a revolutionary vanguard. "I'd much rather—if you have a handful of communists in a student body of thousands—that it be out in the open and in the sunlight where they can be confronted in arguments," Graham said. "I think democracy and freedom can take care of themselves."[34]

Critics sometimes portrayed Graham as a radical, but Graham's social activism made him more of a New Dealer than a leftist. "His activism was visceral," wrote historians Julian Pleasants and Augustus Burns. "It was an emotional response to the Depression's misery and the world's turbulence. Ideologically, he never went beyond Franklin Roosevelt and the Democratic Party."[35]

Roosevelt, and later Truman, held Graham in high regard, giving him several sensitive assignments. FDR named him to the War Labor Board, on which he helped settle disputes between industry and organized labor during World War II. From 1942 to 1945, Graham had two nearly full-time jobs, spending his week in Washington and then taking a seven-hour train trip home to Chapel Hill for most weekends. Graham could be a tough mediator. After a twelve-hour negotiating session with Graham, the formidable labor leader John L. Lewis of the United Mine Workers asked: "Who locked me in with that sweet little SOB?"

Secretary of State George Marshall in 1947 named Graham to a three-person United Nations team to negotiate a truce between the Dutch and the anticolonialist forces in Indonesia. Graham spent several months in Southeast Asia hammering out a truce that would eventually lead to an independent Indonesia.

Truman also appointed Graham as one of two southerners to the President's Committee on Civil Rights. The fifteen-member committee in October 1947 delivered a landmark report, called "To Secure These Rights," which recommended "the elimination of segregation based on race, color, creed, or national origin, from American life." Graham agreed with the basic premise of ending segregation. He endorsed the elimination of segregation in interstate travel and in the armed forces, the creation of better economic opportunities for blacks, an end to the poll tax, and the admission of blacks to graduate schools where there were no comparable separate schools for blacks. But he wrote a dissenting opinion against the use of federal sanctions to force integration, saying integration should be accomplished gradually as people's minds changed through "religion and education."

Like most southern liberals in the 1940s, Graham accepted the social conventions of the South and did not publicly attack segregation—an action that would have been unthinkable for a leader of a major southern institution in the age of Jim Crow. But he worked around the edges to help break it down. In January 1947 Graham approved the use of a UNC auditorium for an interracial group of churchmen to listen to black singer Dorothy Maynor.

By the end of the 1940s, as writer Samuel Lubell put it, "no man had been more representative of liberalism in Dixie Land" than Graham.[36] And yet, as the son of a Confederate veteran, Graham was enough of a southern boy that he kept small busts of Confederate heroes Stonewall Jackson and Robert E. Lee in his big, airy office in South Building, with its view of such campus landmarks as the Old Well and the Davie Poplar.

Graham's growing national profile made him a target of conservatives across the country. In June 1947 the House Committee on Un-American Activities issued a report calling the Southern Conference for Human Welfare "perhaps the most deviously camouflaged Communist-front organization." The report said that while Graham is not a communist, "he is however, one of those liberals who show a predilection for affiliation with various communist-inspired front organizations." The report cited twelve suspicious organizations with which Graham had been associated.[37]

Efforts to discredit Graham increased in early 1949, when conservative commentator Fulton Lewis Jr. charged that Graham was a security risk who could not be trusted with atomic secrets. Graham was elected in 1946 as the first president and chairman of the Oak Ridge Institute of Nuclear Studies, which was sponsored by fourteen southern universities. Although the Atomic Energy Commission granted Graham security clearance, Lewis disclosed that the commission's Security Advisory Board had recommended against it. Truman came to Graham's defense, but southern conservatives such as Senator James Eastland of Mississippi and Representative Edward Hebert of Louisiana attacked Graham as an "ultra liberal" who was "on the pinkish side."

Graham was becoming a political lightning rod on the left at a time that the country was about to make a rightward turn. "That he is the best loved man in the state admits of no more doubt than that he is the best hated man there too; and both emotions he has richly earned," wrote journalist Gerald Johnson.[38]

Senator

Senator Melville Broughton, a former governor, died in Washington on March 6, 1949. Graham had initially resisted Kerr Scott's overtures concerning the Senate seat. At age sixty-two, Graham was nearing retirement age, and after several years of national assignments he wanted to put the university in shape for his successor.

Why had Scott made such a politically risky appointment? Scott said he was tired of the state being run by corporate lawyers, he wanted an ideological counterweight to the conservative U.S. senator Clyde Hoey, and he wanted to send to Washington someone with a national reputation who could be a peacemaker in times of heightening world tensions.[39]

Congratulations for his Senate appointment poured in from Graham's wide circle of friends and supporters—Truman, Eleanor Roosevelt, and Marshall. The fulsome praise was enough to make a person blush. Senator Wayne Morse of Oregon called Graham "one of the most Christ-like men" he had ever met. Others compared him to Indian leader Mahatma Gandhi. "I never thought I'd live to see the hand of the Lord in North Carolina politics," said Hazel Valentine of Raleigh.[40]

On March 27 the Grahams held their last Sunday open house in Chapel Hill. More than 1,500 students and local residents gathered outside the president's house on Franklin Street to wish him farewell. "As I said to the governor," Graham told the gathering, "this has been the most difficult decision of my life—to leave this place, these institutions and these people which have been part of my life for over 40 years." The college band started playing, and the Grahams joined the crowd in singing an emotional version of UNC's fight song: "I'm a Tar Heel born, I'm a Tar Heel bred, and when I die I'm a Tar Heel dead."[41]

But gaining the appointment from the liberal-leaning Scott and winning the support of conservative-leaning North Carolina voters were two different things. And the brief postwar liberal moment in North Carolina and in the South was drawing to a close. "Evidently you are trying to weld a group of Negros [*sic*], Labor and other radicals with your farm support into a machine," Hill Scoggin of Greenville wrote to Scott. "Of all your acts, the appointment of Fellow Traveling Frank Graham to the office of United States

Senator caps the climax. I will make you any reasonable wager that he will be defeated if he tries to run for senator in 1950."[42]

The Storm Clouds Gather

Well before the civil rights movement began in the 1950s, black North Carolinians began pushing for their rights. The National Association for the Advancement of Colored People (NAACP), which opened its first branches in North Carolina in 1917, had 10,000 members by 1946, even though joining the organization could cost a public schoolteacher his or her job.[43]

By the 1930s, African Americans were protesting their second-class status. Black ministers boycotted the dedication of Raleigh's Memorial Auditorium in 1932 because blacks were confined to a small section of the balcony. In 1938 black students in Greensboro boycotted downtown movie theaters to protest Hollywood's use of black stereotypes.

In 1942, fifty-nine prominent black leaders from across the South gathered at what is now known as N.C. Central University in Durham for three days of discussion on what needed to be done to advance the cause of African Americans. As an outgrowth of the meeting, a committee called the Southern Conference on Race Relations issued a statement, known as the Durham Manifesto. The manifesto noted that the war had "increased racial tensions, fears and aggressions, and an opening up of the basic questions of racial segregation and discrimination, Negro minority rights and democratic freedom." The group called for complete voting rights for blacks, the end of all-white primaries, equalization of black and white teacher salaries and black and white schools, and equal access to all jobs, and it encouraged service workers to unionize.

World War II greatly heightened racial tensions in North Carolina, which had more military training camps than any state in the country. With numerous black soldiers from the North confronting Jim Crow laws for the first time, social combustion was inevitable. There were numerous riots across the state. In Durham, the murder of a black soldier who refused to move to the back of the bus touched off a riot in 1944. It took 4,000 soldiers, police officers, and civilians to contain the fires and stop the looting.[44]

The system of segregation was also coming under renewed scrutiny in Washington. Black voting strength was growing in the North. Jim Crow had become a liability in the Cold War, in which the United States was trying to win the hearts and minds of millions of people of color around the world. Truman was infuriated over the brutal beatings and even the murder of returning black World War II veterans, in some cases still wearing their uniforms.

In February 1948 Truman became the first president to submit a special message on civil rights to Congress. Based on the recommendations of his Civil Rights Committee, Truman proposed a federal law against lynching, a ban on poll taxes then being used in seven southern states (not North Carolina), an end to discrimination in interstate travel by bus, rail, and airplanes, and the creation of a Fair Employment Practices Commission with the power to end job discrimination.

By March, angry southern congressional leaders threatened a revolt against the party if Truman was nominated for a full term. "Southern senators are solid all right in their fight against anti-poll tax, anti-lynching, anti-segregation and fair employment practices commission proposals," said Senator Clyde Hoey.[45] The state's other senator, William B. Umstead, suggested that Truman quit the race. Umstead told a state party leader that he would not back Truman. When asked why, Umstead replied: "Well, people around me in Durham say that they'll never vote again for that civil rights S.O.B."[46]

But the rhetoric coming from North Carolina political leaders was far more muted than from the politicians in most other southern states. When southern governors gathered in Jackson, Mississippi, to threaten a revolt against the national Democratic Party, North Carolina governor Gregg Cherry was conspicuously absent. Cherry's moderation did not sit well with some conservatives. "All around us we have true Southern states that don't want to sell out to the Red Democrats of the North, and some of our top leaders appease," complained H. C. Dale of Seven Springs. "We have top leadership, who say they love North Carolina, but are working hand and glove with Yankee Red Democrats to break the democratic backbone of the South where the only true democracy exists."[47]

But other North Carolinians applauded the state's moderate approach. "Some say the South can take care of its own problems," wrote Hubert Ellis of Wilson. "Perhaps they can in the 21st century. They've had the same argument for the past 40 years concerning civil rights. As yet, they haven't advanced a foot. Judging the future by the past, it will be the 22nd century before they advance a yard."[48]

The atmosphere was charged when 3,000 delegates to the state Democratic convention gathered in Raleigh's Memorial Auditorium in May 1948. To help keep the convention in line for Truman, the party leaders trotted out their oldest war horse: seventy-nine-year-old Cameron Morrison, the former Red Shirt leader, governor, and U.S. senator. "I swear that I'll never vote for the nomination of Truman," Morrison said. "[But] I don't want any more of this revolting business. We did it in the [Grover] Cleveland and [Al] Smith elections and we suffered. We don't want any more of this Populist and Al Smith business. If we can't beat Truman [at the national convention] let's step under the Democratic flag and help elect him. Then we'll let our congressmen and senators beat him down when he needs beating."[49]

During the national Democratic convention in Philadelphia, Cherry firmly grasped the state's banner to help prevent the North Carolina delegation from taking part in a walkout of southern segregationists from Mississippi and Alabama. The only thirteen southern votes for Truman at the convention were cast by North Carolina delegates.

While party leaders were able to maintain discipline at the state convention, as 1948 progressed it was clear that the state's politics were polarizing. South Carolina governor Strom Thurmond was nominated in July as the States' Rights Democratic, or Dixiecrat, nominee for president. His first presidential campaign foray was Cherryville's Watermelon Festival. Like South Carolina senator "Pitchfork" Ben Tillman—who also hailed from Thurmond's hometown of Edgefield—Thurmond headed across the state line to spread the gospel of white supremacy to Tar Heels. "If the segregation program of the president is enforced," he told the crowd of 1,500 people, "the results of civil strife may be horrible beyond imagination. Lawlessness will be rampant. Chaos will prevail. Our streets will be unsafe. And there will be the greatest breakdown of law enforcement in the history of the nation. Let us also tell them, that in the South, the intermingling of the races in our homes, in our schools and in our theaters is impractical and impossible."[50]

Thurmond's message struck a chord with Democrats such as R. S. Hood of Chapel Hill. "The South is fighting its most desperate fight with northern meddlers since 1861," Hood wrote. "We are nearer a shooting match then any time since the War Between the States."[51]

The reception accorded former vice president Henry Wallace when he visited North Carolina in August was just short of a shooting match. Wallace had been Roosevelt's agriculture secretary, secretary of commerce, and vice president, before he was dumped from the ticket in 1944 by FDR and replaced with Truman. Four years later, Wallace was the presidential candidate of the Progressive Party, a left-wing party that included communists and pushed for racial integration, world peace, and other causes. Formed in 1948 to push the Wallace presidential bid, the state chapter of the Progressive Party nominated North Carolina's first racially integrated ticket of the twentieth century, nominating blacks for the U.S. Senate and for attorney general.

Mary Watkins Price, a thirty-nine-year-old white woman from Greensboro, was chosen as the state's first female candidate for governor. Raised on a Rockingham County tobacco farm, Price earned a journalism degree from UNC. Moving to New York City, she worked as a reporter and became involved in left-wing circles after joining the labor movement. She later moved to Washington, D.C., to become the confidential and editorial secretary to the influential and widely respected national newspaper columnist Walter Lippmann. Returning to North Carolina in 1945, Price organized the state chapter of the Committee of the Southern Conference for Human Welfare—the same group that earlier had been headed nationally by Graham. She lobbied for liberal causes in the General Assembly, and in 1948 she became president of the state Progressive Party.

In July 1948, North Carolinians opened their newspapers to read some startling charges: Elizabeth Bentley, a former communist and ex–Soviet agent who had become an FBI informant, testified before a Senate committee that Price had spied for the Soviet Union while she was Lippmann's secretary, providing the Russians with information about national leaders with whom the columnist spoke. Price called the spying charges "fantastic" and said it was an obvious effort to discredit the Progressive Party. But she would not say whether she was a communist, saying "to make a public statement that I am not a Communist would in effect place me among the Red-baiters."[52]

After losing the governor's race, Price moved to Washington, D.C., where she worked as a social secretary at the embassy of Czechoslovakia, then a communist country. Price had difficulty holding a job after that. Claiming she was a victim of McCarthyism, Price said the FBI kept getting her fired. She eventually went to work for the National Council of Churches until she retired in 1970. She died in Oakland, California, in 1980, active in left-wing causes until the end.

Was Price a traitor or a victim of McCarthyism? The evidence that has emerged since the end of the Cold War strongly suggests that she was a Soviet agent. In 1995 the U.S. government declassified the files of what was known as the Venona Project—the decoded secret cables between Moscow and its agents in America.

Price's code name was "Dir," and she supplied the KGB with information about Lippmann's contacts with high government officials, according to

KGB cables found in the Venona Project. She worked directly for Bentley and also met several times with one of the top KGB spymasters working in the United States, Iskak Abdulovich Akhmerov. She served as a courier, at one point in June 1943 taking information to a KGB agent in Mexico City. She was also said to have assisted in the Soviet recruitment of Duncan Lee, a descendant of the Lees of Virginia and a former Rhodes Scholar. Lee became a highly placed Soviet spy while working as an aide to General William Donovan, the head of the Office of Strategic Services, the forerunner to the Central Intelligence Agency. Price's sister Mildred also became a Soviet agent, according to the documents.

By July 1944, the stress of spying was threatening Price's health, and she asked to retire. The KGB was reluctant to let her go because "she has been working for a long time and had acquired considerable experience." But they relented, and Price went to work in 1945 as director of the legislative and education department of the United Office and Professional Workers of America, a communist-dominated union. A year later she returned to North Carolina.[53]

Price was at Wallace's side when he opened his three-day North Carolina campaign at the end of August. The trip to North Carolina was part of a southern tour that was an open challenge to the system of segregation. Calling for the end of Jim Crow, Wallace said he would only speak to racially integrated audiences. Wallace made the front pages of North Carolina newspapers when he said he would stay at the home of a black supporter in Durham rather than in a hotel.

Probably never before or since has a presidential candidate received such a hostile reception in North Carolina. His first stop was the state Progressive Party convention, held in a Durham armory. Wallace could hardly be heard above the heckling from outsiders. Fights broke out, and one student acting as a Wallace bodyguard was stabbed eight times. A National Guard sergeant was so unnerved that he unsheathed his 45-caliber pistol.

The next day in the textile town of Burlington, Wallace was not allowed to speak at all. Accompanied by folksinger Pete Seeger and a small group of supporters, Wallace was pummeled by a barrage of eggs, tomatoes, ice cream cones, peach stones, and green peppers. At one point, Wallace waved his finger at the audience and said: "Remember that you are in the United States."

"Get your communists and your Negroes out of this town," one person shouted. Giving up, Wallace said, "Good-bye folks." The crowd of 500 broke past police and began pounding on the car windows and blocking the path.

It was only after a motorcycle patrolman brandished his pistol that the crowd made way.

In Greensboro, Winston-Salem, High Point, Hickory, and Charlotte, Wallace was heckled, shouted down, and splattered with rotten eggs and spoiled fruit. He showed personal courage, standing up to angry crowds even as his gray hair became stained with egg yolk. When he called for federal aid for southern hospitals, he was jeered as a communist. "Any one who wants to call that a Bolshevik plot is welcome to do so," Wallace shot back. "I say it is a Christian thought."[54]

In Charlotte, Wallace noted that Price was wearing a pin of an eagle on her dress. "That eagle there is an American eagle and it has a left wing and a right wing. That is the way of American politics. It has left and right wings." Minutes later, someone in the crowd ripped the eagle pin off her dress.[55]

When he called for allowing all people to vote in Hickory, Wallace was again met with a barrage of eggs and tomatoes. "Use all your eggs, use all your fruit to feed your children," Wallace shouted. Before leaving, Wallace paraphrased the Bible. "As Jesus Christ told his disciples, when you enter a town that will not hear you willingly, then shake the dust of this town from your feet and go elsewhere."[56]

The violence in North Carolina made the front pages of newspapers across the country. In Washington, Truman called the treatment of his former vice president "a highly un-American business." Governor Cherry promised beefed-up protection and declared that "a man ought to have the right to talk." By the time Wallace made his last stop in Asheville, there was a cordon of thirty city policemen and ten highway patrolmen. For the first time, Wallace was able to hold a peaceful rally and be heard. As the train pulled out of Asheville, the traveling reporters from New York and Washington sang their own version of the Tin Pan Alley tune, emending the famous line: "Nothing could be finer than to get out of Carolina in the morning."

Wallace continued on to Alabama, Mississippi, and Louisiana without experiencing the rude treatment that he had received in North Carolina. A few days later, speaking before 48,000 supporters at a "Yankee Doodle" rally at New York's Yankee Stadium, Wallace recalled his North Carolina tour. "Fascism has become an ugly reality—a reality which I have tasted," Wallace said.

> I have tasted it neither so fully nor so bitterly as millions of others. But I have tasted it. I learned what prejudice and hatred can mean. I learned

to know the face of violence, although I was spared the full force of violence. I saw the ugly reality of how hate prejudice can warp good men and women, turn Christian gentlemen into raving beasts; turn good mothers and wives into Jezebels. I didn't like what I saw. I didn't like to see men and women fall victims to the catch words of prejudice and the slogans of hate, even as the poor people of Germany were victimized by the catchwords and slogans of Hitler and Streicher.[57]

President Truman—despite his unpopular stand on civil rights—received a far different reception when he made a campaign appearance in Raleigh shortly before the election. A crowd of 25,000 greeted Truman at the state fairgrounds—the first president to visit the city since Teddy Roosevelt in 1905. Seeking to stymie the Dixiecrats, Truman said a vote for a third party "is the same as a vote for the Republican candidates." Scott halfheartedly endorsed Truman shortly before the election.

Truman carried the state with 58 percent of the vote. Republican Thomas Dewey won 33 percent. Thurmond received 9 percent, while Wallace received only 3,915 votes, or less than .5 percent. Thurmond carried Alabama, Louisiana, Mississippi, and South Carolina. Thurmond's weakest southern states were North Carolina and Texas. North Carolina voters avoided the extremes of Thurmond or Wallace. Despite the mobs during the Wallace visit, the state's reputation for racial moderation was battered but still intact—for the time being.

The 1950 Senate Race

That reputation would be severely tested in the 1950 Senate race, when Graham faced the voters. Perhaps Democratic leaders were blinded by outsiders' praise of North Carolina's race relations. Or perhaps Thurmond's poor showing or the election of Scott buoyed them. But for whatever reason, they misjudged how the attacks on segregation had inflamed racial feelings. Jonathan Daniels, in a letter to Eleanor Roosevelt, wrote that the only way Graham could be defeated was by "a horrible nigger-Communist campaign." He said North Carolina citizens were too intelligent to allow that to occur.[58]

North Carolina's image had moved beyond the white supremacy campaigns at the turn of the century and the periodical race-baiting in later races. By midcentury, North Carolina had an image as the southern state with the most forward-looking race relations. "The state has a reputation for fair dealings with its Negro citizens," wrote V. O. Key in *Southern Poli-*

tics. "Its racial relations have been a two-sided picture, but no where has cooperation between white and Negro leadership been more effective."[59]

North Carolina had avoided some of the worst racial demagogues who had afflicted the Deep South. The pay gap between black and white teachers was smaller than in other southern states. Blacks were registering to vote in the metropolitan areas in increasing numbers, even if they were largely barred from the polls in most rural areas. But North Carolina's reputation for moderate race relations was built on the foundation of racial segregation. When the system of Jim Crow laws began to crack, so did the state's racial climate.

The 1950 election was one of those rare occasions when both North Carolina Senate seats were up for election—one desired by the liberal Graham, who was seeking to finish the remaining four years of Broughton's term, and the other by the conservative Hoey, who was seeking a full six-year term. Some Graham backers thought there was a tacit understanding that if the Scott wing of the party would not work against Hoey, conservatives would not oppose Graham. But they were naive to think conservative-leaning North Carolina voters would meekly elect the South's leading liberal to a full Senate term.

Graham's political assets were significant. Scott swung his political organization behind Graham. He arranged for one of his protégés, Lauch Faircloth, a young Clinton businessman, to become Graham's campaign driver. He tried unsuccessfully to talk Jesse Helms, then a young radio reporter, into becoming Graham's press secretary.

The Truman administration did all it could to keep Graham in the Senate. Truman kept close tabs on the race, calling Graham and other North Carolinians for updates and making sure federal pork was handed out to North Carolina, including awarding a surplus U.S. Navy floating dry dock to the port of Wilmington.[60]

Graham had other advantages. Although organized labor was not a potent political force, it was particularly active for Graham. The NAACP promised to register 250,000 new voters in North Carolina, mainly in the urban areas. Graham was also supported by influential news organizations. Daniels, editor of the *News and Observer* and Scott's appointee to the Democratic National Committee, irregularly attended Graham campaign meetings even as he made sure the influential state capital newspaper gave Graham favorable coverage.

Graham was the very stereotype of an absent-minded, somewhat eccentric professor who talked in high-minded principles but would not sully himself with more practical matters. Graham never learned to drive, needed help in laying out his clothes in the morning, and was chronically forgetting his hat, coat, or airline tickets. "Part of his naivete, or innocence, stemmed from his personal habits, habits that reflected the man," wrote historians Pleasants and Burns.

In the age of the unfiltered cigarette, he did not smoke. In the age of the three-finger bourbon shot, chased with water, he did not drink. In the glory days of fountain-mixed soft drinks, he did not partake. Indeed, on one campaign foray, an exhausted Graham shocked his companions by asking for a "dope" (a Coca-Cola), believing the beverage would pep him up. His surprised aides complied, and Graham drank his Coke. After a few minutes, a perplexed Graham approached his assistants and asked, "How long does it take for it to have an effect?"[61]

Graham's chief challenger was Raleighite Willis Smith, a sixty-three-year-old corporate attorney. A handsome, distinguished-looking man, Smith in 1945 became the first North Carolinian to serve as president of the American Bar Association. His friend, U.S. Supreme Court justice Robert Jackson, named him as an American observer to the Nuremberg war crime trials of the Nazis. President Truman appointed him to the Amnesty Board to review the cases of those convicted of violating draft laws during World War II. Active in civic and political affairs, Smith served three terms in the N.C. House, culminating with a term as House Speaker from 1931 to 1933.

The Smith-Graham race offered a sharp liberal-versus-conservative choice for Democratic primary voters. Smith started the race widely regarded as the underdog. He could count on the conservative wing of the Democratic Party, which by the 1970s would become the core of the Republicans' resurgence in the state. To defeat Graham, Smith needed some issues. Senator Joe McCarthy of Wisconsin provided him with one.

Reds and Race

In February 1950 at Wheeling, West Virginia, McCarthy ushered in an era that would soon be known as McCarthyism. McCarthy alleged that the U.S. government, particularly the State Department, was honeycombed with communists or their fellow travelers. Many Americans were traumatized by the events following World War II. The Chinese Civil War had resulted in a communist victory. Eastern Europe lay under Soviet control. American traitors and spies had helped steal U.S. atomic bomb secrets for the Russians. Newspapers were filled with allegations of spying by such Americans as Alger Hiss.

Graham's careless left-wing connections made him a perfect target. While Smith did not charge that Graham was a communist, he did portray him as a naive left-winger with socialistic leanings. One Smith newspaper ad named seventeen Communist Front organizations—as identified by the House Committee on Un-American Activities—to which Graham had lent his name. They ranged from the Committee to Free Earl Browder, the American communist leader, to the American Friends of Spanish Democracy and his support for a 1944 dinner honoring the Red Army.[62]

The Graham campaign did not try to answer in detail every charge, knowing that some of the answers could be embarrassing for Graham. They instead launched a more general defense, portraying Graham as a patriotic American. In March, Graham tried to deflate the charges in a speech in Dunn. Graham said he was not a communist or a socialist, nor had he ever been "a member of any organization known or suspected by me of being controlled by Communists or socialists."[63]

As the May 27, 1950, primary neared, the red-baiting appeared to be making little headway with voters. The Smith campaign shifted strategy and began to attack Graham as a proponent of racial integration.

Graham was particularly vulnerable on the race issue. As a member of Truman's Civil Rights Committee, Graham supported the creation of the federal Fair Employment Practices Commission (FEPC), which would have power to mediate disputes in which employees claimed discriminatory treatment based on race, religion, or ethnic background. Graham, one of two southerners on the Civil Rights Committee, had not signed the report but had written a minority report in opposition to giving FEPC compulsory powers. Graham was also one of three southern liberals in the Senate, along with Claude Pepper of Florida and Estes Kefauver of Tennessee, who refused to participate in a filibuster against the bill. The Smith campaign attacked Graham's participation on the civil rights committee and for failing to oppose the FEPC. To make sure the issue filtered down to the country stores and mill gates, Smith supporters began using tactics that made the Senate race so infamous.

One anonymous handbill distributed by Smith supporters pictured black GIs dancing with white women in England during World War II with a caption that said Graham favored the same activity in North Carolina. Hundreds of white North Carolinians received a phony postcard mailed from New York City that read: "Dear Voter: Your vote and active support of Senator Frank Graham in the North Carolina primary, May 27, will be greatly appreciated. You know, just as we do, that Dr. Frank has done much to advance the place of the Negro in North Carolina. The Negro is a useful, tax-paying citizen! [signed] W. Wite [*sic*], executive secretary, National Society for the Advancement of Colored People."[64]

Smith supporters also distributed 50,000 handbills alleging that Graham had appointed a young black man named Leroy Jones to West Point. In fact, Graham employed a color-blind system of ranking applicants based on their exam scores. Jones was named a second alternate based on his score, but he never was appointed to or attended the military academy.

Smith's supporters have long maintained that neither Smith nor his top campaign aides had anything to do with the racial smear tactics, which they attributed to local county backers who acted without the knowledge or approval of Smith headquarters in Raleigh. "Every county manager had his idea of how to win the campaign, and we left it up to him to win the campaign in each county," said Hoover Adams, a Harnett County newspaperman who was Smith's campaign press aide. "And they would put out racial stuff, and even the county managers would exchange ideas on how to do it. And we had no control over it—no way we could control it."[65] Adams recalls Smith telling staffers that he did not want racial material distributed by his campaign, but he never denounced such activity during the campaign or afterwards.

With Graham's early lead beginning to melt away under the withering attacks on reds and race, the Scott administration abandoned any pretense of neutrality in the Democratic primary and did everything it could to help Graham. The governor's heavy involvement became an issue. The *Durham Sun*, a pro-Smith paper, called Scott the "Huey Long of Haw River."

In an effort to raise money for Graham, Scott dispatched two of his political lieutenants to Philadelphia, New York, and Washington, D.C., to collect political contributions from liquor distillers doing business with the state. They were tailed by a private detective hired by the Smith campaign, which leaked the story to the press. Scott claimed that all that he knew about the affair was that his political aides had taken vacation time.[66] The Smith campaign claimed Scott's highway appointees were using highway construction as a club to keep local Democratic Party county leaders in line for Graham. The Truman administration also tried to help Graham. It sent House Speaker Sam Rayburn, Vice President Alben Barkley, and Tennessee senator Estes Kefauver into the state to give speeches. While they did not endorse Graham, they criticized the red-baiting tactics being used around the country—and by inference, Smith.

Graham experienced difficulties in the cotton-mill towns, where many workers feared his views on race and where mill owners remembered his advocacy on behalf of the striking workers in the bloody Gastonia textile strike of 1929. The opposition of textile magnate Charlie Cannon, the owner of both Cannon Mills and the town in which it was located, Kannapolis, had its comic aspects. A Graham worker was arrested for loitering at a mill gate, where he was trying to distribute campaign literature. A second Graham worker was arrested for vagrancy, and a third was arrested for littering the streets. Finally, Graham backers chartered an airplane and dropped circulars on mill hands leaving work. "Charlie Cannon missed the boat," said one Graham worker. "He forgot to install anti-aircraft devices."[67]

But Graham also created his own problems. During a visit to a cotton mill in Wadesboro, where the air was filled with lint, Graham wet his handkerchief, holding it to his face as he shook the workers' hands—unmindful that the workers labored in the mill every day without such protection.[68]

As the election drew near, there were several troubling signs for Graham. On May 5, liberal New Deal senator Claude Pepper was defeated in Florida by conservative Democrat George Smathers in a race in which many of the same red-baiting and race-baiting techniques were used. Graham, who seemed to have one major illness every year, missed most of the final two weeks of the primary campaign when he came down with pneumonia.

There was also Graham's martyr-like decision on Truman's FEPC bill. Although sick at home in North Carolina, Graham was asked to pair his vote with a bill's supporter on a key cloture motion. The vote should not have been difficult for Graham, who had voiced opposition to the coercive nature of the FEPC bill. Such an action would have sent a reassuring signal to many of the state's white voters. Hoey said such a gesture would have been worth 50,000 votes to Graham. But during the crucial days before the primary, Graham angered and perplexed his friends by refusing to pair his vote and thereby align himself with the other southern senators. After he lost the primary, Graham voted against cloture, anyway. The move may have cost him the election. But Graham saw himself as a man above politics and would not lower himself to anything that smacked of political expediency. "Perhaps he felt such an act would be self-serving and that he would later find it hard to justify to himself," wrote his biographer Warren Ashby. "Perhaps, also, there had been at the base of his character a touch of the desire for self-immolation."[69]

While Graham steadfastly declined to criticize Smith, his campaign felt no such compunction. It produced ads impugning the integrity of Smith and portraying him as a greedy corporate lawyer. It said Smith was looking after the interests of thirty-six corporate clients, while Graham was helping the average North Carolinian. And they said a Smith election would turn back the state's progress. "They must not crucify North Carolina and its half century of progress in economics and racial amity, on the cross of bigotry, hate and greed," said one Graham ad.[70]

Many North Carolinians rallied to Graham's support. "In plain English, my reason for supporting Mr. Graham is this," wrote L. J. Moore, the owner of a New Bern barbecue restaurant. "He is for the little man and that is me. His stand on the color situation suits me to a T, not forceful but educational."[71]

With the approach of the May 27 primary, emotions were at the breaking point—even at the *News and Observer*, where Daniels directed relentlessly pro-Graham coverage. Columnist Nell Battle Lewis, a Smith supporter who had become a conservative in her later years, screamed at Daniels in the newsroom: "I hope all your children have nigger babies!" At the exclusive Carolina Country Club in Raleigh, a female Smith supporter spat in the face of Frank Daniels Sr., Jonathan's brother, who was also an executive with the newspaper.[72]

The voter turnout was the heaviest ever for a Democratic primary in North Carolina. Despite the attacks, Graham led the primary with 48.9 percent. Smith received 40.5 percent, and former senator Robert Reynolds won 9.3 percent.

Under a North Carolina law passed in 1913, the runner-up could call for a runoff if the leader did not win a majority, and Graham was short of 50 percent. All eyes in the state turned to Smith, who remained noncommittal about whether he would call for a second primary. As Smith tried to decide, the U.S. Supreme Court handed down decisions on three civil rights cases that chipped away at racial segregation. In the most important of the cases, the Supreme Court ruled that the University of Texas must admit a black student to its law school. The decision was a major blow to the separate-but-equal doctrine, and it shocked much of the South.

Despite the rulings on June 6, Smith initially decided privately not to challenge Graham. He drafted a telegram conceding the race and gave it to Hoover Adams to send to Graham. Disobeying his boss, his campaign press aide pocketed the telegram and called a meeting of a handful of supporters to discuss how they could change Smith's mind.

One of the supporters, Jesse Helms, the news director of WRAL radio, bought air time to run thirty-second advertising spots urging people to show up at Smith's house in Raleigh's Hayes Barton neighborhood that evening for a rally. By the time Helms arrived at Smith's house, there were between 200 and 500 people gathered, chanting "We want Smith!" or "All the way with Willis!"

Smith came out of his house three times to address the crowd. He first expressed gratitude to his supporters. Later he said he might reconsider his decision not to call for a runoff. Finally, he asked for peace and quiet to give him time to think about the decision. He told them, "Don't be surprised if I go with you." The next day, Smith called for a runoff.

Runoff

In his first campaign appearance of the runoff, Smith criticized what he called bloc voting by blacks for Graham and declared his devotion to the principles of segregated schools. To win, Smith said he would have to run against a number of political machines: the Scott Machine, the Truman Machine, organized labor, the NAACP, and the Old Well network of UNC grads.

In a hard-edged advertising campaign, Smith portrayed Graham as both un-American and antisouthern. "Associated with 18 groups labeled Communist Fronts by Un-American Activities Committee," read one Smith ad. "Studied under Harold Laski, England's leading Socialist. Voted steadily with 'left-wingers' Pepper and Kefauver. Long recognized as a 'social planner.' Always favored an end to segregation of white and negro. Signed Civil Rights Report in 1947, which included FEPC. Did not join other Southern senators in their fight against FEPC. In 1949 voted on Eastland amendment against all other Southern senators except Pepper and Kefauver. Received solid Negro bloc vote in First Primary."[73]

Dirty tricks abounded. In some eastern towns, well-dressed blacks wearing large hats and conspicuous jewelry rode through town in big cars with "Graham for Senate" banners. In Washington, North Carolina, a phony newspaper ad was placed for the "Colored Committee for Dr. Frank Graham." There were doctored photographs purporting to show Marian Graham, the senator's wife, dancing with a black man.

A week before the election, the most famous flier of the campaign was circulated across the state. "WHITE PEOPLE WAKE UP," cried the circular distributed by the "Know the Truth Committee." "Do you want Negroes working beside you, your wife and daughters in your mills and factories? Negroes eating beside you in all public eating-places? Negroes riding beside you, your wife and your daughters in buses, cabs and trains? Negroes sleeping in the same hotels and rooming houses? Negroes teaching and disciplining your children in school? . . . Negroes going to white schools and white children going to Negro schools? Negroes to occupy the same hospital rooms with you and your wife and your daughters? Negroes as your foremen and overseers in the mills? Negroes using your toilet facilities?" If so, said the circular, "vote for Frank Graham. But if you don't, vote for and help elect WILLIS SMITH FOR SENATOR. He will uphold the traditions of the South."[74]

Daniels accused the Smith forces of trying "to turn North Carolina into Mississippi." "This is something new in North Carolina," Daniels wrote. "Indeed it is something new even in the deeper, darker reaches of the South. It is not the natural passion of violent men like Bilbo and Talmadge. It is the cold-blooded, advertising technique employed to arouse prejudices for the purpose of reactionary politics."[75]

The Smith-Graham campaign took on the atmosphere of a traveling circus. One week before the runoff, Smith and Graham barnstormed the dusty roads of rural Wake County, stopping at the tobacco towns that ringed the state capital.

Smith was accompanied by a caravan of seventy-five cars, complete with a flatbed truck transporting Homer Briarhopper's country band, which invariably played "Dixie," the Smith campaign song. Smith climbed on the back of the truck that sported a banner: "Save Our South — Get on the Smith Bandwagon." "Do you want socialism in Washington?" Smith asked. "Do you want people telling you what to do every hour of the day? My opponent has stood for everything socialistic that has been proposed in Congress for years."[76]

Graham, speaking from a flatbed truck in Wendell, shot back: "In Grover Cleveland's time, when they were trying to get the mail delivered to the farmer, the opponents called that socialism. Now, if you're for rural electrification or rural telephones somebody calls you a socialist."

Among Graham's supporters in the town of Fuquay was Robert E. Prince, the president of the local bank, who climbed on a pickup truck to introduce Graham. "If you are a Communist," Prince said, "then I would like to be a Communist. If you are guilty of un-American activity then I would like to bear your guilt."[77]

In the town of Holly Springs, Graham called his wife Marian to his side. "Look at her," Graham said. "She's been a member of the same church for 56 years. Does she look like a woman who would marry a Communist?"[78]

Graham was facing a new level of hostility on the campaign trail. Audiences were often sullen and even angry. Some turned aside when he tried to introduce his wife. In a Craven County filling station, the proprietor just spit a big wad of tobacco juice and walked away when Graham introduced himself. He was occasionally spat upon.

North Carolina was once again staring into what Walter Hines Page had once called "a dark and unfathomable abyss of race feeling." Wrote journalist Samuel Lubell:

> The mob mood that was built up in the final days of the campaign was not unlike that preceding a lynching. In Wilmington a precinct worker telephoned the Graham manager and demanded hysterically, "Come and take all your literature out of my house! My neighbors won't talk to me." Graham stickers came off automobiles as people found it uncomfortable to say they were for him. In Raleigh, an eight-year-old schoolboy who spoke up for Graham was beaten up as a "nigger lover" by other children. A Durham election official, favorable to Graham, was awakened during the night by the jangling telephone. When his wife answered, she was asked: "How would you like a little stewed nigger for breakfast?" The day before the voting, Graham was scheduled to speak at High Point to some mill workers. His party stopped at a filling station. Five men were sitting around. Introducing himself, Graham offered to shake hands. The men turned their backs. Muttered on: "We're all Willis Smith men here. We'll have nothing to do with nigger lovers here."[79]

On a sweltering June day, 550,000 people went to the polls, a state record for a runoff. Graham's lead in the first primary had evaporated in the racial hysteria. By 9:30 P.M., the results were in. Smith had won 281,114 votes to Graham's 261,789. In the Manteo ballroom at Raleigh's Sir Walter Hotel, Smith supporters whistled "Dixie." "Tell ole' Kerr Scott to go to hell," someone shouted.

After comforting his supporters on the sixth floor, Graham took the elevator down to the ballroom to appear with Smith and congratulate him. Graham didn't say a word as he was driven home to his sister-in-law's house near Hillsborough.[80]

Senator Frank Graham campaigning, 1950. (Photograph by Allard Lowenstein; courtesy of the Lowenstein Family and the Manuscripts Department, Wilson Library, UNC–Chapel Hill)

Aftermath

Graham lost the race in rural eastern North Carolina, the region of the state with the largest black population and where sensitivity toward racial questions was most acute. In the first primary, the Coastal Plain had voted for Graham. Many of them were country people who were strong Scott supporters. But in the runoff, 17 of the 27 counties Graham had carried in the east in the first primary went for Smith.[81]

"People became inflamed and aroused," said Howard Godwin, the Harnett County clerk of court. "It was impossible to head off the stampede. . . . You could not reach them by appeals to reason, because there was no reason in them. You had as well try to beat out a forest fire with a pine bough."[82]

The race issue played not just with farmers and mill hands, but also with middle-class people in some of the upscale urban neighborhoods. Fanny Knight Thomas of Raleigh visited 300 homes on behalf of Graham and made numerous phone calls. "I was asked at least 50 or 100 times if it were true that Negro children were to go to white schools if Dr. Frank was elected," Thomas recalled. "One lady told me she loved Dr. Frank like a brother, but that she would have to fire her maid on Monday if he was nominated on Saturday. She said the maid talked all the time about how they gave him such a big majority in the first primary and what a celebration they were planning on Sunday if he were nominated."[83]

If the Red Shirt campaigns were the last battles of the Civil War fought in North Carolina, then the 1950 Democratic Senate primary was the opening salvo of the civil rights movement that would soon rock the state. And Graham's role, as Pleasants and Burns describe, was unique.

No politician could question segregation's wisdom and expect to continue his political career. Indeed, any other candidate for public office in North Carolina who held Frank Graham's racial views would have been dismissed from the first as a fringe figure, a political oddity. In his own campaign, Frank Graham was careful to appear cautious, skeptical of too rapid racial change. But events—and the logic of his public life—caught up with him in the second primary. He was undone by the panic-driven association that linked him to the effort—now fully launched in the nation—to overturn statutory segregation. The irony of the campaign rests in the realization that Graham's critics—and his defamers—correctly assessed his true racial sentiments.[84]

Aside from the question of race, observers such as Lubell also saw the Smith-Graham race as a harbinger of the rise of North Carolina's Republican Party—an affluent urban middle class more in tune with the national GOP. Graham's worst showing in Charlotte was in the affluent Myers Park neighborhood.[85]

The Smith-Graham race left scars on the state's political psyche that never completely healed. When Smith, the senator-elect, came through a receiving line at the Executive Mansion, he stuck out his hand to First Lady Mary Scott. She looked at his hand for a moment, then at his face and said, "Oh, I couldn't do that," and turned away.[86]

"In the past half century the only campaigns comparable in bitterness to this last one were those of 1898 and 1900," wrote Nell Battle Lewis. "I wonder how long it took for the bad feeling engendered by those two to subside. That might give us some idea of how long it will be before we'll be on an even keel again. For all the political vitality of the state that this campaign showed, I hope we won't have another like it in North Carolina in my lifetime. Once every 50 years is quite enough."[87]

In fact, North Carolina, or at least the older generation, has still not gotten over it. The election made a powerful impression on such future leaders as Terry Sanford, Bill Friday, and Jim Hunt. Friday was later to remark that the bitter election "drove me away from political involvement."[88] The 1950 race was where Helms and his political alter ego, Raleigh attorney Tom Ellis, cut their teeth on politics. Helms and Ellis would be instrumental in the rise of the Republican Party in the 1970s, both nationally and in North Carolina, helping launch the Reagan Revolution, which in turn led to the presidential elections of George H. W. Bush and George W. Bush.

Helms's role in the campaign has always been a matter of dispute, with supporters diminishing his role and foes exaggerating it. Sanford contended that Helms was "one of the principal architects" of the Smith campaign. Helms says his role was minimal, although he said he did sit in on some campaign meetings. He said he had no involvement with any of the racist literature. "None of it," Helms said in a 1999 interview. "I didn't even see it. I haven't even seen to this good day some of the stuff they still talk. But I am not apologizing for anything I did in the campaign because I was proud to help a friend who turned out to be a senator."[89]

Others have different recollections. Pou Bailey, a Raleigh judge, son of former U.S. senator Josiah Bailey, and a longtime poker-playing buddy of Helms, remembers that Helms was "up to his neck" in the Smith cam-

paign. "He had no official position, but I don't think there was any substantive publicity that he didn't see and advise on. He was deeply involved."
Bailey said that Helms was involved in practically every ad that was run.[90]

In his biography of Helms, journalist Ernest Furgurson talked with
R. H. Carson, the seventy-six-year-old retired advertising manager of the
News and Observer. He knew Helms from his days when Helms had worked
as a sportswriter for the newspaper. Carson remembered Hoover Adams
bringing Smith ads to the newspaper. "Adams sometimes was accompanied by Jesse Helms," Carson recalled. "Jesse and I were on a first-name
basis. Often Jesse would alter copy right at the counter. It was never really
very professional copy. Jesse would alter it, and one day I loaned him my
scissors and he took and outlined around the figure of Mrs. Graham with a
Negro. He cut out two or three others in the picture. I was figuring out how
much this was going to cost, four hundred or five hundred dollars maybe.
We didn't run that ad in the *N&O*. We set a lot of ads and made mats, sometimes 50 or 60 of them, for them to send to local papers around the state or
whatever."[91]

Whatever their true roles, Helms and Ellis learned their politics from the
1950 Senate campaign. They learned to defeat progressives by using racial
appeals to split off white farmers and mill workers. And they learned that
tough, negative campaigns could be very effective, whether conducted by
using circulars and newspaper ads in 1950 or by television and radio advertising in the 1980s and 1990s.

Graham's post-Senate career was an anticlimax. Some suggest his loss
took something out of Graham's irrepressible spirit. He would never talk
about the Senate race. "Some of his closest friends sensed, however, despite his silence, that he had been deeply personally hurt," wrote Ashby,
Graham's biographer. "It was not primarily the tactics of the opposition,
for he had met such tactics before. For the first time in his life he, who had
been lavished with love, was publicly rejected, apparently hated—and in
North Carolina. The hurt was greatest of all because he was rejected by the
very people—the textile workers, the farmers and sharecroppers, the small
businessmen—for whom he had lived and fought."

He felt he could not stay in North Carolina. "The South," wrote Ashby,
"had a way of exiling those who threatened the fixed Southern patterns
of race and economics." After turning down numerous job offers, including the presidency of the American Red Cross and college presidencies,
Graham accepted an appointment to serve as a United Nations mediator
in the dispute between India and Pakistan over Kashmir. Graham spent the

next sixteen years working for the UN and living in an apartment in New York. Despite his best efforts, his work did little to advance peace in the region. Near the end of his career, his work on the Kashmir question was sadly ignored.

He continued to give numerous speeches around the country on behalf of the United Nations, and he also spoke out on the issues of the day. He urged support for the U.S. Supreme Court ruling outlawing school segregation. He compared the civil rights protests to the American patriots of 1776. When he spoke at Winthrop College in South Carolina in 1961, a cross was burned in the front yard of the house where he was staying. The South Carolina legislature passed a resolution condemning the college for inviting him and banning his appearance at any public university.

A Weakened Scott

Kerr Scott put his prestige on the line for Graham, and the Smith-Graham race left him politically weakened among voters such as Edwin H. Powell of Rocky Mount. "Worked hard to get you elected, we thought breaking the old machine," Powell wrote the governor. "Then after the election you named Graham as senator—taking one rated as Communist and Socialist and negro lover. On top of that you put a nigger on the State Board of Education to meet with white people. Now if you think the people of NC are going to put up with that you are unjustly kidding yourself."[92]

Scott shrugged off the defeat. "I've been in a lot of scraps. It's not the first time I've been run over." He later greeted reporters in his shirt sleeves, telling them, "I pulled off my coat just to show you that I had not lost my shirt."[93] Scott also made enemies by sweeping out of state government many of the conservative Democrats closely aligned with the Shelby Dynasty and replacing them with his own supporters. "He might just as well have been a Republican or something, because see, he's the one that broke up the machine, as they call it," recalled his brother, Ralph Scott.[94]

By 1951, many conservatives in the legislature hoped to embarrass Scott. Although he entered office with a large budget surplus, by 1951 the state had spent so much so fast that it had to borrow money to pay expenses in anticipation of tax revenues. Scott offered a more modest legislative program in 1951. He called for increased salaries for teachers and state employees, expanded programs for health, repeal of the right-to-work law, creation of a state minimum-wage law, and funds to create a state-sponsored art museum.

Scott once again took to the radio to rail against conservative legislators as "Hold-the-Liners" and the Senate Appropriations Committee as the "Do Nothing for Nobody Club." While Scott's tactics worked in 1949 when he was at the height of his political power, his confrontational style only seemed to stiffen the legislative opposition in 1951. Although some of his legislative proposals passed, Scott found the plowing much more difficult the second time around.

Nearing the end of his term in 1952, Scott had no desire to turn the governor's office back to the conservative wing of the Democratic Party that he had spent four years battling. He recruited an old friend from Lexington, superior court judge Hubert Olive, to run as his successor. But the conservatives had had enough of what they called the "wild bull from Alamance." Conservatives helped nominate and elect a loyal machine candidate, former congressman and senator William Umstead of Durham—the colorless, teetotaling son of a Methodist minister.

In his last radio address as governor in December 1952, Scott's voice became so choked with emotion that radio audiences could hardly hear his last 100 words. Tears trickled down his ruddy face. "I became a candidate because of these two convictions—that rural North Carolina was a land of forgotten people, and that what is bad for two-thirds of the people is bad for all," Scott said. "And now my friends, as we approach the end of the row that we have been plowing together for the past four years . . ."

"He was," wrote Simmons Fentress, "the century's most cussed governor. Columnists and commentators attacked him as a political accident, a notorious spender of other people's money, a dangerous liberal tied to Harry Truman's coattail, a governor of only half the people. Many will be glad to see him go. The gladdest of all probably are the men in the front offices of the big utilities."[95]

In January, after turning over the governor's office, Scott climbed into the new tan Ford sedan that state employees had bought him. He was momentarily confused by the car's automatic transmission. He was escorted to the Wake County line by a highway patrol car. After the trooper left, Scott pulled the car over to the side of the road, and he and Miss Mary pulled out sandwiches and fruit prepared by the mansion staff and enjoyed a picnic meal. But they had to rely on a passing truck driver to lend them a bottle opener for their soft drinks. After arriving at Haw River, Scott quipped to reporters that he was now on relief and had to find some meat to eat. He went out and bagged eight rabbits.

The Third Primary

On June 24, 1953, after giving twenty-four speeches in twenty days, Smith suffered a heart attack in Washington. Two days later he had a second attack and died, three years to the day after his primary victory over Graham. Among those attending his funeral service at Edenton Street Methodist Church in Raleigh was Vice President Richard M. Nixon. Helms was a pallbearer. After flying down from New York, Graham sat on the back pew.

Umstead chose Alton Lennon, a conservative Wilmington attorney, as Smith's replacement. Lennon would have to face voters in 1954 if he wanted to fill the remaining two years of Smith's term. But in the view of the Scott wing of the Democratic Party, Lennon was holding Dr. Frank's seat—stolen from him in a racist campaign. They had hoped to challenge Smith in 1954. But Lennon would have to do as a stand-in.

After spending two and a half years back on his farm, Scott decided to run. In case anyone missed the revenge factor, the Scott faction nicknamed the 1954 Senate race the "Third Primary." Asked by a reporter if he was worried that Lennon would engage in the kind of race-baiting that Smith had four years earlier, Scott smiled and replied: "I'll take care of it son. I'm not as good a Christian as Frank Graham."[96]

Among those who were itching to avenge Graham's defeat was a thirty-seven-year-old, politically ambitious Fayetteville attorney and state senator named Terry Sanford. Shortly after his defeat, Sanford visited Graham and promised "to get even, to rectify that injustice." Sanford became Scott's campaign manager and quickly moved to muzzle Scott's sharp-edged tongue and convince him to deliver his speeches from a script. It was one thing to be entertaining, Sanford said. It was quite another to win a political race. But that didn't mean Scott couldn't be folksy, stopping at country stores to spin stories and remind locals of what he had done to help rural people.

In the small Lenoir County town of Pink Hill, Scott told a radio audience that he once walked twenty-one miles in 1919 because a taxi driver wanted a dollar-per-mile fare. As a campaign gimmick, Scott offered a bull calf to anyone who could walk twenty-one miles in less than six hours—the time it took him to walk that distance in 1919. So began what was to become known as the Great Bull Calf Walk. In Pink Hill, Scott gave away thirty-nine bull calves—most of which were donated by supporters. Knowing a good publicity stunt when he saw one, Scott arrived in town in a sulky pulled by two mules and accompanied by a local high school band. The mayor inducted Scott into the Athletic Order of the Survivors of the Great Bull Calf Walk. "There were thousands of people lining the road and cheering people on," said Lauch Faircloth, a Scott lieutenant. "There were truckloads of those calves. I think a lot of people won a calf who didn't know quite what to do with it."[97]

On May 17, the U.S. Supreme Court handed down the *Brown v. Board of Education* ruling, outlawing public school segregation just two weeks before the primary. The ruling brought cries of outrage from southern politicians.

Scott never appealed to racial prejudice in his campaigns. But neither could any southern politician voice support for the end of segregation and hope to survive at the polls. So Scott, in a statement that Sanford helped draft, walked a fine line. "I have always been opposed, and I am still opposed to Negro and white children going to school together," Scott said.

> It is my belief that most white and Negro citizens of North Carolina agree on this point. I feel certain that no candidate would favor the end of segregation, and I am sure they will join me in hope and prayer that we can avoid stirring up fear and bad feeling between races in North Carolina. As a member of the United States Senate I would work in close cooperation with other like-minded senators to preserve our traditions. I urge that all fellow citizens, regardless of race, color or creed, remain calm and work together in an orderly fashion while machinery is being set up to avoid disruption of our pattern of school life. To this end, I shall fight.[98]

Even a feisty liberal such as Scott was forced to compromise on the volatile issue of race in order to win public office in North Carolina. But such discretion did not earn Scott a pass. At a campaign rally two days after the *Brown* ruling, Lennon said Scott "and certain of his top advisors and political associates have encouraged the abolition of segregation in our public schools for many years."

Would the Third Primary be like the first two—an orgy of emotional race-baiting? Sanford gave a lot of thought to how to handle the race issue if it was used against Scott. In the 1950 Senate campaign, Sanford had led the Graham effort in the Cumberland Mills precinct, a tough mill village located south of Fayetteville. The mill village voted for Graham, despite the racist appeals. Sanford kept a small, ring-bound notebook in his bedroom bureau to jot down the political lessons he was learning. By the end of the Smith-Graham race, Sanford had compiled twenty-five to thirty pages of notes. "I learned one thing," Sanford said. "That is, don't ever let them get off the defensive. Frank Graham let them get off the defensive. He was just so nice and sweet. Well, we . . . gave them blow for blow."[99]

Preparing for an expected last-minute barrage of racial campaign literature against Scott, Sanford asked his county leaders to contact him immediately at the first sign of trouble. During the final week of the primary, the Scott campaign learned that a bundle of leaflets had been dropped off at a service station in the small eastern North Carolina town of Columbia. The leaflets were reprinted from an advertisement that had appeared in the *Winston-Salem Journal*. The ad was a letter signed by an H. R. Gleaves, president of the city's Progressive Civic League, a black political organization. The ad said Scott "has demonstrated his interest in our race and has aided our case of non segregation."

Sanford engaged in some campaign skullduggery and spin control to put the Lennon campaign on the defensive. To make certain the Lennon campaign was the source of the leaflets, Sanford recruited a trusted member of the tobacco workers' union to pose as a Lennon supporter. The union man showed up at Lennon headquarters and asked for and received a bundle of leaflets along with instructions on how they should be left in rural mailboxes and on the front porches of houses in textile-mill towns.

After obtaining a pile of the leaflets, Sanford had the union man hidden away in a Raleigh hotel room with some steaks and beer—and with a Scott political operative babysitting him like a witness about to testify against the mob—for the final two days of the campaign. Sanford couldn't afford for the press to find out that the leaflets were obtained under false pretenses.

Sanford leaked the leaflets to the *News and Observer* in Raleigh, which obliged with a front-page headline the day before the election that read: "Alton Lennon Forces Flood State with 'Phony' Race Issue Leaflets." Sanford, a former FBI agent, called for an FBI investigation, offered a $100 reward for further information, and sent telegrams to Lennon county managers threatening to sue any of them that distributed the leaflets. Scott squeaked through the Democratic primary by only 8,374 votes, and Sanford always believed that it was this bit of trickery that made the difference. "We put that prairie fire out," Sanford said. "We might have gotten our hands a little burned doing it, but we damn well put it out in two days' time. Everything broke just right."[100]

Scott's victory was sweet revenge for the Smith-Graham campaign of four years earlier. Scott twice sent an aide to Hillsborough to try to convince Graham to stand by his side on election night, but Graham would not come. But Graham was in the Senate gallery, sitting next to Miss Mary, in November 1954 when Scott took the oath of office, and he was later brought down to the floor.[101]

Scott served only a little over three years of his Senate term. He seemed to leave his fiery populism back home, concentrating on farming issues and water projects. Journalist Tom Wicker described a Scott-like figure in his novel *Facing the Lions*: "In his shiny blue serge, his trousers not quite touching the tops of his clodhopper shoes, with his Southern molasses-drip of a voice rumbling around a lump in his jaw that anybody looking at him could tell was a chaw of tobacco, [Scott] had been the last senator to use the old cuspidors in the chamber—which was a kind of immortality, and maybe as good as any other kind."[102]

For an eight-year period, representing North Carolina in the U.S. Senate almost seemed like a death sentence: Josiah Bailey died in 1946, Melville Broughton in 1948, Willis Smith in 1953, Clyde Hoey in 1954. When Scott moved into Alton Lennon's Senate office, there were newspaper stories about the three-room suite being "jinxed" because he was the fifth senator to occupy it during one six-year period.

No one would have suspected that Kerr Scott would be next. At age sixty-one, Kerr Scott still looked hale and healthy—frequently walking more than five miles to work from the Westchester apartments in Northwest Washington to his office on Capitol Hill. But a lifetime of country cooking and unending cigars and chewing tobacco had taken their toll. On April 9, 1958, while home on Easter recess, Scott suffered a heart attack. On April 17, while still in the hospital, Scott experienced a second and fatal heart attack.

Legacy

Although the Squire of Haw River had passed from the scene, the Scott clan continued to influence North Carolina politics for the rest of the century. Two years after Kerr Scott's death, Sanford, his protégé, was elected governor—partly with the help of Scott's Branchhead Boy organization. Ralph Scott, a blunt-spoken, gravel-voiced wit and country-boy populist like his brother Kerr, remained a powerful member of the General Assembly into the 1970s. "Uncle Ralph," as he became widely known, was a champion of the dairy industry, N.C. State University, the mentally ill, and civil rights for blacks.

Ralph was in Raleigh to help show the political ropes to both Sanford and Kerr's son, Robert W. Scott, who was elected lieutenant governor in

1964 and governor in 1968. Previously, Bob Scott had been groomed to take over the family dairy farm; his father had always said that one politician in the family was enough, and they rarely talked politics.

Bob Scott had many of his father's attributes—an independent streak, the love of a good joke, and a penchant for speaking bluntly. But he was not a populist, and his politics were not as liberal as those of his father, in part because he served during more conservative times. "Like the younger generation of Longs of Louisiana and Talmadges of Georgia, he reflected the gray flannel suit, post–World War II generation," wrote William Snider.[103]

Bob Scott proved to be a risk-taking governor like his father. He raised the gasoline tax to build more roads, pushed through the state's first tax on cigarettes, started the first pilot kindergarten programs, and led the consolidation of the sixteen state-supported college campuses into one system. The latter was a fierce battle between education fiefdoms that required all of Scott's political skills. But much of Scott's efforts were devoted to trying to maintain law and order as the state was racked by anti–Vietnam War protests on the college campuses and civil rights demonstrations in the black community.

The Scotts tried to keep the family legacy alive, but the era of red-eyed, gravy liberalism—and the era of the powerful farm vote—had passed. Bob Scott made an ill-advised Democratic primary challenge to sitting governor Jim Hunt in 1980, getting slaughtered. He finished with a stint as president of the state community college system. His wife, Jesse Rae Scott, unsuccessfully sought the Democratic primary nomination for state labor commissioner in 1976.

But the Scott influence went far beyond their immediate family mini-dynasty. Kerr Scott had transformed the old populism of Marion Butler, Daniel Russell, Bob Reynolds, and Ralph McDonald and created the modern progressive wing of the Democratic Party.

"Kerr Scott was our political savior—that's the way we looked at him," Jim Hunt said. "This man is saving us. He's giving us a whole new life by bringing in these opportunities. There was a fervor and a passion about Kerr Scott and the change he would make in our lives that is very unusual in politics."[104]

chapter 4 **The Last of the Conservative Democrats**

n May 17, 1954, the U.S. Supreme Court handed down its thunderclap decision of *Brown v. the Board of Education*, outlawing segregation in the public schools. On that day, I. Beverly Lake Sr., forty-eight, was walking down a Raleigh street carrying a clear garment bag from the cleaners containing his grandfather's Confederate uniform. A man stopped Lake on the street and quipped: "Mr. Lake. I didn't know we were going to war so soon." The *Brown* decision would transform Lake's life from that of a scholarly public utilities lawyer with the state attorney general's office to North Carolina's leading segregationist politician.[1]

The life of Sam J. Ervin Jr. would be dramatically altered as well. Ervin was an associate justice on the N.C. Supreme Court—a political tomb where the fifty-six-year-old Burke County native was expecting to quietly finish his law career. Soon, Ervin would emerge as the chief legal theoretician in Congress in the battle to preserve segregation. He would eventually become so famous that he would inspire the creation of fan clubs, and his homespun humor would be captured for posterity in books.

Luther H. Hodges, also fifty-six, was lieutenant governor. Not that anyone much noticed. During his seventeen months on the job, Hodges was nearly invisible, treated by the sitting governor as if he were a potted plant. But Hodges would soon be leading the state as governor during the school desegregation crisis. His handling of the crisis would help elevate him into President John F. Kennedy's cabinet.

The Supreme Court's decision would transform daily life in the South, helping spark one of the great social revolutions in American history. But the movement also would revive southern sectionalism. The 1950s saw North Carolina pull back from its midcentury liberalism, in which leaders such as Governor Kerr Scott and Senator Frank Porter Graham embraced many of the New Deal policies of Franklin Roosevelt and Harry Truman.

With the system of legal segregation crumbling, North Carolinians returned to safe, conservative Democrats to help keep in place the legal framework of the social caste system. This was the last generation of North Carolina leaders who could be truly called southern Democrats when the description meant something more than just a geographic or cultural distinction.

Starting in the 1960s, many conservative voters would turn to the Republican Party. But the GOP, while growing in strength, was still not in a position to compete. So in the 1950s voters cast their ballots for such conservative Democrats as Governors Luther Hodges (1954–61) and William Umstead (1953–54), U.S. Senators Sam J. Ervin (1954–74) and B. Everett Jordan (1958–73), and would-be governors such as Lake.

When the civil rights movement threatened North Carolina's social structure, the state moved swiftly to the right. North Carolina had one of the most active Klans in the country. The homes of civil rights leaders were bombed. Politicians who dared defend the U.S. Supreme Court would find their political careers in tatters. North Carolina congressmen were as hardened in their opposition to civil rights legislation as any race-baiting Deep South lawmakers. While avoiding the demagoguery of other states, North Carolina's leaders quietly managed to delay racial integration of its schools.

But even during this period of ideological retrenchment, North Carolina remained a battleground state where center-left Democrats such as Kerr Scott could be elected to the Senate in 1954 and Terry Sanford could be elected as governor in 1960. Both men, however, had to pay lip service to segregation in order to win.

Brown v. Board of Education

Perhaps no other issue in the twentieth century so divided the country as did public school desegregation. In its landmark case, *Brown v. Board of Education of Topeka, Kansas*, the Supreme Court reversed its stance of 1895 in *Plessy v. Ferguson* that had approved the separate-but-equal doctrine for the races. "We conclude," the court ruled, "that in the field of public education that doctrine of 'separate but equal' has no place. Separate but equal facilities are inherently unequal."

North Carolina's schools were in fact unequal, although the gap between white and black school systems had been closing. In 1900 North Carolina spent more than twice as much on its white students as its black students. In 1940 the state spent 65 cents per black child for every dollar spent on a white child. By 1950 that figure had risen to 85 cents.[2]

For those who argued that North Carolina's dual public school systems were nearing parity, Thurgood Marshall had a wager. "I'll make North Carolina an offer," said the NAACP's legal counsel (and future U.S. Supreme Court justice) in Raleigh in 1956. "Let's next year reverse all the schools, let the whites go to Negro schools, and Negroes go to white schools."[3]

Although not unexpected, the Supreme Court ruling set off a firestorm across the South that was felt for the rest of the century. It gave a new lease to race-baiting politicians, revived the Ku Klux Klan, and led to the creation of White Citizens Councils to fight integration. Southern governors began digging up early nineteenth-century doctrines of states' rights that most legal experts thought had been buried with John C. Calhoun. In Virginia, powerful senator Harry Byrd issued a call for "massive resistance," and the school system in Prince Edward County, just a three-hour drive north of Raleigh, closed for five years rather than be integrated. In Little Rock, Arkansas, President Dwight Eisenhower sent in paratroopers to restore order when a local high school was integrated.

In North Carolina, cooler heads prevailed. Governor Umstead said he was "terribly disappointed" but was cautious and temperate in his response. But many ordinary people worried whether the South could survive such a blow. "Let us all pray together that the Northern forces now directed against our public schools shall not also be turned against our churches, hospitals, social clubs and our very homes," said Carson McCoy of Rocky Mount. "Monday, May 17, 1954, will go down in history as a Black Day."[4]

Luther Hodges

At the time of the *Brown* decision, Umstead had been North Carolina's governor for sixteen months. But he would not live long enough to deal with its consequences. The Durham attorney was one of the political warhorses of the Shelby Dynasty, having served as a congressman and state party chairman and briefly filling a U.S. Senate vacancy, losing the seat in 1948 to former governor Melville Broughton.

Even during his inauguration in January 1953, Umstead did not look like a healthy man. But Umstead soldiered through a long day of activities that included standing in line for four hours greeting well-wishers and attending an inaugural ball, where he played several tunes on his harmonica. Hodges described the day's grueling activities as "somewhat barbaric." The next day Umstead suffered a heart attack that was first reported to the press as "a heavy cold." Umstead never fully recovered from the heart attack, but his sense of duty would not permit him to ease up. On Thursday, November 4, 1954, a frail and sickly Umstead left his office and went home to his bed in the mansion. Later in the day, his doctor ordered him admitted to Watts Hospital in Durham. On Sunday morning, Umstead died of congestive heart failure at age fifty-nine, the only North Carolina governor to die in office in the twentieth century.

Hodges was reading his Sunday morning newspaper in his home in Leaksville (now Eden) when he received a telephone call from an aide to the governor. After hanging up the phone, a stunned Hodges collapsed back in his chair. Two days later, Hodges was North Carolina's accidental governor.

Max Gardner had brought Hodges into politics. Gardner may have seen something of himself in Hodges—a broad-chested young businessman with a commanding presence who was at home in northern corporate boardrooms. Gardner appointed Hodges to the State Board of Education, and he was later named to the State Highway Commission. Hodges, in turn, had helped Gardner and his allies raise political money. Hodges and Gardner were the only two corporate executives to serve as North Carolina's chief executive during the twentieth century—a position dominated by lawyers.

Television commentator Jesse Helms once remarked that Hodges's life was "a bit of story-book Americana, a story of drama of rags to riches." He was one of nine children of a Virginia tenant farmer who moved across the border to Spray to work in the local textile mill and eventually operate a small grocery store.

After working his way through UNC–Chapel Hill, Hodges began a career with Fieldcrest Mills, the textile firm owned by Marshall Field Company of Chicago, working mostly in North Carolina. He spent the last seven years of his career in New York City, where he was a vice president overseeing the operation of twenty-nine Fieldcrest mills in six states and three countries. He lived in a house in Bronxville that was previously owned by Broadway composer Jerome Kern. In the library was a piano where Kern is said to have composed "Smoke Gets in Your Eyes."

Taking early retirement in 1950 at age fifty-two, Hodges entered public life. At the invitation of Winston-Salem banker Robert Hanes, a longtime Gardner intimate who was then U.S. mission chief to Germany, Hodges spent more than a year in West Germany working for the Marshall Plan, providing advice on how to rebuild that country's war-shattered economy.

Hanes, who was also head of Wachovia, the state's largest bank, was among several business people who recruited Hodges to run for lieutenant governor. Hanes was by some accounts looking for an insurance policy in case the sickly Umstead should die in office. That may explain why Umstead froze his lieutenant governor out of any decisions or discussions, treating him as a virtual nonperson. Even as it was becoming obvious that his health was failing, Hodges was a reminder of his own mortality.

After a lifetime as a corporate executive, Hodges was an odd fit in Raleigh's back-scratching political culture. As a governor who had incurred few debts while running for office, Hodges confounded party regulars with his independence and angered Democratic courthouse leaders by frequently appointing the growing class of Republican businessmen to state posts. In a meeting in 1957, forty Democratic chairs complained that Hodges was not feeding the Democratic patronage machine. "The Democratic Party in North Carolina, in my opinion, is losing a lot of its power, its source of revenue and its prestige because we've got too many Republicans working for the state of North Carolina," one former state legislator told the governor.[5]

Hodges's brusque, no-nonsense manner—Helms described him as "autocratic"—sometimes rubbed people the wrong way. As one state official put it: "He has absolutely no patience with people who don't move at the same pace he does. He's a strange man, that man. I think he eats a lot of spinach."[6] The conservative-leaning business executive would help North Carolina devise a new economic development strategy.

During the first half of the twentieth century, North Carolina had led the South in industrialization. North Carolina's 428 hosiery plants were producing 40 percent of the nation's knit goods. Burlington Industries was the world's largest textile company. Half of the nation's cigarettes were made in North Carolina. And there were 300 furniture companies providing more wood house furnishings than any other state.[7] Industrialization had paid off in some respects. In 1930 North Carolina's per capita income was 43 percent of the national average. By the 1950s it was two-thirds of the national average.

But North Carolina's industrialization had not produced the prosperity that civic and political leaders had envisioned. Hodges was shocked to learn that North Carolina ranked forty-forth among the forty-eight states in per capita income in 1953, the same ranking it had in 1929. North Carolina factory workers were paid the lowest wages of any state in the country in 1954, earning $47.88 per week compared to a national average of $71.68 for production workers—a result of low-skill jobs in poor-paying industries, small plants, and lack of unionization.[8]

North Carolina may have been a leader in southern industrialization

Governor Luther Hodges (seated) fishing.
(Courtesy of the *Raleigh News and Observer*)

in the early part of the twentieth century, but it now lagged behind the industrial growth of other southern states and risked potential stagnation if something was not done, according to the Tax Study Commission appointed by the legislature in 1955. "Unless our human resources are used to a far greater extent we cannot hope to lift ourselves by a tug on our economic boot straps," the commission concluded.[9]

Hodges helped develop a new business model for the state, seeking to improve North Carolina's economy by recruiting higher-paying industries, creating a better-trained workforce, and using the state's collection of universities to attract businesses that relied more on brain power. Although industrial recruiting is now commonplace, Hodges was one of the first governors to view his job as the state's chief salesman—leading industrial recruitment trips around the country and to Europe.

Time magazine called him the "South's number one salesman." For a *Life* magazine photo layout, Hodges took a shower in a wrinkle-free suit manufactured in the state. He pulled down his pants far enough so a photographer could shoot his Carolina-made underwear. He handed out cuff links made of miniature Tar Heel bricks. Hodges pushed a cut in corporate income taxes through the legislature and rejuvenated the State Department of Conservation and Development, the main industrial recruitment agency.

Hodges convinced a reluctant legislature in 1958 to create a system of seven "Industrial Education Centers," which were designed to equip people coming off the farms with the skills necessary to work in industrial jobs. The centers would eventually become the state's community college system under his successor Terry Sanford and would grow to fifty-eight campuses.

Hodges's greatest lasting legacy was his role in helping create the Research Triangle Park, taking advantage of the cluster of research universities in the Raleigh-Durham area. The idea of a regional research park was first proposed in the mid-1950s by Greensboro real estate developer Romeo Guest, who was looking for more construction business. Hodges had the business connections to put together a corporation and purchase a 4,000-acre tract of land. Although it got off to a slow start after its creation in 1957, the park became one of the nation's leading research-and-development centers and a magnet for manufacturing and research in computers, pharmaceuticals, and telecommunications that states across the country tried to emulate. By the end of the century, the Research Triangle Park had 137 companies or research organizations with 41,600 employees and had transformed the region into one of the fastest-growing metropolitan areas in the country. "The heart and hope of North Carolina's industrial future is the Research Triangle," Hodges prophesied in 1962.[10]

Hodges's new business plan, however, did not include being any friendlier to organized labor. One of North Carolina's selling points to industrial prospects was that only 9 percent of its workforce was unionized—the lowest percentage in the nation—and Hodges aimed to keep it that way. Hodges sent in the Highway Patrol and National Guard to quell violence during a strike at the Harriet-Henderson Textile Mills in 1958. The strike had turned violent, with instances of rock throwing, acid poured on machines, and dynamite blasts. Boyd Payton, the regional director of the American Textile Workers' Union, was convicted of conspiring to bomb the mill's power plant and was sentenced to seven-to-ten years in prison. Critics said there was little evidence against Payton, and there were appeals for clemency by U.S. labor secretary Arthur Goldberg and evangelist Billy Graham. Sanford commuted Payton's sentence and pardoned him.

When it came to civil rights, Hodges was as traditional as the white carnation he wore in his lapel every day. He never publicly questioned the wisdom of segregation, but he was concerned about the state's ability to attract northern industry. And he wanted to avoid the disruption and violence that was occurring in other southern states. "Moderation" became his mantra— an approach that satisfied neither the defenders nor the critics of segregation but which in the end made Hodges a champion of the status quo.

The legal edifice of segregation had been under attack in the courts for decades in North Carolina and across the South, starting with the graduate schools of the state universities. In 1937 the NAACP supported a suit by a Durham man who sought admittance to the School of Pharmacy at UNC–Chapel Hill. That suit failed, but other legal challenges across the South were more successful. In April 1951, the UNC School of Medicine admitted a black student, and later that year the UNC Law School admitted four black students. In 1955 UNC became the first state-supported undergraduate college campus in the South to admit blacks, when a federal court ordered three blacks to be enrolled as undergraduates at Chapel Hill. Federally controlled schools at the Fort Bragg army base near Fayetteville were integrated in 1951, and the state's Catholic secondary and elementary schools were integrated in 1953.

Shortly after the *Brown* decision, Umstead appointed an eighteen-member committee, which included three blacks, to study the question of racial integration of the schools and make recommendations. Umstead was the only southern governor to name blacks to a committee studying integration.

The chairman of the committee was Thomas J. Pearsall, a Rocky Mount lawyer and former N.C. House speaker. The owner of large holdings of tenant farms in the state's eastern Black Belt, Pearsall might have been expected to be a hard-line segregationist. But Pearsall represented the best of the eastern North Carolina landed gentry—a sophisticated, thoughtful man who ran model tenant farms and who had a reputation as a conciliator. His wife, Elizabeth, had raised eyebrows when she invited a leading black woman educator to speak on racial amity at their Episcopal church during the Depression.

The plan developed by the Pearsall Commission, called the Pupil Assignment Act, gave local school boards the authority to assign students, thereby making it more difficult for the state to be sued for desegregation. That meant civil rights groups would potentially have to sue 175 school districts to accomplish desegregation.

The U.S. Supreme Court followed its 1954 *Brown* decision with a second decision on May 31, 1955, ordering that segregated school systems be dismantled "with all deliberate speed." Hodges reconstituted the Pearsall Commission, this time as a seven-member, all-white committee. "The white citizens of the state will resist integration strenuously, resourcefully, and with growing bitterness," Hodges told a TV audience.[11]

The second Pearsall Commission's plan offered an escape valve for white parents who did not want to send their children to public schools. The key provision in the plan was a constitutional amendment allowing local public schools to be closed by a majority vote. The state would provide tuition grants to parents to send their children to private schools if the public schools were closed. Voters approved the Pearsall Plan, as it became known, by a 4 to 1 margin in September 1956.

The Pearsall Plan was an obvious ruse to avoid the Supreme Court decision, and it was later declared unconstitutional. But it did act as an escape valve, and no North Carolina school district ever closed its schools.

In September 1957, twelve black children enrolled in previously all-white public schools in Charlotte, Greensboro, and Winston-Salem. They were greeted with ugly taunts and threats. But it was a peaceful affair compared to events in other southern states, and North Carolina received favorable national attention.

Hodges's approach was to try to minimize racial unrest so it would not detract from his economic recruitment—a view supported by many business leaders. In an address to the General Assembly, broadcast statewide in July 1956, Hodges called for "common ground" to save the schools. "I know there are extremes on this issue: those who would go far to the left, and those who would get equally as far to the right," Hodges said. "It is neither fear nor lack of conviction that makes me stay nearer the middle. It a sincere desire to be the governor of all the people of whatever belief, of whatever extremes, and to lead as best I can the state in a moderate fashion to help solve this problem pressing down upon us."[12]

But critics noted that despite all the talk of moderation, North Carolina's public schools were not any more integrated than schools elsewhere in the South. The middle turned out to be token integration. To qualify as a moderate in the South of the 1950s, one just had to avoid being a rabid segregationist.

"In the end, the Pearsall Plan accomplished all the objectives its sponsors had envisioned," wrote historian William Chafe. "It postponed meaningful desegregation in North Carolina for more than a decade—longer than in some states where massive resistance was practiced. . . . For Hodges, it proved a brilliant success. In the country at large as well as in North Carolina, he was viewed as a moderate and enlightened governor who had found a peaceful way to handle school desegregation."[13]

While Hodges could easily withstand criticism from white liberals and African Americans, the governor had much to fear from his political right flank. All across the South, white racial views were hardening as the threat of segregation became increasingly real. In North Carolina, a segregationist group called the White Patriots of North Carolina was formed—a group that included three former speakers of the N.C. House and other political figures. Its most visible spokesman was state senator Julian Allsbrook of Halifax County, who would serve in the legislature until his death in 1984. Allsbrook chaired the state Democratic Party's platform committee, which at their annual convention in May 1956 declared that the "fundamental issue is whether the Anglo-Saxon race is to become a mongrel race." The language seemed to be lifted straight out of the white supremacy campaigns of 1898 and 1900.[14]

In November 1955 the homes of four Charlotte civil rights lawyers were bombed. No arrests were ever made in the bombing of the houses of Kelly Alexander, the longtime head of the state NAACP; his brother, future state senator Fred Alexander; future gubernatorial candidate Reginald Hawkins; or attorney Julius Chambers, the future head of the NAACP Legal Defense Fund and future chancellor of N.C. Central University.

In Washington, D.C., the southern bloc in Congress drew up a "Declaration of Constitutional Principles" (otherwise known as the Southern Manifesto) voicing opposition to *Brown*. The manifesto declared that *Brown* was a "clear abuse of judicial power" and a threat destructive of "the amicable relations between the Negro and white races." Nineteen of the South's twenty-two senators signed it, including Ervin, one of the manifesto's authors, and Kerr Scott of North Carolina. Scott tried at the last minute to remove his name from the manifesto but the news release had already gone out, according to aide Bill Cochrane. Whether that was true or whether that was Cochrane just trying to cover for his old boss, Scott certainly had learned firsthand that one could be progressive in North Carolina politics only if one didn't question the system of segregation.

In the U.S. House, 101 of the 128 southern congressmen signed the manifesto. Two of the North Carolina congressmen who declined to sign the manifesto, Charles Deane and Thurmond Chatham, were defeated in the Democratic primary in May 1956—a clear signal of the political dangers of supporting integration. The state's third nonsigner, Representative Harold Cooley of Nashville, survived by campaigning against the court decision. For Deane, a five-term congressman and Richmond County attorney, standing up against the tide was a matter of principle. In a letter to his pastor, Deane, a devout Baptist lay leader, wrote: "I do not have to remain in Washington but I do have to live with myself. I shall not sign my name to any document which will make any man anywhere a second class citizen."[15]

The defeat of Deane and Chatham drew headlines across the country. Segregationists warned that their losses should serve as a warning to the national Democratic Party to leave the South alone. Said Mississippi governor J. P. Coleman: "The action of the voters in a moderate state like North Carolina in defeating two members of Congress because of their refusal to sign the Southern Manifesto should be notice to the nation and to certain figures in the Democratic Party that the South has no intention of submitting to an unconstitutional Supreme Court decision."[16]

The lessons were clear enough. Question segregation, like Deane and Chatham, and you would be severely punished by the voters.

Beverly Lake

Hodges's chief nemesis on school integration was Lake, a balding man who had spent much of his life as a beloved law professor at Wake Forest University. Lake, the son of a Wake Forest University physics professor, lived nearly all his life in the small college town located just north of Raleigh. Lake was proud of his southern heritage. His stepmother's father had been a colonel in a Kentucky regiment during the Civil War.

Lake was not always such a racial hard-liner. During the infamous 1950 Senate Democratic primary, Lake had supported liberal and fellow professor Frank Porter Graham over conservative Willis Smith. In a radio speech on behalf of Graham, Lake criticized Smith's race-baiting. "For the first time in the memory of most North Carolinians an effort is being made to gain votes for a candidate for high political office in this state by stirring from its 50-year sleep the dreadful monster of race hatred," Lake said. Years later, Lake said he regretted backing Graham.

Lake left his beloved Wake Forest University only when it left him—when tobacco millionaires moved the campus 100 miles west to Winston-Salem. In 1952 he joined the state attorney general's staff, becoming an expert on utility law and a consumer advocate, representing the public in rate hearings before the State Utilities Commission.

Lake joined the school integration fight when state attorney general Harry McMullen asked him to write North Carolina's friend-of-the-court brief in the second round of the *Brown* case. Lake defended segregation in front of his old Harvard law professor, the great liberal justice Felix Frankfurter.

Lake argued that integration of the schools could lead "to a second civil war." He was not alone in that belief. Of the 198 North Carolina sheriffs and police officers that responded to a survey, 191 believed that an effort to integrate their schools would lead to violence. Of 165 school superintendents polled, only seven believed desegregation would occur peacefully.[17]

By the mid-1950s, Lake's role had expanded from the state's lawyer to the leading Tar Heel critic of school integration. In speeches around the state, Lake defended segregation, attacked the NAACP as an enemy of amicable race relations, and called for communities to charter nonprofit corporations to operate segregated schools. Lake was soon being mentioned as a possible gubernatorial challenger to Hodges in the 1956 Democratic primary. Lake claimed Hodges was "blinded by the glitter of moderation," and his plan offered appeasement and "retreat, retreat, retreat."

Hodges tried to walk a very narrow line, co-opting segregationist sentiment at home while presenting a moderate image to the nation. Hodges had been the subject of several glowing stories in national news magazines. "To Luther Hodges," said an article in *Reader's Digest* magazine, "the South's great tragedy is that it spends so much precious energy on racial issues."[18] Increasingly, Hodges was being mentioned as a possible vice presidential choice in 1960 as a way of preventing southern Democrats from bolting.[19]

Black politics, however, seemed to stump Hodges. He was shocked when, while making a speech at North Carolina A&T College, a state-supported college (now university) for black students in Greensboro, the students interrupted his remarks by snickering and shuffling their feet. The governor asked A&T president F. D. Bluford whether he should continue or stop. Bluford deeply angered Hodges by replying: "Suit yourself." Students said they objected to Hodges's pronunciation of the word "Negro" as "Nigra." Hodges later said that if he had used the pronunciation, he had not done so intentionally.[20] An angry Hodges later wrote a friend, "I am through making speeches to colored people, certainly for the time being."[21]

Hodges criticized the NAACP as a threat to North Carolina's racial order. But he was also worried about the Ku Klux Klan's potential for undermining North Carolina's image. Following the *Brown* decision, the Klan experienced a revival in the state under the direction of James "Catfish" Cole, a former carnival barker and tent evangelist from South Carolina. Cole had some success as long as he was denouncing blacks, integration, and movie star Ava Gardner, an eastern North Carolina native who was rumored to be having an affair with black actor-singer Sammy Davis Jr. But Cole ran into trouble when he declared war on the Lumbee, an Indian tribe centered in southeastern North Carolina's Robeson County.

"There are about 30,000 half breeds in Robeson County and we are going to have a cross burning and scare them up," said Cole. He announced that on January 18, 1958, 5,000 heavily armed Klansman would hold a rally to remind the Indians of "their place" in the racial order.[22]

"He said that, did he?" drawled Simeon Oxendine, a Lumbee who had flown more than thirty missions against the Germans in World War II. "Well, we'll just wait and see."

On the appointed night, a few dozen Klansmen were greeted in a roadside field by 500 armed Lumbee Indians. The Indians let out a war whoop and began firing their rifles into the air. The Klansmen dropped their guns, abandoned their unlit cross, and fled into the woods. The victorious Lumbees celebrated by lighting the cross, hanging Catfish Cole in effigy, and trying on the captured KKK robes. The Indian victory drew national publicity and much laughter. A photograph of a grinning Oxendine wrapped in a KKK banner made the cover of *Life* magazine. Alabama governor "Big Jim" Folsom wired his congratulations to the tribe, saying he "hope[d] the

Indians continue to beat the paleface." Hodges issued a four-page denunciation of the Klan, and the state indicted Cole on charges of inciting to riot. He was sentenced to eighteen to twenty-four months in prison and served more than a year.[23]

But Hodges had far more trouble with the celebrated "kissing case." In 1958 two black boys, eight and ten years old, were sent to reform school for allegedly forcing a seven-year-old white girl to kiss them. Although evidence suggested it was just a harmless childhood game, the incident produced near hysteria among some whites in the town of Monroe, near Charlotte. The boys were beaten while in custody, and their mothers lost their jobs and were evicted from their homes.

The kissing case, fanned by northern left-wing groups, caused a national and international sensation, making front pages across the world. It also was seized upon by communist countries for propaganda purposes. A worldwide campaign was begun to free the boys, with committees formed, petitions signed, and embassies picketed in a number of European countries. Hodges's office was so inundated with letters that he had to hire translators to help him respond.

Hodges's first inclination was to discredit the boys by suggesting that they were incorrigibles, that their parents were of bad character, that northern papers had sensationalized the case, and that the boys' supporters were communists. But Hodges had to dispose of a problem that was harming the state's reputation and possibly ruining his own national aspirations. His solution was to release the boys to their mothers—now forced to live in another community—with a state official announcing that their home life had now sufficiently improved for them to return. This maintained the state's fiction that the boys were locked up for nearly four months for their own welfare, rather than as punishment for kissing a white girl. "This posture was vintage Luther Hodges—a central claim to honest, capable, business-like government accompanied by a heartfelt gesture to his right flank," writes historian Timothy Tyson.[24]

Hodges won election for a full term in 1956 by the widest margin since Gardner was elected in 1928. Hodges's tenure was the longest of any elected North Carolina governor until the state constitution was changed in 1977 to allow governors to serve two consecutive terms. Hodges may have spent his career in business, but he had quickly learned politics during some treacherous times. While blacks and white liberals never saw Hodges as a progressive figure, his Brooks Brothers brand of segregationist policies might have been the best North Carolina could have done under the circumstances.

"The moderate course—the middle way, as it was known in North Carolina—tried to thread between the extremes of massive resistance and rapid desegregation," writes historian Numan Bartley. "As such, moderation inherently lacked stability, but at the same time it was the only effective political alternative to massive resistance."[25]

President Kennedy in 1961 appointed Hodges as commerce secretary, a post he held for four years under both Kennedy and Lyndon Johnson. While in Washington, Hodges was frequently criticized by conservative TV commentator Jesse Helms, who attacked him for helping Kennedy push civil rights legislation and other initiatives.

Although Hodges did more than any governor to help shape the burgeoning Research Triangle, his name was largely forgotten by the twenty-first century. Hodges had requested that no highways, bridges, airports, or other public works be named after him. But in 2003 his son succeeded in getting a portion of Interstate 540, the new Outer Loop around Raleigh, named after him.

The Rise of Sam Ervin

Five days before the *Brown* decision, Senator Clyde Hoey, the old Shelby Dynasty stem-winder, died while sitting at his desk in the Senate office building. Among those rumored to be in line for Hoey's seat was Irving Carlyle, a prominent Winston-Salem attorney and former state legislator. The gossip was fanned when Umstead asked Carlyle to take Hoey's place as the keynote speaker at the state Democratic convention held in Raleigh three days after the *Brown* decision.

Carlyle had prepared a standard partisan speech, but when the *Brown* decision came down, he decided he could not ignore it despite the political risks. Although mild by today's standards, his remarks were considered highly provocative in the South of 1954. "I would like to say this," Carlyle told the convention. "The Supreme Court has spoken. As good citizens we have no other course except to obey the law as laid down by the Court. To do otherwise would cost us our respect for law and order, and if we lost that in these critical times, we have lost that quality which is the source of our strength as a state and as a nation."[26] Carlyle won broad applause from the convention delegates. But as a friend remarked: "That's not approval of what you said. They're just admiring your stinkin' courage."[27]

Umstead appointed state supreme court justice Sam Ervin to the Senate seat, but it is not clear that Carlyle's courage cost him the seat. Ed Rankin,

Umstead's chief of staff, thinks it was always more likely that Umstead would appoint Ervin, a fellow conservative and close personal friend, than a liberal like Carlyle.[28]

During his storied twenty-year Senate career, Ervin never disappointed southern segregationists. Nor did Ervin ever have a close election. It was a Faustian bargain. Ervin's opposition to civil rights protected his political base, enabling him to lead the fight against McCarthyism, to become the Senate's leading civil libertarian, and to investigate the abuses of Watergate.

Ervin was born in 1896, the fifth of ten children of Samuel and Laura Ervin. His father was a prominent circuit-riding lawyer in Morganton, then a town of about 4,000 in the shadow of the Blue Ridge Mountains. It was in the trenches of France during World War I that Sam Jr. first made a name for himself. After graduating from UNC in 1917, Ervin volunteered for the army and was one of the doughboys shipped overseas. Frustrated by a lack of action, Ervin resigned his commission as lieutenant and reenlisted as a private so he could go to the front.

Ervin was wounded at Cantigny, where he was shot in the left foot while helping a German soldier. But it could have been worse: the shell hole that he had left only moments before exploded after receiving a direct hit, killing all five of Ervin's comrades. He returned to action in the Second Battle of the Marne, where he participated in an offensive against German lines. Ervin, in charge of a platoon although he was only a private, led his comrades out of the trenches and advanced behind a line of French tanks into murderous German machine-gun fire.

Facing a German machine-gun emplacement that was wreaking havoc, Ervin asked for four volunteers to accompany him in charging the machine gun. During the 100-yard dash, two of the men were killed and a shell fragment ripped into Ervin's left thigh, knocking him to the ground. But two of the men got through and killed the German machine gunners. Ervin crawled back to the American lines and reached a trench, only to have a French tank that was rolling over him hit by a German shell and flip over on its side. Reaching a rock quarry at the end of the trench, Ervin encountered an old classmate from Chapel Hill, Samuel I. Parker of Concord, who had just led a different group in capturing several machine guns.

"The first thing I knew I saw Sam Ervin standing down there and he was leaning on his rifle and he was bent over," Parker recalled. "Blood was all over him. I just saw it was Sam and I told him he ought to go to the rear. He said, 'No, I want to stay with you. I'll help you organize for a counterattack.' I said, 'Okay, you lay here and organize this point.' So he did and he just stayed with me until we had the strong point reorganized."[29]

Ervin spent the rest of the war in a series of hospitals. He underwent an operation to remove the shell fragments, but his wound kept getting reinfected. Ervin was awarded the Distinguished Service Cross for extraordinary heroism. It took him years, however, to get over his war experience. He was often nervous and couldn't sleep at night, leaving his bed to smoke in the backyard.

Planning to follow his father into the law, Ervin took a refresher course and passed the state bar exam. But wanting more legal training, he enrolled in Harvard Law School. He took his courses in reverse order, starting with the third year first, because he did not know if his girlfriend and future wife, Margaret Bell of Concord, would wait for him the entire three years.

While studying for his final exams at Harvard, Ervin received a telegram from the Burke County Democratic chairman informing him that he had been nominated as a candidate for the N.C. House. Ervin returned to Morganton to go into law practice with his father, and the voters elected the twenty-five-year-old war hero to the legislature. Ervin served in the 1923, 1925, and 1931 legislatures, where he most famously opposed a resolution against the teaching of evolution in the public schools.

Building a small addition to his father's law office, Ervin practiced law off and on from the 1920s through the 1940s. He also remained active in Democratic Party politics, serving as a lieutenant in the Shelby Dynasty.

In 1935 Ervin became a part-time county judge, and in January 1937 Hoey appointed him a special superior court judge. Ervin traveled across the state, filling in for other judges and relieving crowded court dockets. He often spent forty-two weeks a year on the road in forty-five counties and claimed he knew nearly every lawyer in the state. In the evenings before television, Ervin often joined the courtroom crowd on the porches of hotels and rooming houses to exchange stories. It was there—and through his voluminous readings—that Ervin collected his treasure trove of stories of the countryside, the Bible, and life in general for which he would become famous as a senator.

But holding court across the state eventually took a toll on Ervin. He developed his nervous twitching eyebrows that became one of his trademarks during the Watergate hearings. After developing a bleeding ulcer, he resigned from the bench at the end of 1943.

For seven months in 1946, Ervin served in Congress, filling out the remaining term of his brother, Joe, who had committed suicide. In 1948 Governor Gregg Cherry offered Ervin a seat on the N.C. Supreme Court. During his six years on the court, he became one of its most forceful members, known for his literate and colorful opinions.

Senator Sam

Ervin was a conservative whose career is difficult for many people to ideologically categorize. Liberals cheered Ervin, the civil libertarian, who helped remove from power President Nixon and Senator Joe McCarthy. But it was conservatives who applauded when Ervin opposed extending the power of the federal government. He fought laws aimed at ending racial segregation and discrimination, the passage of the Equal Rights Amendment for women, and new consumer protection laws. As the country became divided over the Vietnam War, Ervin steadfastly supported American military involvement.

Ervin arrived in Washington in June 1954, when the tide was turning against the red-scare tactics of McCarthy. The Wisconsin senator had exploited Americans' uneasiness about the onset of the Cold War, the spread of Communism to China, and a few sensational spy cases. McCarthy made a series of wild charges that the State Department and other government agencies were honeycombed with Soviet agents. But he eventually went too far with his ruthless tactics, and his inability to back up his allegations proved his undoing.

Because of his background as a judge, Ervin was asked by Senate Democratic leader Lyndon Johnson of Texas to serve on the Senate select committee investigating McCarthy. It was an unattractive assignment because McCarthy could be counted upon to smear any senator who opposed him.

Appearing on the nationally televised program *Meet the Press*, McCarthy went after Ervin and two other committee members, calling them "unwitting handmaidens" of the Communist Party. Even as a freshman, Ervin was not easily intimidated. On a subsequent appearance of *Meet the Press*, Ervin said McCarthy was out to ruin the reputation of any senator who opposed him. "If Senator McCarthy did not believe those things when he said them about the Senate Committee, then there is a pretty solid ground to say that he ought to be expelled from the Senate for moral incapacity," Ervin said. "On the contrary, if he put those things in there honestly believing them to be true, then he has evidently suffered gigantic mental delusions, and it may be argued with much force that he should be expelled from the Senate for mental difficulty."[30]

It fell to Ervin, a senator for a mere five months, to argue the committee's case for censure before the full U.S. Senate. It was a moment that made Ervin's reputation in Washington. The one-hour speech before a Senate gallery packed with McCarthy supporters was 100-proof Ervin, peppered with Bible stories and mountain characters such as Uncle Ephraim. Ervin didn't mince words when summing up the case. "The Senate is trying this issue: Was Senator McCarthy guilty of disorderly behavior in his senatorial office? The American people are trying another issue. The issue before the American people transcends in importance the issue before the Senate. The issue before the American people is simply this: Does the Senate of the United States have enough manhood to stand up to Senator McCarthy? . . . Mr. President, the honor of the Senate is in our keeping. I pray that senators will not soil it by permitting Senator McCarthy to go unwhipped of senatorial justice."

After the Senate voted 67 to 22 to censure McCarthy, Johnson told Ervin: "You showed you don't scare easily."

The censure vote broke McCarthy's political power and turned McCarthy into a pitiful, heavy-drinking shadow of himself during his final three years. Ervin felt sorry for McCarthy and befriended him at committee meetings. When he died, Ervin was one of three Democrats invited by McCarthy's widow to attend his funeral.

In 1960 Ervin became chairman of the Constitutional Rights Subcommittee of the Senate Judiciary Committee. The subcommittee had been formed four years earlier by Chairman James Eastland of Mississippi for the purpose of discrediting civil rights legislation, and he had packed the subcommittee with southerners such as Ervin. But Ervin had other ideas about the subcommittee, turning it into a forum for protecting civil liberties. Ervin brought a constitutional scholar's love of the law and the Bill of Rights and a mountaineer's sense of independence. In case after case, Ervin stood up against government efforts to impinge on people's lives in a way that defied easy liberal/conservative labels.

He helped enact laws to provide lawyers for defendants too poor to pay for their own counsel in federal court. He made it easier for poor people accused of a crime to be released on bail before their trial. He broadened the legal rights of patients in mental hospitals, of Indians living on federal reservations, and of soldiers and sailors accused of crimes. He took up for federal employees when the government intruded into their privacy. Although a deeply religious man, Ervin opposed state-sponsored prayer in the public schools.

Ervin often disagreed with the U.S. Supreme Court, which was located across the street from his drafty Washington apartment. Ervin once literally assaulted the Supreme Court building when the brakes failed on his old Plymouth and he went careening over the curb into the side of the building.

He increasingly condemned the activist tendencies of the federal courts, which he thought had moved from interpreting existing laws to making new ones. But where he and the Supreme Court most clearly went their separate ways was on the question of civil rights.

Ervin was a man of his times. He lived most of his life in the era of segregation and thought separation of the races was the natural result of the free association of people. Ervin fought every civil rights bill that came before Congress, trying to kill them, water them down, or delay them. He fought them with dignity, arguing constitutional law rather than engaging in racial demagoguery. He denounced the lunch-counter sit-ins as a lawless trespassing on private property, he helped lead a filibuster against a modest 1960 civil rights bill backed by the Eisenhower administration, and he led the fight at the 1956 and 1960 Democratic National Conventions against a civil rights plank. In 1967 Ervin opposed Lyndon Johnson's nomination of Thurgood Marshall as the first black to sit on the U.S. Supreme Court. Ervin fought court-ordered school busing for integration and was against giving the Equal Employment Opportunity Commission the power to order companies to stop discriminating. Even though most black North Carolinians were denied the right to vote through nearly two-thirds of the twentieth century, Ervin claimed to have "never known a single man to be denied the right to register to vote on account of his race."

Participating in the anti–civil rights filibuster in 1960, Ervin acknowledged that integration was not necessarily a bad thing but said it should be accomplished voluntarily. And he confessed that the political middle ground in the South had nearly vanished. "A person who is interested in public service," Ervin told the Senate, "is compelled to take a stand for or against compulsory integration of the races whether he is for it or against it. So he can no longer stand on a middle ground and try to do something for the welfare of the community. He is driven to an extreme, one way or the other."[31]

Attorney General Robert F. Kennedy, in a pointed exchange with Ervin during Senate hearings on a civil rights bill in 1963, asked Ervin to reconsider his opposition.

Kennedy: "How are we going to bring up our children, Senator, if there

Former senator Sam Ervin speaking against the Equal Rights
Amendment at a rally at Dorton Arena in Raleigh, 1977.
(Photograph by Steve Murray; courtesy of the *Raleigh News and Observer*)

is not going to be some leadership and assistance from somebody such as yourself? Senator, with the kind of prestige you have in the United States, you could make a major difference in ending these kinds of practices as well as bringing this country through a very difficult period of transition. That is all I ask of you, Senator."

Ervin: "The only thing you have a right to ask of me is that I stand and fight for the Constitution and for the basic rights of Americans. That is what I'm doing now. . . . You are not correct in saying I have never spoken out against discrimination. All of my life I have fought against it." Ervin noted that he had introduced a bill in the state legislature to provide for bonds to defray the costs of construction of black schools, to equalize pay between black and white teachers, and to increase appropriations for black schools.

"As a citizen, lawyer, and judge in North Carolina," Ervin said, "I have always stood for the right of all men to stand equal before the law. As a citizen and a public official, I have always stood for the right of every qualified voter to register and vote. So you are not very just to me in saying I have not fought discrimination."[32]

But there were many North Carolinians, particularly blacks, who felt it was Ervin who was not being very just. Ervin cloaked his segregationist stands in the high-minded language of constitutional principles. But his arguments had the musty smell of the Old South and John C. Calhoun's orations about states' rights. And Ervin seemed to have little sensitivity for the plight of hundreds of thousands of his black constituents whose liberties had been tightly constrained by racist laws.

Like Lake, Ervin used his Harvard education to defend segregation, thereby providing respectability to those whose views on segregation were rooted in generations-old racial prejudice. Like his brilliant Senate colleague William Fulbright of Arkansas, Ervin's considerable record of accomplishments will always be tarnished by being on the wrong side of history on the great question of his time.

Watergate

History has been kind to Ervin. His role as a leading legal theoretician in the battle against the civil rights movement has faded, and he ended his career as a folk hero to many. From the time he entered the Senate, Ervin distrusted Richard Nixon. He had watched with skepticism as Nixon rose in politics by conducting red-baiting campaigns to win election to the U.S. House and the U.S. Senate. After Nixon was elected president in 1968 on a platform of law and order, the administration began proposing a series of laws or executive orders that were in response to the urban riots and protests against the Vietnam War. Although a fellow conservative, Ervin found his own libertarian views increasingly in conflict with Nixon's initiatives.

Ervin waged a legislative guerilla war against the Nixon administration's effort to pass laws to allow preventive detention of criminal suspects and to allow police to enter the homes of suspects without knocking. He railed against the president's executive order expanding the activities of the Subversive Activities Control Board. He was critical of administration efforts to stop the leaking of information to the news media, saying such leaks helped preserve a free society. He was scandalized by the use of military intelligence units to spy on civilian antiwar protesters. "The supreme value of civilization is the freedom of the individual, which is simply the right of the individual to be free from government tyranny," Ervin told the Senate.[33]

But it was the Watergate scandal that led Ervin to his ultimate showdown. The scandal involved much more than the break-in of the national Democratic headquarters at the Watergate apartment complex in Washington, D.C., where former CIA operatives tapped phones and photographed documents. Watergate came to mean a whole series of illegal activities by a paranoid White House that felt under siege by antiwar protesters and was worried about the president's reelection in 1972. The president's men were involved in burglarizing private psychiatric files, accepting illegal corporate contributions, tapping phones of reporters, faking evidence against political opponents, planting agent-provocateurs to incite radicals to illegal activities, and using the Internal Revenue Service as a tool to attack the administration's enemies. When the Watergate burglars were caught, the White House began paying illegal hush money to cover up their links to the crimes.

In January 1973 Ervin was appointed to head the Senate Select Committee on Watergate. Ervin didn't particularly want the assignment—he felt he had more important issues to deal with as his career wound down. "Sam is the only man we could have picked on either side who would have the respect of the Senate as a whole," said Senate Majority Leader Mike Mansfield.[34]

The Watergate hearings began in May 1973, televised nationally to a daytime audience who watched enthralled as a parade of White House aides, political operatives, CIA and FBI agents, fund-raisers, and former cabinet members offered contradictory testimony. The picture that emerged was of the democratic process being subverted.

Ervin seemed perfectly cast for the role—an old-fashioned Uncle Sam full of homespun stories and humor and with a Founding Father's knowledge of the Constitution. "In pursuing its task," Ervin said in opening the two months of hearings in the ornate Senate Caucus Room, "it is clear that the committee will be dealing with the working of the democratic process under which we operate in a nation that still is the last, best hope of mankind in his eternal struggle to govern himself decently and effectively." He concluded: "The nation and history are watching us. We cannot fail our mission." [35]

As the new star of daytime TV, Ervin became something of a national folk hero, with T-shirts and books of his wit and wisdom published. He was so besieged that he secured an unlisted telephone number, and a bodyguard was assigned to him. Ervin became the nationally best-known North Carolina political figure of the twentieth century—perhaps surpassed in later years by Senator Jesse Helms, or by Senator John Edwards in the early twenty-first century.

"Watching him pursue a witness or scowling at one in a pantomime of outrage was like holding up a mirror to our own consciences," wrote his biographer Paul Clancy. "We had grown accustomed to seeing our public officials with their masks on, but Ervin was different. That rough sea of a face, with the nervous eyebrows flying like wings of a hawk, the hound-dog cheeks quivering, the lips racing, and the sparkling eyes darting, seemed to be responding to some inner critical mass of moral indignation." [36]

Ervin could play country boy, as he did when his sharp grilling of former commerce secretary Maurice Stans drew a complaint from Republican senator Edward Gurney of Florida. "Well," Ervin replied. "I'm sorry that my distinguished friend from Florida doesn't approve of my method of examining the witness. I'm just an old country lawyer and I don't know the finer ways to do it. I just have to do it my way."

Or he could sound very much like a judge passing down a verdict from on high. "The evidence thus far introduced before this committee," Ervin said, "tends to show that men upon whom fortune had smiled benevolently and who possessed great financial power, great political power, and great governmental power; undertook to nullify the laws of man and the laws of God for the purpose of gaining what history will call a very temporary political advantage." [37]

Ervin always downplayed his role in Watergate, saying that much of the credit for uncovering the scandal should go to U.S. district judge John J. Sirica and to *Washington Post* reporters Bob Woodward and Carl Bernstein. The Watergate scandal enabled Ervin to leave the Senate in a blaze of glory. He announced that he would retire at age seventy-eight when his term ended at the end of 1974.

"He brought the stern values of another age into the latter half of the twentieth century at a time when unprincipled men had been permitted to flourish by chicanery and the arrogant abuse of power," wrote Clancy. "He found that those older values were more valid than ever during the Watergate era and that people like himself, who were schooled in them, were in great demand. Many in the nation reached out for his guidance and in doing so reached out for the guidance of the Founding Fathers." [38]

chapter 5 **Dixie Dynamo**

n February 1, 1960, four freshmen at N.C. A&T State University purchased school supplies at a Woolworth's five-and-dime store in Greensboro and then sat at the lunch counter and asked to be served, challenging the southern system of segregation. The lunch-counter manager, following local custom, refused the students service. "I beg your pardon but you just served us at [that] counter," said Ezell Blair Jr., one of the students. "Why can't we be served at the [food] counter here?"[1]

As word spread of the students' resistance, the lunch-counter sit-ins became a mass movement of civil disobedience borrowed from Indian leader Mahatma Gandhi's campaign against British rule. The lunch-counter movement spread to fifty-four cities in nine states, with students being splattered with eggs in Raleigh, hit with bricks in High Point, and suffering verbal abuse in most places.

Three days after the sit-ins began, Terry Sanford announced that he was running for governor. Sanford helped set a tone of moderation in North Carolina in the sixties, as shell-shocked whites saw their world and the world of their parents crumbling down around them.

While much of the South exploded with anger at the civil rights movement, Sanford pushed the state toward racial reconciliation. While Alabama governor George Wallace stood in the schoolhouse door, Sanford sent his son to one of the state's first racially integrated elementary schools. While Birmingham police commissioner Eugene "Bull" Connor turned fire hoses on demonstrators, Sanford quietly integrated the state park system. And while churches were being bombed in Mississippi, Sanford became the first southern governor to call for equal job opportunities for blacks.

But there were limits to progressivism. Sanford could only get elected by providing lip service to segregation. Despite moving cautiously, Sanford had to deal with a white backlash against the civil rights movement—an outraged legislature, a drumbeat of criticism from TV commentator Jesse Helms, and an invigorated Ku Klux Klan that spread flaming crosses and terror across the state.

The Rise of Sanford

One could hardly have predicted Sanford's politics from his background. He was born in 1917, growing up in the small farming town of Laurinburg surrounded by flat cotton fields in the racially conservative southeastern part of the state, where the Red Shirts and the Klan once had a strong following. His father, Cecil Sanford, owned a hardware store before losing it during the Depression. He later held a series of modest jobs, including salesman. Sanford's mother, Betsy, was a schoolteacher.

Life in the segregated South was often far more nuanced than it is often portrayed. Sanford's parents, active Methodists, taught him that black people should be treated with decency. In 1928 his father registered the first black voter in Laurinburg since African Americans had been disfranchised after the white supremacy campaigns. The elder Sanford was sometimes called by Laurinburg black residents who had landed in jail and needed a white friend to vouch for them.

Sanford's intellectual awakening began in Chapel Hill in 1935. Like so many of the best and brightest of his generation in North Carolina, he came under the spell of liberal UNC president Frank Porter Graham, who opened his mind to the problems of race, labor, and women's rights. But politics would have to wait until after World War II. In 1942 he took a leave of absence from his job as a special agent with the FBI and became an army paratrooper. The freshly minted lieutenant saw heavy action in Italy, Belgium, and France, winning the Bronze Star and suffering a wound during the Battle of the Bulge.

After the war, Sanford began a law practice in Fayetteville and started his rapid climb in politics, winning a North Carolina Senate seat in 1952 and managing Kerr Scott's U.S. Senate campaign in 1954. By the mid-1950s, Sanford was building his own organization to run for governor—a precursor of modern campaigns where candidates begin running several years before the election.

Sanford inherited the old Branchhead Boys organization. One Christmas he sent each of the former senator's county contacts a plastic-encased plug of Scott's favorite chewing tobacco, Peach and Honey. But Sanford's organization also included people he had met through the Jaycees, the American

Legion, the Methodists, and the Young Democrat Club. He was the first Tar Heel candidate to hire a pollster, Lou Harris, an old college classmate. Sanford, who was never more than an average public speaker, took lessons from a professional speech coach in New York City. He was the first North Carolina candidate to extensively use television advertising. "It's not true that Mr. Sanford has been running since he was 12 years old as some cynics insist," observed the *Charlotte News*. "But we are fairly certain that he broke into a kind of dog-trot in 1954 and has been picking up speed ever since."[2]

Governor's Race

The 1960 governor's race was wide open. Governor Luther Hodges was the last remnant of the old Shelby Dynasty. Several leading lights of the liberal wing of the Democratic Party were no longer on the scene. Kerr Scott had died and Frank Graham was working for the United Nations in New York. The Republican Party had not yet emerged as a strong factor in North Carolina politics, so the race would be decided in the Democratic primary.

When Sanford announced for governor before a hometown crowd in Fayetteville and called for a "New Day," it was more than just the standard political sloganeering. Sanford was the first World War II veteran to be elected as North Carolina governor. The war helped shape the view of many veterans. "We came back with a lot of confidence," said Clint Newton, a Shelby businessman who was a fighter pilot during the war.

> We had gotten the job done. Here you have all these people coming back, having been so provincial and suddenly exposed to France, Italy, Sicily, North Africa, England—you name it. We found our respective towns were not the center of the universe. We wanted to make North Carolina better. So many of us went to UNC and with its liberalism and seeing the racial factors and this sort of thing. Our state lacked a good educational system. There was a small group of idealists. Sanford was at the core of the idealism. When Sanford said he wanted to run for governor, we got together and expanded the group and divided the state up.[3]

When Sanford filed for governor, he donned his paratrooper ring and pin and attached an old Frank Graham campaign button to the underside of his lapel. Throughout his political career, Sanford hearkened back to his days in the Airborne—both as a sense of who he was and because it was a way to connect with the state's conservative cultural values. When he ran for the U.S. Senate in 1986, he handed out paratrooper pins to supporters. And when he was in trouble in his 1992 reelection campaign, he donned his old paratrooper jacket.

Although Sanford was part of a crowded Democratic field, the man who would emerge as his chief competitor was segregationist I. Beverly Lake. The lunch-counter sit-ins—combined with continuing pressure to integrate the schools—had raised the anxiety level of many whites. A poll taken by Lou Harris in April 1960 showed that 54 percent of North Carolinians believed that blacks should not be served at lunch counters, while 22 percent thought they should be served.[4]

Lake said Hodges's approach to integration set the wrong tone. North Carolina was the focus of the lunch-counter sit-ins, Lake said, because the NAACP was "led by the present administration's professed love for moderation to believe that North Carolina is the softest spot in the South."[5]

Sanford focused his campaign on how to improve the public schools, not on how they should remain segregated. Despite advice from his pollster, Sanford took the risky step of saying he would support a tax hike for education if elected. Throughout his political career, Sanford was a gambler, willing to take stands that would unnerve most politicians. But he was also building support for his legislative program even as he was campaigning—a melding of politics and governing. "While you don't stir up as many enemies, you don't develop as many enthusiastic friends by taking that cautious, middle-of-the-road thing, and it just never suited my nature," Sanford later remarked. "I've always been a 51 percent man, and thought that if we could move as far as we could and still carry 51 percent, that was the responsibility of leadership."[6]

As the front runner in the Democratic primary, Sanford was called by his rivals "Terrible Tax Terry" or "High Tax Terry" or "Tall Talking Terry." But the other candidates could not match his drive. Sanford spent years campaigning for governor, shaking so many hands—he estimated 40,000 hands—that he developed blisters that turned purple, black, and then brown. At one campaign event, Sanford received a call from his wife, Margaret Rose, saying he needed to spend more time with his two young children. Bert Bennett scribbled on a napkin a question for Sanford: "Terry, what makes you stay in this business?" Sanford jotted a reply and pushed the napkin back to Bennett that was short and to the point: "To keep the SOBS out."[7]

Sanford led the primary field with 41.3 percent in the May 28 primary, short of the majority needed to clinch the nomination. Lake finished second with 27.8 percent, followed by Attorney General Malcolm Seawell and former state Democratic chairman John Larkins.

In the first primary, Sanford and Lake were civil, with both men offering modest praise for each other's character and background. But in the runoff, the facade of gentility was torn away and the race issue came to the fore. This was cultural warfare long before the term became popular in later years. This was not just about who would be the next governor; this was about who might be seated next to your child at school. There were echoes of past brutal campaigns — the white supremacy campaigns of 1898 and 1900 and the 1950 Smith-Graham Senate brawl.

For a month, the two candidates went after each other, largely without the benefit of speechwriters and spin doctors. Lake ridiculed Sanford's slogan of wanting a "New Day" in North Carolina. "The NAACP also wants to see a new day in North Carolina," Lake said. "The NAACP believes the new day it wants to bring about in your schools, your eating establishments, your barber shops, your beauty parlors, your parks, your beaches, your ballrooms and your children's homes can dawn in North Carolina if Mr. Sanford is your governor."[8]

Sanford called Lake a "bigot" who was making a "naked and immoral appeal to raw race prejudice. . . . We do not need the climate of hate that Dr. Lake is talking about. We don't need the climate of fear — of hysteria that Dr. Lake proposes. Dr. Lake is leading us down the path of closed schools or integrated schools — bloodshed and disorder."[9]

Sanford portrayed himself as a defender of segregation, but as a moderate who would avoid the kind of violence, disruption, and introduction of federal troops that occurred during the court-ordered integration of public schools in Little Rock, Arkansas. "The people of North Carolina do not want integration and we cannot afford to close our schools, but this is where the professor would lead us," Sanford said. "He is injecting a false issue on integration and it is false because he knows I am opposed to integration. The difference is that I know how to handle it, and he doesn't."[10] In one of his favorite lines of the campaign, Sanford said what the state needed was not massive resistance, but massive intelligence.

While Lake was driving hard on the issue of segregation, Sanford tried his best to finesse the explosive issue — placating white-segregationist sentiment while not alienating black voters, who now composed 10 percent of the electorate. "I saw political sudden death," Sanford recalled near the end of his life. "Dr. Frank Graham let the issue get the upper hand. It wasn't that I wanted to avoid that issue. I just didn't want that issue to be dominant."[11]

Later in his life, Sanford defended his misrepresentations and evasions, saying that if he had openly supported integration he could never have been elected governor. "You couldn't get too far ahead of the people and you couldn't say anything that you'd later feel bad about. . . . Under the circumstances, I was cautiously going as far as I could go."[12]

In the end, the state's political and business establishment, including Hodges operating behind the scenes, rallied to Sanford, fearing that a Lake victory would lead to massive resistance to segregation, an end to the state's reputation for racial moderation, and damage to the state's cherished business climate. Sanford, who won 56 percent of the vote, would later say his victory was "the first time that a racist campaign had ever been defeated." Sanford called New York to tell Frank Porter Graham that his defeat a decade ago had paved the way for Sanford's own victory. At Lake's headquarters on election night, supporters gathered to sadly sing "Dixie."[13]

With his hard-won victory over Lake, Sanford's election in the fall should have been assured in what was still a one-party state. But Sanford once again rolled the dice, agreeing to become one of the first major southern political figures to support Massachusetts senator John F. Kennedy for the Democratic nomination for president.

Sanford, like most other southern and North Carolina Democratic leaders, had first been inclined to take the politically safe route and support Texas senator Lyndon Johnson for president. The practical pols in Sanford's camp told the candidate that backing a northeastern Catholic like Kennedy would be political poison. But others argued that Sanford's politics and style matched those of Kennedy—not LBJ. The two men were the same age, and both were World War II veterans. "History knocks seldom and when it does, you'd better open up," Bert Bennett told Sanford. "History is knocking in this opportunity to associate with Kennedy."[14]

Sanford endorsed Kennedy at the Democratic convention in Los Angeles and seconded his nomination at the national convention. Sanford was a national Democrat who thought that the South had too long isolated itself from the mainstream. Kennedy looked like a winner.

Sanford's endorsement of Kennedy at the Democratic Convention set off a firestorm back home. North Carolina was one of the most heavily Protestant states in the country. Sanford received 450 cards, letters, and telegrams from North Carolina when he was in Los Angeles. About half were favorable, but many telegrams were in the vein of one sent by a Chapel Hill man: "In supporting Kennedy you are betraying North Carolina. You are undeserving of the recent confidence expressed in you by this people. Apparently you are ignorant of the facts of life regarding international Catholicism. The Vatican philosophy is as dangerous as Moscow's despotism. Hope rest of the North Carolina delegation uses better judgment and support Johnson."[15]

The Kennedy-Catholic issue breathed new life into the campaign of Robert Gavin, a former federal prosecutor who was the Republican nominee for governor. Gavin claimed Sanford had joined the "radical-socialist wing of the Kennedys" and would not speak unless he had been "briefed by the Sen. John Kennedy machine." He said if the Democrats were elected, Congressman Adam Clayton Powell—the only black in Congress—would try to integrate every public school in North Carolina.[16] Anti-Catholic literature was widely distributed, although apparently neither the state Republican Party nor the Gavin campaign was involved.

Barbara Rohrman, a Catholic who was a little girl in Charlotte during the election, remembers her parents attending a social function at a facility owned by the Knights of Columbus in what was then rural Mecklenburg County. As they were turning into the club's driveway, a bullet came crashing through their windshield. "When the police were called, they sloughed it off," Rohrman said. "They said, 'Well it's because you have a Kennedy bumper sticker and you're going into a Catholic country club.'"[17]

Mike Easley was a ten-year-old Catholic altar boy in Rocky Mount in 1960 when his father, H. A. Easley, the owner of a tobacco warehouse, campaigned for Sanford and Kennedy. "I remember one time we were talking to one particular farmer," said Easley, a future governor. "The guy said, 'I don't know about this integration stuff with Sanford, but I'll take a chance on him. But I can't go with no Catholic.'"

"I looked up, and Daddy—with his body language—said 'Be quiet.' He said 'we are going to hear a lot of that and just keep moving.'"[18]

Even Sanford's minister at Hay Street Methodist Church in Fayetteville fretted over whether Sanford should keep his commitment to give the Layman's Day Speech in October. Sanford withdrew and was still angry over his treatment years later. "The Methodist Church virtually excommunicated me," Sanford later recalled.[19]

But as the campaign wore on, the anti-Catholic hysteria dissipated. Sanford campaigned at Kennedy's side as he drew large and enthusiastic audiences in Greenville, Charlotte, and Greensboro. On the other hand, his Republican opponent, Richard Nixon, seemed snakebitten. Nixon injured his knee getting in an automobile in Greensboro, preventing him from campaigning during several crucial days near the end of the campaign. Kennedy, who started the race well behind Nixon in the state, carried North Carolina with 52 percent—a crucial victory in one of the closest presidential contests in American history. The new president owed a large debt to Sanford. Sanford paid a price for backing Kennedy as well as for his racial moderation. Sanford's initial post-primary lead was sliced in half. Sanford won with 54.5 percent—the closest race for governor in the South since Republican Alf Taylor had been elected governor of Tennessee in 1920.[20] A grateful Kennedy administration helped Sanford land a major Environmental Protection Agency facility near Durham and Raleigh in 1965, giving a boost to the fledgling Research Triangle Park.

Governor Sanford

When Sanford moved into his office in the Capitol, he prominently displayed the portraits of three of his heroes—Kerr Scott, Frank Porter Graham, and Charles Brantley Aycock, the "Holy Trinity" of Tar Heel progressives—as well as that of former governor O. Max Gardner. "If it takes more taxes to give our children this quality education, we must face that fact and provide the money," Sanford said in his inaugural address. "We must never lose sight of the fact that our children are our best investment. This is no age for the faint of heart."[21]

Like his predecessor, Luther Hodges, Sanford was looking for ways to move North Carolina off the bottom rungs in income. Like Hodges, Sanford continued to emphasize industrial recruitment and the creation of the community college system. But unlike Hodges, he raised taxes rather than cutting them—using the revenue to improve the secondary and elementary schools.

North Carolina's public school system had been starved for funds by decades of conservative state government. There had been surges of support under such governors as Aycock, Morrison, and Scott, but no sustained effort had taken place. In 1960, while New York was spending $562 per year on each student, North Carolina was spending $237. Teacher salaries were among the lowest in the nation. Mississippi and Alabama had smaller high school classes than North Carolina. And North Carolina was last—by a wide margin—in the average number of years of education completed by its citizens.[22]

Terry Sanford campaigning with John F. Kennedy in Charlotte, 1960; governor
Luther Hodges is in the front seat. (Photograph by Bruce Roberts; courtesy of
Roberts and the Center for American History, University of Texas, Austin)

At the heart of Sanford's ambitious agenda was his $100 million (or $631 million in 2006 dollars) Quality Education Program, adding teachers, raising average teacher pay by 22 percent, increasing money for instructional supplies by 33 percent, and doubling school library money. To pay for his new programs, Sanford asked the legislature to remove the exemptions on the state's 3 percent sales tax, including those on food and prescription drugs. The food tax was regressive, hit the poor the hardest, and would be criticized by liberals for the next three decades. (The tax was repealed in 1995 after Republicans gained control of the N.C. House for the first time in the century.)

To sell his program to the General Assembly, Sanford conducted a series of education rallies across the state, including one broadcast on statewide radio. He rattled off one statistic after another, detailing how North Carolina trailed most of the country in education. The state ranked forty-fifth in spending for education and forty-first in teacher-pupil ratio, and it had raised teacher salaries less than any state during the 1950s. He argued that removing the food tax exemption had the best chance of passing and was less objectionable than raising the sales tax for every item from three cents to four cents. "I hope also that they will remember that if we tax bread we also will be taxing cake; if we tax fatback, we also will tax caviar; if we tax cornmeal, we also will tax filet mignon," Sanford said.[23]

Faced with a conservative-leaning legislature, Sanford was an aggressive lobbyist. He often invited legislators to the mansion for a breakfast of eggs, grits, sausage, ham, bacon, and biscuits. He visited the Sir Walter Hotel, where most legislators lived while the General Assembly was in session. He sat in cushioned chairs swapping stories, smoking stogies, and selling his program. Nor did he have any of the do-gooder's qualms of engaging in political horse-trading for votes. "I did have people with road problems, parole problems, problems of admission to the schools for the retarded and jobs for constituents," Sanford said later. "I did what I could to help them. They are entitled to have influence in behalf of their constituents who elected them, and I held up their hands whenever I could."[24] Sanford also had strong ties to the Democratic County courthouse machines that still held sway in North Carolina.

The power of some of the sheriffs—such as Raymond Goodman of Richmond County, a tough farming and textile area along the South Carolina border—was legendary. From 1950 until 1994, Goodman ruled the county from the furniture store he owned, sitting across the street from the courthouse in Rockingham. Day in and day out, Goodman sat on a sofa, an unlit cigar in his mouth, as deputies arrived with law-enforcement business, customers inspected furniture, and constituents sought favors, advice, or just the latest political gossip. Although of humble roots, Goodman eventually became a prominent businessman, owning a local textile mill and clothing store.

A slim, balding, bespectacled man in a coat and tie who looked more like a retiring English professor than a sheriff, Goodman never forgot a name, could recite family histories, and did numerous small favors, such as distributing 1,000 turkeys each Christmas and extending credit at his stores. Goodman stopped the head-cracking tactics of his predecessors, and in the sixties he began making room for blacks in county politics. If you lived in Richmond County and wanted something from state government, you went to the sheriff, who called the governor or his lieutenants in Raleigh. In return, Sanford could call up the local political bosses and ask for their help.

The legislature passed Sanford's program and the tax hike to pay for it. But not before his foes invented a little ditty.

> Did he feed you tax expansion, when you ate up the mansion?
> Did he put the food tax square upon your plate?
> If he fed you tax expansion, when he fed you at the mansion,
> Then we hope you choke on what you really ate.[25]

There was a public backlash against the tax hike. In November 1961 voters overwhelmingly defeated ten state bond issues that would have provided $61.5 million for university buildings, community colleges, state ports, and other projects. It was the first time since 1924 that Tar Heel voters had rejected a statewide bond issue, and it was the first major test of Sanford's popularity since the tax increase. A statewide poll showed that three out of five North Carolina voters were dissatisfied with Sanford's job performance.

Despite those yellow cautionary flags, Sanford didn't take his foot off the accelerator. His role model was Kerr Scott. "[Scott] said we could do things that we didn't imagine we could do," Sanford recalled. "That was a good lesson. We can be just about anything we try to be. He only had four years to get his licks in."[26]

Sanford put together a team of unusually bright and creative young aides that came to be known as "Terry's Kindergarten." Perhaps his most unlikely aide was John Ehle, a writer and novelist whom Sanford recruited to be his idea man. At Ehle's suggestion, the state set up a film board modeled after the National Film Board of Canada to promote the movie industry here. The North Carolina Governor's School was created, allowing gifted high school students to take specialized summer enrichment courses. The N.C. School of the Arts was created in Winston-Salem—a sort of Juilliard for the South for music, dance, and dramatic arts students in high school and college.

Legislative opponents ridiculed what they called the "toe-dance bill." "Do you think I could go back home and tell my people that I voted to spend $325,000 of their tax money so some guy in a bikini can get on the stage and do a toe dance?" asked one lawmaker.[27] Ben Roney, a hard-bitten political pro from Rocky Mount whom Sanford had made his secondary-roads chief, pushed the bill through with some judicious financing of local roads. He was jokingly called "Maestro Roney," and it was said that he had literally paved the way for the arts school.

One of the Sanford administration's most enduring accomplishments was transforming a system of industrial training centers started under Hodges into a state community college system that would be widely regarded as one of the nation's finest. Sanford expanded the idea of providing industrial training to include affordable junior college classes for commuter students.

The community college system provided an inexpensive system of two-year higher education for the post–World War II Baby Boom generation, in many cases the sons and daughters of tobacco farmers and textile workers. Sanford would live to see the system meet its goal of providing fifty-eight campuses, with a school within commuting distance of every state resident.

North Carolina's voyage from poverty to the national economic mainstream was a long, hard, multigenerational struggle. North Carolina was rapidly catching up to the rest of the country; only South Carolina and Georgia had seen their per capita income grow faster than North Carolina's from 1929 to 1960. Still, North Carolinians earned only 71 percent of the national average. The state also had nearly twice the share of poor people as the national average.[28]

With the help of the Ford Foundation, Sanford started one of the nation's first antipoverty programs. The program sought to break the cycle of poverty by providing extra attention to children from poor families by improving teaching methods, reducing class sizes, and creating preschool programs. The North Carolina Fund by design lasted only six years. But its success influenced President Johnson to create the Head Start Program as part of his national "War on Poverty." A generation later, Jim Hunt used some of the same ideas to create Smart Start, another effort to help preschoolers from poor backgrounds. The North Carolina Fund also financed community-action programs, and a program that put college students — sometimes working in interracial teams — to work in impoverished neighborhoods. That became the forerunner of VISTA, another of Johnson's Great Society programs.

In many ways, North Carolina in the early 1960s was a small-scale laboratory for programs tried later nationally. With his reputation as the leading moderate in the South, Sanford became expert in getting foundation executives to open up their purses for North Carolina. *National Geographic* magazine labeled North Carolina the "Dixie Dynamo" in 1962. The magazine said there seemed to be "something exciting, dynamic and somehow youthful" about the state.[29]

Sanford's leading critic was Jesse Helms, who became a TV editorialist in Raleigh shortly before Sanford took office. The two men were products of small-town North Carolina and were of the same generation. But the two could not have viewed the world more differently.

Helms saw little in Sanford's administration that pleased him. He criticized Sanford's push for government expansion and higher taxes, as well as Sanford's support for creating a state community college system. He criticized Sanford for snubbing segregationist Mississippi governor Ross Barnett when he delivered a speech in Raleigh. He criticized him for not joining other southern politicians in Washington in testifying against a Kennedy administration civil rights bill. And he ridiculed Sanford when voters rejected the bond issues.

He warned that Sanford's efforts to move the Democratic Party to the left would alienate conservative Democrats and could lead to growth in the Republican Party. "There may be enough people in North Carolina to win an election who believe in higher and higher taxes, more government control and less individual freedom, and blind obedience to political orders handed down from above," Helms said in 1961. "But we doubt it. The liberal wing of the party, which should be wearing its crown uneasily, should recognize that conservative Democrats do not believe in such things and that conservative Democrats have held the party together in this state for most of the century. It should be obvious to all that a two-party movement is under way in North Carolina."[30]

Civil Rights

While Sanford focused his efforts on education, the overpowering issue of the day was the civil rights movement. During his inaugural address, Sanford set a moderate tone on race relations, calling for mutual respect and understanding and demanding that in the years ahead "no group of our citizens can be denied the right to participate in the opportunities of first-class citizenship."

Sanford drew worldwide attention when he enrolled Terry Jr. in Raleigh's Murphy School, one of the few integrated public schools in the state and in the South. Sanford took steps that did not require approval of the legislature, appointing increasing numbers of blacks to boards and commissions. Sanford and Hargrove Bowles, his director of Conservation and Development, quietly integrated the state's park system in the summer of 1961.

"The most difficult thing I did was the most invisible thing," Sanford said. "That was to turn the attitude on the race issue. I realized that the lines of history were intersecting right there as I took the governorship. The leadership that was needed had to come from the top. It gave me what I considered just a priceless opportunity. I think we did turn it in that direction."[31]

The task was easier in a border state like North Carolina than it was in the Deep South. North Carolina had a smaller black population, and white racial views were not as hardened. "North Carolina had never had the same level of passion on that issue that, say, South Carolina had," Sanford said. "There was somewhat of a different climate here, making it somewhat easier for Governor Hodges and me to take those positions than it was for, say, the governor of Mississippi or Alabama, or Virginia, South Carolina, Georgia."[32]

But it was the civil rights revolution, not Sanford, dictating the pace of events. In North Carolina's cities, the system of segregation was crumbling under pressure from civil rights demonstrators. Challenging segregated seating on buses, a group of civil rights activists, calling themselves Freedom Riders, rode public buses across the South in 1961, including a stop in Raleigh.

But that was just a taste of things to come. In 1962 the Congress of Racial Equality (CORE), a civil rights group led by James Farmer, targeted North Carolina's restaurants and hotels, particularly the Howard Johnson's chain. CORE staged protests in Raleigh, Durham, Greensboro, Burlington-Graham, and Statesville. In the spring of 1963, CORE organized a campaign of massive sit-ins in the major North Carolina cities. Protesters jammed hotels, restaurants, and public accommodations in the hope of being arrested—a tactic of civil disobedience designed to overload the jail system.

The largest protests occurred in Greensboro in May, where 1,200 people were arrested during eleven consecutive nights of protests that eventually pressured city leaders to integrate its downtown stores. When the jails were filled, the protesters were taken to an old polio hospital, then to a prison farm, and then to a National Guard Armory. During the Greensboro sit-ins, student leaders recruited as their spokesman a charismatic and flamboyant South Carolina native named Jesse Jackson, the president of the student council and a football star at what is now N.C. A&T State University.

While Sanford twice alerted the National Guard for possible deployment in Greensboro, he never ordered them out on the streets. Sanford sought to channel the student protesters' feelings in less confrontational directions. He hired Jackson to coordinate the production of a series of films in which black students talked about discrimination and why they were involved in the civil rights protests.

The civil rights demonstrations reawakened the ghosts of the Red Shirts. A resurgent Ku Klux Klan claimed more than 6,000 members and even more sympathizers in North Carolina. In 1965, 6,000 attended a cross burning in Sampson County, and 5,000 attended a Klan wedding outside Farmville. The Klan set up a booth at the state fair in Raleigh.[33]

A congressional investigation by the House Committee on Un-American Activities found that in 1965 "North Carolina is by far the most active state for the United Klans of America." Investigators counted 112 active "klaverns" (or local organizations) in the state, most of them located in eastern North Carolina. Raleigh and Greensboro each had three klaverns.[34]

The Klan thumbed its nose at civil authority. On October 14, 1964, a cross was burned on the grounds of the Executive Mansion. Seven months later, on the night of May 28, 1965, the Klan burned crosses on the lawns of courthouses or city halls in Burgaw, Currie, Elizabethtown, Henderson, Oxford, Roxboro, Salisbury, Southport, Statesville, Tarboro, Ward's Corner, Whiteville, and Wilmington.[35] In the summer of 1966, in the northeastern corner of the state, there were Klan rallies in Moyock, Sunbury, Elizabeth City, Murfreesboro, Ahoskie, Weeksville, Hertford, Lewiston, Windsor, Plymouth, Columbia, Williamston, Englehard, Pantego, Pinetown, Washington, Greenville, Chocowinity, Ayden, Grifton, Dover, Jasper, and Ernul.[36]

The Klan could impose a reign of terror. In Craven County in 1965, a black funeral parlor was bombed, a house where a dozen antipoverty workers lived was riddled with shotgun blasts, and the mayor—who also ran a job-training program that served blacks—had his chicken houses torched.[37] Klan night riders tortured at gun point a black man and a white man in Harnett County for socializing together; black schools in Mars Hill and Johnston County were torched. The Klan tried to kill civil rights lawyer James Ferguson.[38]

Some reacted to threats with humor. When Raleigh city court judge Pretlow Winborne, who had been critical of the KKK, returned home to find a burning cross, he called together neighbors and roasted wieners. "The least they could have done was burn it while I was at home and could enjoy it," Winborne quipped.[39]

Sanford walked a political tightrope. He called for an end to the civil rights demonstrations, saying the protests "had reached the point of diminishing returns in its latter days, destroying good will, creating resentment, losing friends and not influencing people." But he also worked behind the scenes to help further negotiations with major hotels and retailers to integrate.[40]

In city after city, the owners of department stores, restaurants, and hotels agreed to integrate their businesses. Sanford was helped immeasurably by many business people who chose, however reluctantly, to accommodate change rather than see the state wracked by violent demonstrations. Gene Patterson, the liberal editor of the *Atlanta Constitution*, urged business leaders in his city to follow the model of business people in North Carolina in calmly working to ease the transition. "This emergence of business leadership in a progressive role in race relations is a vastly important new factor in the development of the South," Patterson wrote in 1963. "In Raleigh, Charlotte and elsewhere the power structures have acted to prevent fires instead of waiting to fight them."[41]

Sanford did not deliver the usual antisegregation jeremiads of other embattled southern governors. In a speech to the N.C. Press Association meeting in Chapel Hill in January 1963, he became the first southern governor to call for the end of racially discriminatory hiring practices. "The time has come for American citizens to give up their reluctance, to quit unfair discriminations, and to give the Negro a full chance to earn a decent living for his family and to contribute to higher standards for himself and all men," Sanford said in a speech delivered on the 100th anniversary of Lincoln's Emancipation Proclamation.[42]

Sanford called for voluntary efforts, rather then new laws, through the creation of a statewide Good Neighbor Council and similar local councils to encourage the employment of black people. His leading critic, Jesse

Helms, suggested that Sanford was a hypocrite who was playing to the national news media. He asked why Sanford had not hired more blacks in his administration or any blacks in his Fayetteville law firm. Others came to see Sanford's initiatives as fairly weak beer. "In the end, Terry Sanford's positive contribution to North Carolina's race relations involved primarily the areas of atmosphere and leadership style," wrote historian William Chafe. While Sanford helped legitimatize the aspirations of blacks, Chafee said he "produced little in the way of substantive change in the personnel and policies of state government."[43]

For many young black people, Sanford was moving far too slowly. One evening in May 1963, the students brought their protests to the Executive Mansion. Sanford was hosting a black-tie ball to benefit the N.C. Symphony, and many of the state's leading citizens had turned out to listen to Eleanor Steber, a soprano with the Metropolitan Opera. But the music was at times nearly drowned out by 500 clapping civil rights protesters, who had gathered on the mansion lawn and were singing freedom songs and gospel tunes. "We want the governor. We want the governor," the protesters chanted for twenty minutes.

For those with an eye toward history, the evening was rich with symbolism. In 1898 the Red Shirts, the vigilantes of the white supremacy movement, had surrounded the Executive Mansion. Now, sixty-five years later, the grandsons and granddaughters of disfranchised black citizens had showed up at the governor's doorstep, demanding their rights. The wheel of history was turning.

Sanford, wearing a tuxedo, stepped on to the south porch to face the protesters. There was no fence around the mansion at that time. Sanford told his bodyguard to stay inside, but the highway patrolman followed him anyway. On the second floor balcony, Sanford's two children, Terry and Betsee, watched as Sanford stood silently on the porch as some in the crowd booed and hurled epithets at him. "Let our great governor speak," someone shouted sarcastically.

A clearly miffed Sanford said: "I'll be glad to talk to you about any of your problems, any of your grievances, any of your hopes. This is not the time, or the place. You are not bothering me at all. You can stay here another hour or so, if you like. I've enjoyed the singing."

"We are not here to entertain you, governor," someone shouted from the crowd. "You are not here at my request either, friend," Sanford shot back. "If you want to talk to me at any time about your plans and your problems, let my office know. You have not come to me with any requests."

One of the demonstrators yelled that the governor "should have known our troubles" without any request. "I'm not dictator, son," Sanford said. "You're in a democracy." Again there were more boos. The demonstrators stayed around a little longer, and the demonstration ended inconclusively, with the students heading back to nearby Shaw University.

In June Sanford asked 150 black leaders to the Capitol, where he warned that he would not "let mass demonstrations destroy us." The enemy of black people, Sanford said, is not white people. "Your enemy and mine is a system bequeathed us by a cotton economy, kindled by stubbornness, intolerance, hot headedness, north and south exploding into war and leaving to our generation the ashes of vengeance, retribution and poverty. The way to fight this common enemy is education."[44]

If the civil rights protests were trying the patience of a racial moderate like Sanford, it was infuriating many members of the General Assembly, which was dominated by rural conservatives. With Sanford nudging the state along a moderate path on civil rights, the General Assembly became the center of the segregationist backlash.

Conservative legislators felt under siege when the civil rights protesters began to target the venerable Sir Walter Hotel, the state's "political hotel" and the Raleigh residence of many lawmakers. The Sir Walter, opened in 1924 just three blocks from the Capitol, was known as the "Third House" of the legislature. For decades, the Sir Walter was where the deals were cut, satchels of campaign money were distributed, hookers plied their trade, and gossip was exchanged over bourbon. Every Monday morning, liquor salesmen dropped off nine cases in room 215, which was permanently rented by the liquor lobby. From there, the bottles were delivered in brown paper bags to slake the lawmakers' thirst. U.S. senator Sam Ervin Jr. once called it "the most politically saturated inn in America."

Returning to the Sir Walter after a hard day at the legislature, lawmakers often had to weave their way through singing, clapping demonstrators in the lobby. On several occasions, hundreds of protesters marched around the state's modernistic Legislative Building, which opened in 1963.

Lawmakers looked for ways to voice their displeasure. The N.C. House passed a resolution calling for creation of a new court—a so-called Court of the Union composed of the fifty state chief justices—that could overrule the U.S. Supreme Court. On another occasion, the legislature abolished funding for UNC-TV, the university-supported public television network, when they learned that a staff member had participated in a civil rights demonstration (the funding was later restored).

Conservative lawmakers gained their revenge in the closing days of the 1963 session, when they passed the Speaker Ban Law, which barred communists from speaking on state-supported campuses. The "Act to Regulate Visiting Speakers at State Supported Colleges and Universities" was introduced and rushed through the legislature in a single day in order to prevent any debate or allow university officials time to organize opposition. A recall effort the next day fell short. The measure had little to do with communists on campuses—the overwhelming evidence suggests there were only a handful of radicals—but to express conservative discontent with the civil rights movement. Some rural lawmakers equated the civil rights movement with communism—part of an incomprehensible plot to destroy the southern way of life.

The key figure behind the speaker ban was state senator Clarence Stone, who had been elected president of the Senate after the death of Lieutenant Governor Cloyd Philpott. An ardent segregationist who ran the family grocery store and an oil distributorship in Rockingham County, Stone was an admirer of Alabama governor George Wallace. Stone corresponded with such leading segregationists as future Georgia governor Lester Maddox, Arkansas governor Orval Faubus, and Virginia senator Harry F. Byrd. During the centennial reenactment of the Battle of Gettysburg, Stone traveled to the battlefield, where in broad daylight he relieved himself on a monument of a Union general who had raided his hometown. "We are still a conquered province," Stone said at a Confederate Memorial Day speech at the Capitol in May. "We do not have any states' rights any more."[45]

Among Stone's segregationist allies was Helms, who said UNC deserved the speaker ban because of its failure to investigate complaints about communist influence in Chapel Hill. "It was not an idle exercise when orders were sent out from Moscow in 1961 directing Communist agents to infiltrate the college campuses of America, to brainwash fertile and immature minds, to spread confusion and unrest," Helms said. "The communists are in business and they mean business."[46]

Among the speakers banned under the new law was playwright Arthur Miller, who had refused to answer questions before the House Committee on Un-American Activities. Only when the Southern Association of Colleges and Schools threatened to withdraw the university's accreditation did Governor Dan Moore (1965–69) create a commission to study the law. Several hundred UNC faculty members signed a petition threatening to resign en masse if the university lost its accreditation. The speaker ban law was modified in 1965, and a federal court found it unconstitutional in 1968.

North Carolina was one of the few states in the country without a gubernatorial veto. But governors still had bully pulpits to influence public opinion. Sanford had little to say about the speaker ban at the time, preferring not to alienate his legislative allies whom he needed to support his legislative programs. Sanford picked his battles, and this was one that he did not want.

As he was preparing to leave office, Sanford wanted to be certain that the segregationist Lake would not succeed him. Sanford chose federal Judge L. Richardson Preyer, a Greensboro blue blood who was the grandson of Vick Chemical Company's founder. But Preyer had little good ol' boy appeal, and he was also saddled with Sanford's unpopularity over the food tax and his moderate stand on civil rights. Preyer led the first primary, but in the runoff Lake, who finished third, threw his support to moderate Mountain conservative Dan Moore, a former superior court judge who had resigned from the bench to become corporate attorney for Champion Paper Company in Canton. Conservatives gloated at Moore's 62 to 38 percent trouncing of Preyer. "The conservative majority of North Carolina's people has been a long time getting together as a collective voice," Helms said. "They have too often been lured away from reality by false promises and by cunning wedges driven amidst them. But on Saturday an aroused majority spoke—clearly, militantly and finally. The people are fed up."[47] In a closely divided state such as North Carolina, activist governors such as Kerr Scott and Sanford might get elected, but they could not pass on their legacies to successors.

A year after taking office, Moore appointed Lake to a seat on the N.C. Supreme Court. Lake served on the supreme court until he retired in 1978 at age seventy-two. In 1969 Lake declined to give his papers to East Carolina University because of a dispute with the school over emblems of the Old South. "I do not care to have anything belonging to me in the custody of an institution that finds it necessary to apologize for displaying the Confederate flag and singing 'Dixie,'" Lake said.[48]

After meeting at Moore's funeral in 1986, Sanford and Lake exchanged cordial letters. Lake wrote to Sanford that there were broad differences between the two men. "That, not personal ill will, brought us to the leadership of the opposing forces in the 1960 campaigns, just as former classmates at West Point fought so fiercely against each other a century earlier. I still believe the losing side was right in each instance."[49]

The Lake family would remain influential in Tar Heel politics the rest of the century. In 1980 Lake's son, I. Beverly Lake Jr., an attorney and state senator, switched his registration from the Democratic Party to the Repub-lican Party and unsuccessfully challenged Democratic governor Jim Hunt, a Sanford protégé, for the governorship in 1980. The younger Lake did not campaign on a segregation platform, but he also declined to repudiate his father's views, saying he was "proud of his [father's] public record."[50]

Twenty years later, the younger Lake, by then a member of the N.C. Supreme Court, was elected chief justice by defeating Henry Frye, the state's first black chief justice. But by then race was no longer a spoken factor in the contest, and Lake Jr. and Frye were occasional golf partners.

Sanford's four years had been a whirlwind of activism. *Time* magazine called his term "one of the most memorable instances of progressive south-ern leadership in recent history." *Look* magazine said Sanford had "sup-ported the Negro first for equality more vigorously then any public official in Southern history." A 1981 Harvard University study rated Sanford one of the country's ten best governors of the twentieth century, along with po-litical heavyweights such as Woodrow Wilson and Huey Long. He served as a role model for a number of younger southerners who became governor, such as William Winter of Mississippi, Jim Hunt of North Carolina, and Bill Clinton of Arkansas.[51]

Running for President

Sanford's creative juices didn't stop flowing when, at age forty-seven, he left the governor's office. He started a law firm in Raleigh and wrote several books about government. In 1967 he organized the Education Commission of the States, a national compact to share information on education. To help the South find solutions to regional problems, he launched the South-ern Growth Policies Board in 1971.

He also kept a sharp eye out for his next political opportunity. In 1968 Sanford considered challenging conservative U.S. senator Sam Ervin Jr., with whom he had a long-running feud. He regarded Ervin to be a "con-stitutional racist." But Sanford concluded that it would a divisive, difficult primary, especially in the atmosphere of 1968, when there were strong con-servative feelings because of the civil rights movement and anti–Vietnam War protests.[52]

Sanford and Ervin were both Democrats, but they might as well have been members of different political parties. Ervin's low regard for Sanford dated at least from Sanford's decision to support Kennedy. In August 1964, when Ervin was asked by a Johnson administration official about the pos-sible appointment of Sanford to an antipoverty post, Ervin said the people of North Carolina in the Moore-Preyer Democratic primary had overwhelmingly repudiated Sanford. "I would say politically he is somewhat poverty-stricken." Ervin told the White House that appointing Sanford to an ambassadorship might be good because it would get him "out of the state and get him far away." Senator B. Everett Jordan gave Sanford no higher recommendation. When asked about Sanford, an LBJ aide wrote: "Senator Jordan, without a second's hesitation, replied: 'I don't think much of him' and asked not be quoted."[53]

National Democrats held Sanford in higher regard. He was on Democratic presidential nominee Hubert Humphrey's short list of possible vice presidential candidates in 1968. Although he was passed over, Sanford moved to Washington that fall to become chairman of the Citizens for Humphrey-Muskie Committee.

Undeterred by his role in the losing Humphrey campaign, Sanford began thinking seriously about running for president himself. No southerner had been elected to the White House since the Civil War. Woodrow Wilson, a Virginian, was elected in 1912, but he had been governor of New Jersey at the time. Lyndon Johnson of Texas was president, but in political terms he was often regarded as more of a westerner. "The time had come when a Southerner could contend because we had put the race issue behind us," Sanford would later recall. "It wasn't solved, of course, but no longer was it on the backs of Southern political officeholders as it had been for two generations."[54]

But Sanford's timing was off. He was entering national politics just as the country was being torn apart by the Vietnam War, and black riots in the major cities were causing a white backlash. Sanford may have been one of the southern lieutenants in the New Frontier, but now the country was entering the era of Republican Richard Nixon and his Silent Majority.

Concerned about the growing strength of George Wallace, the segregationist governor of Alabama, in the 1972 Democratic primaries, Sanford belatedly entered the presidential race. Sanford saw Wallace as the wrong kind of southern politician, a "pure hypocrite" who played the race card for his own political benefit. If he could defeat Wallace in the North Carolina presidential primary in March, then perhaps lightning could strike and he would emerge as a compromise candidate at the Democratic National Convention in Miami.

But it was a long shot at best. Sanford started out months behind the other candidates, with no organization and no money. The "Dixie Classic" was what the *News and Observer* dubbed the Sanford-Wallace primary in

North Carolina. Wallace campaigned against pointy-headed intellectuals, antiwar protesters, and busing for school integration purposes and urged voters to send Washington a message. He virtually ignored Sanford. Sanford campaigned for establishing national health insurance, for ending tax loopholes for the rich, for equal rights for women, for putting price controls on food, and for a 25 percent increase in Social Security benefits.

But Sanford was politically hemmed in, with Wallace on his right and Congresswoman Shirley Chisholm, an African American, winning the support of black voters on the left. And the polarized politics of 1972 was not fertile ground for political moderates such as Sanford. Wallace defeated Sanford by a 50 percent to 37 percent margin. Friends described this as one of the low moments of Sanford's life—rejected by his own people by the type of racial demagogue that he had spent his life opposing. North Carolina voters were never willing to put a Wallace-like racial demagogue in control of state government, but they were willing to send a message to Washington that they didn't like the social turmoil of the past decade.

Sanford's dark-horse candidacy was finished, although he remained in the race, hoping a deadlocked convention might turn to him. Instead, liberal South Dakota senator George McGovern won the nomination, leading his party to a disastrous defeat.

In June 1975, Sanford announced a second try for the presidency. Campaigning in Marblehead, Massachusetts, in January 1976, Sanford was hospitalized after complaining of chest pains. Tests discovered a heart murmur. Two weeks after returning home, Sanford withdrew his candidacy. "The ordeal of running a political campaign from a non-political position is tougher than I anticipated," Sanford said.

Sanford's quest for the presidency—the most serious of any North Carolina political figure in the twentieth century—was finished. "Personable and politically astute at close range, Sanford lost something on the stump," wrote veteran political writer Jules Whitcover. "His invocations in 1975–76 of his record on civil rights fifteen years earlier, with pointed references to the New Frontier, only reinforced the impression that he was a politician of the past."[55]

In the North Carolina presidential primary in 1976, George Wallace—now wheelchair bound as a result of a would-be assassin's bullet—lost to former Georgia governor Jimmy Carter by a 54 to 35 percent margin. For Sanford, the state rejected the racial demagogue four years too late.

Sanford focused his attention on a more modest presidency, presiding for sixteen years over Duke University and helping build that Durham institution into one of the country's elite institutions of higher learning. Leading the campus from 1969 until 1985, Sanford proved a master fund-raiser, more than doubling the university's endowment from $70 million to $200 million and overseeing a major construction plan.

When he was elected governor in 1960, Sanford had been one of the young Turks challenging the Democratic establishment. But by the mid-1980s, Sanford was the grand old man of the party who took a paternal interest in its success. In the fall of 1985, with the Democratic Party in disarray, Sanford was busy working the phones trying to recruit a strong Democratic challenger to Republican senator John East.

Failing to find an acceptable recruit, the sixty-eight-year-old Sanford announced his candidacy—a move that was greeted with skepticism by many of his former supporters, who noted that he had not won an election in a quarter of a century. The old Democratic warhorse proved his political skills had not rusted, defeating Republican senator Jim Broyhill of Lenoir, a respected legislator but a lackluster candidate, in the fall. In January 1987 Sanford joined his archenemy, Jesse Helms, in representing North Carolina in the Senate.

chapter 6 **Jessecrats**

hen Jesse Helms was born in 1921, North Carolina, like the rest of the South, was a one-party state, and it would remain so for the next two generations. To be a Republican in North Carolina was something that set you apart as a freethinker or maybe a Yankee transplant—unless one lived in the GOP enclaves of the Appalachian Mountains or its foothills.

Helms helped change that. Helms was a political surgeon, transplanting the old conservative Democratic tradition into the Republican Party—making sure that Robert E. Lee was honored at GOP Lincoln Day dinners. For many people, Helms became the authentic voice of the old Cotton South. It was a South where people still stood up when "Dixie" was played, where social life still revolved around the church, and where white and black people knew their place in the social structure. Helms, who was a Democrat until age forty-nine, made it so acceptable for conservative Democrats like himself to vote Republican that state Republican Party chairman Frank Rouse coined a name for them: "Jessecrats." The name stuck.

Helms became North Carolina's most famous national political figure of the twentieth century. He helped transform the state into a Republican stronghold instrumental in the elevation of Ronald Reagan to the presidency, shifted the GOP to the political right, and contributed to the polarization of the nation's politics.

Rise of the Republicans

Even during its years in the wilderness, the Republican Party was stronger in North Carolina than in most of the rest of the South—a legacy of the pro-Unionist sentiments in the nonslaveholding areas of the Mountains and foothills. Despite temporary gains during the 1928 Herbert

Hoover presidential landslide, the Republican Party did not begin to grow substantially until after 1948, when the Democratic Party began its long march toward dismantling Jim Crow and the state experienced postwar prosperity.

As North Carolina continued its transformation from a state of poor farmers and mill workers into a middle-class state after World War II, it was only natural that it would move toward two-party competition. Starting in its historical redoubt in the Mountains and foothills, Republicanism spread eastward into the increasingly affluent Piedmont cities, where business executives and suburbanites felt a greater kinship with the GOP.

In 1952 Republican Charles Jonas, a Lincolnton attorney, won the Ninth Congressional District in the Charlotte area—a seat he held for twenty years. Ten years later, Republican Jim Broyhill, a member of a prominent Lenoir furniture-manufacturing family, was elected to the Tenth Congressional District in the foothills, a seat he held for twenty-four years. Both seats became reliably Republican. In 1968 the Republicans picked up two more Piedmont seats when Wilmer "Vinegar Bend" Mizell and Earl Ruth were elected. All four congressional seats were won in areas with only modest black populations, and where the civil rights backlash was presumably minimal. During the 1950s, Republican president Dwight Eisenhower twice came close to carrying the state.

But even with natural Republican growth, the civil rights movement was to play a pivotal role in changing North Carolina into a two-party state. Southern Democrats had long warned their northern compatriots that they would remain loyal to the Democratic Party only so long as it supported white supremacy in the South. North Carolina senator Josiah Bailey issued one such warning during a southern filibuster against an antilynching bill in 1938. "In the hour that you come down to North Carolina and try to impose your will upon us about the Negro, so help me God, you are going to learn a lesson which no political party will ever again forget," Bailey told the Senate. "That is the truth. Some may not like me for saying it now, but one of these days those who do not like it will say, 'Would to God we had listened to the warning.' The civilization in the South is going to be a white civilization; its government is going to be a white man's government."[1]

A harbinger of the rising Republican tide in North Carolina was the 1964 presidential campaign of Barry Goldwater, the conservative Republican senator from Arizona. Although not a southerner, his opposition to civil rights legislation and his talk of states' rights and property rights struck a chord with many conservative Democrats. "If he accomplishes nothing else in this strange and frustrating year," Helms told his TV audience after a Goldwater appearance in Raleigh in 1964, "he has at least brought to life in North Carolina a heretofore slumbering and virtually motionless two-party system."[2]

Although Democrat Lyndon Johnson carried North Carolina, Goldwater won many converts. Among them was Jim Gardner, a handsome, smooth, and charming young businessman from Rocky Mount. Gardner married advantageously and made millions as one of the cofounders of Hardee's restaurants, which began in 1960 with a Greenville restaurant selling fifteen-cent "charco-broiled" hamburgers and would grow into one of the nation's largest fast-food chains. With his fortune, Gardner became an owner of the Carolina Cougars, North Carolina's first professional basketball franchise.

From 1963 until 1972, Gardner was the leading political voice for the Goldwater-style conservative Republicanism in North Carolina. In 1963 Gardner led a group of Rocky Mount businessmen who broke away from the Democratic Party. In 1965 Gardner became the state Republican chairman. The following year, the thirty-three-year-old Gardner defeated Democratic Congressman Harold Cooley, the chairman of the U.S. House Agriculture Committee, becoming the first Republican to win a House seat in eastern North Carolina since 1898.

Gardner tapped into the same vein of discontent that Helms would mine in the 1970s—the divisions over the Vietnam War, rising crime, urban riots, the expansion of the welfare state, and, most of all discontent, over the civil rights movement. "You don't want to hear this," said Frank Rouse, a Kinston contractor who was the state Republican Party chairman in the 1970s, when asked about the reason for Republican growth.

It's race in North Carolina. That is not supposition. That is fact. The Democrats by and large were pro-busing, pro-integration, pro-welfare, pro-something for nothing. The Republicans resent the fact that blacks bloc vote for Democrats and white Democrats resent the fact that blacks have such a stranglehold on their party. Folks who live in suburbia or folks who have moved to North Carolina don't understand it, but it is an absolute fact. If you in 1960 were a white tobacco farmer in eastern North Carolina you were a Democrat. In 1996, if you are a white tobacco farmer in eastern North Carolina you are a Republican. Now there has been a lot of other things that have been factors. But race has been far bigger than everything else. That is why Jesse's campaigns have been so successful because they understand that.[3]

Few people understood the power of the white political backlash better than Helms. Robert Gavin, the moderate GOP nominee for governor in 1960 and 1964, earned an admonishment from Helms when he expressed puzzlement as to why—given his forward-looking views on race—he didn't do better among black voters. "He seems to us to be missing the point if he implies that his party ought to undertake to appeal to minority bloc votes," Helms said. "Such a course, we would warn, would surely disrupt the modern growth experienced by Mr. Gavin's party in this state during the past several years."[4]

As the Democratic Party moved away from its segregationist tradition, it rapidly lost support. "I've voted Democratic since 1928," said Wilton Duke, chairman of the Pitt County Board of Commissioners in the heart of the eastern tobacco country. "But the Democratic Party left the white people. When they left, that is what caused the new wave of Republicans."[5]

By the 1968 elections, North Carolina Democrats were pulling the Republican lever in numbers that would have astonished their parents' generation. Richard Nixon, appealing to whites with his Southern Strategy, became the first Republican to carry North Carolina since Hoover. Segregationist Alabama governor George Wallace, running as a third-party candidate, finished second, and the standard-bearer for the Democratic Party, Vice President Hubert Humphrey, a longtime civil rights advocate, finished third.

In the governor's race, Gardner expressed "outrage that this country has to deal with a second front at home against rioters and beatniks when its fighting men are risking death overseas" in Vietnam.[6] Gardner openly courted Wallace supporters, saying "I don't disagree with Mr. Wallace on anything he says." Foreshadowing Helms, Gardner vigorously criticized the state's newspapers, calling them "left-wing rags." On several occasions, his campaigns left newspaper reporters who were covering him stranded at airports and rallies without transportation. "We are going to pave the street all the way to the governor's mansion with every one of them," Gardner said.[7]

But Gardner's campaign was also plagued by mistakes and embarrassments. The most sensational example occurred in October, when one of his campaign advisors, Craig Knowles, an Alabama public relations executive, committed suicide in Mexico City after having been caught robbing a hotel of $2,800.[8]

Gardner lost to Lieutenant Governor Bob Scott, the son of former governor Kerr Scott, by a 53 to 47 percent margin. Helms praised Gardner's strong showing and predicted correctly that it was another indicator of the sea change that was coming in North Carolina politics. "So conservatism, which was the bedrock upon which the state Democratic Party in North Carolina was years ago built originally, is on the rise again in our state," Helms said. "The people are simply beginning to return to what they have subconsciously believed all along."[9]

Gardner represented the new insurgent brand of Republicanism in the South that would give rise to Helms. Rather than backing Nixon in the 1968 GOP presidential primary, Gardner supported the conservative challenge of California governor Ronald Reagan. Gardner served as Reagan's southern leader and flew with Reagan to the GOP convention in Miami Beach that year, giving a speech seconding Reagan's nomination.

The Rise of Jesse Helms

If Gardner was the glamour boy of the conservative movement in North Carolina, Helms was just plain folk. He was not slick, nor was he particularly handsome with his horn-rimmed glasses, stooped shoulders, and thinning hair. Helms seemed more likely to scowl in public than to smile. The shy Helms never much liked working a crowd. But to his supporters, Helms's brown-shoes style made him more real and underscored his political persona as the antipolitician—despite the fact that he had spent nearly his entire career in the political arena as a reporter, Senate aide, presidential campaign aide, banking industry spokesman, city councilman, political commentator, and senator. Helms, in fact, loved politics. "Men may complain about the frustrations and disappointments of politics," Helms once remarked, "but it is the adrenaline that quickens their pulse and spurs their imagination."[10]

Helms's father, Jesse Sr., was a tough, strapping, 6' 4" man who was the symbol of civil authority in Monroe, a town located just east of Charlotte. "Mr. Jesse," as he was known, was one of the town's three patrolmen, eventually rising to become both the police and fire chief. White Helms contemporaries describe Monroe as a wholesome place to grow up—Saturday matinees at the Strand or Pastime theaters watching Westerns starring Hoot Gibson and Buck Jones, services at the First Baptist Church on Sunday, and Wednesday prayer meetings. Monroe in the 1920s had "five churches, four Republicans, one pool hall, and one whorehouse."[11] For a small county seat of about 6,000 people, Monroe produced an unusual group of high achievers. Consider Helms's high school band. The cornet player was Hargrove "Skipper" Bowles, who was the Democratic nominee for governor in 1972. On the oboe was Henry Hall Wilson, who became chairman of the Chicago

Board of Trade and a U.S. Senate candidate. The clarinet player was James "Bud" Nance, who became a rear admiral, skipper of an aircraft carrier, and acting national security advisor to President Ronald Reagan. Another band member was John Bowles, who became president of the national Rexall pharmacy chain. The tuba player was Helms, who won a statewide competition for his rendition of "The Flight of the Bumblebee." For African Americans, Monroe was like a lot of tough cotton towns. Blacks who stepped out of line could expect to be treated roughly. There was an active Ku Klux Klan, and even as late as the 1950s black people by custom often walked in Monroe's streets rather than on the sidewalks with the whites.[12]

After a year at Wingate College, a nearby Baptist junior college, Helms enrolled at Wake Forest College, which was then located near Raleigh. Working his way through college, Helms washed dishes, wrote news releases for the school as part of a New Deal program, and worked as a copyeditor for the *News and Observer*. A college education was a luxury for a 1940s newspaperman, so Helms quit Wake Forest in 1940 to begin a journalism career. Although he would later became a vociferous critic of the news media, journalism was a ticket to success for a young, ambitious man from a modest background—a chance to display his talents, to observe politics up close, and to meet famous men who would become valuable contacts. Helms worked for eleven years as a newspaper and radio reporter, counting a three-year hitch in the navy. He labored in the *News and Observer*'s sports department before switching over to news coverage and eventually moving to the *Raleigh Times*, the more conservative afternoon newspaper, as assistant city editor and then city editor. While at the *News and Observer*, Helms began dating and later married Dorothy Coble, the editor of the women's section.

Traveling around the state giving radio interviews during World War II as a navy recruiter, Helms fell in love with the microphone. After the war, Helms went into radio reporting. Starting out as apolitical, Helms became increasingly conservative in his later twenties. One influence was his father-in-law Jacob Coble, a Raleigh shoe wholesaler and an avid conservative. Another was Alvin Wingfield, a Raleigh gadfly and sometime radio commentator, who introduced Helms to the books of Austrian libertarian economist Ludwig von Mises. A year after helping conservative Democrat Willis Smith win a Senate seat in 1950, Helms moved to Washington, D.C., as Smith's administrative assistant.

On Smith's small staff, Helms was a jack-of-all-trades—driver, legislative aide, and producer of one of the first radio broadcasts for constituents. In

Smith's office, Helms learned the importance of good constituent services, which became one of his strengths as a senator. In the smaller Washington of the 1950s, Helms chatted with such senators as Richard Nixon of California, Robert Taft of Ohio, and Richard Russell of Georgia. Russell, the leader of the southern bloc and one of the Senate's giants, borrowed Helms for his unsuccessful campaign for the Democratic nomination for president in 1952.

Shortly after Smith died in June 1953, Helms returned to Raleigh as executive director of the North Carolina Bankers Association. Helms spent the rest of the 1950s lobbying for the bankers in the General Assembly and editing the association's monthly magazine, the *Tarheel Banker*. Few would have guessed that his face would one day appear on the cover of *Time* magazine.

Helms and his wife Dot settled into a comfortable life in Raleigh, raising a family, attending church, playing an occasional round of golf, and playing poker. Helms's poker buddies were men of substance—judges, lawyers, and bankers. But there was little evidence that the police chief's son was a social climber; in general, he eschewed country clubs and Raleigh society.

Helms built a modest house in Raleigh's upper-middle-class Hayes Barton neighborhood, next door to his father-in-law. He and Dot had two daughters of their own, and they also adopted a nine-year-old Greensboro boy afflicted with cerebral palsy after reading a newspaper story about how he wanted a mother and father for Christmas. Helms served two terms on the Raleigh City Council.

The man most responsible for Helms's political rise was A. J. Fletcher (1887–1979). The son of a Baptist minister in North Carolina's mountains, Fletcher was a successful Raleigh attorney, entrepreneur, and opera and theater buff who sang and acted in local productions and started a professional opera company. In 1939 Fletcher bankrolled a small, 250-watt radio station in Raleigh called WRAL. Eighteen years later, Fletcher surprised many when he beat out larger competitors to obtain a Federal Communications Commission (FCC) license to start Raleigh's first major television station.

After Fletcher hired Helms as the news director of his radio station in the 1940s, the two men grew extremely close. Fletcher encouraged Helms to go to Washington with Smith. Helms in turn had talked to two or three senators to help Fletcher get his FCC license. In 1960 Fletcher wanted Helms back on his payroll—this time as an on-air editorialist.

Fletcher, like Helms, wanted a conservative voice in the state capital as a counterweight to the *News and Observer*, which had long been regarded as one of the more liberal newspapers in the South despite its involvement in the white supremacy campaigns at the turn of the century. "I am determined, to the extent possible, to convince our viewers that the so-called Welfare State is simply another name for Socialism, and that Socialism is another name for Communism, but without the machine gun; that is, the implementation by force of the State's decrees," Fletcher wrote to a friend. "For fifty years no voice like this has been heard in this area, since the morning and afternoon newspapers, both owned by the same family, headed by Jonathan Daniels, former assistant to President Truman, have been so far to the left that they barely escape being behind the Iron or Bamboo curtains."[13]

WRAL was only the second television station in the country to hire an editorialist, and it was unclear whether the FCC would permit hard-hitting opinions during its newscasts. The first of Helms's 2,800 *Viewpoint* commentaries aired on November 21, 1960, without any fanfare.

For the next eleven years, Helms ended the 6 P.M. news broadcast five nights a week with a four-and-half-minute editorial across eastern North Carolina. His commentaries were also heard on more than fifty radio stations on the Tobacco Radio Network as well as published in forty weekly and ten daily newspapers. Although Helms did not host a talk show, in some ways he was a forerunner to Rush Limbaugh, Bill O'Reilly, and other national conservative commentators who would emerge in the 1990s, giving voice to conservative anger.

Helms and the 1960s were made for each other. The civil rights movement, race riots, the anti–Vietnam War protests, the feminist movement, the Great Society programs, the sexual revolution, and the drug culture provided rich material for a conservative commentator. "He was good at his trade," writes his biographer, Ernest Furgurson.

> At first, he was better at the substance than the style. He had the editorial writer's knack of making one point per piece, rather than cluttering his efforts with a series of morals that left the listener in a fog. He was seldom stylistically ornate, and did not spend much time dredging up instructive quotations from the classics. Rather, he was direct, often sarcastic, more folksy than learned, in both message and delivery. He knew his audience, because his target was hundreds of thousands of people in places like Monroe. He understood their daily conversations—at the service station and supermarket, at the courthouse, at the tailgate of

pickup trucks parked in the shade of pine trees behind sandy tobacco fields.[14]

Helms's favorite targets were what he termed the "so-called civil rights movement," the Reverend Martin Luther King Jr., President Lyndon Johnson, Governor Terry Sanford, the news media, antiwar protesters, unmarried students who were living together, and liberal folksingers such as Joan Baez. Helms preached an unvarnished libertarian conservatism. He called Social Security "nothing more than doles and handouts." Rural electrification cooperatives were termed "socialistic electric power," and Medicare was a "step over into the swampy field of socialized medicine." "The destruction of this country can be pinpointed in terms of its beginning to the time that our political leadership turned to socialism," Helms said in an editorial. "They didn't call it socialism, of course. It was given deceptive names and adorned with fancy slogans. We heard about New Deals, and Fair Deals and New Frontiers and the Great Society."[15]

Helms's tendency to go after his adversaries with a meat cleaver earned him a reputation for meanness—a reputation that followed him into the Senate and marked his later political style. Not content with disagreeing with a person's views, Helms sought to discredit them by dredging up past incidents from an adversary's life, such as a person's homosexuality (civil rights activist Bayard Rustin), past arrests (author Harry Golden), or efforts to seek freedom of a communist (playwright Paul Green). "Observe, for example, the television reports of almost any protest march or demonstration," Helms said in a 1968 commentary in which he criticized antiwar protesters. "Look carefully into the faces of the people participating. What you will see, for the most part, are dirty, unshaven, often-crude young men, and stringy-haired awkward young women who cannot attract attention any other way. They are strictly second-rate, all the way."[16]

Helms's editorials prompted complaints to the FCC, which twice investigated the station—once delaying its license renewal. During one FCC investigation, WRAL announced that it would begin airing viewer responses to Helms. But Fletcher backed Helms, and Helms never muted his comments.

Raleigh lawyer Tom Ellis, one of Helms's poker buddies, began to notice the Helms phenomenon when he lunched with him at a popular cafeteria in the Hudson Belk department store in downtown Raleigh. The servers, mainly white country women in their fifties and sixties, began treating Helms as a celebrity. The women's "eyes would light up" when Helms came along with his tray, telling him how much they agreed with his editorials. Ellis had long watched in frustration as popular Republicans such as Dwight Eisenhower had built up substantial margins in the western part of North Carolina and the Piedmont, only to lose the state because of a poor showing in the heavily Democratic east. What was needed, Ellis believed, was a candidate who could appeal to conservative eastern Democrats. And he believed Helms was that man.

In 1970 Helms changed his registration to Republican, and two years later he took a leave of absence from WRAL and entered the Republican primary for the U.S. Senate seat held by Democratic senator B. Everett Jordan.

Breakthrough

Jordan had been appointed to the Senate in 1958 by Governor Luther Hodges, a fellow textile executive and business partner. Jordan was a pragmatic conservative who voted with business interests and against civil rights legislation. He was perhaps best known for his ability to bring home federal money for North Carolina projects. But critics such as Helms had charged that as chairman of the Senate Rules Committee he had protected his friend, President Lyndon Johnson, from scandals involving LBJ aide Bobby Baker. Facing reelection in 1972, the seventy-six-year-old Jordan was fighting cancer and was politically vulnerable. Two years after his defeat, Jordan would be dead.

Jordan lost a Democratic primary challenge to Nick Galifianakis, a forty-two-year-old son of a Greek immigrant who ran a restaurant in Durham. A Duke-educated attorney, Galifianakis was an ex-Marine who served eight years in the state legislature and three terms in the U.S. House before deciding to challenge Jordan. Like Jordan, Galifianakis had turned against the Vietnam War.

The Jordan upset left the Democrats splintered. Such Democratic Party divisions would repeatedly aid in the Republican Party's rise. Galifianakis was a far more attractive opponent for Helms than Jordan would have been. He was more liberal than Jordan, and his ethnic background was unusual for someone running for office in one of the most ethnically homogeneous states in the country. For Tar Heel residents not used to his Greek name, Galifianakis helpfully said it "began with a gal and ended with a kiss."

But Galifianakis needed more than charm to win in 1972, which was shaping up as a Republican landslide. President Nixon looked even stronger than he had four years earlier, when had carried the state. This time he faced South Dakota senator George McGovern, an unpopular liberal Democratic nominee.

The Helms campaign tied itself as closely as possible to Nixon's coattails, while joining Galifianakis and McGovern together at the hips. The Helms campaign took out newspaper ads criticizing "McGovernGalifianakis welfare giveaways" and "McGovernGalifianakis cut and run" policies in Vietnam. The Helms campaign slogan, repeated over and over, was "Elect Jesse Helms—He's One of Us." The slogan was vague enough to mean different things to different people. Did it mean that Helms was a conservative? Or that he came from old Scotch-Irish stock that was more deeply rooted in North Carolina than a Greek American? Helms trimmed his ideological sails for the Senate race. No longer did he attack Social Security and Medicare. The WRAL-TV recordings of his editorials—which would have provided fodder for the Democrats—mysteriously disappeared.

On the Saturday before the election, Nixon campaigned in Greensboro with Helms and Jim Holshouser, the GOP nominee for governor, at his side. The Sunday newspapers carried photographs of Nixon, Helms, and Holshouser together, their hands held high in the traditional victory pose. It was powerful imagery. Nixon carried the state by an astounding 71 percent, winning all but two counties. Helms won with 54 percent of the vote. Holshouser pulled in 51 percent.

The day after the election, the eighty-five-year-old A. J. Fletcher accepted congratulations on having helped elevate his surrogate son to the U.S. Senate. "This morning my thoughts go back to the afternoon when you came in my room in our law offices and talked about your dream to build WRAL-TV and give the *real* North Carolina a voice with which to combat socialism and other issues in the *News and Observer* philosophy," wrote his old law partner I. Beverly Lake Sr., the former segregationist candidate for governor who was by then a state supreme court justice. "Jesse's election is a major step in making your dream a reality."[17]

Leading the Conservative Revolution

North Carolina's first Republican senator of the century held no allegiance to the party of Lincoln, Taft, Eisenhower, or even Nixon. A few days before taking his oath of office, Helms declared: "I'm not a Nixon Republican. I'm nobody's Republican or anything else."[18]

Helms was a conservative Democrat in Republican clothing. He carried to Washington the southern conservative and segregationist tradition of a Sam Ervin, coupled with the angry belligerence of a George Wallace. Dismissed as a right-wing crank when he first arrived in Washington in 1973, Helms was viewed by many as a likely one-term senator who rode into office holding fast to Nixon's coattails. But Helms would prove his critics wrong. By the beginning of the 1980s, Helms was the leader of a powerful political movement that would soon be dubbed the New Right. Helms had helped install Ronald Reagan in the White House. At his command was a network of conservative activists across the country. His political lieutenants at home controlled the nation's largest political action committee.

Helms filled the leadership gap in the conservative movement between Goldwater's defeat in 1964 and Reagan's election in 1980. He also provided leadership to the Republican Party after Nixon resigned from office and the GOP ranks were decimated by the Watergate scandal.

Helms emerged as a conservative critic of both Nixon and his successor, Republican Gerald Ford. He regularly criticized Henry Kissinger, Nixon's and Ford's chief foreign-policy advisor, for his role in pushing détente with the Soviet Union. He was a foe of foreign aid, the Panama Canal Treaty, and arms limitation treaties. When Ford chose former New York governor Nelson Rockefeller as his vice president, Helms denounced the once-divorced Rockefeller for having "stole another man's wife." Helms hardly liked anything Ford did. "Under the Republican Party's present course, the party is out of tune with its own rank and file membership, and out of tune with the growing conservative majority," Helms said.[19]

From the very beginning, Helms earned the nickname "Senator No"—bestowed upon him by *News and Observer* editor Claude Sitton—because he was often one of only a handful of senators to cast negative votes. Helms spent long hours on the Senate floor giving speeches to an empty Senate chamber on the need to return to the gold standard, on the perils of communism, on the evils of spendthrift government, or the machinations of the Trilateral Commission. It was as if the WRAL-TV studios in Raleigh had been moved to the middle of the Senate floor.

In his first year alone, Helms introduced ninety-six bills and twenty-one amendments and gave 138 speeches on the Senate floor. He fought relentlessly against any expansion of government, except for the military. Throughout his career, he was an ardent foe of nearly every social program, from food stamps to child nutrition programs; opposed nearly every consumer program, including the creation of the Consumer Protection Agency; and voted against nearly every environmental bill.

Helms organized like-minded senators into a conservative caucus, called the Republican Steering Committee. That same year he became chairman

President Richard Nixon campaigning with Jesse Helms and Jim Holshouser in Greensboro, 1972. (Courtesy of the *Raleigh News and Observer*)

of a seventeen-member Committee on Conservative Alternatives—where he served as a liaison among sharply conservative groups interested in such issues as abortion, school prayer, and busing. He helped them develop a national strategy against what he called the "discount Republicans." "Those were dark days," said New Right activist Connaught Marshner, who was chairman of the National Pro-Family Coalition. "There weren't many conservatives in Washington. He sort of became the standard-bearer for the movement."[20]

In 1975 Helms toyed with the idea of creating a third political party. His political organization researched how to get a third-party candidate on the ballot in all fifty states. "Conservatives in both parties feel that they have no place to go," Helms said.[21] But Helms abandoned the third-party idea when he found his man in the Republican Party—California governor Ronald Reagan. Helms first met Reagan in Southern Pines when Reagan was on the after-dinner speaking circuit and Helms was still a TV editorialist. Although Reagan was far more glamorous, the two men shared some similarities: both were small-town boys who got their starts in sports reporting or broadcasting, became spokesmen for big business, and became deeply immersed in conservative politics. And both understood the power of television.

Reagan had cut an ad for Helms during his 1972 Senate campaign. In July 1975 Reagan came to Raleigh to help Helms raise money for his fledgling political organization, then called the North Carolina Congressional Club. Helms introduced Reagan to the crowd of 2,000 people at a $100-per-plate pork barbecue and fried chicken dinner at the Kerr Scott Building at the State Fairgrounds as "a man who, faced with the choice, would rather be right than president. But I know it has not escaped your notice that there is a very good chance he can and will be both."[22]

In 1976 Reagan challenged President Ford. By the time North Carolina's presidential primary was held in March, Reagan's campaign had lost a string of primaries, his campaign was broke, and party leaders were urging him to abandon his conservative insurgency. Much of the North Carolina GOP establishment, including Holshouser and the state's two Republican Congressmen, lined up behind the president.

Tom Ellis, who headed Helms's political organization, commandeered the Reagan North Carolina primary campaign. Ellis had been fuming for months that Reagan's national handlers had been bungling the campaign, talking about his record as California governor rather than using Reagan's best asset: talking into a camera about his conservative values. Severing

Senator Jesse Helms with California governor Ronald Reagan at a rally at Dorton Arena in Raleigh, 1975 (Photograph by the *Raleigh News and Observer*; courtesy of the North Carolina State Archives)

communications with the national Reagan campaign, Ellis began airing a thirty-minute commercial that Reagan had made for Goldwater in 1964.

Helms's organization launched a sophisticated get-out-the-vote effort. Helms convinced Reagan to spend the week before the primary campaigning in the state. Reagan stepped up his criticism of Ford for backing a treaty to return control of the Panama Canal to the Panamanians. "We bought it, we paid for it, it's ours and we're going to keep it," Reagan said in one of his favorite lines.

Ford meanwhile virtually ignored North Carolina. Thinking that Reagan was finished, the Ford campaign eased up to provide Reagan room to make a strategic withdrawal. "We thought we were going to win in North Carolina and sew up the whole thing," Dick Cheney, a top Ford lieutenant (and later vice president) recalled.[23]

As he would repeatedly do throughout his political career, Helms and his organization also played the race card. The Ford campaign released a list of potential vice presidential running mates that included Edward Brooke of Massachusetts, the first black senator of the twentieth century. The Helms organization printed leaflets bearing the headline: "Ford suggests Brooke as a possible partner." Reagan ordered a halt to the flyer's distribution. "The governor has never campaigned on race, never used it as an issue and never will and feels strongly about it," Michael Deaver, Reagan's chief of staff, said at the time.[24]

The day before the North Carolina primary, a headline in the *New York Times* read: "Reagan Virtually Concedes Defeat in North Carolina." Reagan's upset of Ford in North Carolina by 52 to 48 percent was so surprising that at first the Reagan campaign team — by this time campaigning in Wisconsin — did not believe the news. But when it began to sink in, Reagan began tossing a football around his campaign plane. His aides broke out the champagne and began singing the Tin Pan Alley tune with new lyrics: "Nothing could be finer than to give Ford a shiner, in the primary."[25]

Helms continued to battle for Reagan and the conservative cause right up to the national convention in Kansas City. Working with the Reagan forces at the convention, Helms and his allies helped force through a series of conservative platform positions on issues such as China, Panama, and the Soviet Union. When Reagan outraged his conservative allies by announcing that liberal GOP senator Richard Schweiker of Pennsylvania was his vice presidential choice, Helms allowed his name to be put into nomination. Helms withdrew his name at the podium, but it gave him a chance to give a conservative-call-to-arms speech. He received 103 delegate votes for vice president anyway.

Four years later, Reagan won the nomination in Detroit. At the convention, Helms and his aides helped draft a platform that contained some thirty Helms-sponsored amendments, ditching the party's support for the Equal Rights Amendment for women and hardening the party's antiabortion position. Helms also allowed another vice presidential drive on his behalf. His staff traveled to New Hampshire to collect petitions to get Helms on the ballot for vice president. As he had at the 1976 convention, Helms addressed the convention in Detroit before withdrawing his name in favor of Reagan's choice of George H. W. Bush. Helms and his allies were pushing the national party to the political right.

Helms put his political organization at Reagan's disposal in the fall, raising $4.6 million (or $11.1 million in 2006 dollars) in an independent campaign to help Reagan win the White House. Reagan always showed his gratitude toward Helms, crediting him for saving his political career. When Helms was in the fight of his political life in 1984, Reagan came into the state to campaign for him. Lou Cannon, a Reagan biographer, wrote that the 1976 North Carolina primary was the "turning point" of Reagan's political career. "Without his performance in North Carolina, both in person and on television, Reagan would have faded from contention before Kansas City, and it is unlikely that he would have won the presidential nomination four years later."[26]

The state's 1976 presidential primary was the most consequential in North Carolina history and one of the most important in American history. It was the only time that a sitting president was defeated in a primary election. Reagan became a pivotal figure in American politics in the late twentieth century, leading a conservative revolution that helped elect the two George Bushes as president and helping Republicans gain control of Congress.

The National Congressional Club

No one in North Carolina had ever seen anything like the National Congressional Club. There had been political machines in the state before, but those were traditional courthouse organizations. The Helms organization was a high-tech machine, bankrolled by tens of millions of dollars from around the country. It relied on cutting-edge television advertising, with a payroll of seasoned political operatives working out of a three-story brick office building at 3825 Barrett Drive in a nondescript suburban North Raleigh office park. One of its creators would later boast that it was the most powerful political machine the South had seen since Louisiana governor Huey Long's—and maybe even greater than the Kingfish's empire.[27]

The Congressional Club not only engineered Helms's reelection in 1978, 1984, and 1990, but it also elected John East, a political science professor at East Carolina University, to the U.S. Senate in 1980 and Clinton businessman Lauch Faircloth to the U.S. Senate in 1992. In the process, it defeated Democrat after Democrat. The Congressional Club handed four-term governor Jim Hunt his only defeat in 1984. It unseated Senator Robert Morgan, a moderate Democrat, and Senator Terry Sanford, a liberal. It scotched the hopes of John Ingram, a white populist, and Harvey Gantt, a black candidate. The Congressional Club also had a national reach. It helped elect Reagan, but it failed in its attempt to elect Steve Forbes as president in 1996. The Congressional Club tried in 1985 to buy the giant television network CBS because it wanted more conservative national news broadcasted. The club became a training ground for a generation of young conservatives—people such as Charles Black, Alex Castellanos, Carter Wrenn, Arthur Finkelstein, Richard Viguerie, and Ralph Reed—who later ran the campaigns of U.S. presidents as well as those of prime ministers of other countries. "Raleigh was the center of The Cause," Castellanos said. "At the end of the day, The Cause helped balance the budget, knock down the Berlin Wall, elect Ronald Reagan president and make conservatives mainstream. That is where the movement started in America—in Raleigh with Jesse Helms."[28]

Helms's organization, the National Congressional Club, was only nominally Republican. Rather, it served as a bridge between the Republicans and the conservative Democrats who were looking for a new home. At the height of its power, the Congressional Club had more Democratic members than Republicans, according to Ellis.

The National Congressional Club began humbly as a political action committee formed in 1973 to help retire $160,000 in debts (or $766,000 in 2006 dollars) from Helms's 1972 campaign. The organization's name underwent several permutations before it closed its doors in 1995, starting out as the North Carolina Congressional Club before becoming the National Congressional Club and, finally, the National Conservative Club. The two leading figures in the club were Ellis and Wrenn.

Ellis was born in 1920 in Alameda, California, the son of an explosives engineer who worked on the Hoover Dam. During the Depression, the family moved to Delaware. Ellis graduated from the University of North

Carolina at Chapel Hill and the University of Virginia School of Law before beginning a law practice in Raleigh in 1948. As a young volunteer, Ellis worked in the 1950 Smith campaign, researching Senator Frank Porter Graham's connections to various left-wing causes.

During that race, Ellis first met Helms, and they began a political partnership that would stretch across a half century. During the 1950s, Ellis was an attorney for the state commission that helped draft North Carolina's response to the Supreme Court's decision ordering school integration. Ellis was a hard-liner who pushed for strong resistance to integration, including possible closing of the public schools. He worked for segregationist candidates, lost a state Senate race in 1956, and switched to the Republican Party in 1970.

For the next quarter of a century, Ellis became Helms's political alter ego—and the closest thing North Carolina had to a political boss in that era. Ellis made and unmade senators. He dictated who would be state Republican Party chairman. He blocked a Republican governor from attending a national GOP convention. Crusty, blunt, shrewd, and tough, the pipe-smoking Ellis once described himself as politically to the right of Helms. He also could be ruthless. He never hesitated skewering an opponent—even if it was an old comrade in arms like Democratic senator Robert Morgan or Republican congressman Jim Broyhill. He was both feared and respected by his staff of young conservatives. He was an innovator, willing to try new political techniques—such as direct mail and television. And he was a riverboat gambler, willing to go deeply into debt in campaigns with the hope that the money could be raised later.

Like some northern transplants, Ellis became more southern than most southerners. A portrait of Robert E. Lee hung behind his desk in his law office. His views on race also seemed to be out of the Old South. In 1983 President Reagan nominated Ellis to the Board for International Broadcasting. The board oversaw Radio Free Europe and Radio Liberty, which beamed broadcasts into communist countries. But Ellis asked that his nomination be withdrawn after Senate Democrats questioned his role as a board member of the Pioneer Fund, which sponsored genetics research into questions of whether blacks were inferior to whites.

While Ellis was the head of the Helms organization, Wrenn oversaw daily operations. A heavy-set, slow-talking, cigar-smoking history buff, Wrenn became the most respected and feared political operative in the state. He was a native of Danville, Virginia, and later moved with his family to Durham. The son of a construction-company owner and a bookkeeper, Wrenn described himself as "pretty liberal" when he enrolled at UNC–Chapel Hill. But his politics soon turned conservative, influenced by friends and his work as a student volunteer in Helms's 1972 campaign. In December 1974, the twenty-two-year-old Wrenn went to work for the National Congressional Club as its only employee.

The third key figure in the National Congressional Club—and probably the most creative—was Arthur Finkelstein, a mysterious figure who rarely talked to the press. A gay Jewish New Yorker, Finkelstein made his reputation in conservative circles as Helms's chief political consultant. He was known for hard-edged ideological campaigns portraying Democrats as out-of-touch liberals. He also became an important figure in national and Israeli politics, helping elect conservatives Benjamin Netanyahu and Ariel Sharon as prime minister. Finkelstein's sexuality became public in 1996, when a Boston magazine reported that he and his partner had adopted and raised two children in a suburb of Ipswich, Massachusetts.

Direct Mail

The National Congressional Club started with the technology of an earlier age—index cards neatly filed in boxes with the names of 1,000 people who had given $100 each. Fund-raising letters were laboriously written on an electric typewriter. Several people who worked in Helms's 1972 campaign had been active in the Young Americans for Freedom (YAF), a college group active in conservative politics. YAF successfully raised money using a direct-mail specialist named Richard Viguerie, a Virginia political consultant. The idea of mail solicitations was not new. But the development of computer technology had made it much easier to churn out mass mailings, which were often personalized.

The Congressional Club made its first mailing in June 1975, an appeal signed by South Carolina senator Strom Thurmond. Using $25,000 from the Reagan dinner, Viguerie did a test mailing, and the checks started rolling in. Then he made a larger mailing, and the checks really poured in. Not only was the Congressional Club no longer in debt, but it also was flush. Encouraged by the results, the club hired Viguerie to raise money for Helms's 1978 campaign. "It wasn't like somebody sat down and said this is a great idea and we ought to test it," Wrenn said. "It was like a step at a time. Once you had a computer and you could put a list of 250,000 names on it, Viguerie figured out how to run those damn things through a printer and personalize them."

From then on, Helms typically raised 75 percent of his money from outside of North Carolina. Often, the fund-raising appeals used alarmist rhetoric and stressed hot-button issues warning conservatives that militant blacks, homosexuals, labor bosses, and bra-burning feminists were about to take over the country. With their appeals to people's fears, the Helms fund-raising letters contributed to the negative and corrosive tone of American politics.

But direct mail also tended to make campaign fund-raising more democratic. Helms did not have to go hat in hand and beg money from big corporations or fat-cat donors—although he received lots of corporate contributions. The contributors tended to be average citizens, such as Harvey Buckwalter, a retired farmer from Pennsylvania who was worried about abortions, the spread of the AIDS virus, and other concerns. He wrote twenty-eight checks to Helms's reelection effort between 1987 and 1989, totaling $804. "There is too much wickedness, waste and disgrace," Buckwalter said. "Unless we get back to fundamental principles based on the Bible, we are all doomed."[29]

During his 1990 reelection campaign, there were 211 people who made twenty-five contributions or more to Helms. Daniel W. Kupsche, sixty-seven, owner of a vending-machine company in Illinois, contributed at least eighty-four times; Violet M. Chesler, eighty-nine, a retired secretary from Ohio, contributed at least sixty-six times; and Robert Stewart, ninety-one, a retired businessman from Florida, made at least sixty-one contributions.[30]

Direct-mail fund-raising was costly and time-consuming, often losing money through the first three mailings, until the list could be honed to proven donors. There were years in the 1970s and 1980s when the National Congressional Club was the nation's largest political action committee. The Helms reelection campaigns raised $60 million over four elections, according to federal election records. Wrenn estimates that it brought in an additional $40 million for conservative causes—or $100 million total. "This was sending out paper and getting back money," said Castellanos, a longtime Congressional Club operative. "It was almost as good as turning water into wine."[31]

Helms was able to raise large sums because he created a national following soon after arriving in the Senate. On the advice of Senator Jim Allen of Alabama, Helms became a master of the Senate rules—learned in part by volunteering for the largely thankless task of presiding over the Senate. Conservative southern Democrats had long used the Senate rules to block civil rights legislation. Now Helms used the rules to force the Senate to vote on controversial amendments dealing with issues that most politicians preferred to ignore. Helms forced votes on abortion, school prayer, court-ordered busing for school integration, homosexuality, federal funding of the arts, and a host of other issues. While other senators snickered when Helms went down to defeat by wide margins, Helms used the votes to help raise money for his political organization and for other conservative groups for which he permitted his name to be used. By the late 1970s, Helms was likely the only American political figure who could mobilize a half-million-member army of supporters within days.[32]

Although the Senate had long been a cozy club, Helms did not mind taking lonely stands, nor did he mind incurring the wrath of his colleagues when he tied the Senate up in parliamentary knots. Some senators, such as Dale Bumpers of Arkansas, openly attacked Helms on the Senate floor, accusing him of tying up the Senate with amendments so his political organization could raise money. "His presses are running, his letters are going out," Bumpers told the Senate. "He is going after all the troglodytes in the Senate who are opposed to school prayer."[33] Nor did Helms mind breaking other rules of the gentlemen's club. In 1989 he campaigned in twenty-two states, at times stumping against an incumbent.

Television

If raising vast amounts of money through direct mail was the first light-bulb that went off, the use of television was the Helms organization's second insight. Preparing for Helms's first reelection campaign in 1978, the Congressional Club spent a year building county organizations and holding numerous fund-raising dinners featuring Helms. After all of that work, Helms's own internal campaign polls showed he had gained only five percentage points.

In the spring of 1978, Finkelstein, Helms's campaign pollster, proposed a TV advertising campaign. Helms's political advisors were stunned at the results. They had spent $1 million over a year on traditional politics and seen little results. After spending $200,000 on TV ads, they saw Helms rise fifteen points in the polls in a matter of weeks. "It was like a revolution in a moment," Wrenn recalls. "Our whole conception of political campaigns changed when that poll came back and they were never the same again."[34]

From then on, the Helms political organizations poured money into television campaigns and spent as little as possible on such traditional politics as county organizations, dinners, yard signs, and buttons. Money and television, and more money and more television; the media age had arrived in politics. What mattered was raising money to get your message on television. County chairmen no longer mattered. Building local organizations hardly mattered. They were just the middlemen. This was the new politics, and the Congressional Club understood it sooner than anybody else in North Carolina.

Unburdened by the baggage of traditional political organizations, and run at the top basically by two men who had to answer to no one—except perhaps informally to Helms—the National Congressional Club was free to reinvent North Carolina politics. As Ellis liked to say, necessity was the mother of invention. Democrats still held a large advantage in voter registration. The Democrats still had the only viable statewide political organization. And most of the major newspapers in the state were lined up against Helms. Unlike traditional organizations, the Congressional Club never shut down between elections, keeping its key political operatives on the payroll for as long as twenty years.

The Congressional Club's organizational chart at times resembled General Motors, with numerous offshoot groups. It was an organization drawn by a blue-chip Washington law firm and included several for-profit corporations. The intricate organization shielded much of the Congressional Club's financial dealings from public view, provided cut-rate political services to candidates, and helped the club avoid violating federal election laws—not always successfully. Helms and his aides also set up several Washington think tanks to influence public policy and also provide additional money-raising organizations. Helms, Inc., it was dubbed by *Congressional Quarterly* magazine.

"I think Republicans in general had a pretty solid advantage from the mid-70s to the mid-80s over Democrats in terms of tactical politics—in use of computers, the use of negative ads, campaign strategies and issues," Wrenn said. "The agenda was really lining up for Republicans then. It wasn't so much that we were brilliant. The opportunities were there. We were gamblers."[35]

Helms—Winning Reelection

Backed by a political organization attuned to the new politics, Helms won reelection four times. But with his confrontational and sharply conservative brand of politics, it was never easy. In retaining office, Helms won 55 percent, 52 percent, 53 percent, and 53 percent of the votes—figures far below most established Senate incumbents. Like many successful politicians, Helms was blessed with good timing. In his two most difficult campaigns, 1972 and 1984, he was helped by national Republican landslides. In 1978 he faced a Democrat who was virtually disowned by his party. And in his last two reelection campaigns he defeated a black candidate during a century in which only two African Americans were elected to the Senate, neither from the South.

But Helms's success was based on far more than luck or even his political machine. Helms mastered constituent politics, with his staff helping thousands of North Carolinians obtain their Social Security checks or passports or assistance with other problems. A workaholic, Helms often labored late into the evening, pecking with two fingers on his trusty manual Royal typewriter, sending out personal notes to people across the state. "When I was elected to Senate, I made a commitment to myself that I would not be a big-shot senator," Helms said. "I wanted to do what I could for the so-called little people."[36]

Helms had a finely tuned political ear. He could appeal to people's finer qualities such as love of country, respect for religious sensibilities, and reverence for the state's rural roots. On the campaign trail, Helms articulated small-town values. His folksy stories of growing up in Monroe had a Norman Rockwell character—tales about turkeys being taken to market or a little boy buying flowers for his mother's grave. Such nostalgia made Helms an almost grandfatherly figure to many in North Carolina, despite his national reputation as the "Prince of Darkness," as one national Democratic Party chairman labeled him.

Helms's unambiguous stands on controversial issues such as abortion, and his often strident rhetoric, sometimes snarling delivery, and willingness to disrupt the flow of Senate business to get his way, helped make him a popular figure among conservatives across the country and raise millions of dollars. But it was a risky strategy back home, where voters were increasingly becoming polarized about Helms. Some voters admired Helms's give-'em-hell style. The cliché became: "You may not agree with Jesse, but at least you know where he stands." But many voters who agreed with Helms on the issues were turned off by his style. Reagan could deliver conservatism with a sunny, feel-good optimism. Helms's politics had a darker tone. On one occasion, the Helms organization took a poll asking North Carolina voters how they felt about having homosexuals teaching in the public schools. Seventy percent were opposed to gay teachers. But when Helms started talking about the issue, internal campaign polls showed him losing popularity because voters didn't like his Elmer Gantryism and moral smugness.

"The problem that made Helms so hard to re-elect was not that he had all of these positions that people disagreed with, but that he had this style," Wrenn said. "The reaction to your base was hallelujah and pass the plate. But the reaction of the undecided voter was that he was not a nice person. That he was a mean-spirited, intolerant, arrogant sort of person."[37]

Republican Growth

North Carolina, like the rest of the South, was undergoing a political sea change. During the last third of the twentieth century, the Democratic advantage over Republicans in voter registration in North Carolina shrank from a 4.5-to-1 ratio to a 1.5-to-1 ratio. And registration did not fully reflect the shifts. In 1968, 60 percent of Tar Heels viewed themselves as Democrats, 21 percent considered themselves Republicans, and 19 percent were independent. By 1998, 32 percent considered themselves Democrats, 36 percent Republicans, and 22 percent independents.[38]

The Democratic Party's abandonment of white supremacy helped trigger the shift—along with race-related issues such as racial quotas, welfare, and busing for school-integration purposes. But there were also a host of other factors.

North Carolina was growing more affluent, and more people identified with the Republican Party based on economic class and self-interest, just as they did in other parts of the country. In 1940 North Carolinians earned 54 percent of the national average wage. By 1980 Tar Heel wage earners had narrowed the gap to 80 percent of the national average. By 2000 state wage earners were taking home 92 percent of the national average in pay.[39]

North Carolina insurance salesmen living in colonial houses on cul de sacs and driving station wagons—and later sport utility vehicles—began voting like their counterparts elsewhere in the country. Many whites had moved out of poverty into the middle class and were for the first time feeling the bite of substantial taxes. "It was the class background of white citizens, not the racial composition of their electoral surroundings, that was underpinning Republicans gains," concluded political scientists Bryon Shafer and Richard Johnston in a 2006 study.[40]

The Republican Party's call for less government and lower taxes appealed to a strong individualistic streak in many white Tar Heels, many of whom had grown up imbued with the self-sufficiency of the farm. And southern skepticism about the federal government reaches back generations to before the Civil War. GOP support for large defense budgets appealed to southerners' innate respect for the military. North Carolina was a state bristling with military bases, such as the army's Fort Bragg near Fayetteville, the Marines' Camp Lejeune near Jacksonville, and Seymour Johnson Air Base near Goldsboro.

The Republican Party's calls for allowing group prayer in the public schools and banning abortions appealed to many conservative, church-going Tar Heels. And the GOP's promise to get tougher on criminals and to oppose gun-control laws struck a chord with many whites. Nor was there much sentiment for collective bargaining among white Tar Heels. Several surveys have shown that North Carolinians are more satisfied with their lot than residents in other states—a result of mild weather, small-town friend-liness, and one of most homogeneous populations in the country. Orga-nized labor, never able to gain a strong foothold in the state, remained only a marginal influence in Tar Heel politics.

North Carolina had also seen an influx of people from the Northeast and Midwest who tended to be more Republican than native Tar Heels. Republican transplants not only made their presence felt in major metro-politan areas, but retirees also helped make the golfing and Coastal and Mountain resort areas more Republican. By the 1980s it was not unusual to hear Yankee accents at Republican gatherings. The state GOP elected chair-men who were natives of Massachusetts, Pennsylvania, and Maryland. John East, an Illinois native, was elected to the U.S. Senate; Fred Heineman, a native New Yorker, was elected to the U.S. House from the Raleigh area; and Sue Myrick, an Ohio native, was elected to the U.S. House from the Char-lotte area. North Carolina House speaker Harold Brubaker was a Pennsylva-nia native. Democratic leaders, who had made almost a religion of chasing northern industries for decades, now saw as a by-product of their efforts a decline of their own political power.

The Republican Party had become the party of *Southern Living* magazine, in the phrase of political science professors Merle and Earle Black. The new GOP-leaning middle class was a mixture of conservative and liberal themes, they wrote. Many North Carolinians were for low taxes and minimal regu-lation on business and were opposed to unions and programs for the poor. But they also wanted government to spend money to stimulate economic growth—on highways, airports, harbors, colleges and universities, research parks, and health complexes.[41] The new Republicans sounded a lot like the old business progressives who dominated state politics.

North Carolina began electing moderate Republican governors. The Re-publican landslide of 1972 not only launched Helms's career; it fulfilled other GOP aspirations as well. Republican strength in the N.C. General Assembly rose to what was at the time the highest level of the twentieth century, with the GOP controlling 50 out of 170 seats. The GOP won four of the state's eleven congressional seats. And most importantly, the Republican Party elected its first governor since Daniel Russell.

If Helms was the fire-and-brimstone preacher, Holshouser was the cheerful church youth director. Holshouser, a thirty-eight-year-old attorney from the Mountain town of Boone, represented a different strain of Republicanism from that of Goldwater, Gardner, and Helms. Unlike Helms, Holshouser came from a long line of prominent Mountain Republicans.

Two years out of law school, Holshouser was elected in 1962 to the N.C. House, where he rose rapidly in the GOP ranks that had been depleted by the Barry Goldwater debacle in 1964. He became House Republican leader in 1965 and state Republican chairman a year later. He became widely known in state GOP circles when, as party chairman, he campaigned across the state in 1969 against the state's first cigarette tax, pushed through the legislature by Democratic governor Bob Scott.

In 1972 Holshouser upset Jim Gardner, the 1968 GOP gubernatorial nominee, in a runoff by outworking his opponent and winning the traditional Republican base. In the fall, Holshouser was aided by the Nixon landslide, the Helms victory, and a primary-fractured Democratic Party to upset Hargrove "Skipper" Bowles. With his gentlemanly style and his tinge of mountain populism, Holshouser had an ability to reach out to many swing voters that other Republicans missed. He ran well among women and young people, and he competed toe-to-toe with Bowles in liberal Orange County, the home of the University of North Carolina at Chapel Hill. The AFL-CIO endorsed every Democrat on the ballot that year but remained neutral in the governor's race. Unlike the Helms-Gardner-Goldwater wing of the GOP, Holshouser also cultivated black voters.

The transition to power in Raleigh was sometimes a rocky one for the Republicans because the party had not run state government in several generations and had no bench of experience. Holshouser rewarded hundreds of Republican Party workers who had been shut out of political patronage jobs over the century. There were several highly publicized mass firings. The Holshouser administration was also plagued by some minor scandals at the start. But it eventually found its sea legs. Holshouser established a record as one of the South's moderate Republican governors, along with the likes of Linwood Holton of Virginia and Winfield Dunn of Tennessee.

Holshouser's record was not markedly different from that of a moderate-conservative Democrat and was well within North Carolina's business-

progressive tradition. He supported the creation of a statewide kindergarten program. He backed the Coastal Area Management Act, regarded as
national landmark environmental legislation to protect the state's fragile
seacoast. He helped start the rural health-center program to provide more
medical care in the countryside. He oversaw a major expansion of the state
park system. He appointed several blacks and women to high visibility
posts in state government. And he supported the creation of black-oriented
enterprises such as Soul City, a federally funded New Town project started
in Warren County by former civil rights leader Floyd McKissick.

Just as the Helms forces attempted to move the national Republican
Party away from Eisenhower-Nixon-Ford Republicanism to the more conservative Goldwater-Reagan model, they also engaged in bitter intraparty
warfare in North Carolina.

There was an ideological and cultural component to the party strife:
social conservatives versus fiscal conservatives; the corporate boardroom
versus fundamentalist churches; Chablis versus sweet tea. There was also
a geographical split. Traditional Republicans tended to be from the western foothills and mountains and businesspeople in North Carolina's cities
and suburbs. The Helms wing tended to be more from the traditional conservative Democratic strongholds in eastern North Carolina or from the
mill towns of the Piedmont. "There was never any comity or communications or amicability between the Holshouser people or the Helms people,"
said Wrenn. "It was like there was these two separate islands. They were
in the same nation, but they didn't talk. If one of the boats from the other
island sailed toward you, you'd roll out a cannon just out of reflex. It was
vicious."[42]

So divided was the Republican Party in 1976 that Holshouser and the
two GOP congressmen, Jim Martin and Jim Broyhill, were prevented from
becoming delegates to the national convention because they backed President Ford. The fight became so intense that Holshouser, the state's first
Republican governor elected in the twentieth century, was booed by Helms
forces, causing First Lady Pat Holshouser to break into tears.

The civil war within the GOP would periodically flare up. During the
GOP Senate primary in 1986, the National Congressional Club ran a candi-
date against Broyhill. Although the Congressional Club–backed candidate,
David Funderburk, a former U.S. ambassador to Romania, didn't win, it
left Broyhill a weakened figure in the fall. Broyhill lost to Democrat Terry
Sanford.

During the 1988 presidential primary, the warfare erupted into a brawl at

Jim Gardner (at podium), the newly elected lieutenant governor, with former governor Jim Holshouser at a Raleigh news conference, 1988 (Photograph by Harry Lynch; courtesy of the *Raleigh News and Observer*)

a Fourth District GOP convention in the National Guard Armory in Louisburg. Believing that the traditional Republicans were using undemocratic methods to control the convention and elect pro–George H. W. Bush delegates, the supporters of evangelist-presidential candidate Pat Robertson got down on their knees in prayer, sang "Onward Christian Soldiers," and then stormed the platform, prompting several fistfights. At one point, after the Democratic sheriff was called in to restore order, the Robertson supporters began chanting "police state, police state." Echoes of the factional GOP warfare would continue into the twenty-first century, as House Republicans fought for control of the N.C. House of Representatives.

But the Republican Party gradually began to mature, thanks in large part to the election of Jim Martin in 1984, a business progressive who was a consensus builder. By the 1990s, the party's two factions were working together to support GOP candidates.

Martin may have been as highly educated as any man who has occupied the governor's office in North Carolina. The straight-arrow son of a Presbyterian minister who grew up in South Carolina, Martin earned a PhD in chemistry from Princeton University before beginning a career as a chemistry professor at Davidson College. For relaxation, Martin composed classical music. Martin began working his way up in politics in the mid-1960s in the Republican-leaning Charlotte area. He was elected to the Mecklenburg County board of commissioners, eventually becoming its chairman before serving twelve years as a U.S. congressman. Martin, then forty-nine, was elected as governor in 1984 during a Reagan landslide, defeating Democratic attorney general Rufus Edmisten, a former aide to Senator Sam Ervin Jr., by a 54 to 45 percent margin.

North Carolinians elected two Republicans as governor in the twentieth century, and in both instances they were pragmatists who governed from the center-right. North Carolina voters have repeatedly rejected ideologues of the left and the right in choosing their governor. As the Republican Party moved to the political right, the GOP found it increasingly difficult to put its nominees into the governor's mansion.

Martin became the state's first two-term Republican governor. His record was moderate—pushing tax cuts for business and efficiencies in state government. But he also successfully championed more than $1 billion in bond issues for school construction and road improvements. And Martin helped pushed through a 5.25-cent-per-gallon motor fuels tax hike in 1989 to step up road construction.

Martin had more difficulty dealing with a Democratic-controlled legislature than had his GOP predecessor. Holshouser was a veteran legislative leader who knew all the players and political folkways of Raleigh and was trusted. Martin's political career had been in Charlotte and Washington, D.C. Although bright and well informed, Martin, the scientist-politician, was never adept at practical legislative politics or horse-trading.

But Martin exacted his revenge, ousting his two major Democratic rivals—House Speaker Liston Ramsey and Lieutenant Governor Bob Jordan. Martin won a second term in 1988, riding another national GOP landslide to defeat Jordan by a 56 to 44 percent margin. He replaced Jordan with an ally, former congressman Jim Gardner, who became North Carolina's only Republican lieutenant governor of the century. The following year, Martin helped remove Ramsey from power by supporting a coalition of House Republicans and nineteen dissident Democrats tired of Ramsey's long tenure. The bipartisan revolt led to the election of Joe Mavretic, a Democratic lawmaker and retired Marine Corps pilot from Edgecombe County.

The ouster of Ramsey in 1989 marked the beginning of a period of intense competition for control of the N.C. House. The House became ground zero in the battle for control of the state. The Republicans won control of the House in 1994, electing Harold Brubaker, a cattle farmer and appraiser from Randolph County, as the first Republican speaker since Fusion days. The Democrats regained the House in 1998. But the margins were so small that there was always suspense even after the election as both parties wheeled and dealed in an attempt to assemble a bipartisan governing coalition. There was even a co-speakership between Democrats and Republicans in 2003.

Following his reelection in 1988, Martin was an established star in the GOP firmament. Most people expected him to challenge Democratic U.S. senator Terry Sanford in 1992. But in February 1990, the *News and Observer* reported that the governor's tax-paid state research office—which was run by his former campaign research director—had compiled information on Martin's political opponents, mainly newspaper clippings. Democratic attorney general Lacy Thornburg, who ran for governor two years later, said he would investigate. The use of the research office to gather political material was a minor infraction, not a major scandal. And Thornburg's response was predictable political maneuvering.

But Martin's overblown reaction was anything but predictable. Martin left his sickbed, where he was recovering from a throat infection, and, without consulting aides, called together reporters. During a rambling ninety-minute news conference, Martin, sweating and seeming at times to be incoherent, invited the attorney general, the state auditor, the chairman of the state Democratic Party, and the Wake District Attorney to join the conference so he could ask them some questions. Two days later, angered over the *News and Observer*'s coverage of the news conference, Martin hand delivered a letter to Claude Sitton, the paper's editor. Martin wrote that when his term as governor ended he would be finished with politics, saying, "It's too brutal for me." The governor hearkened back to the *News and Observer*'s efforts ninety years earlier to drive governor Daniel Russell and other Republicans from office. "Were you convinced that it was necessary to drive the stake through my heart so that I would never terrorize your beloved Democrat Party again?" Martin wrote. "Were you so exhilarated that at last here was your best opportunity, as Reliable Keeper of the Redshirt Democrat Faith for a hundred years, to administer now the coup de grace to Governor Daniel Russell's successor?"[43]

The mild-mannered former chemistry professor had never cared for the rough-and-tumble of politics, and later he said he had always intended to retire from politics at the end of his second term. After his term ended in 1993, Martin returned to Charlotte and, true to his word, left behind his political career to pursue his business interests.

chapter 7 **Jim Hunt and the Democratic Revival**

The he Republican Party in North Carolina was on the march in the 1980s and the Democratic Party was reeling. By the end of the decade, North Carolina Republicans had won the last two governor's races and five of the last six U.S. Senate races. Jesse Helms was the national face of Tar Heel politics. North Carolina had become a reliable Republican state in presidential politics.

At a fund-raiser in a restored, white-columned mansion in Nash County in March 1988, Jim Gardner, the former hamburger tycoon and two-time gubernatorial candidate, stood on an oak staircase and laid out his dreams of a Republican era — a generation of GOP control of the executive branch that would change the state's political culture.

Eight years of Jim Martin as governor would be followed by eight years with Gardner in the Executive Mansion, Gardner told the crowd. "What you have is an opportunity this year to have a Republican administration in Raleigh for 16 years," Gardner said. "This is a big [election] that could change the political landscape of the state."[1]

But there was no sixteen-year run of Republican governors. Instead, the state in 1992 began a sixteen-year run of Democratic governors — a string seen nowhere else in the South during this period. While Republicans continued to gather strength, North Carolina began the twenty-first century with the strongest Democratic Party in the South. The Democrats would produce a serious presidential candidate in U.S. senator John Edwards. And four-term Democratic governor Jim Hunt competed with Helms for political dominance of the state.

The Democrats survived by becoming ideological centrists and artful coalition builders. To win the backing of African Americans, teachers' groups, and party liberals, the Democratic candidates pushed education improvements and supported black initiatives. To hold the support of moderates of both parties, the Democrats allied themselves with business, pushed economic development, and stressed law-and-order issues, such as support for the death penalty. The Democrats largely avoided divisive cultural issues and attempted to put distance between themselves and the national ticket.

The Republicans had a clear tactical advantage from the mid-1970s until the mid-1980s in the new politics—the use of television advertising, fund-raising, direct mail, and attack politics. But the Democrats learned from the Republicans how to run modern campaigns, shedding their old county courthouse machines for high-tech media campaigns. The architect of the Democratic revival was Jim Hunt.

The Rise of Jim Hunt

In 1950 thirteen-year-old Jimmy Hunt watched with fascination as the graders paved N.C. 42, the road that ran by the Hunt family farm in Wilson County. The tar being laid down was part of populist governor Kerr Scott's ambitious farm-to-market roads program. In today's world of four-, six-, and eight-lane interstate highways crisscrossing North Carolina, it is hard to fully appreciate the importance of paving dusty, two-lane country roads. "When you lived on a dirt road as I did, probably the biggest thing that could happen in your life is to get a paved road," Hunt recalled decades later. "I remember people used to get stuck in the middle of the dirt road, the mud was so bad. The dust in the summer when everything was dry, you couldn't keep the washing out on the lines. We didn't have any dryers in those days. Country people would just give their right arm to have their road paved. I stood up at the end of the driveway and watched the road-paving machines come along and pave my country road. It just hit me—if you work in politics you can do some wonderful things to help people—tangible things that people really need and want." The country road that Scott had paved is now called Governor Hunt Road.[2]

In the early twenty-first century, it is often said that the country is divided into two political cultures: Republican "red" states and Democratic "blue" states. But Hunt grew up in a world where conservative values and liberal politics melded together. Born in 1937, Hunt was raised on a tobacco and dairy farm near the tiny Wilson County town of Rock Ridge, located in the flat eastern part of the state. Hunt grew up milking cows, planting, suckering, and curing tobacco, and attending revivals and church picnics. His father, James B. Hunt Sr., was a soil and water conservation agent who helped start the local Grange and a farmer's co-op. His mother, Elsie Brame Hunt, was an English teacher and librarian. Both were college educated, a rarity during that time, active members of the Marsh Swamp Free Will Baptist Church, and teetotalers. The church was not fundamentalist, but it was so conservative that men sat on one side of the aisle and women on the other.

They were also liberal Roosevelt New Dealers. Among Hunt's earliest political memories was his mother weeping when she learned that Senator Frank Porter Graham had been defeated by Willis Smith in the bitter 1950 Democratic primary. Through his work in the Grange, Hunt's father had befriended Kerr Scott. The Hunts sometimes stopped at Haw River to visit the governor on his farm. Scott appointed Hunt's mother to the State Board of Health, the first woman to serve on that board. Jim Hunt later named one of his cows after Kerr Scott. After Scott's death, Hunt wrote in the *Agriculturalist*: "As we traveled up to Haw River on that beautiful morning that they laid him to rest, it seemed that a little part of our own heart and spirit were gone."[3]

Hunt was ambitious from an early age. He was the quarterback on a six-man football team, and at halftime, while still wearing his helmet and pads, he played the trumpet in the band. He was also captain of the basketball team, senior-class president, yearbook editor, and class valedictorian. Hunt was state president of the Future Farmers of America and the Grange Youth. He met his future wife, an Iowa farm girl named Carolyn Leonard, while attending a national Grange convention in Ohio. During their courtship, Hunt frequently hitchhiked thirty-six hours, a switchblade in his pocket for protection, to visit her in Iowa. The two married while Hunt was a sophomore at N.C. State University in Raleigh, and they had the first of three children while they were students.

N.C. State University, a land-grant college in Raleigh, was in the 1950s still called "a cow college" by the snootier students at the University of North Carolina at Chapel Hill. And Hunt seemed to fit the bill, from the huge pompadour that crowned his head to his foot-washing earnestness, unwillingness to drink, and the two degrees he earned in agriculture education and economics.

But it was politics more than tobacco-poundage controls that intrigued Hunt. He was the ultimate campus politician and networker, winning an unprecedented two terms as student body president. Even as an undergraduate, the faculty marked him as a future governor. He was part of a clique of farm-boy politicians who a generation later would help run the state. They included Phil Carlton of Pinetops, whom Hunt appointed to the N.C. Supreme Court and secretary of crime control and public safety; Eddie

Knox, a future Charlotte mayor and gubernatorial candidate; Tom Gilmore, a future state representative and gubernatorial candidate; J. K. Sherron, a future state senator; Wendell Murphy, a future state senator; and Norris Tolson, who would become a cabinet secretary under two governors.

As a graduate student in 1960, Hunt worked in the gubernatorial campaign of Terry Sanford, traveling across the state and organizing the state's campuses for Sanford. Just as Sanford learned from Kerr Scott how to organize the state, Hunt apprenticed himself to Sanford. The early sixties were heady days for Democrats. In Raleigh, Sanford was an activist and innovative governor, while in Washington the charismatic John F. Kennedy was creating excitement with his New Frontier. After a year at the UNC law school, Hunt moved his family to Washington to work as college director of the Democratic National Committee. He spent a year in Washington and traveling around the country organizing for the Democratic Party. "I learned a lot about how you do campaigns," Hunt said. "I learned how the Kennedys worked. I learned how you went at it full bore. They meant business about politics."[4]

Although trained as an economist and a lawyer, Hunt spent most of his adult life as a professional politician. He mastered the business of politics at an early age. Hunt quite literally wrote the book on political organizing—authoring the precinct-organizing manual for the state Democratic Party. By 1968 Hunt was conducting workshops across North Carolina on organizing. At the end of his political career, Hunt would say he knew political organizing "like the back of my hand."[5]

Returning to UNC to finish law school, Hunt experienced one of the few reversals in his life. Although he finished near the top of his law-school class, he failed the state bar exam, which he blamed on spending too much time working in the 1964 gubernatorial campaign of former federal judge L. Richardson Preyer. Surprised by the setback, Hunt took time off for public service. He worked for a short time training Peace Corps volunteers in Hilo, Hawaii, and Davis, California—a very New Frontier thing to do. But the Peace Corps did not accept married couples for overseas assignments. So Hunt spent two years with his family in the Himalayan nation of Nepal, where he worked as a Ford Foundation economic advisor. He and his family lived in a foundation-provided house with mud walls, electricity provided two or three hours per day, and no telephone. Their third child was born in a missionary hospital in Katmandu. Thirteen-mile walks to a nearby village were common, as was stretching out on a sleeping bag on the floor under mosquito nets for weeks at a time while on the road. The lessons

Hunt learned working to develop a third-world country would help shape his views on governing. He came believe that government could be a tool for economic development, government and business must work together, and political leaders must constantly travel among their people.

Public-private partnerships would become a mark of Hunt's administrations, leading to the creation of the Microelectronics Center of North Carolina and the N.C. Biotechnology Center. Both used public money to encourage private investment. He also laid the groundwork for the creation of the Centennial Campus at N.C. State University to allow private industry to place research units on state-owned land.

Hunt's pro-business political philosophy was also beginning to take shape. Unlike his hero, Kerr Scott, Hunt was never a populist railing against the big corporations. He was an ally of the big banks and large utility companies and other businesses in the state, many of which he recruited for his proeducation efforts—and which helped finance his political career. While Scott criticized the N.C. Citizens for Business and Industry, the state's chamber of commerce, Hunt named its president to chair his State Board of Education. "Instead of just dividing up the pie differently, and fighting over the pie, we have to grow the pie," Hunt said. "That is probably one of the reasons that my approach was a little different from other progressive leaders. I didn't just want to fight by taking something from somebody and give to somebody else. I wanted to grow the whole pie."[6]

Returning to Wilson in 1966, Hunt passed the bar exam, set up a law practice, and quickly began building a political career. In 1968 he was elected president of the state Young Democrats Club, the organization that Sanford had used as a political stepping stone.

When civil rights leader Martin Luther King Jr. was assassinated that year, Hunt, as a member of the Good Neighbor Council, was one of the few whites who participated in a candlelight vigil, marching from a black church to the Wilson County courthouse for prayers. Hunt's views on race had been evolving since high school. During his senior year at the rural, segregated school, Hunt wrote an essay supporting racial integration. Influencing Hunt was a speech he had heard on race relations by liberal activist Allard Lowenstein at a meeting of the National Student Association in Ohio. To persuade his father, who still believed in segregation, Hunt gave him a copy of John Howard Griffin's *Black Like Me*, in which a white author disguised as a black described traveling around the South. "He said it was the right thing to do, and we ought to accept it," recalled his father. "It wasn't the most popular view around."[7]

By late 1970, Hunt was weighing his moves. The lieutenant governor's office had once been regarded as a dead-end job. But Bob Scott demonstrated how it could be used as a political springboard to the Executive Mansion. The post had recently been made a full-time position. To make the jump from a little-known, small-town lawyer to governor-in-waiting, Hunt needed a powerful political sponsor. Fortunately, he had one in Bert Bennett.

Vice President Hubert Humphrey had once called Bert Bennett "the Lord God Almighty of politics" in North Carolina. When he ran for president in 1968, Humphrey lured Bennett and Sanford to Washington to run his campaign. Bennett, a Winston-Salem oil distributor, had helped put Sanford in the governor's mansion in 1960 and had served as state party chairman. Bennett and Sanford had failed to elect Richardson Preyer governor in 1964, but they had kept together their network. A salty, tough, former naval officer from one of Winston-Salem's more prominent families, Bennett kept on his desk a carved wooden fist with its middle finger extended.

During the Sanford campaign, Bennett had spotted Hunt as a young talent and put him to work in his organization. In early 1971 Hunt sat down at his kitchen table at his Wilson County farmhouse and wrote a letter in longhand to Bennett, expressing his interest in running for statewide office. Bennett agreed to back him. "There was no question about the eagerness," Bennett said. "He had the burning desire. When you are a natural and you work like hell—that is a hard combination to beat."[8]

Given his political drive and talents, eventually Hunt might very well have been elected governor on his own. But without the Bennett organization, it would have been a much longer climb. "He was the most important person in my political career—he and Terry and the Sanford group," Hunt said.[9]

Hunt's political career was born in the midst of a powerful Republican tide that in 1972 also propelled Helms and Jim Holshouser into office. At age thirty-five, Hunt was the highest-elected Democrat in state government and the Democrat's leading spokesman.

The rise in Republicanism influenced Hunt's political career, making him more cautious than Kerr Scott, his hero, or Sanford, his mentor. One misstep could mean disaster for Hunt and the Democrats. So Hunt learned to rely on extensive public opinion polls, talk guardedly, outwork his opponents, avoid divisive issues, and rarely stray from the political middle.

With the backing of the Bennett Machine, Hunt easily won the 1976 Democratic primary for governor by defeating two millionaires, George

Wood and Ed O'Herron. Hunt's timing could not have been better: helped by a backlash against the Watergate scandal, Democratic presidential candidate Jimmy Carter was the last Democrat to carry the state in the twentieth century. Blessed with a weak and underfinanced opponent, Hunt defeated David Flaherty, a Massachusetts-born textile executive, by a 65 to 34 percent margin.

Hunt was part of a Democratic revival of moderate, post–civil rights southern governors that were learning to negotiate through the changed political landscape—a group that included Reubin Askew of Florida, Dale Bumpers of Arkansas, and William Winter of Mississippi.

Governor Hunt

There was little that was striking about Hunt. He was of average height and build. Editorial cartoonists loved to enlarge his pompadour in their caricatures, routinely inserting a comb in his hair. Hunt had the relentless sincerity of an evangelist or an encyclopedia salesman, always preaching about how we need to help "the li'l children." Rarely did he let glimpses of humor shine through. Because he never seemed to let his hair down in public or in private, some came to see Hunt as a bit plastic. His workaholic hours were the stuff of legend, with aides, legislators, and others accustomed to receiving postmidnight or early-morning calls.

The secular religion of southern governors such as Hunt was education, and that is where Hunt focused most of his energies. Despite efforts by governors from Aycock to Sanford to improve public education, North Carolina continued to lag—a legacy of its rural poverty. North Carolina started the century spending only 21 percent of the U.S average per child on education. By 1960 North Carolina was spending 63 percent of the national average. By the time Hunt took office, education spending had risen to 76 percent of the national average but still trailed four other southern states.[10]

As lieutenant governor, Hunt helped push through the legislature a state kindergarten program. During his first term as governor, he put into place the Primary Reading Program, which placed reading aides in every classroom in grades one through three. During his last two terms, Hunt supported Smart Start, another early childhood program designed to give preschoolers from impoverished backgrounds a better start in life.

Hunt raised teacher salaries to the national average by the end of his fourth term. He expanded Sanford's efforts to provide programs for the brightest students by creating the North Carolina School of Science and Mathematics, the first state-supported residential school for science and math students in the country. Each week, he spent an hour tutoring a student at Raleigh's Broughton High School. He began a regimen of testing and school report cards, trying to instill more accountability into schools. Near the end of his reign, Hunt was still pushing the state to do better, calling for North Carolina to set a goal of having the best schools in the nation by 2010.

After the state poured billions of dollars into education, there were indications Hunt's efforts were paying off. Between 1992 and 2000, North Carolina led the nation in student improvement in mathematics in the fourth and eighth grades, as measured by standardized tests. Texas governor George W. Bush used Texas's increase in the same test scores—Texas was second to North Carolina in gains—to help win the presidency in 2000.

By 2003, eighth-grade North Carolina students were performing above the national average on math proficiency tests and on fourth-grade reading tests. In the South, only Virginia children performed better.[11] By the end of Hunt's term as governor, North Carolina was spending 86 percent the national average on its students.[12]

Hunt came to be regarded as a national expert on education, his advice sought by elected officials across the country. When he stepped down as governor for the second time, he created an institute at the University of North Carolina at Chapel Hill to help elected officials across the country reform their own education systems.

Hunt's reputation as a progressive was based largely on the increased spending on public education during his administration and his championing of the rights of blacks and women. Hunt named the first black cabinet secretary, appointing former Chapel Hill mayor Howard Lee as secretary of the Department of Natural Resources and Community Development. He appointed state representative Henry Frye of Greensboro to the state supreme court. Frye was later elevated to chief justice with Hunt's help.

He lobbied for state ratification of the Equal Rights Amendment, but the constitutional amendment providing guarantees of equality for women was defeated four times by the legislature. Hunt was one of the favorite governors of NARAL, the abortion-rights group, for supporting the only state-supported abortion funds for poor women in the South and one of the few in the country.

But Hunt illustrated the limits of progressivism in North Carolina. Like other southern moderates, Hunt was adept at walking the tightrope of holding white moderates while attracting black voters. He invoked conservative

Jim Hunt fires up a Democratic rally in downtown Raleigh, November 1996.
(Photograph by Scott Sharpe; courtesy of the *Raleigh News and Observer*)

cultural values, frequently asking for the blessings of God in his speeches and banning the serving of alcohol in the Executive Mansion.

When Hunt ran in 1976, he pledged not to raise taxes, and he kept his pledge in his first term. But in 1981 he supported a 2.75-cent increase in the motor fuels tax in what he has described as his most difficult battle as governor. When the country experienced an economic recession in 1982, Hunt cut spending and froze the salaries of state employees and teachers rather than raise taxes—a move that angered both groups.

He presented a stern image on law-and-order issues, supporting the death penalty, creating the Department of Crime Control and Public Safety, and starting the most extensive prison construction program in state history. He won plaudits from conservatives when he withstood an international pressure campaign by liberals to pardon the Wilmington Ten, nine black men and one white woman convicted of firebombing a grocery store and conspiring to shoot at police during a racial disturbance in the port city in 1970. Among the ten was the Reverend Ben Chavis, who later would become national president of the NAACP. In typical Hunt fashion, he compromised and reduced their sentences in 1978. A federal court later overturned their convictions.

When Republicans won control of the N.C. House in 1994 during a national GOP landslide, they proposed the largest tax cut in North Carolina history. Hunt trumped them by proposing even larger tax cuts, including eliminating the sales tax on food that Sanford had pushed through a generation earlier.

Veering left and then right, Hunt was never easy to pigeonhole. While many liberals ground their teeth at Hunt's conservative feints, Hunt says he leans a bit to the left. "I am a progressive who believes in providing full and equal opportunity for all people to become all that they can be and all God wants them to be," Hunt said in an interview after leaving the governor's office. "I believe government has major responsibilities in making that happen. But public leaders should also encourage the private sector and the faith sector."[13]

While there was a strain of Kennedy-Sanford liberal idealism in Hunt, he was no political reformer. Hunt's purpose was to harness the power of the old political machine and use it to advance education and economic development.

Hunt did not invent the old-style politics that had dominated state politics for generations, but he did not try to change it as he assembled the last of the old-fashioned statewide political machines. His organization was based in part on political patronage and pork barrel: the hiring of highway workers, the appointment of judges, the distribution of roads, and some 3,000 appointments to boards and commissions.

The main cog in the Hunt Machine was the old Sanford organization headed by Bennett. After taking office, Hunt swept out hundreds of Republican state government workers and replaced them with Democrats. Hunt sharply increased the number of state workers under his patronage control. And his political lieutenants were masters at putting the arm on state workers for political contributions.

Hunt's ascent in politics coincided with the final days of the old courthouse politicians, such as Sheriff Raymond W. Goodman of Richmond County and brothers Zeno and E. Y. Ponder, who ruled mountainous Madison County bordering Tennessee.

Sometimes the county bosses would embarrass Hunt. Zeno Ponder, whom Hunt appointed to the State Board of Transportation, was indicted by federal prosecutors on charges related to his sale of land that was in the path of a state highway. When he was acquitted, Ponder went before the TV cameras and held up a buckeye. The federal prosecutor, Ponder said, was just like a buckeye—a worthless nut.

The Ponder brothers ran the most famous courthouse machine in the state from the 1950s through the 1980s. Politics was rough in the Mountain county. Men sometimes carried guns to voting places, Zeno Ponder's house was once dynamited, and there was no end to the jokes about graveyard voting.

Zeno, who favored a pencil-thin mustache, was a college graduate who once worked on the Manhattan Project that developed the atomic bomb. Zeno helped his brother get elected sheriff in 1950 by thirty-one votes in a county that had been Republican. The Republicans were so distraught that they wouldn't give up the office, but E. Y. was sworn in anyway. For a short while there was a Republican jail and a Democratic jail. The Republicans set up a machine gun outside the jail, and the Democrats would drive by after dark and throw firecrackers to spook the Republicans. "This was our nightly pastime," Zeno said. "We got E. Y. in office. We stripped them down a four bushel sack of pistols off the Republican deputies and sent them back to plowing."[14]

E. Y. was the good cop, presiding daily over gatherings of men who would stop by for a lunch of beans and cornbread or in the evenings to swap stories. Zeno was the hard-nosed political operative whose election to the N.C. Senate was overturned by the State Board of Elections because of gross voting irregularities. "I believe in a two-party system," Zeno once remarked, "a great big Democratic Party and a little bitty Republican Party."[15]

Keeping the Democratic Party Machine fed sometimes got Hunt in trouble. Hunt was embarrassed when it was disclosed that one of his political appointees, Mather Slaughter, was writing memorandums evaluating the political loyalties of various sheriffs. State AFL-CIO president Wilbur Hobby went to jail for misusing $1 million in job-training money that the Hunt administration had funneled to two companies that Hobby controlled. So vast was Hunt's political organization that during the 1984 Senate race, his campaign estimated that it had 50,000 to 60,000 volunteers working for his election.

Once in office, Hunt's organization allowed him to quickly consolidate power. North Carolina's founding fathers, suspicious of concentrated power, had given the state one of the weakest chief executives in the country. The powers had grown since the 1700s, but even in the twentieth century North Carolina governors' lack of institutional influence astonished their contemporaries across the country.

No North Carolina governor could serve two consecutive terms, which meant that by his third year in office, the governor was already a lame duck with waning influence. North Carolina was also the only state where the governor had no veto. So whatever laws the General Assembly passed became law as the governor watched from the sidelines. Generations of North Carolina governors had enviously eyed the powers of their contemporaries in other states, but none could conceive of convincing a powerful state legislature to reduce its powers.

Hunt changed all that. In 1977 he overrode the opposition of conservative Democrats to convince the legislature, and then the voters, to pass a constitutional amendment allowing governors and lieutenant governors to be elected to two consecutive terms. In the 1990s, Hunt pushed through a constitutional amendment that gave governors veto power.

The impact of gubernatorial succession rippled throughout state government, changing the political culture of the state legislature. By tradition, N.C. House speakers served only one two-year term in what was expected to be the crowning moment of their legislative careers. The Senate leadership post changed every four years. But with governors now potentially serving eight consecutive years, legislative leaders argued they needed to be in office longer to maintain the balance of power. So the General Assembly began producing influential lawmakers who stayed in office for years, creating their own political organizations that rivaled the power of the governor.

The first major legislative mandarin was House Speaker Liston Ramsey, a paunchy, taciturn, mumbling old political lion who was more comfortable in the back rooms cutting deals than in front of a television camera. A product of the Ponder brothers' Democratic machine in Madison County, Ramsey sold his small business in 1960 and began a forty-year career in the N.C. House. When he lost in 1964 as part of a backlash against the Ponder brothers trying to steal an election, he continued to attend House and committee sessions.

Ramsey served eight years as N.C. House Speaker, starting in 1981. As a Kerr Scott Democratic populist, Ramsey sought to protect his Mountains from exploitation, frequently siding with the environmentalists against big business. He championed education and rural North Carolina, trying to funnel as much state money as possible into the Mountain hollows.

In the 1990s, the power fulcrum shifted across the state from Madison County to the Outer Banks, the home of N.C. Senate leader Marc Basnight, a Manteo restaurant owner who rose in politics as a lieutenant in Hunt's political organization. Basnight garnered even more influence than Ramsey, with his organization helping to elect governors and recruiting and dispersing campaign cash to keep the Senate in Democratic hands.

Basnight was taken lightly when he first arrived in the N.C. Senate in 1985, with his "hoi-toider" accent, a reputation for wearing "Outer Banks argyles" (going sockless), and a penchant for mangling the English language, such as when he talks about having a "prescription" to the *Economist* magazine. But the shrewd Basnight knew how to read men and women, and by 1993 he was leading the Senate. He worked to protect the coast's fragile environment, championed a $3.1 billion higher-education bond issue, and got so many state offices and jobs put in his northeastern district that people joked that it might sink into the salt marshes. The Basnight organization was the last political machine in North Carolina that was still operating by 2007.

By 1999 a third legislative machine arose, headed by Jim Black, an optometrist from the Charlotte suburbs. Black would be elected four terms as a speaker, keeping the N.C. House barely in Democratic hands through a mixture of probusiness policies and support for expanding education. A key ally of Democratic governors Jim Hunt and Mike Easley, Black's aggressive political fund-raising would land him in prison in 2007.

Showdown

By the end of his first term in 1980, Hunt had become so powerful that he simply steamrollered his opposition. When former governor Bob Scott—piqued at Hunt for not using his influence to make him president of the community college system—challenged him in the Democratic primary, Hunt defeated the bearer of one of North Carolina's most famous political names by a 70 to 29 percent margin. Despite a national Republican landslide in the fall of 1980 led by Ronald Reagan, Hunt easily defeated Republican I. Beverly Lake Jr., a future chief justice of the state supreme court and the son of the segregationist gubernatorial candidate, by a 62 to 37 percent margin.

Hunt was increasingly regarded as unstoppable at home and a rising star in national politics. It seemed inevitable that the two major figures of Tar Heel politics would clash in 1984 when Jesse Helms faced reelection. The Helms organization had long recognized Hunt as a threat. The Congressional Club had recruited Lake to run against Hunt in 1980. It ran ads criticizing Hunt in 1981 for pushing a gas tax through the legislature.

But the epic Hunt-Helms Senate race almost never happened. Things had started to sour for Helms after the triumphal moment in 1980 when his organization helped elect Reagan and replaced Democratic senator Robert B. Morgan with Republican John East. Helms had always been at his best as a conservative, bomb-throwing outsider. Now Helms was part of the new Republican establishment in Reagan's Washington, and he was agriculture committee chairman in the new Republican-controlled Senate.

Helms seemed off balance. The role of inside deal maker was foreign to Helms. He had difficulty in traditional back-scratching farm politics. His instincts were to lash out, not build fences. In December 1982, when an internal poll showed him twenty-five points behind Hunt, Helms told his advisors he would not seek a third term, only later being convinced to run.

Everything about the Helms-Hunt race was larger than life—its candidates, the money spent, and its duration. At times it more closely resembled a presidential campaign than a Senate race. The race cost $26 million, a national record for a Senate race at the time and the equivalent of $51 million in 2007. The advertising lasted nineteen straight months, breaking only for a week-long 1983 Christmas truce.

It spawned a country song: "Mudslinging at Mayberry—The Ballad of Jim and Jesse." Entrepreneurs hawked a Jesse Helms watch—with the hands running backward. Japanese and Swedish reporters fumbled with North Carolina road maps. And Hollywood actors Charlton Heston and

Andy Griffith showed up on TV screens extolling the virtues of Helms and Hunt, respectively.

When conservatives are in trouble in North Carolina, they frequently turn to racially charged issues. The momentum in the race began to shift in October 1983, when Helms launched a heavily publicized filibuster against legislation making slain civil rights leader Martin Luther King Jr.'s birthday a national holiday. For several days, Helms attracted headlines as he hammered away at King's alleged communist connections. "King's view of American society was thus not fundamentally different from that of the CPUSA [the American Communist Party] or of other Marxists," Helms told the Senate. "While he is generally remembered today as the pioneer of civil rights for blacks and as the architect of nonviolent techniques of dissent and political agitation, his hostility to and hatred for America should be made clear."[16]

Helms's comments were no different from those he had frequently made in the 1960s from the WRAL-TV studios. But during the fifteen years since King's assassination, the civil rights leader had achieved a special status in American life. Senate Democrats, many of whom relied on the support of black votes, lashed out at Helms in ways not often seen on the Senate floor. Senator Daniel Patrick Moynihan of New York took a 350-page stack of FBI documents about King that Helms had placed on each senator's desk and threw them on the ground, dismissing them as "trash." Senator Bill Bradley of New Jersey accused Helms of "playing up the old Jim Crow."

But if Helms was taking heat in Washington, his anti-King holiday filibuster was playing well in the tobacco warehouses, textile mills, and barbecue joints back home. The holiday was opposed by 85 percent of North Carolina's white voters, according to polls. Helms's standing in the polls jumped 10 percent after his filibuster against the holiday.

Keeping Hunt on the defensive, the Helms campaign in the fall of 1983 ran a series of TV commercials going after one of Hunt's vulnerabilities—his desire to seem to be all things to all people. The Helms ads were short and simple. They laid out Helms's views on a controversial issue such as the King holiday, school prayer, school busing, or the nuclear freeze and then asked the question: "Where do you stand, Jim?" Soon people everywhere could recite the "Where Do You Stand, Jim" mantra just like an advertising jingle for Coca-Cola.

Helms stayed on the air month after month with his advertising campaign, which was often innovative and sometimes used humor. One ad included film footage of Hunt raising his hand at a National Governor's Association meeting in Washington to vote in favor of a meaningless resolution to reduce the deficit through budget cuts and tax increases. "This is actual TV news footage in slow motion of Jim Hunt voting to raise your taxes," said the announcer. Another commercial featured a woman singing the song "Look for the Union Label," which was borrowed from a garment workers' union TV campaign urging consumers to buy products made in unionized plants. As the women sang, a list of unions who had contributed to Hunt's campaign scrolled down the screen.

The Helms campaign overtook Hunt in July. That summer the stilettos came out.

Bob Windsor, the publisher of a free weekly published in Chapel Hill called the *Landmark*, was a character—a large man who wore bib overalls. He practiced a personal brand of highly partisan journalism reminiscent of nineteenth-century newspapers in which he viciously attacked his enemies and glorified his friends such as Helms. In July Windsor ran a sensational story alleging Hunt had an unnamed homosexual lover while in college; the man supposedly went on to work in the State Department. It also alleged Hunt kept a "call girl" on his staff. The story that ran with the headline, "Jim Hunt is Sissy, Prissy, Girlish and Effeminate," was a smear lacking even a smidgen of evidence. During Hunt's long career in politics, there had never even been a hint of sexual misconduct. Near the end of the article, Windsor acknowledged that his story was based on rumors and that "I made no effort to check them out and do not claim they are the truth or factual in any way." When the Hunt campaign threatened a libel suit, Windsor retracted the story and made a written apology. Whispering campaigns of this sort are common in politics. But in the case of the Windsor affair, the slur was made in print and the story made headlines in the traditional press. "It was just about the worst smear in North Carolina history," Wrenn recalled later.[17] But it was not easy for the Helms campaign to distance itself from the article. Windsor hung out at the Helms campaign headquarters and regularly carried stories praising the senator. The issue containing the allegation included one and a half pages of advertising from the Helms campaign.

Helms and his allies used the homosexuality issue throughout the campaign by tying Hunt to gay rights activists in fund-raising letters, newspaper ads, and news conferences. In an interview fifteen years after the election, Wrenn said the Windsor article was not a dirty trick sanctioned by the Helms campaign, although he said he could not rule out a rogue operation by one of Helms's campaign staff members.

Foreign Policy

The Hunt campaign had their own rusty knife, tying Helms to right-wing death squads in Latin America.

Helms's first love as a senator had always been foreign affairs. During his thirty years in the Senate, Helms was an anticommunist hard-liner—from opposing détente with the Soviet Union during the Nixon administration to fighting friendlier relations with China during the administration of George W. Bush. Helms worked actively against every socialist regime from Angola and Mozambique to Nicaragua and Afghanistan and opposed nearly every nuclear-arms agreement with the Soviet Union and most international treaties (including an antigenocide pact), which he feared would impinge on American sovereignty. He operated on the principle that any foe of communism was a friend of his. So Helms befriended not only brave dissidents such as Russian writer Alexander Solzhenitsyn and Chinese protester Harry Wu, but also right-wing thugs around the world. Because of his friendship with the Argentine generals who were fighting a left-wing insurgency, he was the only senator to vote against a resolution favoring Great Britain in its war to reclaim the Falkland Islands that had been seized by Argentina. Helms strongly supported Chile's dictator Augusto Pinochet, traveling to Chile in 1986 to defend the regime against charges of human rights violations, calling on President Reagan to fire his envoy, accusing the State Department of aiding Marxist groups, and later claiming that the CIA had spied on him during his trip.

He was an unceasing foe of Fidel Castro, the communist Cuban dictator. In 1996 Helms pushed through Congress the Helms-Burton Act that codified the U.S. trade embargo against Cuba and allowed lawsuits against foreign companies that benefited from American property expropriated by Castro's government. Helms received a hero's welcome from an adoring crowd of Cuban exiles when he visited Miami's Little Havana neighborhood in 1995 to lay a wreath at a monument to slain veterans of the failed Bay of Pigs invasion.

Unconcerned about diplomatic niceties, Helms was often among the first to point out unpleasant truths—that the Mexican government was corrupt, that Panamanian dictator Manuel Noriega was dealing drugs, and that communist China sponsored slave labor. Helms operated his own mini–State Department, with a group of multilingual aides such as James Lucier, John Carbaugh, Christopher Manion, and Deborah DeMoss, who traveled around the world establishing contacts with conservative businessmen, army colonels, tribal chieftains, and guerrilla fighters. At times,

Helms had better intelligence than the State Department because of his far-flung sources—some of whom liked Helms but detested U.S. official policy.

But Helms's alliance with assorted dictators provided an opening for the Democrats. Hunt began running TV commercials portraying Helms as an extremist and linking him to pariah nations around the world, from Argentine dictators to the apartheid regime in South Africa. The most strident ad tied Helms to Roberto D'Aubuisson, an army major in El Salvador who the CIA said directed right-wing death squads that murdered several thousand suspected leftists or their supporters during civil unrest in that country.[18] Helms foreign policy aides helped D'Aubuisson set up his ARENA party in 1981. The Reagan administration backed the more moderate José Napoleon Duarte in his victory in 1984 over D'Aubuisson for president.

The Hunt campaign TV ad was timed to coincide with D'Aubuisson's arrival in the United States at Helms's invitation. The Hunt ad began with the crack of rifle shots and black-and-white photographs of dead bodies. "This is what they do," said the announcer. "Death squads in El Salvador. Innocent men, women, and children murdered in cold blood. This is the man accused of directing those death squads, Roberto D'Aubuisson. And this [a photo of Helms] is the man whose aides helped D'Aubuisson set up his political party in El Salvador. This is Roberto D'Aubuisson's best friend in Washington, maybe his only friend. Now, Jesse Helms may be a crusader, but that's not what our senator should be crusading for." The ad created a sensation in North Carolina, with even many of Hunt's supporters demanding that the commercial be pulled. *Newsweek* magazine called the ad "savage."

After two and a half days and worried about a backlash, the Hunt campaign pulled the ad. But the campaign continued until the end to portray Helms as a handmaiden to jackbooted dictators.

Debates

After a summer marked by charges of gay lovers and a TV commercial with photographs of dead bodies, Hunt and Helms held four debates, each televised across the state. Helms deliberately set out in the first debate to present a kinder, gentler image—keeping a picture of his grandchildren in front of him to remind himself to be grandfatherly. But this was a case of Helms not being Helms. Hunt easily won the first debate, playing the role of the aggressor and keeping Helms on the defensive, accusing him of favoring tax cuts for the rich, opposing all arms control agreements, not supporting Social Security, and opposing President Reagan's Central American policies.

The Helms campaign managed to reduce the number of debates from the originally planned five to four. And Helms's performance improved as the debates wore on, with the incumbent finishing strongly. In the most famous line of the debates, Helms questioned Hunt's support of the military, and Hunt responded that he had the backing of veteran's organizations.

"Which war did you serve in?" Helms asked.

In the second debate, Helms began by questioning Hunt's support for a King holiday. The interplay echoed past North Carolina political exchanges: George White and Furnifold Simmons, Frank Porter Graham and Willis Smith, Bobby Kennedy and Sam Ervin Jr., Terry Sanford and I. Beverly Lake Sr.

> HUNT: "I support [it] not just in [King's] honor but in honor of all citizens, black and white, who have worked for equal opportunity, have worked for the future of this state and this country, where people can work together. Now Jesse, North Carolina's been making a lot of progress. I know you've been up there in Washington these 12 years and maybe you don't know what's been going on here. The people have been working together . . . black and white. . . . Jesse, this is 1984. This is a progressive state. We're not going to go back now and open those old wounds. That's what you want to do."
>
> HELMS: "Governor, I want to congratulate you on a fine political speech. That's typical of you. You're proud, you say, of your support of a national holiday for Martin Luther King, notwithstanding all of the aspects against it. Now you're doing the same thing about the so-called Voting Rights Act extension. Let's bear in mind that Senator Sam Ervin described that legislation as the most atrocious assault on constitutional principles ever committed by Congress. Now which is more important to you governor, getting yourself elected with the enormous black vote, or protecting the Constitution and the people of North Carolina?"
>
> HUNT: "Jesse, which is most important to you, getting re-elected or having the people of this state upset and fighting and set at odds against each other? My gracious, how far back do you want to take us? Hey, this is a state that is making progress, Jesse. You're just out of touch with it. And the reason we're growing and making progress the way we are is because people are working together; they care

about each other; and they're not following the kind of negative, divisive leadership that you've been giving."[19]

Helms repeatedly tried to tie Hunt to former vice president Walter Mondale, the Democrats' unpopular presidential nominee. Helms mentioned Mondale's name forty times in the final debate. While Hunt avoided the national Democratic ticket, the Republican Party threw its weight behind Helms. Reagan, Vice President George Bush, and more than thirty Republican senators campaigned for Helms. Television ads featuring Reagan praising Helms's courage and comparing him with Sam Ervin were beamed repeatedly into North Carolina living rooms.

On the campaign trail Helms, the consummate outsider, reminded voters of his close ties to Reagan and of his chairmanship of the Senate Agriculture Committee. "If I am not there in January, you can kiss the tobacco program and the peanut program goodbye," Helms said.[20]

Trailing through most of the summer, the Hunt campaign was becoming increasingly desperate. One Hunt poll in late September showed Helms leading 51 to 43 percent. In early October, an increasingly grim Hunt high command gathered in the Executive Mansion to see if the race could be salvaged. Hunt's top advisors brought in a new face—a New York consultant named Dick Morris, who had a reputation as a gut fighter.

Morris was a rarity in the world of politics: a consultant who worked for candidates of both parties. Six years later, Helms hired Morris when he was in a tough reelection fight against Harvey Gantt. In the mid-1990s, Morris helped revive the presidency of Bill Clinton—although Clinton would be forced to throw Morris overboard in 1996 because of a toe-sucking sex scandal with a call girl.

Morris, armed with polling data, said the magic bullet for defeating Helms was the abortion issue. "It's obvious what is happening here," Morris told the Hunt advisors. "Their view of [Hunt] is weak, indecisive, wishy-washy. You've got to make them afraid of Helms. The thing that cuts deepest is this thing about abortion."[21]

During Helms's first year in office in 1973, the U.S. Supreme Court handed down its landmark *Roe v. Wade* decision legalizing abortion. Helms immediately became the Senate champion of those opposed to abortions. During his career, he sponsored twenty-seven antiabortion amendments or bills.[22] Helms called the legalization of abortions a "human holocaust with no parallel in history." And he said abortion should not be permitted under any circumstance. "Rape does not justify murder of an unborn child,"

Helms said in 1988. To work on Helms's Senate staff, one had to pass an abortion litmus test.[23]

Helms's willingness to be an antiabortion leader was an important part of his appeal to social conservatives and one reason he was able to raise millions of dollars across the country for his political organization. But Helms's political handlers feared that issue more than any other because nearly every public opinion poll showed that the majority of North Carolinians did not want to outlaw abortions.

Despite Morris's advice, the Hunt campaign was afraid to make abortion the major issue in the closing days of the campaign, although it did run a tough radio ad alleging that Helms's position would outlaw some forms of birth control. Deciding not to roll the dice on abortion, Hunt in the final weeks attacked Helms on Social Security and portrayed Helms as part of a sinister network of "radical right-wing groups" that they dubbed "Helms, Inc."

On the final day of the campaign, Helms flew around the state and tied Hunt to "homosexuals," "labor union bosses," and "crooks." And he said Hunt would only win if he got "an enormous bloc vote"—Helms's euphemism for black voters. "The man is not to be trusted," Helms told reporters in Charlotte. "And I hope that he never has another day in public office after he's finished his term as governor."[24]

In the end, Reagan swept the state with a 62 percent margin, and in doing so helped Helms win a 52 to 48 percent victory. Larger than life, the Hunt-Helms race was sometimes billed as a battle for North Carolina's political soul. If so, the state at its core was conservative. In nearly every major ideological showdown in the twentieth century, North Carolina opted for conservatives—whether in the white supremacy campaigns of 1898 and 1900, the Smith-Graham Senate primary in 1950, or the Helms-Gantt Senate races in 1990 and 1996. The Sanford-Lake contest was the exception. But what made North Carolina different from much of the South was that North Carolina progressives could compete almost equally with conservatives, and in some instances they could win.

Hunt's consensus brand of politics was more suited for running state government, while Helms's more ideological mode was a better fit in Washington. Sixteen years after his only defeat, Hunt was still puzzled by the loss. "Truth be told," Hunt said, "I'm still not completely sure what happened. I guess people liked me as governor, but they didn't quite see me in the U.S. Senate."[25]

Jim Hunt Redux

Hunt watched a rising Republican tide during his eight years out of political office. He had gone to work as a corporate lawyer in Raleigh, commuting daily from his Wilson County cattle farm, the Tarheel Double H. He remained in the public eye, staying involved in education and other causes. Democrats repeatedly tried to recruit him to run again and rescue the party. By 1990, Hunt seriously began to consider a second act in his political career.

In 1992 the Republican candidate for governor was Jim Gardner, who had been lured out of political retirement four years earlier to be lieutenant governor and Jim Martin's heir apparent. Gardner had been out of politics for sixteen years, recovering from a series of financial failures in real estate and hotels in the early 1970s that had nearly wiped him out. He had slowly built back his businesses, most notably a chain of barbecue restaurants. He was no longer the promising young Turk who had been elected to Congress and had run two strong races for governor in 1968 and 1972. But he had never entirely lost his taste for politics.

Gardner accused Hunt of being a big spender and soft on criminals. But Gardner's business failures in the 1970s had hurt him, and Hunt won the support of important elements of the state's business community, including the major banks, which had backed GOP governor Jim Martin for eight years. "State government should be run like a business," Hunt said during one debate with Gardner. "But I hope you don't get to run it like one of your businesses."

The Democrats, desperate after being out of power for eight years, used increasingly negative tactics. The Hunt campaign dredged up Gardner's list of business failures, noting he had been sued for fraud and back taxes. The Democratic sheriff in Nash County discussed the driving violations of Gardner's son. The Democrats distributed a bumper sticker that read: "Honk if Jim Gardner owes you money." The two candidates routinely called each other liars. "Adolph Hitler built up everything he did based on lies," Gardner said. "James Hunt did the same thing this year."[26]

Hunt proved adept at changing with the times. He had risen in politics in the 1970s with an old-fashioned political organization that relied on courthouse organizations. But by the 1990s those organizations were largely dead, and Hunt relied on high-priced media campaigns funded by business leaders. His politics had also shifted subtly to the political right, reflecting the national change that had occurred in the Reagan era. Hunt still called for spending more money on the public schools. But he also mixed in more conservative themes. He criticized the Democratic-controlled General Assembly for raising taxes in 1991 during the recession, saying the budgetary shortfall was "sheer government mismanagement."

The stakes in the Democratic comeback were so high that the Hunt camp resorted to illegal political espionage. The Gardner campaign disclosed that a Hunt supporter had been listening on her police scanner to telephone calls between Gardner and key supporters that were made on cellular phones. The political snooping was discovered when a jilted former boyfriend exposed the Hunt supporter's electronic eavesdropping. Although Hunt was never tied to the operation, a close political advisor pled guilty to illegally receiving transcripts of the telephone conversations.

Despite the revelations about the eavesdropping, Hunt easily defeated Gardner by a 53 to 43 percent margin in what turned out to be a Democratic year with the election of Bill Clinton as president. As he had sixteen years earlier when GOP governor Jim Holshouser left office, Hunt returned the executive branch to the Democrats.

Gardner was a tantalizing figure for Tar Heel Republicans—a natural political talent who never quite fulfilled his promise. He helped make North Carolina a two-party state, but in the end his sharp ideological style, his business failures, and his image of being a tad too slick made too many Tar Heel voters nervous about putting him in charge of the state.

Hunt survived a powerful midterm political earthquake, which sharply weakened his party while leaving Republicans in a more powerful position. During the 1994 elections, there was a national Republican landslide—a backlash against President Clinton's overreaching national health care program and several congressional scandals. Voters elected a Republican majority in Congress. Nowhere in the country were the tremors from the Republican landslide more strongly felt than in North Carolina—where there was no statewide race to shield the Democrats from the national GOP tide. Overnight, the state's U.S. House delegation went from eight Democrats and four Republicans to eight Republicans and four Democrats. The GOP also won control of the N.C. House for the first time in the twentieth century, changing from a 78 to 42 Democratic majority to a 68 to 52 Republican majority. The N.C. Senate narrowly remained Democratic by a 26 to 24 margin, although the GOP achieved a thirteen-seat gain. This proved to be the high-water mark in the General Assembly and Congress for the North Carolina Republican Party in the twentieth century.

Hunt shifted quickly to his right. When the Republicans proposed a major tax cut, Hunt trumped them by proposing and pushing through the

Governor Jim Hunt congratulates former governor Terry Sanford
at Sanford's eightieth birthday party in Durham, 1997.
(Photograph by John Rottet; courtesy of the *Raleigh News and Observer*)

legislature the largest tax cut in Tar Heel history—a move he later said was a mistake when the state hit a recession at the start of the twenty-first century. He also co-opted the Republicans by seizing the issue of welfare reform—requiring people to get off public assistance and helping them get back into the workforce. When Hunt gave his State of the State Address to the General Assembly in 1995, Republicans jokingly asked who would give the Democratic response.

While many Democrats openly scoffed at his ideological gymnastics, Hunt proved to be a Democratic firewall, preventing a complete Republican sweep of the state. In 1996 Hunt easily won reelection. Under Hunt's leadership, the Democrats edged their way back from the precipice. In 1996 the party took back two of the congressional seats they had lost. And in 1998, they won back control of the N.C. House.

With Dixie becoming an increasingly Republican bastion, Hunt showed southern Democrats how to win with carefully calibrated appeals to both the rural whites he grew up with and African Americans. In doing so, Hunt paved the way for a new generation of Democrats, most notably Senator John Edwards and Governor Mike Easley.

There had been dynasties in North Carolina politics before—the Simmons Machine and the Shelby Dynasty. But in many ways, Hunt was a one-man dynasty, dominating Tar Heel politics for a generation. Hunt mastered the old-time politics of courting powerful, cigar-smoking courthouse bosses, winning over city machines in black neighborhoods, and providing political patronage to highway workers. But by the time he returned to power in 1993, North Carolina's politics had changed, becoming more urban, sophisticated, and television-oriented—and more Republican. When Hunt first was elected governor, Democrats had a 3-to-1 edge in voter registration. By the time he left, the Democratic advantage had melted to a 1.5-to-1 margin.[27]

Hunt learned to operate in that environment as well. He patched together coalitions of Democratic-leaning interest groups, including teachers, organized labor, and African American leaders. But he also reached out to the executives of Charlotte banks, the high-tech companies of the Research Triangle Park, and other business leaders—many of whom helped Hunt raise the more than $30 million he needed to finance his campaigns.

Hunt kept the Democratic Party from going under during a Republican tide by his political skills, ideological nimbleness, and the fact that he never stopped working. But even as he became more conservative, Hunt remained committed to his central goals of improving North Carolina's public schools, enforcing civil rights, and bringing in new jobs. "Jim Hunt's achievement was to figure out how to survive in the changing economy and the changing political landscape of the South and still remain a Democrat," said Ferrel Guillory, director of the Program on Southern Politics, Media and Public Life at the University of North Carolina at Chapel Hill. "He picked his spots. He broadened his base. Yet he remained a Democrat."[28]

chapter 8 **Phoenix Rising**

arvey Gantt was one of the few black racial pioneers for whom Jesse Helms had kind words.

Gantt, a native of Charleston, South Carolina, made national headlines when he enrolled at Clemson University in 1963, becoming the first black student to attend a white public college in South Carolina. Three months earlier, rioting had erupted when James Meredith had integrated the University of Mississippi. To avoid a repetition, 200 police set up roadblocks around Clemson to keep out troublemakers. Gantt's enrollment drew 150 reporters, and the twenty-year-old transfer student was soon giving interviews on network television and to national magazines.

In a WRAL-TV editorial, Helms praised Gantt's behavior, especially in comparison with that of Meredith. "If ever a man put his best foot forward, Harvey Gantt has done so," Helms said. "His conduct will not cause South Carolinians to relish court orders relating to integration. But he has done a great deal, probably more than he himself realizes, to establish respectful communications across sensitive barriers in human relations."[1]

Gantt's rise in politics says much about how North Carolina had changed. By 1990, North Carolina was squarely in the country's economic mainstream. The median income in North Carolina was $37,604, compared to the U.S. average of $42,765. North Carolina's poverty rate was nearly identical to the national average. The state now had a slight urban majority.[2]

Just as importantly, attitudes toward race had shifted with integration of the schools and workplaces. In a state without big cities, Charlotte had developed into the largest metropolitan area of the Carolinas. It is a city with a lot of commercial hustle and swagger, and boasts some of the largest skyscrapers in the South. By the end of the century, only New York was a bigger banking center.

Charlotte saw itself as a Sun Belt dynamo that was moving beyond the old politics. In some ways, Charlotte liked to view itself as the informal capital of the Carolinas—with Raleigh and Columbia, South Carolina, mere government outposts. And it attracted some of the brightest people of the region. Among them was Gantt. After graduating with a degree in architecture from Clemson and obtaining a master's degree in urban planning from the Massachusetts Institute of Technology, Gantt started North Carolina's first racially integrated architectural firm in Charlotte.

Gantt fit right in with Charlotte's influential business community. He was an articulate, upbeat professional with a Volvo in his driveway and a tennis court in his backyard. With the backing of the city's white business establishment, Gantt was appointed to the Charlotte City Council in 1975 before being elected in 1983 as mayor of the Republican-leaning city that was 75 percent white. During his two terms as mayor of North Carolina's largest city, Gantt championed downtown redevelopment and helped bring a National Basketball Association team to the city.

Seeking a third term as mayor in 1987, Gantt was defeated by Republican Sue Myrick, a future member of Congress. She criticized Gantt for not doing enough to ease traffic congestion and also attacked him for using his race and political position to gain a license to start a Charlotte television station—an issue that would come back to haunt Gantt again.

Despite his reelection defeat, Gantt was buoyed in 1989 by the election of Virginia governor Douglas Wilder as the first African American governor in the nation's history. Gantt decided to challenge Helms the following year. The fact that a black man could be a serious U.S. Senate candidate in the 1990s showed just how much the political terrain had changed since George White left Congress in 1901, predicting that blacks, "Phoenix-like," would rise again.

The Reentry of Blacks into Politics

The rising would take decades because of the literacy test passed by the voters in an election marked by violence and voter intimidation. Although ostensibly aimed at illiterate blacks, the constitutional amendment was used to bar most African Americans—from illiterate tenant farmers to college professors—from voting. Whether a black person passed the literacy test depended on the interpretation of the white registrar.

Registrars could make the literacy test as difficult or as easy as they liked. The literacy tests were most rigorously applied in the eastern counties with the largest black populations. A survey of county registration officials by the North Carolina Advisory Committee to the U.S. Commission on Civil Rights in 1961 found the most difficult literacy tests were administered in the rural eastern counties of Bertie, Camden, Currituck, Franklin, Gates, Greene, Halifax, Northampton, and Warren. "Some county registrars in North Carolina reported that they administered literary tests which included such requirements as the taking of oral dictation, extensive reading aloud, and answering questions on the meaning of words and phrases," the committee reported. "Others settled for an ability to fill out an application form properly and to sign one's name. Several county registration officials reported that they did not enforce the constitutionally required literacy test at all."[3]

In Franklin County, a black person seeking to register was asked to define "habeas corpus." In Bertie County, blacks were disqualified for spelling or punctuation errors. One black woman failed the literacy test when she mispronounced the words "contingency" and "constitutionality" in reading the state constitution.

Henry Frye, a future chief justice of the N.C. Supreme Court and an African American, had just been mustered out of the Air Force as a second lieutenant and admitted to the law school at the University of North Carolina when he entered the municipal building of his hometown of Ellerbe in Richmond County on August 25, 1956. "You had to be able to read and write to the satisfaction of the registrar," Frye said. "Some registrars were very hard to satisfy."[4]

Frye was asked to name five signers of the Declaration of Independence and the twelfth president of the United States. Presumably, if Frye had been able to answer those questions, there would have been others. Several weeks later, after Frye complained, the local political boss allowed Frye to register.

Nor did blacks who were arbitrarily denied the rights of citizenship have much recourse in the courts. After being denied registration, two black Iredell County schoolteachers in 1936 sued the county and the board of elections. In upholding the literacy test, the N.C. Supreme Court attributed the state's progress in education during the first third of the century to the disfranchisement of black voters. "It would not be amiss to say that the constitutional amendment providing for an educational test brought light out of darkness as to education for all the people of the state. Religious, educational, and material uplift went forward by leaps and bounds," the court said.[5]

As late as 1965, Jesse Helms was still defending the use of literacy tests.

The real question, Helms said, "is whether illiterates ought to be allowed to vote. And that raises the question of what kind of politician is likely to benefit from a system in which people who cannot possibly understand their responsibility are allowed and encouraged to register and vote without question."[6]

In 1964 Congress passed the Voting Rights Act, outlawing literacy tests in areas with a history of discrimination, and in 1970 it extended the ban everywhere. At the urging of Frye, the first black elected to the N.C. General Assembly in the twentieth century, a referendum repealing the literacy test was placed on the ballot in 1970. But voters rejected the constitutional amendment. At the end of the twentieth century, the literacy test was still part of North Carolina's constitution, even though it was no longer enforceable.

While the literacy test was the chief means of denying the ballot to black North Carolinians, there were other devices as well. Local election boards often kept irregular or very restricted hours, making it difficult for people to register to vote. North Carolina had a poll tax until 1920. While much of the South excluded blacks from all-white Democratic primaries, North Carolina allowed optional all-white local Democratic primaries until the practice was abandoned in 1930—fourteen years before the U.S. Supreme Court ruled such primaries to be unconstitutional.

Despite the impediments, North Carolina allowed far more blacks to register and vote than most southern states. That was particularly true in the cities, where there was a more tolerant attitude toward black voting and where white political dominance was not threatened.

North Carolina practiced a form of gradualism, slowly extending the right to vote to black residents well before Congress passed a second Voting Rights Act in 1965, outlawing racial discrimination in voter registration. In 1940 an estimated 10 percent of voting-age African Americans were registered to vote in North Carolina. Only Tennessee had a higher percentage among southern states. Black registration in North Carolina increased to 14 percent in 1947, 18 percent in 1952, 24 percent in 1956, 32 percent in 1958, 38 percent in 1960, and 47 percent in 1964.[7]

In North Carolina's cities, African Americans were able to run for political office during the first half of the twentieth century, although they had no chance of winning. In 1919 Calvin Lightner, a funeral-home operator, whose son would become the first black mayor of Raleigh fifty-four years later, ran for Raleigh City Council, as did two other black Raleigh residents.

In North Carolina's cities, even though they had white majorities, blacks began making their reentry into politics. The first signs of the rising were in the 1930s and 1940s, when African Americans began to organize politically in cities such as Raleigh, Durham, Greensboro, Winston-Salem, and Charlotte, forming civic committees to press for action on issues important to the black community. In 1947 Kenneth R. Williams, a black minister and professor at historically black Winston-Salem State College, was elected to the Winston-Salem Board of Alderman. He was the first black candidate in the twentieth-century South to outpoll a white candidate in a city election. By 1953 Greensboro, Fayetteville, Durham, Wilson, Gastonia, and Chapel Hill had African Americans on their councils.[8]

But it was not until congressional passage of the Voting Rights Act of 1965—placing the power of the federal government behind black voting rights—that African Americans began to succeed on the statewide level. By 1966, statewide voter registration was 14.5 percent black, by 1976 it was 15.5 percent, and by the end of the century it was 19.1 percent.

In 1966, Henry Frye, then a thirty-four-year-old Greensboro lawyer, ran for the N.C. House and lost. Two years later, Frye tried again and was elected. At the end of the century, there were twenty-four blacks in the 120-member state legislature, many of them representing black majority districts created as a result of the Voting Rights Act.

Howard Lee was elected mayor of Chapel Hill, a liberal college town, in 1969. In a more striking development, Clarence Lightner, a black mortician and city councilman, in 1973 was elected mayor of Raleigh—a city where blacks composed only 16 percent of the electorate. From 1970 until the end of the century, the number of black elected officials in North Carolina grew from 62 to 498.

The early election of blacks to public office was often cited as another sign of North Carolina's progressive tradition. But it was a thin veneer of liberalism. Lee failed to capture the Democratic nomination for lieutenant governor. Lightner was defeated for reelection after his family was touched by scandal. Nevertheless, he had paved the way for Gantt.

Helms and Race

The Helms-Gantt races caught the imagination of the country. By the 1990s, the South's other leading segregationist politicians had either passed from the scene, modified their politics (like South Carolina senator Strom Thurmond), or apologized for their past views (like former Alabama governor George Wallace). While Helms may have toned down his rhetoric from his days on WRAL-TV, he was one of the last national figures still willing to sing "Dixie" in the ear of a black colleague.

Throughout his political career, Helms reacted angrily whenever a reporter brought up his use of race. But it is hard to imagine Helms's career without race anymore than one could consider Senator Furnifold Simmons's career without white supremacy.

Helms's political baptism was the Smith-Graham Senate race in 1950, where he participated in one of the most racist campaigns in state history. Whether Helms was a bit player or an important behind-the-scenes strategist—and the debate still continues more than a half century later—is nearly irrelevant. When it came to race, Helms hardly hid his segregationist views.

When he was editing the *Tarheel Banker*, Helms argued that the public school system would collapse if the courts forced white and black children to attend the same schools. When federal troops were sent to enforce the desegregation of Little Rock's Central High School in 1957, Helms wrote: "What is happening in America is exactly in tune with the forecasts of Karl Marx. The America which should be concerned by the curtain of Communism falling throughout the world is, instead, ripping itself to shreds over a false and completely phony issue called 'integration.' The cackles you hear have a Russian accent."

Helms seemed to embrace the views of racial superiority. In 1967 statistics showed a high percentage of North Carolina draftees were rejected for the draft for mental reasons. Helms said most of those who flunked were black. "No intelligent Negro citizen should be insulted by a reference to this very plain fact of life," Helms said. "It is time to face, honestly and sincerely, the purely scientific statistical evidence of natural racial distinction in group intellect."[9]

During his Senate career, Helms managed never to find a civil rights bill that met with his approval. In 1982 he staged a filibuster against an extension of the Voting Rights Act, even though it was supported by seventy-five senators and endorsed by President Reagan. Helms sponsored bills that would have banned court-ordered busing for racial integration. He was a major backer of the apartheid regimes in South Africa and Rhodesia (now called Zimbabwe). For years, he blocked efforts to put a black judge on the conservative, all-white Fourth U.S. Circuit Court of Appeals in Richmond, Virginia, prompting President Clinton to call his actions "outrageous."

Helms frequently targeted black political figures. During his 1978 reelection effort, his favorite foil was the U.S. ambassador to the United Nations,

Andrew Young, the highest-ranking black in government. At political rallies in eastern North Carolina, Helms drew out Young's title in mock reverence: "Am-bas-sa-dor Andrew Young." Recovering from a back operation, Helms said he had received a get-well card from Young. "He [Young] said some of his African friends wanted to have me for dinner."[10]

In 1983, when Helms was in the deepest political trouble of his political career, he led a four-day fight in the Senate against making Martin Luther King Jr.'s birthday a national holiday. Helms filed suit asking the federal government to open raw FBI files on King, which had been sealed for fifty years. Helms continued to campaign against King throughout his political career.

During his 1984 reelection campaign, Helms repeatedly tied Hunt to the Reverend Jesse Jackson, reprinting in campaign literature a photograph of Hunt meeting with Jackson. The literature included such messages as "Jesse Jackson All Out to Help Hunt" or "Jackson-Hunt Voter Drive Threatens Reagan-Helms." One Helms fund-raising letter mentioned Jackson's name twenty-four times. Another warned: "Yes. Black voting power is spreading like wildfire."[11]

During his two races against Gantt, Helms once again stressed issues that touched on the great American divide, such as racial quotas. As he prepared for his 1990 reelection campaign, Helms's organization asked for donations to offset a "massive bloc voter registration drive. . . . Reverend Jesse Jackson will soon have thousands of Rainbow Coalition 'activists' roaming the streets of virtually every small town in North Carolina registering thousands of anti-Helms voters just like he did in 1984 when he registered over 100,000 voters to defeat Jesse Helms."[12]

Helms's segregationist views in the 1960s reflected those of a majority of white North Carolinians, according to public opinion polls. But in the years following, Helms gave little indication that his views had evolved. Helms seemed at times to be a walking sandwich board for racial insensitivity. In 1993 Senator Carol Moseley Braun, a Democrat from Illinois and the first black woman elected to the Senate, objected to a Helms amendment extending a congressional patent on using the Confederate flag on the emblem of the United Daughters of the Confederacy. Riding on a Capitol elevator with Helms, she recalled, "He started to sing, 'I wish I was in the land of cotton.' . . . And he looked at Sen. [Orrin] Hatch and said, 'I'm going to make her cry. I'm going to sing "Dixie" until she cries.'" Helms later said he was just teasing her, and that Moseley-Braun had laughed about it in the elevator but turned it into a controversy for political purposes.[13]

Helms often bristled when questioned about the use of race in his political campaigns. When the author wrote a newspaper story in 1989 that catalogued his use of race, Helms declined to talk to the author for several years. Like many of his generation, Helms points to his personal relationships with many black people. But Helms seemed to get along best with black people who were in subservient roles, such as the elevator operators around the Capitol. He notes that when his office helped people with their constituent problems, it did not ask their race. "I have repeatedly suggested to numerous reporters that they interview blacks who know me," Helms wrote in a letter to the author. "Ask them whether I am a 'racist.' Ask the blacks who work in and with the United States Senate. No reporter or editor for the *News and Observer* has been willing to do that."[14]

But Helms critics dismissed such sentiments. "The Helms reply to accusations of racism is a vow of admiration and respect for blacks," wrote Claude Sitton, editor of the *News and Observer*. "And why not? That was a stock in trade of Southern segregationists. The reply assumed, of course, that the listener well knew that these sentiments extended only to the Uncle Toms who shuffled off the sidewalk when Miss Ann walked by and who came, hat in hand, to Mr. Charlie's back door when looking for a handout."[15]

There have been numerous incidents that occurred in Helms's personal life that raised questions about his views on the white/black divide. He opposed the racial integration of his church, First Baptist Church, in the 1960s, although it should be noted that the incident involved a civil rights activist who was testing the church's policies rather than someone genuinely wanting to join the congregation. When a *Charlotte Observer* reporter and photographer visited him in his Raleigh home for an interview during the 1984 Senate campaign, Helms quickly pulled an illustration off the wall of his den. "That'll get me in trouble," he said. The picture showed a black man in a rocking chair on the veranda of a plantation, sipping a mint julep and saying, "This is what me and Martin Luther had in mind."[16]

Helms was one of the last senators to hire blacks on his staff, although undoubtedly there was a small pool of blacks who would have felt comfortable working for a conservative with his history on race. In 1983 Helms hired a black typist to work on his Senate Agriculture Committee staff. It was only after the 1984 election, when he had been in office more than twelve years, that he hired his first black professional, Claude Allen, his young campaign press secretary, to work on the Senate Foreign Relations Committee. Allen would later become White House domestic advisor under President George W. Bush. During his 1990 reelection campaign, Helms hired an increasingly eccentric James Meredith on his Senate staff. Meredith was forced out shortly after Helms beat Gantt.

In 1995, during a rare appearance on a nationally televised talk show, Helms was unexpectedly confronted with raw racial feelings. On the Larry King show broadcast on the CNN network—that night guest hosted by conservative columnist Robert Novak—an unidentified caller told Helms that "you should get a Nobel Peace Prize for everything you've done to help keep down the niggers." Nearly every political figure of note in America in the 1990s, liberal or conservative, would have denounced such language and vigorously denied any such intent. But Helms was a man whose views were fixed in a different era, and one who seemed to have a tin ear for modern sensibilities. This was how the conversation went:

NOVAK: "Oh dear."
HELMS: "Whoops. Well, thank you, I think."
NOVAK: "Ha, ha, ha."
HELMS: "Ha, ha, ha."
NOVAK: "That was the bad word. That was politically incorrect. Can you, we really don't condone that kind of language though, do we?"
HELMS: "No, no, no."
NOVAK: "Absolutely."
HELMS: "No. My father didn't condone it. When I was a little boy one of the worst spankings I ever got is when I used that word and I don't think I've used it ever since."
NOVAK: "And you had African Americans on your staff a long time ago, didn't you? As I remember."
HELMS: "Yep. I hired several. But during the Bush and Reagan administrations every time I would hire one they would take him away from me, you know, because they wanted them to be able to say that they had them. But I don't hire anybody because of race or anything else. I hire them on the basis of ability and dedication."[17]

Helms never apologized for supporting segregation. The institution, he once remarked, was right for its time. He maintained throughout his life that the civil rights movement was unnecessary. "I don't think that forced desegregation would work, and it hasn't worked," Helms said in a 1999 interview with UNC-TV. "It is not working today and you can look around you and see what is happening. The worst sin of the federal government was getting into private business. And that did not work. And then came affirmative action, which is not fair to anybody. What I am saying is that government cannot enforce, nor should it try to dictate human relations."[18]

If Helms ever had any reservations about government dictating human relations during the days of segregation, he did not voice it.

Whenever black voters in North Carolina were asked at election time what they thought about Helms, their answer was always loud and clear. "All his public life, he has done and said things offensive to blacks, and to anyone sensitive to racial nuance," wrote Ernest B. Furgurson, his biographer. "He does them, says them, and eventually people complain. He either denies his action or its racial intent. But he never says he is sorry. Instead, he turns around and does it again, and the process is repeated, over and over. Its effect is to assure those whose base motive is race that while he has to be polite and deny those accusations in public, down deep he is one of them. It is one reason why Helms has won every election he has ever run."[19]

Helms-Gantt

The North Carolina Democratic Party had moved considerably to the left by the 1990s, partly because so many conservatives had fled to the Republican Party and because of the influence of African American voters, who tended to see a greater need for government programs. To capture the nominations in 1990 and again in 1996, Gantt defeated two respected white moderates—Mike Easley, a small-town district attorney who would later become governor, and Charles Sanders, the retired chairman of one of the nation's largest drug companies. Both Easley and Sanders were backed by much of the white liberal establishment, including Terry Sanford, who felt a black man could not defeat Helms.

The Helms-Gantt races were once again national media circuses. The Old South/New South story lines were obvious. Gantt kept the drama alive by running smart, tough campaigns, raising $15.7 million from liberals across the country during his two races. (Helms raised $32.2 million.) Through much of the 1990 race, Gantt made Helms defend his votes against education and environmental legislation.

With his grandfatherly appearance and gray-flecked hair, Gantt was a candidate with considerable crossover appeal to whites. Gantt projected an upbeat attitude, which contrasted with the sense of anger that was never far from Helms. African Americans sometimes complained that Gantt was too middle-class to easily connect with the average black voter. Gantt seemed uncomfortable with emotional appeals favored by some black politicians and preachers. But he reminded black voters that he once lived in a public housing project as a child. A member of his church choir, Gantt sometimes sang solos while visiting black churches.

Gantt was civilly received wherever he campaigned. "I expected more heckling," Gantt said. "I didn't get it. I remember walking into boat shows or greasy spoon restaurants in small towns in North Carolina where I didn't expect to get a single vote, but it was just curiosity for me to talk to people and shake hands. Folks treated me like a celebrity—and told me right away how they disagreed with me and were going to vote for Helms—but they were civil about it."[20]

Gantt portrayed Helms as an ideological crusader whose causes were irrelevant to the interests of the average North Carolinian. "Mr. Helms seems to be more interested in what's going on in Mozambique, Argentina and Chile and in El Salvador than he is about what is going on with the tobacco farmers in the east, the textile workers in the Piedmont and the apple growers in the west," Gantt said.[21]

Both sides created national networks, with Helms turning to Washington and Gantt to Hollywood. The first President George Bush raised more than a $1 million for Helms at a Charlotte fund-raiser. The president characterized Helms as a defender of small-town values. "For 18 years," Bush said, "Jesse Helms has done his duty, acting as a U.S. Senator to protect what Mayberry's Aunt Bea of the beloved *Andy Griffith Show* called, 'home and people's feelings and how they grew up.'"[22]

Gantt countered Helms's political power with celluloid celebrity. Actor Christopher Reeve held a fund-raiser for Gantt in New York City. Actor Paul Newman and his wife, actress Joanne Woodward, hosted another New York fund-raiser. Also anteing up for Gantt were comedian Bill Cosby, actors Gregory Peck and Danny Glover, singer Barbara Streisand, playwright Edward Albee, and astronomer and TV personality Carl Sagan. At the close of a Broadway performance of the Tennessee Williams play *Cat on a Hot Tin Roof*, actress Kathleen Turner asked if there were any North Carolinians in the audience, and if so would they vote against Helms? A number of well-known artists, including Roy Lichtenstein and Robert Rauschenberg, gave money to defeat Helms.

One key reason why Hollywood and artists disliked Helms was because of his opposition to federal arts funding. Helms spoke for many when he criticized the use of tax dollars to subsidize such works as Andres Serrano's photograph "Piss Christ," featuring the image of a crucifix submerged in a liquid that looked like urine. At a political rally at the Carolina Tobacco

Senate candidate Harvey Gantt campaigns at UNC–Chapel Hill, 1996.
(Photograph by Jim Bounds; courtesy of the *Raleigh News and Observer*)

Warehouse in Goldsboro, Helms had some advice for a San Francisco woman who wrote a letter to the senator to tell him she threw up at every mention of Helms's name: "I wrote her back and said . . . [t]he next time it happens, frame it and send it to the National Endowment for the Arts, and they'll give you $5,000."[23]

There was also a bit of prudery in Helms's politics. A Helms aide once called the Shakespeare Theater at the Folger Library in Washington, D.C., after viewing a performance of *The Merry Wives of Windsor*. She wanted to know whether she correctly heard the word "erection" in act 3, scene 5, and, if so, was that part of Shakespearean text or the director's addition? She was assured that it was the words of the Bard. ("She does so take on with her men; they mistook their erection.")[24]

The twin issues of tax-funded art and homosexuality came together in the works of Robert Mapplethorpe, providing Helms with a potent political issue. Mapplethorpe had received a $30,000 grant from the National Endowment for the Arts to help put on an exhibition of his work in Washington, D.C., which included homoerotic and sadomasochistic photographs. The exhibition featured photos of male genitals, a partially exposed young girl, and a young boy standing naked in a chair. Helms was sure Main Street, church-going North Carolina would be repulsed by such art and wouldn't want their tax money subsidizing it. He waged a highly publicized campaign in Congress to bar federal funding for art deemed "obscene or indecent" or which "denigrates, debases or reviles" people's religious beliefs.

Most of his constituents almost certainly agreed with Helms. But as in so many cases, he carried the issue to extremes. At some campaign functions, Helms aides carried black notebooks filled with Mapplethorpe's art and invited the men, but not the women, to have a peek. "If you think I'm shooting bull . . . you men step up here and take one look at the pictures here," Helms said after a barbecue dinner in a gym in Burlington. "You'll be sick."[25] For Helms, it was a matter of convincing people of the rightness of his position. But it also made Helms look like a zealot. An angry Tom Ellis, his chief strategist, went behind the senator's back and ordered campaign aides to stop carrying the Mapplethorpe books to rallies and fund-raisers.

Perhaps no member of Congress was more dismissive of the movement by homosexuals to gain acceptance in society than Helms. He frequently railed against homosexuals as "disgusting" and "unnatural," described them as "sodomites," and warned that the "sodomy crowd" was opposing his reelection. "We have got to call a spade a spade and a perverted human being a perverted human being," Helms told the Senate in 1987. Helms fought the appointment of openly gay persons to high public office. He forced President Clinton to withdraw his nomination of Robert Hormel as ambassador to Fiji because Hormel was a homosexual. He opposed a gay activist for a position in the Department of Housing and Urban Development, saying: "She's not your garden-variety lesbian. She's a militant-activist-mean lesbian, working her whole career to advance the homosexual agenda. Now you think I'm going to sit still and let her be confirmed by the Senate? If you want to call me a bigot, go ahead."[26]

Helms fought additional public-health funding to deal with the AIDS epidemic that was especially widespread among homosexuals. He tried to block the distribution of syringes to prevent the spread of AIDS and backed a bill that would eliminate confidentiality in AIDS testing. He sought to cut off federal funding to school systems that used curricula that placed homosexuality in a positive light. He succeeded in adding AIDS to a list of diseases for which immigrants can be denied entry to the United States, and he made it a crime for people who know they have AIDS to donate blood or organs.

Two Raleigh mothers who lost their sons to AIDS ran a highly publicized campaign against Helms in 1996 called Mothers Against Jesse in Congress, or MAJIC. Gay organizations launched independent efforts against Helms in both 1990 and 1996. Gay activists often played into Helms's hands with their own stridency. In 1991 gay activists launched a fifteen-foot balloon in the shape of a condom over his Arlington, Virginia, home to tastelessly protest his opposition to AIDS research. His feud with the gay community was political gravy for Helms. It not only helped Helms raise money, but in culturally conservative North Carolina it also was the perfect wedge issue to attract conservative Democrats. "Gantt has run fund-raising ads in gay newspapers," said one Helms ad. "Gantt has raised thousands of dollars in gay and lesbian bars in San Francisco, New York and Washington. And Harvey Gantt has promised to back mandatory gay-rights laws."[27]

Gantt responded to the attacks by saying that Helms must create a bogey-man. "If this were 25 years ago, he'd be talking about blacks," Gantt said. "If this were 18 years ago, he'd be talking about the communists or those civil rights agitators. This year, it's artists, architects and maybe extreme liberals. Somehow we've got to make them terrible people, bad people to be with. Homosexuals: bad people. That's nothing new. I think the public sees through that."[28]

The Helms campaign, in fact, was becoming increasingly nervous about the election. Helms supporters had taken the election too lightly. There seemed little excitement or interest in the country bars or conservative churches. Gantt kept up a barrage of criticisms of Helms's record, depicting him as the foe of the environment, education, and health care. On October 20, the *Charlotte Observer* published a poll showing Gantt leading by a 49 to 41 percent margin. It was a wake-up call to the Helms campaign.

Close Call

Always wary of the news media, the Helms campaign became almost paranoid. It declined to disclose the senator's campaign appearances, prompting the Associated Press to issue a request to its member newspapers to help track Helms's campaign stops. The Helms campaign only responded to questions from reporters that were submitted in writing.

Helms's internal campaign polls never showed Gantt in the lead. But the race was uncomfortably close. "Helms has always had this trouble," said Castellanos, Helms's media consultant. "North Carolina is a state that is changing out from under him in many ways. There is a generation growing up in the state that doesn't know him. And on some cultural issues, [it] has not shared his views. There are people coming in the Research Triangle and other parts of the state from the North and other places who do not share his views."[29]

Communism had collapsed in Eastern Europe with the Soviet Union, and Helms's image as a cold warrior no longer seemed as important. The Helms campaign also seemed uncertain about how to run against a black man.

About ten days before the 1990 election, four of Helms's top advisors—Ellis, Wrenn, and TV consultants Castellanos and Earl Ashe—gathered in a hotel room in the Washington suburb of Alexandria to find the silver bullet that would defeat Gantt. The Helms advisors produced two new TV ads, both raising questions about governmental favoritism toward African Americans. But the ads needed to start right away if they were to have time to penetrate the consciousness of North Carolina voters. Ashe's late-night flight from Dulles Airport was canceled at the last minute, and the ads had already been checked with the luggage. This produced the midnight ride to save Helms's political career that has become folklore in conservative circles. Ellis took copies of the ads, rented a limousine—unheated as it turned out—and was driven back to Raleigh. By 6 A.M. Ellis was back in

Raleigh, and by noon the new ads were at North Carolina television stations.

One TV ad dealing with racial quotas became perhaps the best-known political commercial in North Carolina history. The ad featured a pair of white hands crumbling a job application as the announcer says: "You needed that job, and you were the best qualified. But they had to give it to a minority because of a racial quota. Is that really fair? Harvey Gantt says it is. Gantt supports Ted Kennedy's racial quota law that makes the color of your skin more important than your qualifications. You'll vote on this issue next Tuesday. For racial quotas: Harvey Gantt. Against racial quotas: Jesse Helms."

The chief architect of the ad was Castellanos, whose parents had fled Cuba after Castro's takeover. He had grown up in Harnett County, attended UNC–Chapel Hill as a National Merit Scholar, and soon thereafter had joined the staff of the National Congressional Club. Later he became one of the best-known Republican political consultants in the country, working for several presidential campaigns. Castellanos filmed the racial-quota ad himself, after he decided to use the hands of his cameraman—with his plaid shirt and wedding ring—in the ad. Asked about the ad several years later, Castellanos dismissed the idea that it was intended to appeal to white prejudices. "It was easier for me to do that ad than someone else because I don't feel any tremendous racial guilt about that," Castellanos said, noting that he is Hispanic. "I think it's bullshit basically. It's just real simple. If it's wrong for people to discriminate it's wrong for government. And Harvey Gantt says no."[30]

The national news media played the ad over and over again and portrayed it as the commercial that saved Helms's career. Gantt said the racial-quota ad cost him the race. But Helms's advisors say the quota commercial was only mildly successful and ran for just three nights. "The hands ad got everybody all stirred up," Ellis said. "But that is not what did it. The mileage we got was: 'How did Harvey Gantt become a millionaire?'"[31]

Helms advisors said the commercial that saved Helms career was the second ad produced in the Alexandria hotel room, which aired three times as often as the quota ad. Gantt was part of a group of mainly white investors that sought a Federal Communications Commission license to start a TV station in Charlotte that later merged with a minority-owned group. Four months after the newly merged group won the license in 1985, the station was sold to Capital Broadcasting Company, the company that owned

Helms's old station in Raleigh. The Helms ad charged that Gantt had used his minority status and his position as mayor to make a bundle of money. Gantt denied the charge, saying the group was awarded the FCC license not because of race but because in the end it was the only applicant.

At the beginning of the campaign, Helms promised "that some heads will be cracked if anything is done that even appears to be racist." But Helms had said that when he was confident that he could win easily against a black opponent. Now that the race was tight, Helms was once again using racial cues. Helms's campaign fund-raising letters focused on black figures such as Jesse Jackson and Virginia governor Douglas Wilder. One Helms television commercial featured a video of Mel Watt, Gantt's campaign manager (and a future congressman), who is black.

"If you want quotas to dominate and dictate whether you get a job or whether you get a promotion, you vote for Mr. Gantt," Helms told supporters at King's Restaurant in Kinston.[32] The Helms performance played well with C. W. Palmer, eighty-three, a Kinston businessman who attended the campaign lunch. If Gantt were elected, Palmer said, "he'd give it [tax money] away to the hippies, the Jews, the niggers."[33]

In another tactic apparently designed to depress black turnout, the state Republican Party mailed 125,000 postcards into black neighborhoods, warning them of possible voter fraud and providing misleading information about registration. The state GOP later settled a Bush Administration U.S. Justice Department suit, denying any wrongdoing but promising not to use any similar "ballot security" program in the future.

Gantt called Helms a "desperate man" who was using "hate mongering" to win the election. "They are divisive," Gantt said. "They are designed to scare people along the lines of race. I'm going to let the people of North Carolina judge whether Senator Helms is a racist or not."[34]

As always, Helms indignantly denied playing the race card in the final days. "Race is not an issue in the campaign," Helms said. "That is a contrivance of the news media, and of Mr. Gantt. What am I supposed to do? I was born white. He was born black. Neither of us had any choice about what we were going to be. But we have not once made a racial issue of it. He has, because he's going around encouraging, pleading for a total bloc vote of the black citizens of this state."[35]

For many people who were raised under segregation, the idea of electing a black person to the Senate was a leap they could not make. "I don't think Gantt is capable," said Thurston Quinn, a seventy-year-old tobacco farmer from Wayne County. "I was born and raised on a farm. I've been around black people all of my life. I know there are some smart black people, but Gantt doesn't strike me as one of them."[36]

North Carolina voters reelected Helms by a 53 to 47 percent margin. But from the election-night speeches, it was hard to know who had won. Helms appeared angry, while Gantt was gracious. But then Helms always played the role of the angry, beleaguered white man surrounded by enemies. "The confederation of liberals has struck out again: the homosexuals, the defenders of pornographic artistry—if you want to call it that—the National Organization for Women, the pro-abortion crowd, the labor union bosses, and the left-wing news media," Helms told the state GOP convention in Wilmington in 1991.[37]

Six years later, in 1996, Gantt once again challenged Helms with the same result, losing to Helms by a 53 to 47 percent margin. Helms twice defeated Gantt because he had the backing of a powerful political organization, because he was a famous incumbent able to raise vast sums of money from a nationwide fund-raising network, because North Carolina had a strong conservative streak, and because of the barriers of race.

Once again, North Carolina's progressive image had been tarnished. How could one square the reelection of an old segregationist still using racial cues with the idea that North Carolina was somehow the South's most forward-thinking state?

Despite Helms's reelection, the Senate race showed that North Carolina had come a long way in racial attitudes. No African American had been elected to the U.S. Senate from the South since Reconstruction. But Gantt won 47 percent of the vote, including more than a third of the white vote against a powerful incumbent senator. Gantt received 150,000 more votes in 1990 than Democrat Terry Sanford had received in 1986 when he was elected to the Senate. Gantt also received 66,026 more votes in the state than did Bill Clinton in 1996.

African Americans would continue to make slow but steady gains. A month after Gantt's defeat, the Democratic caucus of the N.C. House elected state representative Dan Blue, a Raleigh attorney and Terry Sanford protégé, as the first African American House Speaker in the South in the twentieth century. In 1992 Ralph Campbell of Raleigh was elected state auditor. In 1984 former state representative Henry Frye was elected to the N.C. Supreme Court, where Hunt elevated him to chief justice in 1999. But in a highly competitive state, black officials seemed more politically vulnerable than their white counterparts. Blue's photograph was prominently displayed in Republican campaign literature when the GOP captured the N.C. House during the 1994 Republican landslide. In 2000 both Campbell and Frye lost their reelection bids to conservative white Republicans.

Congress

The biggest political advances by blacks were in the courthouses and city halls across North Carolina. Nowhere were the advances more striking than in Warren County, an old tobacco and cotton-belt town along the Virginia border. For decades, Warren County had been ruled by the Kerr family. John Kerr Sr. was a prominent congressman who had coauthored the federal to-bacco price-support program. John Kerr Jr. had been N.C. House Speaker and had played a critical role in creating the N.C. Museum of Art. Both were segregationists in a county dotted with fine old antebellum homes, which had produced more than its share of Confederate generals and where people still talk about the time when Robert E. Lee visited the local grave site of his daughter after the War of Northern Aggression.

But by the 1960s, the black majority had begun pushing for integration of restaurants, stores, and schools. The whites did not give up power easily. Eva Clayton, the wife of a local attorney, was teargassed during a local civil rights march. Her husband's law partner, Frank Ballance, was clubbed by a deputy sheriff. But with the 1965 Voting Rights Act, black voter registration in Warren County climbed—to 33 percent in 1966, 42 percent in 1973, and 52 percent in 1980.

The breakthrough occurred in 1982, when African Americans elected a majority to the board of county commissioners and the new board chose Eva Clayton as its chair. Three blacks were elected to the school board. A black was elected sheriff. And Ballance was elected to the N.C. House. The old Kerr organization was replaced by the black-dominated Warren County Political Action Council. "Free At Last" proclaimed the headline in the *Carolina Times*, a black-oriented newspaper published in Durham.

Blacks had been knocking on the door of Congress for years. But win-ning election to Congress was difficult in North Carolina because black voters were not congregated in major cities as elsewhere in the country, but were scattered in cities, towns, and rural areas. Under pressure from the U.S. Justice Department, which was enforcing the Voting Rights Act, the legislature drew two black majority congressional districts during the re-districting that followed the 1990 census. In 1992 Mel Watt, a Yale-educated attorney and Gantt's 1990 campaign manager, was elected to the newly cre-ated Twelfth district that snaked along the Interstate 85 corridor from Durham to Charlotte. The district drew national ridicule for its strange shape and was made more compact following a challenge that went to the U.S. Supreme Court, but it stood. Watt would become chairman of the national congressional black caucus.

The same year, Eva Clayton was elected to the Congress in the First district in eastern North Carolina—much of it George White's old district. A decade later, when Clayton retired to take a position with the United Nations in Rome, Ballance, one of her chief allies, was elected. But Ballance resigned in the middle of his term and went to prison for misusing state funds while a state legislator. He was replaced by G. K. Butterfield, a black Wilson attorney and former judge. Black political organizations could be as crooked as the old white courthouse machines.

The Congressional Club's Last Hurrah

The 1990s saw the end of the National Congressional Club. After helping to defeat Gantt in 1990, the Congressional Club had one last hurrah. In 1992 the club recruited Lauch Faircloth to run against Democratic senator Terry Sanford.

During his six years in the Senate, Sanford took some provocative positions; most notably, he was a leading voice against the highly popular Persian Gulf War, in which a United States–led coalition expelled an invading Iraqi army from Kuwait. Sanford's Senate career was not marked by the successes of his governorship. His strength was as an executive, where he could order aides to implement his steady stream of ideas. The slow pace and the give-and-take of the legislative branch did not suit Sanford's temperament. Writing in his own private journal near the end of his term, Sanford noted that his Senate tenure paled by comparison to his role as governor. "Its usefulness, its contribution to the nation and the state," Sanford wrote, "was marginal."[38]

Faircloth and Sanford had been friends since the days when they were part of Kerr Scott's political organization. Faircloth, a Clinton businessman, had been one of Sanford's chief money raisers during his 1960 campaign for governor. During the 1960 Sanford campaign—much to the amusement of both men—they even had been forced to double up in the same bed at the home of local Democratic leader T. G. "Sonny Boy" Joyner of rural Northampton County.

When Faircloth unsuccessfully sought the Democratic nomination for governor in 1984, Sanford had helped him raise money. But in 1985, Faircloth wanted to run for the U.S. Senate and felt he had been blindsided when his old friend jumped into the race, forcing him out.

Faircloth, always a conservative Democrat despite his associations with Sanford and the Scotts, switched to the Republican Party and received the Helms organization's backing. Faircloth portrayed Sanford as a big-government liberal while emphasizing his own support for reforming the welfare system—an issue that carried racial connotations for some voters who associated welfare programs with blacks. Sanford's age became a factor when he underwent surgery to replace a defective heart valve in October. He lost to Faircloth by a 50 to 46 percent margin in what was largely a Democratic year.

Sanford never publicly expressed any bitterness about his defeat. For one thing, his private life was so rich. In retirement, Sanford started a second Raleigh law firm, became involved in real estate ventures, raised money for the arts, wrote a book on aging called *Outlive Your Enemies*, and taught at Duke University. When he died, he was working on a novel on a man's journey through the twentieth century.

To the end, Sanford was the grand old man of the Democratic Party. He continued to work the phones, dispensing advice to such political figures as Governor Jim Hunt and future governor Mike Easley—whether they wanted it or not. "I suspect that by now he almost certainly has had his orientation session with the Lord—and it was not a one-way conversation," Hunt said at Sanford's funeral. As Sanford was dying of bone cancer in 1998, Democratic Senate candidate John Edwards visited his sick bed for advice on how to defeat Faircloth. And when Sanford died that April, Edwards used his death as a rallying cry to Democrats that they needed to win back the Senate seat "for Terry." Although Sanford never made it to the White House, his funeral at Duke Chapel on the campus of Duke University resembled a farewell to a president, complete with an honor guard from his beloved old World War II outfit, the Eighty-Second Airborne.

Even as the Congressional Club was electing Faircloth to the Senate, it was beginning to break up. "Jesse ended the club," said Carter Wrenn. "That's a fact. The rest of it is a little bit reading why."[39]

Helms had long been ambivalent about the Congressional Club. He was glad that it raised money and helped reelect him, but he felt uncomfortable with the criticism of its unending stream of direct-mail fund-raising and negative ads. Helms frequently argued with his top lieutenants, and there were periods when Ellis and Helms would not talk, according to Wrenn.

The Congressional Club was nearly constantly in debt; desperate pleas for money were part of its stock in trade. A child of the Depression, Helms had always found the debt unsettling. Shortly before he left his job as an editorialist on WRAL-TV, Helms had fondly recalled that it took former senator Clyde Hoey fifteen years to retire his debt from his 1936 campaign for governor. "Those were the days when men considered it a matter of honor to pay their debts," Helms said in 1971. "In fact, the public looked with distrust upon men who failed to do so. But no longer. It has become fashionable in our time for citizens, including those of high station, to run up debts which they have no notion of paying."[40]

Matters came to a head in early 1991. Helms had instructed his organization not to go into the red in the 1990 race. But with liberal money pouring into North Carolina to help Gantt, the Helms campaign borrowed more than $1 million in the closing weeks—a move that enabled Helms to run the quota and TV-station ads that quite possibly saved Helms's career.

The first sign that there was serious trouble between Helms and the Congressional Club, Wrenn said, was when he received a puzzling and rather tart letter from Helms saying that he had not authorized the campaign to go into debt and that the debt belonged to the club. Helms told Wrenn not to use his name in future club mailings. The Congressional Club had already sent out a fund-raising letter in January 1991 that was signed by Helms. As always, Helms insisted on approving letters that went out under his name, often rewriting them. That spring, the club sent out basically the same letter, changing some of the wording and using Helms's name but not seeking Helms's second approval. "I am not going to have that," Helms said at the time.[41] Helms later remarked: "They had a different agenda from me and it was a broader agenda. I think they were using me and my name to raise money for things that I was not interested in."[42]

Ellis said a misunderstanding caused the break. "Does approving it in January hold over until June?" Ellis asked. "Evidently Carter and Helms had a big [fight] about it and Helms said, 'I'm through signing letters' and that was the end of that thing."[43] Wrenn said Helms never understood how the Congressional Club worked, nor why it was necessary to keep the political organization going between elections, maintaining a permanent staff and raising money through continuous fund-raising.

The final break occurred over a personal squabble involving Helms's daughter, Jane Helms Knox, who lost her job as principal of St. Timothy's Episcopal School in Raleigh. Ellis and Wrenn, who were active in St. Timothy's, had helped Helms's daughter get a job in the school, where she later was promoted to principal. In the early 1990s, there was a spat between Knox and the school's founder. The split divided the church's board, and Ellis and Wrenn decided to support the new church rector in upholding the dismissal of Helms's daughter. "We felt it was the only fair way to resolve this without tearing the school apart," Ellis said. "It worked for the school, but there was no way to explain this to Jesse Helms."[44]

Without their star, the National Congressional Club quickly went into decline. The club tried to hold on by using Faircloth as their chief fundraiser. But Faircloth, upset with the progress on retiring his 1992 campaign debt, soon broke with the club as well.

"We kept the Club going for years," Wrenn said. "But basically it was like having an army that you could no longer afford to support. We were continually cutting back and dying on the vine."

The powerful political machine had self-destructed. The machine had been running low on fuel for years because direct-mail fund-raising from conservatives had fallen off. With Republicans in the White House from 1981 to 1993, there was less reason for conservative contributors to believe the appeals that feminists, gays, and black activists were about to storm the gates.

The breakup occurred at a time when the Congressional Club's principal figure, Helms, was in declining health and believed that his political career was winding to a close. He underwent radiation treatment for prostate cancer in the fall of 1991. He had quadruple-bypass heart surgery in 1992. He was also treated for Paget's disease, a bone ailment. About the same time, his wife, Dorothy, had a cancer operation. While Helms was breaking with the Congressional Club, he was also purging his Senate staff. He fired eight aides on his Senate Foreign Relations Committee, including longtime right-hand man James Lucier. Helms also fired the director of the Jesse Helms Center, a museum and research center located near his hometown of Monroe.

"Helms always had the ambivalence about the things that he thought hurt his reputation," Wrenn said. "He got sick and didn't think he would run again and was worried about his legacy and decided to unload all of those things that he thought made him unpopular and tried to create a new, nicer Jesse."[45]

Helms's assumption that 1990 would be his last hurrah changed when his health improved and he realized his dream of becoming chairman of the Senate Foreign Relations Committee in 1995. The senator was reelected in 1996, although this time he did it without the Congressional Club.

Helms's Retirement

By the mid-1990s, Helms was no longer the cutting edge of the conservative movement. He was slowly replaced by a younger generation of conservatives, people such as Congressmen Newt Gingrich of Georgia and Tom Delay of Texas, who defined the outer reaches of American conservatism. With his political machine dismantled, Helms was no longer as feared, either nationally or in North Carolina. And Helms seemed to have slightly mellowed, or at least become a tad less bellicose. But what Helms lost as a conservative movement leader he gained in institutional power. In 1995 after Republicans retook the U.S. Senate, Helms became Foreign Relations Committee chairman—fulfilling an improbable dream.

Helms engaged in his usual conservative crusades as chairman, fighting international treaties against genocide, chemical-weapons testing, and nuclear-weapons testing. He also continued to use his power to block the appointment of his foes. Among the most notable was Republican governor William Weld of Massachusetts, who Helms prevented in 1997 from becoming U.S. ambassador to Mexico during the Clinton administration. But Helms also showed some flexibility, approving the payment of $1 billion in U.S. debt to the United Nations, an organization he had long despised. He became the first U.S. senator to address a meeting of the UN Security Council in 2000. Many of the powerful now paid court to Helms. A steady stream of prominent figures made pilgrimages to speak at Wingate University near his hometown of Monroe, including Secretary of State Madeleine Albright, former secretary of state Henry Kissinger, Supreme Court justice Clarence Thomas, the Dalai Lama (the spiritual leader of Tibet), and former British prime minister Margaret Thatcher. The government of Kuwait contributed $100,000 to the nearby Jesse Helms Center, a museum and research center, and the government of Taiwan gave $225,000.

His Washington office showed how far the son of the Monroe police chief had come. The walls were lined with editorial cartoons lampooning him, as well as personally inscribed photographs from actor John Wayne, Russian novelist Alexander Solzhenitsyn, and evangelist Billy Graham.

While Helms worked with the Democratic administration of Bill Clinton on issues such as reorganizing the State Department, he never lost his tart tongue. Shortly after he assumed the presidency, Clinton took steps to open the doors to homosexuals serving in the military—a move that angered many in the Armed Services. An offhand crack by Helms about the president's unpopularity among the military in 1994 created a national furor.

"Mr. Clinton better watch out if he comes down here," said Helms, alluding to North Carolina's many military bases. "He'd better have a bodyguard."

An outspoken critic of the Clinton administration, he strongly supported efforts to impeach the president during the scandal that grew out of Clinton's affair with White House intern Monica Lewinsky. And yet Helms developed a close working relationship with key Clinton administration figures such as Albright.

With the White House on the defensive, First Lady Hillary Clinton charged on NBC's *Today Show* that there was a "vast right-wing conspiracy" to "get" her husband, singling out North Carolina's senators, Helms and Faircloth, as participants in that conspiracy. Two nights after Hillary Clinton made her charge, Helms attended a state dinner at the White House, for which he had been previously invited. Making his way down the receiving line, Helms quipped to Hillary Clinton: "Right-wing conspiracy reporting, Ma'am. And she said, 'Fool.' And she kissed me on the cheek. You know, you can't argue with people like that."[46]

In 2001 Republican senator James Jeffords of Vermont, angered over some of the conservative policies of President George W. Bush, switched sides, tipping control of the Senate to the Democrats. Helms's loss of the chairmanship of the Senate Foreign Relations Committee was one more reason for him not to seek reelection in 2002. At age eighty, his health was continuing to decline. He used a motorized wheelchair to get around because of peripheral neuropathy, a nerve disease that numbed his feet and affected his balance. Moreover, North Carolina had changed during his three decades in the Senate. Time was taking its toll on his core of conservative Democratic supporters, the Jessecrats. While the state was becoming more Republican, many of the Republicans living in the suburbs of Raleigh, Greensboro, and Charlotte had moved from the North and were moderate in their views on questions of race and on the social issues.

In August 2001 Helms went before the cameras at WRAL-TV in Raleigh— the station where his editorials had made him into a celebrity—and announced his retirement. Helms soon disappeared from the public stage after leaving the Senate, suffering from vascular dementia and other ailments.

Jesse Helms spoke for an older, more rural North Carolina—a place where life revolved around the church and the soil, where the nuclear family was still intact, and where blacks knew their place. It was a place of fierce individualism and deep skepticism toward government.

Helms was both a reliable ally of business and a voice for blue-collar workers and farmers who were suspicious of the social changes sweeping the country—whether it was civil rights, gay rights, or women's rights. Helms channeled conservative Democratic senators Furnifold Simmons, Josiah Bailey, and Sam Ervin Jr. And like those men, on one of the overriding issues of the day—whether this was a democracy for everyone or just the chosen few—Helms was on the wrong side of history.

chapter 9 **White Shirts**

esse Helms and Jim Hunt strolled arm in arm across a lawn one spring day in 1999, like two old friends rather than two aging political warriors who had once tried to destroy each other. Hunt had accepted Helms's invitation to speak at a groundbreaking for the new Jesse Helms Center, a museum and research center honoring Helms near his hometown of Monroe.

Helms and Hunt, the two men who dominated Tar Heel politics during the last three decades of the twentieth century, had learned to accommodate and perhaps even appreciate one another since their bitter Senate race in 1984. Both men had aged since they were first elected to statewide political office in 1972. Hunt's hair had gone gray during his four terms as governor. Helms, nearing the end of his fifth term in the Senate, hobbled along with the aid of a walker. Hunt called Helms "one of the greatest men to come along in our state's history." He called him "a man of honesty, of integrity, of personal courtesy and manners in the finest Southern tradition." Helms recalled their "bipartisan friendship" and their efforts together to recruit industry to the state. "Jim Hunt is a master salesman and a highly respected representative for North Carolina," Helms said.[1]

Neither man anointed a successor when he left office. When it was riding high in the 1980s, Helms's high-tech political organization, the National Congressional Club, could handpick senators. But the machine broke apart in the mid-1990s. The days of the Democratic machines—with their courthouse bosses—had long gone. Democratic dynasty makers such as Furnifold Simmons and O. Max Gardner could determine who would sit in the Executive Mansion. But Hunt, a one-man dynasty, could not. Nor would he try to pick a successor.

The Republicans and Democrats took different paths as they moved forward. The Republicans leapt across the gender line to choose one of the nation's most respected women. The Democrats made the generational shift, becoming the first party to choose members of the post–World War II, baby-boomer generation to lead their party. In both instances, the parties were led by photogenic, made-for-TV political figures who could appeal to the growing number of suburban voters who felt little allegiance to either party.

The health of Helms, the aging gray eminence of the conservative movement, was becoming increasingly precarious. So, in early 2001, the president's men quietly began searching for a successor. The White House's involvement reflected a vacuum that had developed in Tar Heel Republican politics since the mid-1990s: not only had the Helms machine gone out of business, but there was also no Republican governor.

Moving into the vacuum was Karl Rove, the chief political advisor for Republican president George W. Bush. Not since Mark Hanna served as President William McKinley's political strategist at the beginning of the twentieth century had there been such an influential political advisor in the White House. Following one of the closest presidential races in American history in 2000, President Bush had only a one-seat Republican majority in the Senate. The tenuous nature of the GOP's control of the Senate quickly became evident when Republican senator Jim Jeffords of Vermont switched his registration to independent and organized with the Democrats, giving them control of the Senate in May 2001.

When Helms, who was in declining health, announced his retirement in August 2001, the White House had already lined up Elizabeth Dole as his replacement. In recruiting Dole, the White House chose one of the GOP's stars. Dole had held two cabinet posts—secretary of transportation under President Ronald Reagan and secretary of labor under the first President George Bush. She had worked in the White House under four presidents. The Harvard-educated attorney had been president of one of the country's largest institutions, the American Red Cross. And she was married to one of the nation's best-known political leaders, former Senate majority leader Bob Dole. Both she and her husband had run for president.

Beyond her resume, Dole possessed the good looks and charm of the former Duke University beauty queen that she was. Dole was such an accomplished speaker—her trademark was to stroll into the audience with a portable microphone like a television talk show host—that she typically earned $40,000 a speech before the Senate race. Public opinion polls found that she was among the nation's most-respected women. Wherever Dole campaigned—at the state fair, in small-town restaurants, or at country clubs—she was mobbed with well-wishers and autograph seekers. Not even Helms or Hunt drew such crowds.

She also had another powerful factor working for her: gender. In culturally conservative North Carolina, women may have been the foot soldiers in political campaigns, but rarely were they the candidates. North Carolina failed to ratify a constitutional amendment giving women the right to vote in the earlier part of the twentieth century and rejected the Equal Rights Amendment in the later part. Politics, it was often said, was a man's game. Not until 1992, when Eva Clayton, a Democrat, won the First Congressional District seat did North Carolina elect a woman to the U.S. House. (Eliza Pratt, a longtime congressional secretary, was elected to fill out the remaining nine-month term of her Democratic boss, who had died. She served from May 1946 to January 1947 and did not seek election to a full term.) In 1994 Sue Myrick, a Charlotte Republican, was elected to the Ninth Congressional District seat. Elaine Marshall, a Democrat, was elected secretary of state in 1996, the first woman elected to a statewide executive branch position. In 2000 Lieutenant Governor Beverly Perdue and Agriculture Commissioner Meg Scott Phipps, both Democrats, and Labor Commissioner Cherie Berry, a Republican, joined her.

Dole caught the imagination of many of the state's women, attracting large numbers of them everywhere she went. Before female audiences, Dole delivered a soft-edged, self-deprecating feminism—what one might expect if *Ms.* magazine and *Southern Living* magazine were merged into one publication. She talked about a male classmate at Harvard Law School who had asked her why she was taking the space of a man who would actually use his law degree. She recalled how when she was a young Washington, D.C., attorney, a judge sent her down to meet a client in the lockup and she had to brave the jeers of the male inmates. And she recalled how Sandra Day O'Connor had difficulty finding a job after graduating third in her class from Stanford Law School.

"The power of women helping women should never be underestimated," Dole told a campaign luncheon in Cary in September. "We've come a long way, haven't we? But we've got a long way to go."[2]

But Dole was also wary of the feminist label. "I think it depends on how you define the word 'feminist,'" Dole said. "If you are talking about equal rights and equal opportunities—absolutely. My whole career has been spent trying to help women reach their full potential—women and minorities. If you are talking about something like a prepackaged plan handed down by the political correctness club—no."[3]

But if Dole was the Republican Party's dream candidate to replace Helms, there were three unanswered questions about her. Would she be

Senate candidate Elizabeth Dole welcomes kind words from a supporter
at the O. O. Rufty General Store and Market in Salisbury, 2002.
(Photograph by Mel Nathanson; courtesy of the *Raleigh News and Observer*)

regarded as a carpetbagger? Was she conservative enough for Republican primary voters? And was she tough enough for the give-and-take of a major campaign?

Never before had North Carolina political leaders of either party tried to elect to a major public office a candidate who had not lived in the state for forty years. Two years earlier, New York voters had elected another famous woman, former First Lady Hillary Clinton, to the U.S. Senate. But New York is a more transient state that was more likely to be open to newly arrived political candidates.

Dole was born in Salisbury to a well-to-do wholesale florist in 1936. She left the state after graduating from Duke and spent most of her adult life in Washington. She had kept up her home-state ties, frequently visiting relatives and campaigning for GOP candidates, and she was an active Duke alumna.

In the fall of 2001, Dole moved back to her parents' handsome Tudor-style house, settling in with her 100-year-old mother and transferring her voter registration to North Carolina from her husband's home state of Kansas. She dispelled the carpetbagger image by energetically touring all 100 counties.

Dole may have spent decades living in a luxury Watergate condominium in Washington, but she connected to her audiences by frequently talking about her Christian faith. Religion had long been a powerful force in southern politics. Helms's rise to national prominence was due in large part to his alliance with Christian conservatives who believed the country was beset with moral decay. Dole wove religious themes into her stump speeches more than any other major North Carolina politician in recent memory.

"I just want to ask you to be prayer warriors for me in the next seven weeks," Dole told about 700 people at a God and Country Banquet in New Bern sponsored by the Christian Coalition. "Let's be prayer warriors. Just lift me up that I may do God's will, whatever it is."[4]

Her Christian testimony helped reassure conservatives that she was ideologically fit to succeed Helms. Conservatives had been wary of her during her aborted presidential run in 1999, but she moved quickly to her right. She jettisoned her support for gun control that she had voiced while wooing women voters during her presidential campaign. She campaigned as a conservative, supporting partial privatization of Social Security and favoring tax credits for parents who want to send their children to private schools.

Washington insiders questioned whether she had enough grit to engage in a tough political campaign. They had not been impressed by her run for president. She withdrew from the presidential campaign in the fall of 1999 when she failed to compete in money raising with Bush.

During her presidential campaign, Dole often came across as overly scripted and uncomfortable with the give-and-take of political campaigns. Some Democrats thought she was a southern magnolia who would wilt under the heat of a North Carolina campaign.

Dole, in fact, was a lifelong perfectionist who practiced speeches over and over again and didn't like surprises. Her drive for perfection sometimes made Dole look like a martinet—always well rehearsed, always immaculately dressed, and rarely providing an unscripted moment in public. *New York Times* columnist Maureen Dowd dubbed her "Little Miss Perfect," while a Doonesbury political cartoon suggested Dole was such an automaton she had to be "rebooted." Like other virtues, perfectionism could be carried to an extreme. Dole has said she has battled all her life to not let her perfectionism overwhelm her.

Her Democratic opponent was Erskine Bowles, a wealthy Charlotte investment banker from one of North Carolina's more prominent families. His father was Hargrove "Skipper" Bowles, a popular Greensboro businessman who served in the cabinet of Democratic governor Terry Sanford and was the Democratic nominee for governor in 1972. Erskine Bowles had made a name in Washington, working in the Clinton administration as director of the Small Business Administration and eventually as White House chief of staff. Bowles was the kind of probusiness, centrist Democrat who normally does well in elections. He was also wealthy and poured millions of his personal wealth into the campaign.

Bowles sought to focus the race on a troubled economy. During the previous decade, the number of North Carolina manufacturing jobs had declined from 818,100 to 612,000, or about a quarter of the state's industrial base. The loss of manufacturing jobs to Mexico, China, and other countries was happening across the nation. But few industries were harder hit than the textile industry.

But voters were more focused on the war on terrorism, following the September 11, 2001, attacks on New York City and Washington. And much of the country had rallied around President Bush. Bush campaigned five times in North Carolina for Dole—more than in any state except Florida, where the president's brother, Governor Jeb Bush, had a difficult reelection campaign. Bush, who was at the height of his popularity in 2002, was able to nationalize the midterm elections, helping Republicans regain control of the U.S. Senate.

Dole became North Carolina's first woman senator. Her margin of victory against a strong Democratic opponent was impressive. She won 54 percent to 45 percent, the widest margin in a North Carolina Senate race since Helms had defeated John Ingram in the 1978 Senate race.

Dole projected a more consensus-oriented, less ideologically driven, and less-combative brand of conservatism than Helms. Helms had been a warrior, rising in politics in the 1970s before the new conservative movement headed by Ronald Reagan, Newt Gingrich, and the Bushes had changed Washington into a Republican pond.

Dole was now part of a Republican establishment, with the GOP in control of the White House and Congress and a GOP-appointed majority in the U.S. Supreme Court. Taking office at age sixty-five, Dole seemed unlikely to be the North Carolina Republican Party's future. The future might very well belong to Richard Burr, whom Rove recruited to run for North Carolina's open Senate seat in 2004. Burr, a conservative congressman from Winston-Salem, was able, Dole-like, to convey the softer suburban brand of conservatism. And like Dole, he easily defeated Bowles, who would later become president of the University of North Carolina.

Dole and Burr were the new faces of the Republican Party. Neither appealed to race, and both made overtures to African Americans and the growing number of Hispanic voters. The election of Dole and Burr was in keeping with a long North Carolina tradition of sending fiscal and social conservatives who were promilitary and probusiness to Washington. But at the same time, the state continued to elect moderate Democrats to run things in Raleigh.

Prosecutor

Despite four terms as governor, Hunt left no political heir. He saw the efforts of his mentor, Governor Terry Sanford, to name his successor come to grief. Nor was it Hunt's style to meddle in Democratic primaries. Of the two Democrats trying to succeed him, Hunt was close to Lieutenant Governor Dennis Wicker, a small-town attorney from a politically prominent family. Wicker was the favorite of much of the party establishment. But Mike Easley, a two-term attorney general, easily captured the Democratic nomination by going over the heads of local political organizations and connecting with the voters through television advertising.

Easley developed his outsider's political persona during his years as a tough local prosecutor. The isolated coves and inlets of the coast of south-eastern North Carolina were a haven for drug dealers in the early 1980s—especially after federal authorities had cracked down on trafficking along the Florida coast.

Easley, the district attorney living in the small coastal town of South-port, helped prosecute 350 drug traffickers, including forty members of a gang convicted of killing a federal judge in Texas. One cocaine dealer was convicted of putting out a contract on Easley while in federal prison with the instructions "mutilate the motherfucker." Easley learned to sleep with a shotgun next to his bed, stored revolvers in his desk and his automobile's glove compartment, and taught his wife Mary how to shoot. At one point, he sent his wife out of state to live with her parents in New Jersey until the situation cooled down.[5]

The big money from drugs bred corruption in a section of the state that had long had a reputation for a less-than-fastidious brand of politics. Eas-ley helped prosecute thirty-four public officials in his three-county district. He helped prosecute two of the three sheriffs, a popular clerk of court, a state legislator, and Lieutenant Governor Jimmy Green.

Easley, estranged from the local Democratic Party apparatus, developed his own outsider's political style that confounded many of his contempo-raries. But it carried him to two terms as state attorney general and in 2000 to the Executive Mansion. His only loss was to Harvey Gantt in the 1990 Democratic U.S. Senate primary.

The son of a Nash County tobacco warehouseman, Easley grew up an Irish Catholic in heavily Protestant eastern North Carolina. He attended integrated Catholic schools at a time when the public schools were still segregated. He also learned to overcome a serious reading disability that was discovered when he was a student at the University of North Carolina at Chapel Hill. With the help of friends, who read books to him, he graduated with honors from Chapel Hill and the law school at N.C. Central University in Durham. Although his reading improved as he got older, even as attor-ney general and governor he preferred aides to give reports to him orally—sometimes as a recorded telephone message—rather than read a written report. To compensate for his reading problem, Easley developed a facile mind and an unusually sharp memory.

In 2000 Easley defeated former Charlotte mayor Richard Vinroot, a product of the political organization of former governor Jim Martin. And he won reelection in 2004, defeating state senator Patrick Ballantine of Wilmington.

With Easley's reelection, the Democrats were assured of sixteen years of control of the governor's mansion—a feat accomplished nowhere else in the South and surpassed by Democrats only in the states of Oregon and Washington.

Easley's formula for winning in an increasing Republican South was to focus on issues with broad support, like improving public education and recruiting industry, while appealing to conservatives by supporting the death penalty and being business friendly. Unlike previous Tar Heel governors, he also backed a state-run lottery. Socially conservative North Carolina was the last major state in the country to adopt a lottery.

Although pro-choice on abortion, Easley avoided divisive social issues. Like Hunt, Easley was able to appeal to rural whites, suburbanites, and African Americans. He was the first governor to graduate from a historically black university—N.C. Central University, where the first lady later worked as a law professor.

The first baby boomer governor represented the new professional suburban class. Easley and his wife were attorneys. But Easley understood that despite all the new high-tech industries and glass-office towers, North Carolina was still a blue-collar state with deep rural roots. He culturally connected with many traditionalists—whether hunting, swapping country stories, or crashing a NASCAR racing car into the wall at a track in Charlotte during a charity event. Easley had grown up about twenty miles from Hunt in rural eastern North Carolina, and he was in tune with the state's small-town heartbeat. In considering his political strategies, Easley watched a popular TV program called *King of the Hill*, a network animation about a good-old-boy propane salesman from Texas. He once had his pollster poll only *King of the Hill* viewers. "I like to know where I stand among *King of the Hill* voters," Easley said. "It reminds me of so many of my friends."[6]

Easley distanced himself from national Democrats, campaigning only once with Vice President Al Gore in 2000 and not at all with Massachusetts senator John Kerry in 2004. While George W. Bush twice carried North Carolina with 56 percent of the vote, Easley won with 52 and 56 percent of the vote.

Easley was a product of his times, as many voters lost their strong party bonds. The fastest-growing group of voters are those who register as unaffiliated. In 1986 there were 129,728 unaffiliated voters in North Carolina, and by 1998 there were 608,023.[7]

While Easley governed as a Democrat, he nearly divorced himself from the state party organization—thereby underscoring his independent

Mike Easley, the Democratic nominee for governor,
watches Governor Jim Hunt speak at a campaign rally, 2000.
(Photograph by Corey Lowenstein; courtesy of the
Raleigh News and Observer)

image. In 2005 he stopped going to party dinners and conventions when the Democrats rejected his choice for party chairman and elected a more liberal chairman. He often feuded with N.C. Senate leader Marc Basnight.

Easley is one of the more complicated figures in North Carolina politics. He is a talented campaigner, yet one who disdains the barbecue circuit and travels around the state only a fraction of the time that Hunt did. He has a quick wit and is a talented mimic, full of Irish charm, with dead-on impressions of North Carolina political figures, including Hunt. Befriending the prison trustees that man the Executive Mansion, Easley formed a singing trio or quartet, breaking into songs like Louis Armstrong's "What a Wonderful World" for guests.

Easley needed all of his charm, taking office as the state went into its worst economic slump since the Great Depression of the 1930s. While the entire nation slid into a recession to start the new century, the slump was particularly acute in North Carolina, where the three-legged stool that had supported the state's economy—textiles, tobacco, and furniture—was dangerously wobbling.

Easley spent much of his first term managing crises, finding economies in government, cutting funding to state agencies, laying off modest numbers of state employees, and raiding various government trust funds, including money earmarked for local governments. He also showed political courage in pushing through the legislature a temporary tax increase—most notably a half-cent sales tax hike.

Easley fit the mold of most North Carolina governors. He was a business progressive, willing to spend more money to improve education, and at the same time he was an ally of many of the state's business leaders and began offering large incentives to corporations who created jobs in North Carolina.

John Edwards represented a different political strain in the state. He was an updated version of the state's long list of populists that includes Marion Butler, Daniel Russell, Robert Reynolds, Ralph McDonald, and Kerr Scott.

Trial Lawyer

On January 2, 2003, dozens of national reporters and TV satellite trucks crammed into the narrow, leafy residential street in the Country Club Hills section of West Raleigh to watch John Edwards announce his intentions to unseat President Bush in 2004. Just six years before, it is doubtful that Edwards could have gotten even a local cable-access station to show up on his doorstep. Edwards was so apolitical that he didn't even bother to vote half of the time.

Edwards was one of a new breed of politicians, one in which telegenic good looks, personal charisma, and a large bank account replaced the older political virtues of working one's way up the political system. Helms and his political advisors had discovered that the power of television trumped traditional political organizations. Edwards further refined the evolution. Helms at least had been a public figure whose decade as a Raleigh television editorialist had made him a known quantity. Edwards's politics was a mystery before he ran for political office.

Edwards was born in Seneca, South Carolina, in 1953. His ancestors came from Georgia and the hills of South Carolina. Like thousands of other southerners in the early twentieth century, they were sharecroppers who left the farms to work in the textile mills, where at least there was a steady paycheck. His parents began life as common mill workers, although his father worked his way up to become a plant supervisor, working for Roger Milliken, a union-busting billionaire who helped bankroll the rise of the Republicans in the South—from Barry Goldwater to Newt Gingrich.

When he was twelve, Edwards's family moved to the Moore County mill town of Robbins, a plain-shoes industrial town that provided a vivid contrast to nearby Pinehurst, a manicured golf resort that was a magnet for the wealthy. In few other places in America were the two Americas that Edwards would later use as a campaign theme so evident.

Textile work, particularly in the early years, was often dangerous, and it was not uncommon for workers to get their hands or arms mangled in the fast-moving belts and powerful machinery. If a worker was injured on the job, he or she might get help from the owner—or they might not. State worker-compensation benefits were notoriously low in the South, and review boards were often weighted toward employers. North Carolina was the least-unionized state in the country, so workers had little clout with management.

In working-class towns across the South, trial lawyers were often viewed as the equalizers—celebrated in fiction by figures such as Harper Lee's Atticus Finch or author John Grisham's characters—as someone who would stand up for the average working person against the big company and its political allies.

"There is a huge class consciousness to John," said Rich Leonard of Raleigh, a longtime friend and a U.S. bankruptcy judge. "I think it plays out in so many of his political decisions. I think his primary, overriding political view is to put the starting point in the same place for everybody."[8]

From an early age, Edwards had wanted to be a lawyer. He began a remarkable legal career, first in Nashville, Tennessee, and then in Raleigh. He earned millions of dollars as one of the nation's top plaintiffs' lawyers. He sued doctors for medical malpractice and trucking companies whose drivers were involved in fatal accidents; in one case he won $25 million for a little girl whose intestines were sucked out by an uncovered swimming pool drain.

Edwards was so gifted that other lawyers often gathered to watch him deliver the closing arguments to juries. He was known not for courtroom theatrics, but for his calm, skillful presentation, his command of the issues, and his ability to relate to juries. While most plaintiffs' attorneys dream of $1 million awards or settlements, Edwards had at least forty-eight such cases. Edwards handled cases that won $205 million for his clients in settlements and jury verdicts.

Politics had not been important in his life. But that changed in 1996, when his sixteen-year-old son Wade was killed in a freak automobile accident when his jeep flipped over on Interstate 40. The death of their firstborn changed the trajectory of the lives of John and his wife, Elizabeth Edwards. Elizabeth gave up her law practice, and Edwards, after wrapping up a few big cases, ended his legal career. They rediscovered their religious faith. And Elizabeth, after taking hormone shots, started a second family, having children at age forty-eight and fifty.

His son had encouraged Edwards to enter politics. Donning his son's Outward Bound pin, Edwards entered the 1998 Senate race as a political outsider. Much of the Democratic Party establishment was backing D. G. Martin, a popular attorney and former university official. But Martin could not compete financially with Edwards, who put $6 million of his own fortune into the primary and general election. In the fall, Edwards faced Republican senator Lauch Faircloth, a conservative agribusiness man from Clinton, who had been elected with the backing of the Helms organization.

From the moment he declared his candidacy, it was evident that Edwards was a rare political talent—smart, hard-driving, and able to convince voters just as he had swayed juries. "One of the holy grails of politics is the fresh face—Mr. Smith Goes to Washington," said Gary Pearce, a Raleigh political consultant who worked for Edwards, referring to the Frank Capra movie. "I remember thinking, 'I really found it.'"[9]

In the fall, Edwards defeated Faircloth by a 51 to 47 percent margin. Edwards ran as an outsider against the Washington special interests—tapping into voter concerns that Washington was weighted against the average citizen. He would repeatedly describe a scene in which corporate lobbyists stood outside the Senate chambers influencing the votes of lawmakers. He refused to take any contributions from political action committees. He campaigned against the big insurance companies, saying the health decisions should be decided by a patient and his or her doctor and not by faceless insurance bureaucrats working for some insurance company in Hartford. He called for passage of a patient's bill of rights to give people more power in dealing with health-care insurance companies.

Edwards's victory was surprising. For the first time since the arrival of two-party politics in the 1960s, a Democratic challenger in North Carolina had defeated a sitting Republican senator who had been elected.

The generational contrast between the forty-five-year-old Edwards and the seventy-year-old Faircloth was striking. Edwards won the support of many suburban voters, who saw him as someone more like themselves. Edwards also had good timing. He faced the voters in a year when voters were angry with Congressional Republicans, who they felt overreached in impeaching President Clinton.

From the time he arrived in Washington, Edwards was regarded by the national Democratic Party as a rising star. His career was advanced by Senate Democratic leaders who gave him a prominent role in pushing a patients' bill of rights through the Senate, although the measure failed in the House.

Edwards made such an impression that in 2000 Al Gore, the Democratic presidential nominee, seriously considered naming him his vice presidential running mate. (He eventually decided on Connecticut senator Joe Lieberman.) "The reason he got put on the list is he was a fresh, young, new face from the South, articulate," said former California congressman Tony Coelho, the Gore campaign chairman. "He was sort of a nice breath of fresh air."[10]

The brush with the presidential ticket was heady stuff, and Edwards caught the presidential bug. Seven months after his near miss on the vice presidential ticket, and two months after President Bush took office, Edwards made his first foray into Iowa, in March 2001, where the first caucuses would be held in January 2004. By the following year, Edwards was moving across the country, raising money and making speeches.

Edwards's populist pitch, an upbeat message that avoided attacks on his

Democratic rivals, and a fresh appeal made him the most successful presidential candidate North Carolina ever produced—unless one considers James K. Polk, Andrew Jackson, and Andrew Johnson, the three Tar Heel natives who rose to the presidency after migrating to Tennessee. Edwards argued that he was the only presidential candidate who could compete with Bush in the South, boasting that he had defeated the Helms machine.

One of the most enduring images of his campaign was of the pink, three-room mill village house in Seneca, South Carolina, where his family lived when he was born—an image featured heavily in his TV ads as a sort of a modern-day log cabin. Everywhere he went, Edwards asked this question: can the son of a mill worker defeat the son of a president?

Edwards represented the twenty-first century version of populism. Unlike his gallus-snapping antecedents who rallied farmers against Wall Street money and the powerful railroads, Edwards talked about the influence of big oil that gouged drivers, and the HMOs and insurance companies that denied health-insurance claims.

Edwards did not scowl when he talked about the rich. After all, Edwards was rich; his multimillion-dollar mansions were grist for his opponents. It is a populism that Edwards had honed for twenty years in front of small-town juries, convincing them to deliver million-dollar verdicts against doctors, hospitals, trucking companies, and insurance companies.

Edwards's populism—delivered with a smile and the pleasant personality of a suburban evangelist or a midmarket TV news anchor—tapped into the growing insecurities of Joe Lunch Bucket. It was a message that played well in down-at-the-heels industrial towns of the Ohio Valley and the Rust Belt sections of Michigan, Wisconsin, and Minnesota, which were pockmarked by closed factories. While Americans had prided themselves on being a middle-class nation where the lines of class were blurred, the gap between the haves and the have-nots had been widening.

Edwards's populism sought to tap into deep worries about the manufacturing plants closing, of once high-flying CEO's landing with golden parachutes, and of once-secure pensions disappearing. It played on fears that Washington is controlled by powerful corporate interests and that the gap between the wealthy and the struggling working class is growing.

Conservatives charged that Edwards was engaging in class warfare when he gave his "Two Americas" speech that would become the trademark of his 2004 presidential run. But on the campaign trail, heads would nod in agreement as Edwards talked about the widening gap in America. "It seems today we have two Americas," Edwards said in a New Hampshire primary TV ad in early 2004. "With two health care systems, one for the privileged, the other rationed by insurance companies. With two public school systems, one for the haves, one for everybody else. Two governments, one for powerful interests and lobbyists, the other for the rest of us. Two tax systems, where the wealthy corporations pay less, working families pay more."

Edwards won the South Carolina primary and finished a strong second in the Iowa caucuses and in primaries in Wisconsin and Oklahoma. He left in his wake some of the most respected figures in the Democratic Party—Lieberman, Senator Bob Graham of Florida, Representative Dick Gephardt of Missouri, Vermont governor Howard Dean, and former NATO commander Wesley Clark. But he did not have the money, the backing, or the seasoning to catch up with veteran Massachusetts senator John Kerry.

"This time around, voters were not looking for a new face or an outsider," said Alan Lichtman, a presidential scholar at American University in Washington, D.C. "They were looking for someone with a track record, and someone experienced and someone who can stand up to Bush on international issues."[11]

Edwards dropped out of the presidential race in March, but his strong showing helped build support for putting him on the ticket as the vice presidential candidate. In July Kerry chose him as his vice presidential running mate. The choice was a popular one in the Democratic Party, particularly among activists impressed by Edwards's primary showing, trial attorneys who wanted to elevate one of their own to national office, and Democratic senators who thought Edwards could help the Democrats hold several southern Senate seats. But some were disappointed that Edwards did not provide more help to the Democratic ticket, particularly in the South, which once again went strongly for Bush. Some Democrats also criticized Edwards for not running for reelection after his seat was won by Republican Richard Burr.

Edwards was the first North Carolinian to be selected as a vice presidential candidate of a major political party since Andrew Johnson in 1864. Johnson was then a Democratic senator from Tennessee.

Edwards never really stopped running for president. Shortly after the Democratic ticket lost to Bush, Edwards set up an antipoverty think tank at the University of North Carolina at Chapel Hill to examine poverty questions. He also began traveling around the country, laying the groundwork for another presidential run in 2008.

Moving to his political left, Edwards became a key ally of organized labor, often joining organizing efforts or walking on picket lines. He began

Senator John Edwards accepts the nomination for vice president at
the 2004 Democratic National Convention, held at Boston's FleetCenter.
(Photograph by Robert Willett; courtesy of the *Raleigh News and Observer*)

traveling around the world to meet with foreign leaders to broaden his resume. After initially supporting the U.S. war in Iraq, Edwards became an outspoken opponent of the war. He became a favorite of liberal Democrats who used the new technology of the Internet to politically organize. Even the illness of his wife Elizabeth, who was diagnosed with breast cancer at the end of the 2004 campaign—and which, it was revealed, had spread in March 2007—did not deter him.

Heading into the 2008 presidential election year, Edwards was competing with Senators Hillary Clinton of New York and Barack Obama of Illinois for the Democratic nomination. No North Carolinian had ever gone so far in modern American politics.

Epilogue

orth Carolina grappled with two overriding questions during the twentieth century: How can a poor state pull itself into the nation's economic mainstream? And how should a southern state with segregationist roots handle the question of race?

From Cameron Morrison to Jim Hunt, the animating spirit behind North Carolina politics has been business progressivism—a pragmatic centrism that has rarely satisfied either liberals or conservatives. The state's political leadership has greeted industry with open arms, passed business-friendly laws, been hostile to organized labor, and kept state government and taxes at moderate levels. At the same time, the state has spent more money than most southern states on universities, roads, and schools to lay the groundwork for economic growth.

Few states traveled the economic distance that North Carolina did during the twentieth century. North Carolina was among the poorest states in the country in 1900. It led the nation in illiteracy. It was populated mainly by poor farmers—many of them sharecroppers engaged in subsistence farming—and increasingly by textile mill hands that were among the lowest-paid industrial workers in the country. By the end of the twentieth century, North Carolina looked like the rest of America. In 1999 the median household income in North Carolina was $39,184, compared to $41,994 nationally.[1] In 1900 North Carolina was spending 21 percent of the national average on education. By the end of the century it was spending 86 percent of the national average on the schools.[2] Its students were performing above the national average on standardized reading and math tests, although there continue to be deep-seated problems, such as the high dropout rate.

North Carolina grew during the twentieth century from 1.9 million people to 8.4 million—from a rural state to a suburbanized one. Many of the new arrivals came to work in the rapidly expanding high-tech corridor that stretched along Interstate

85 from Raleigh to Charlotte—the so-called Piedmont Urban Crescent. North Carolina's large number of farmers and textile workers diminished, replaced by white-collar workers. The state's traditional industries were in rapid decline. All across North Carolina there were padlocked plant gates, as the textile and furniture industries moved their operations to Mexico, China, or other counties with cheaper labor. The dangers of smoking finally began catching up with the tobacco industry, and fewer people made their living from the so-called golden leaf. By the end of the century, more people worked at computer giant IBM's facility in the Research Triangle Park than grew tobacco in North Carolina.

The Research Triangle Park grew into one of the premier high-tech centers in the country, with such blue-chip firms as GlaxoSmithKline, Nortel, Sony Ericsson, and Cisco. Charlotte became one of the nation's most important banking centers, with Bank of America and Wachovia creating national banking empires that stretched from Boston to Miami and San Francisco.

Tobacco fields were being plowed under to make room for suburban cul-de-sacs. Barbecue joints gave way to supermarkets that sold takeout sushi. During the opening of deer season, you'd be as likely to see Broncos or BMWs heading for the countryside as you would pick-up trucks. With its sprawling but low-density metropolitan areas, North Carolina had become, in the words of author John Herbers, "a countrified city." Herbers called North Carolina the "prototype of America's future" in his 1986 book, *The New American Heartland*.

The state's prosperity, however, was uneven. While the metropolitan areas fretted over how to handle booming growth, many rural areas were worried about survival. One could still find more mobile homes across the state than in most other places in America, including Alabama and Arkansas.[3] Although poverty had been sharply reduced in the twentieth century, one study found that more than 35 percent of North Carolinians, or 1.1 million families, still earned less than the amount needed to achieve a basic standard of living at the end of the century.[4]

Demographers predict that North Carolina will grow to 12.2 million by 2030, surpassing such states as Michigan, New Jersey, Ohio, and Georgia in population. North Carolina's nineteenth-century reputation as the "Rip Van Winkle State" was a distant memory by 2000. The influx of people is reshaping Tar Heel politics. North Carolina has had a net gain of 1.5 million new voters during the past decade. Nearly two-thirds of the voters born outside North Carolina are either registered as Republican or unaffiliated. Among native-born Tar Heel voters, 52 percent are Democrats, 33 percent are Republicans, and 15 percent are unaffiliated. Among those born elsewhere, 37 percent are Republicans, 36 percent are Democrats, and 28 percent are unaffiliated.[5] But the wave of newcomers does not portend a conservative shift. Many of the newcomers are Starbucks–Whole Foods Republicans—not antigovernment–Jesse Helms Republicans—who are more willing than the old conservative Democrats to spend money for roads, schools, public safety, and parks.

Building the new subdivisions and shopping centers were thousands of Hispanic workers, mainly from Mexico. They plucked the chickens in the meat-processing plants, cleaned the office buildings, and waited on residents in fast-food restaurants. North Carolina's Latino population grew faster than that of any other state in recent years, increasing from 77,000 in 1990 to an estimated 600,000 in 2006. An estimated half of the new residents were undocumented workers, and those who were citizens tended not to participate heavily in politics. Latinos may have grown from 1.1 percent of North Carolina's population to 6.1 percent, but it will likely take at least a generation before they have a significant impact on the state's politics.

But there are indications that a backlash against the Hispanic immigration—particularly the illegal immigrants—is forming. Polls show immigration tops the lists of voter concerns. There has long been suspicion of foreigners in North Carolina, and several politicians, most notably Senator Furnifold Simmons and Senator Robert Reynolds, railed against immigrants.

Attitudes toward the black/white racial divide had undergone a sea change since the white supremacy campaigns. North Carolina adopted a milder form of racial segregation than most of the South, as business leaders sought to avoid the violence and disruption that could harm efforts to recruit northern corporations to locate here. But the state's reputation for racial moderation has often been overstated, and there was often a white backlash when the racial code was threatened. Even into the 1990s, race was often a subtext of North Carolina political campaigns; witness the tactics used by Jesse Helms to defeat Harvey Gantt.

The reemergence of blacks into politics has meant that North Carolina politicians could ignore the interests of African Americans only at their own professional peril. Attitudes of many whites changed in the postsegregation South. African Americans were also no longer seen as quite the same threat because of their great migration to the northern states earlier in the century. The percentage of black residents had declined from 38 percent in 1880 to 21.6 percent in 2000. There were eighteen counties with black majorities in 1900 at the time of the disfranchisement vote; by 2000 there were only six.

For generations, the white supremacy campaigns were largely locked away in North Carolina's closet—increasingly becoming an embarrassment to the moderate image the state was selling to northern industrialists. Charles Brantley Aycock was hailed as an education leader, not as a white supremacist. His words are etched in stone on the two buildings in Raleigh that have served as the offices for the N.C. Department of Education during the last half of the twentieth century. His statue sits on Capitol Square and in the statuary hall in the U.S. Capitol. His Wayne County homestead is preserved by the state as a historic site. The Democrats still call their annual western North Carolina fund-raiser the Vance-Aycock dinner. Governor Terry Sanford hung Aycock's portrait in the governor's office in 1961, and Governor Jim Hunt quoted Aycock on education during the last State of the State Address of the twentieth century in 1999.

Only in recent years has North Carolina attempted to come to terms with the racial violence that established the state's political framework for much of the twentieth century. Scholars began writing more critically about the period. There were programs to commemorate the 100th anniversary of the Wilmington Race Riot. In 2000 the state legislature created a commission to investigate the insurrection—patterned after Florida's inquiry into the 1923 Rosewood Massacre and Oklahoma's investigation into the Tulsa Race Riot of 1921. The commission's final report, issued in 2006, recommended greater efforts to educate the public about the violence, providing compensation to the heirs of victims who can prove a loss, creation of economic incentives to help Wilmington areas damaged by the violence, and efforts by newspapers to distribute the report and acknowledge its own role. The Democratic Party apologized for its role in the white supremacy campaign in 2007.

In 1976 a state highway marker was placed near the New Bern home of former congressman George White, who was driven from the state in 1901. In 2004 Congress authorized the renaming of the Tarboro post office after White, and in 2005 a portrait of White was unveiled in the Edgecombe County Courthouse.

Red State–Blue State?

For the first six decades of the twentieth century, North Carolina, like the rest of the South, was virtually a one-party state, and that party was the Democrats. Elections were usually decided in the Democratic primary, and the general election was just an afterthought. But since the 1960s, the GOP has experienced unparalleled growth. By the end of the century, North Carolinians were arguing whether the state was Democratic or Republican—or in the jargon of the day, whether it was a "blue" state or a "red" state.

The state's Republican leanings are most evident in federal races. Like the rest of the South, North Carolina has become a reliable Republican state in presidential elections. In nine of the last ten presidential elections, the state has voted Republican. The only exception was in 1976, when North Carolina went for southerner Jimmy Carter, although Arkansas native Bill Clinton came close to carrying the state in 1992.

Republicans have also won nine of the past twelve Senate races. For a Democrat to win a Senate election in North Carolina, there have to be special circumstances, such as a strong candidate running in a midterm election with the national Democratic tide at his back. The Democrats won in 1974 with Robert Morgan, in 1986 with Terry Sanford, and in 1998 with John Edwards. Both Morgan and Sanford were defeated when they sought reelection in presidential years, and Edwards did not seek a second term.

In races for president and the U.S. Senate, North Carolina's conservative streak—its fierce individualism, its respect for the military, and its Bible Belt social views—come to the fore. The bookends for the twentieth century were two conservative senators, Furnifold Simmons and Jesse Helms, each serving a record of thirty years in the Senate. Each created powerful political machines, each was a master at Bible Belt politics, each was closely aligned with business interests, and each represented the old views on race.

But North Carolina remains a blue state when it comes to Raleigh politics. During the decades when the South was dominated by the Democrats, North Carolina had one of the strongest Republican Parties in the South. Now that Republicans command much of the South, North Carolina has one of the most influential Democratic Parties.

Beginning in 1993, North Carolina has been governed by Democratic governors for sixteen straight years—a feat duplicated only in Oregon and Washington. A key reason for this success is that the Democrats nominated skillful probusiness moderates such as Hunt and Easley, who knew how to appeal to swing voters and continue the philosophy of business progressivism. But the long run of Democratic governors was also the result of missteps by Republicans.

Twice during the twentieth century, North Carolina voters elected Republicans as governor—Jim Holshouser in 1972 and Jim Martin in 1984 (reelected in 1988). Both were attractive moderate conservatives who also fell within the business progressive tradition and who could appeal to swing suburban voters. And both were elected during Republican presidential landslides. Every time Republicans nominated a Helms-style conservative for governor—Jim Gardner in 1968 and 1992, Robin Hayes in 1996, and Richard Vinroot in 2000—they lost. North Carolina voters may want a give-em-hell style in Washington, but they want a give-em-new-roads style in Raleigh.

While the Republicans have dominated federal races and the Democrats have taken out a mortgage on the governor's mansion, the state legislature has become ground zero in the political wars, always teetering between the two parties. The Republicans twice won control of the N.C. House of Representatives in the twentieth century (in 1994 and 1996). The Republicans won a majority of the N.C. House seats in 2002, but they never took control because Republican Michael Decker switched to the Democratic Party and a bipartisan coalition was formed. Decker later went to prison for accepting a $50,000 bribe for switching his vote.

North Carolina has long had a reputation for clean government—no gangs of highwaymen looting the state treasury as in so many other states. But that reputation has been frayed in recent years by a series of scandals. Agriculture Commissioner Meg Scott Phipps, a Democrat and the daughter and granddaughter of governors, went to prison in a fund-raising scandal. Democratic congressman Frank Ballance went to jail for misuse of state money when he was a state legislator. And Democrat Jim Black, a five-term N.C. House Speaker, went to prison for illegally raising money in a Charlotte bathroom. Other lawmakers were the subject of investigation.

Each case was different, and greed was sometimes a factor. But the scandals also cast a light on some larger trends. The decline of the old-fashioned political machines means that candidates can no longer count on political bosses to deliver the vote for them. That means they often have to raise large amounts of political money to make their case to voters on television. Phipps's undoing grew out of her need to raise $1 million for an agriculture commissioner's race, raising it from the people she would regulate—the vendors who operated the amusement rides at the state fair.

When the N.C. House teetered back and forth between control by the Democrats and Republicans, Jim Black became master of raising millions of dollars and wheeling and dealing. Eventually, he crossed the line, accepting illegal cash payments to keep his political machine lubricated. Today's campaign finance laws, and their enforcement, could very well have landed some of the most illustrious names in North Carolina political history in jail. Cash in brown paper bags is no longer winked at.

During the 1980s and 1990s, no southern state had as many close elections as North Carolina. The gap between the winner and loser in North Carolina races for governor, U.S. Senate, and president was an average of 6.8 percentage points in the 1990s and 10.3 percentage points in the 1980s. In fact, no state in the country was as politically competitive as North Carolina in the 1990s.[6]

Exit polls from the 2004 election painted a picture of a closely divided state. Forty percent of the voters questioned identified themselves as Republicans, 39 percent as Democrats, and 21 percent as independents.[7] The political parties are having increasing difficulty commanding the loyalty of their own voters. The candidates who win are those who appeal to suburban swing voters—Republicans such as Elizabeth Dole and Richard Burr and Democrats such as Mike Easley and John Edwards.

A prominent North Carolina newspaper editor once asked me how the same state could elect both a rock-ribbed conservative like Jesse Helms to the Senate five times and a progressive like Jim Hunt as governor four times. The answer is that North Carolina is a closely divided state. The state has a strong conservative streak that has elected the likes of Furnifold Simmons, Josiah Bailey, Sam Ervin, Jesse Helms, and Elizabeth Dole. No one can get elected to high office in North Carolina without keeping the state's social conservatism in mind. It is a God-fearing, gun-owning, lock-em-up-and-throw-away-the-key, military-loving state. And race feelings, while diminished, are still a powerful force. It is a state that loves NASCAR, pick-up trucks, and plainspoken politicians who don't put on too many airs.

But it is more. Somewhere in the state's political soul beats the heart of a commercial hustler. North Carolina is a once-poor state on the make. There is a booster spirit about the state that wants the best universities, the best roads, the biggest skyscrapers, and the best basketball teams. So it has elected a series of business progressives such as Cameron Morrison,

O. Max Gardner, Luther Hodges, Jim Martin, and Jim Hunt to move the state forward.

There is also a little-man streak in a state that never had much of an aristocracy. North Carolinians may now live in cul-de-sacs and drive SUVs and eat sushi, but many are just a generation or two removed from the farm or the textile mill. There is a lingering distrust of the "big boys." So North Carolinians occasionally elect populists such as Marion Butler, Daniel Russell, Robert Reynolds, Kerr Scott, Eva Clayton, and John Edwards to let Wall Street, or the big banks, or the utility companies, or the HMOs know that it's not okay to push people around.

North Carolina remains culturally conservative, more like Alabama than California. But North Carolina is also a state not content with the status quo; nor is it as tied to the past as much of the South. North Carolina is a state caught between its memories of the past and its dreams for the future.

Appendix Endings

Charles Brantley Aycock, Democratic governor from 1901 to 1905. Plagued by heart problems, Aycock was giving an education speech in Birmingham in April 1912 when he collapsed and died at age fifty-two.

Josiah Bailey, Democratic senator from 1931 to 1946 and the principal author of the Conservative Manifesto. He died in office of a cerebral hemorrhage at age seventy-three.

Marion Butler, Populist senator from 1895 to 1901. He gave up his Senate seat to Simmons, his arch enemy, in 1901, although he tried to convince the Senate to block the move by arguing that Simmons had been elected through fraud. Butler moved to Washington, D.C., where he became a progressive Teddy Roosevelt Republican and practiced law until his death of kidney disease in 1938.

Sam Ervin, Democratic senator from 1954 to 1975. He retired to Morganton to peruse the 7,500 books in his personal library and watch the sun set behind Table Rock and Hawksbill Mountain. He died in 1985 in a Winston-Salem hospital.

O. Max Gardner, Democratic governor from 1929 to 1933, suffered a fatal heart attack in New York in 1947, just hours before he was to set sail for London to become ambassador to the Court of St. James. He was sixty-four.

Frank Graham. After his wife Marian died in 1967, Graham returned to Chapel Hill to live in his sister's house. He suffered a heart attack the following year. A new generation of students often came and visited him, talking with him about the Vietnam War, the civil rights movement, education, and other issues. He died in February 1972 at age eighty-six.

Jesse Helms, Republican U.S. senator from 1973 to 2003. Afflicted with memory problems, his last public appearance was to promote his memoirs in 2005.

Luther Hodges, Democratic governor from 1954 to 1961 and U.S. commerce secretary from 1961 to 1965. Returning to his home in Chapel Hill, Hodges went to work for the North Carolina Research Triangle Foundation for a dollar-a-year salary. He helped the Research Triangle Park recruit such major firms as IBM and the research laboratories of the U.S. Environmental Protection Agency.

His son Luther Hodges Jr., a leading banker and businessman, would be an unsuccessful candidate for the U.S. Senate in 1978 and would serve as undersecretary and acting secretary of commerce under President Jimmy Carter. The senior Hodges lost his wife Martha in a house fire in Chapel Hill in 1969; he suffered smoke inhalation and a broken leg after jumping from a second-story bedroom window. He died in 1974.

Clyde Hoey, Democratic governor from 1937 to 1941 and U.S. senator from 1945 to 1954. In his later years, he was sometimes driven back home from Washington by Jesse Helms, then a young senatorial aide. He died in his office at age seventy-six.

Jim Holshouser, Republican governor from 1973 to 1977. Battling a lifelong kidney problem, he had a kidney transplant not long after leaving the governor's office. He practiced law, forming a firm with former governor Terry Sanford. He served on the University of North Carolina Board of Governors and was active in the Presbyterian Church.

Jim Hunt, Democratic governor from 1977 to 1985 and from 1993 to 2001. He has remained active in education, including creating a national education leadership institute in Chapel Hill.

I. Beverly Lake Sr., Democratic candidate for governor in 1960 and 1964. Served on the N.C. Supreme Court. His son I. Beverly Lake Jr. was the Republican nominee for governor in 1980 and later served as chief justice of the N.C. Supreme Court. The elder Lake died in 1996.

Jim Martin, Republican governor from 1985 to 1993. He retired from politics after his final term and now is chairman of the James Cannon Research Center of the Carolinas Medical Center in Charlotte.

Ralph McDonald, Democratic gubernatorial candidate in 1936 and 1944. He contracted tuberculosis in 1937, spending two years in sanitariums. After he recovered, he became a professor at UNC–Chapel Hill, resigning in 1944 to run for governor a second time. But the anti–sales tax and antimachine sentiment had subsided, and his race was a pale shadow of his 1936 campaign. He later held various education posts, including serving ten years as president of Bowling Green State University in Ohio; he then moved to Florida to work as an education consultant. McDonald died in 1977.

Cameron Morrison, Democratic governor from 1921 to 1925 and U.S. senator from 1930 to 1933. He returned to his Charlotte estate after his final term. He made a political comeback in 1942, when at age seventy-three he was elected to the newly created Tenth Congressional District seat. In 1944 he tried to regain his old Senate seat but lost to former governor Clyde Hoey. In 1952, at age eighty-two, Morrison led the North Carolina delegation to the Democratic National Convention in Chicago. He died while vacationing in Canada in 1953.

Robert Reynolds, Democratic U.S. senator from 1933 to 1945. He spent his
remaining years on Reynolds Mountain, raising his daughter and frequently
traveling. When she turned eighteen, "poor-boy" Reynolds threw a "coming-
out" party, flying in a famous New York society orchestra, buying her a
silk gown created for her by Christian Dior of Paris, and treating guests to
caviar—not good old North Carolina hen eggs. He died in 1963 at age seventy-
eight of bladder cancer.

Daniel Russell, Republican governor from 1897 to 1901. He retired to
Wilmington for the final eight years of his life. He lived in his home in
Wilmington and his plantation at Bellville, where he tried unsuccessfully
to grow rice. Russell practiced law and continued to be a thorn in the
Democrats' side. He successfully argued before the U.S. Supreme Court
the South Dakota bond case, which compelled North Carolina to pay its
Reconstruction-era bonds. Quoting a line from Shakespeare's *King Lear*,
Russell told his wife: "We are not the first, who meaning best, have come to
worst." He died in 1908, just short of his sixty-third birthday. Russell's home
in Wilmington became a Catholic school for black students.

Terry Sanford, Democratic governor from 1961 to 1965 and U.S senator from
1987 to 1993. After losing his Senate seat, Sanford was involved in real estate
ventures, raised money for the arts, and wrote a book on aging called *Outlive
Your Enemies.* He died in 1998 of bone cancer and was buried at Duke Chapel.

Kerr Scott, Democratic governor from 1949 to 1953 and U.S senator from 1955 to
1958. A lifetime of country cooking and unending cigars and chewing tobacco
ultimately took their toll. On April 9, 1958, while home on Easter recess,
Scott suffered a heart attack. On April 17, while still in the hospital, Scott
experienced a second and fatal heart attack.

Furnifold Simmons, Democratic senator from 1901 to 1931. He spent the
final decade of his life as a modest country squire, supervising his farms
in Craven and Jones Counties. In what was an interesting twist, Simmons
voiced support for Franklin Roosevelt's programs from his New Bern back
porch, while the man who replaced him, Josiah Bailey, evolved into one of the
leading conservative southern Democratic critics of the New Deal. He was to
say that the final years were some of the happiest of his life. He died at age
eighty-six on April 30, 1940, after an extended illness.

George White, Republican African American congressman from 1897 to 1901.
He moved to Washington, D.C., in 1901, saying, "I cannot live in North
Carolina and be a man and be treated as a man." He started a law practice
and became a real estate developer, starting the all-black town of Whitesboro
near the southern tip of New Jersey. White later moved to Philadelphia, where

he started a bank, practiced law, and was active in civic affairs. He briefly sought the Republican nomination for a congressional seat there in 1912, arguing that black citizens were "entitled to at least one representative in Congress." In 1917, at age sixty-four, White was appointed as assistant city solicitor in Philadelphia. White died on December 28, 1918. He is buried near Philadelphia.

Notes

PROLOGUE

1. David Traxel, *1898: The Birth of the American Century* (New York: Alfred A. Knopf, 1998), p. 281; and LeRae Umfleet (principal researcher), *1898 Wilmington Race Riot Report* (Raleigh: N.C. Department of Cultural Resources, 2006), p. 108.
2. Jeffrey J. Crow and Robert F. Durden, *Maverick Republican in the Old North State: A Political Biography of Daniel L. Russell* (Baton Rouge: Louisiana State University Press, 1977), p. 136.
3. U.S. Bureau of the Census, *Urban and Rural Population: 1900 to 1990*, table 1 (October 1995).
4. Thomas C. Parramore, *Express Lanes and Country Roads: The Way We Lived in North Carolina, 1920–1970* (Chapel Hill: University of North Carolina Press, 1983).
5. U.S. Bureau of the Census, *United States Census of Population, 1900*, vol. 8, pt. 2, "States and Territories."
6. Jacquelyn Dowd Hall, James Leloudis, Robert Korstad, Mary Murphy, Lu Ann Jones, and Christopher B. Daly, *Like a Family: The Making of a Southern Cotton Mill World* (Chapel Hill: University of North Carolina Press, 1987), p. 24.
7. Jeffrey J. Crow, Paul D. Escott, and Charles L. Flynn Jr., *Race, Class, and Politics in Southern History* (Baton Rouge: Louisiana State University Press, 1989), p. 159.
8. Donald R. Matthews, ed., *North Carolina Votes: General Election Returns by County* (Chapel Hill: University of North Carolina Press, 1962), p. 111.
9. William J. Cooper and Thomas E. Terrill, *The American South: A History* (New York: Alfred A. Knopf, 1990), p. 518.
10. Crow and Durden, *Maverick Republican*, p. 111.
11. Ibid., p. 128.
12. Richard L. Watson Jr., "Furnifold M. Simmons and the Politics of White Supremacy," in *Race, Class, and Politics in Southern History*, ed. Jeffrey J. Crow, Paul D. Escott, and Charles L. Flynn Jr. (Baton Rouge: Louisiana State University Press, 1989), p. 38.
13. Oliver H. Orr Jr., *Charles Brantley Aycock* (Chapel Hill: University of North Carolina Press, 1961), p. 108.
14. C. Vann Woodward, *Origins of the New South, 1877–1913* (Baton Rouge: Louisiana State University Press, 1951), p. 325.
15. Traxel, *1898*.
16. Fred Rippy, ed. and comp., *F. M. Simmons, Statesman of the New South: Memoirs and Addresses* (Durham: Duke University Press, 1936), p. 22.

17. Eric D. Anderson, *Race and Politics in North Carolina, 1872–1901: The Black Second* (Baton Rouge: Louisiana State University Press, 1981), p. 206.
18. David Cecelski and Timothy B. Tyson, *Democracy Betrayed: The Wilmington Race Riot of 1898 and Its Legacy* (Chapel Hill: University of North Carolina Press, 1998), p. 23.
19. Josephus Daniels, *Editor in Politics* (Chapel Hill: University of North Carolina Press, 1941), p. 295.
20. Benjamin R. Justesen, *George Henry White: An Even Chance in the Race of Life* (Baton Rouge: Louisiana State University Press, 2001), p. 62.
21. Ibid., p. 262.
22. Daniels, *Editor in Politics*, p. 293.
23. "The Sanford Rally, Lock Shields White Men," *Raleigh News and Observer* (cited hereafter as *N&O*), November 5, 1898.
24. "The Whites Shall Rule," *N&O*, November 6, 1898.
25. Rippy, *F. M Simmons*, p. 86.
26. Crow and Durden, *Maverick Republican*, p. 127.
27. Daniels, *Editor in Politics*, p. 283.
28. "The Governor's Stump Speech," *N&O*, October 27, 1898.
29. Crow and Durden, *Maverick Republican*, p. 130.
30. "Col. Waddell's Speech," *N&O*, November 6, 1898.
31. Ibid.
32. Cecelski and Tyson, *Democracy Betrayed*, p. 28.
33. Umfleet, *1898 Wilmington Race Riot Report*.
34. Cecelski and Tyson, *Democracy Betrayed*, p. 37.
35. Umfleet, *1898 Wilmington Race Riot Report*, p. 1.
36. Alice Sawyer Cooper in collaboration with Louis Goodman, "Daniel Lindsay Russell: A Family and Friend's Memoir" (unpublished manuscript, Daniel L. Russell Papers, Southern Historical Collection, University of North Carolina at Chapel Hill), p. 74.
37. Cecelski and Tyson, *Democracy Betrayed*, p. 87.
38. "Campaign Begun by Candidates," *N&O*, April 17, 1900.
39. Hugh Talmage Lefler and Albert Ray Newsome, *North Carolina: The History of a Southern State* (Chapel Hill: University of North Carolina Press, 1954), p. 525.
40. "Good Will Jubilee," *N&O*, November 16, 1898.
41. J. Morgan Kousser, *The Shaping of Southern Politics: Suffrage Restriction and the Establishment of the One-Party South, 1880–1910* (New Haven: Yale University Press, 1974), p. 55.
42. "A History-Making Day," *N&O*, February 18, 1899.
43. Lindley S. Butler and Alan D. Watson, *The North Carolina Experience: An Interpretive and Documentary History* (Chapel Hill: University of North Carolina Press, 1984), p. 347.
44. "Campaign Begun by Candidates," *N&O*.
45. Orr, *Charles Brantley Aycock*, p. 136.
46. Ibid., p. 181.

47. Janette Thomas Greenwood, *Bittersweet Legacy: The Black and White "Better Classes" in Charlotte, 1850–1910* (Chapel Hill: University of North Carolina Press, 1994), p. 212.

48. Benjamin R. Justesen, "George Henry White, Josephus Daniels, and the Showdown over Disfranchisement, 1900," *North Carolina Historical Review* 77, no. 1 (January 2000): 1.

49. Anderson, *Race and Politics*, p. 294.

50. John Hope Franklin, *From Slavery to Freedom: A History of African Americans* (New York: Alfred A. Knopf, 1947), p. 435.

51. Nicholas Worth (Walter Hines Page), "The Autobiography of a Southerner," *Atlantic Monthly*, July–October 1906, p. 484.

52. Robert W. Winston, *It's a Far Cry* (New York: Henry Holt and Co., 1937), p. 238.

CHAPTER 1

1. W. J. Cash, "Jehovah of the Tar Heels," *American Mercury*, July 1929, p. 310.

2. Eric D. Anderson, *Race and Politics in North Carolina, 1872–1901: The Black Second* (Baton Rouge: Louisiana State University Press, 1981), p. 136.

3. Fred Rippy, ed. and comp., *F. M. Simmons, Statesman of the New South: Memoirs and Addresses* (Durham: Duke University Press, 1936), p. 193.

4. Jonathan Daniels, *Tar Heels: A Portrait of North Carolina* (New York: Dodd, Mead and Company, 1941), p. 324.

5. Samuel Huntington Hobbs Jr., *North Carolina: Economic and Social* (Chapel Hill: University of North Carolina Press, 1930), p. 272.

6. Burke Davis, "Senator Bob Reynolds: A Retrospective View," *Harper's Magazine*, March 1944.

7. Cash, "Jehovah."

8. Donald R. Matthews, ed., *North Carolina Votes: General Election Returns by County* (Chapel Hill: University of North Carolina Press, 1962).

9. William H. Chafe, *Civilities and Civil Rights: Greensboro, North Carolina, and the Black Struggle for Freedom* (New York: Oxford University Press, 1980), p. 32.

10. Jeffrey J. Crow, Paul D. Escott, and Flora J. Hatley, *A History of African Americans in North Carolina* (Raleigh: N.C. Department of Cultural Resources, Office of Archives and History, 1992), p. 133.

11. Ibid., p. 130.

12. U.S. Bureau of the Census, *United States Census of Population, 1900*, vol. 1, "Number of Inhabitants."

13. William J. Cooper and Thomas E. Terrill, *The American South: A History* (New York: Alfred A. Knopf, 1990), p. 584.

14. Rippy, *F. M. Simmons*, p. 304.

15. C. Vann Woodward, *Origins of the New South, 1877–1913* (Baton Rouge: Louisiana State University Press, 1951), p. 400.

16. Oliver H. Orr Jr., *Charles Brantley Aycock* (Chapel Hill: University of North Carolina Press, 1961), p. 18.

17. R. D. W. Connor and Clarence Poe, *The Life and Speeches of Charles Brantley Aycock* (Garden City, N.Y.: Doubleday and Page, 1912), pp. 258–59.
18. Orr, *Charles Brantley Aycock*, p. 320.
19. Ibid.
20. Ibid., pp. 320–21.
21. Ibid., p. 329.
22. Woodward, *Origins*.
23. Louis R. Harlan, *Separate and Unequal: Public School Campaigns and Racism in the Southern Seaboard States, 1901–1905* (Chapel Hill: University of North Carolina Press, 1958), p. 104.
24. Ibid.
25. Cooper and Terrill, *The American South*, p. 584.
26. Rippy, *F. M. Simmons*, p. 52.
27. Cash, "Jehovah."
28. Douglas Carl Abrams, "A Progressive-Conservative Duel: The 1920 Democratic Gubernatorial Primaries in North Carolina," *North Carolina Historical Review* 55 (October 1978): 426.
29. Joseph L. Morrison, *Governor O. Max Gardner: A Power in North Carolina and New Deal Washington* (Chapel Hill: University of North Carolina Press, 1971), p. 32.
30. Abrams, "A Progressive-Conservative Duel."
31. Elena C. Green, "Those Opposed: The Antisuffragists in North Carolina, 1900–1920," *North Carolina Historical Review* 67 (July 1990): 318.
32. Ibid.
33. Morrison, *Governor O. Max Gardner*, p. 32.
34. George B. Tindall, *The Emergence of the New South, 1913–1945* (Baton Rouge: Louisiana State University Press, 1967), p. 226.
35. "Italy Turns to This State for Advice on Highway Work," *N&O*, March 2, 1923.
36. William D. Snider, *Light on the Hill: A History of the University of North Carolina at Chapel Hill* (Chapel Hill: University of North Carolina Press, 1992), p. 203.
37. Tindall, *The Emergence of the New South*, p. 225.
38. Ibid.
39. "First General Session Held at Auditorium: Welcome by Governor," *N&O*, November 24, 1921.
40. Samuel Huntington Hobbs Jr., *North Carolina: Economic and Social* (Chapel Hill: University of North Carolina Press, 1930), p. 165.
41. Nathaniel Fuqua Magruder, "The Administration of Governor Cameron Morrison of North Carolina, 1921–25" (Ph.D. diss., University of North Carolina at Chapel Hill, 1968), p. 245.
42. Lindley S. Butler and Alan D. Watson, *The North Carolina Experience: An Interpretive and Documentary History* (Chapel Hill: University of North Carolina Press, 1984), p. 360.
43. Paul R. Clancy, *Just a Country Lawyer: A Biography of Senator Sam Ervin* (Bloomington: Indiana University Press, 1974), p. 94.

44. "Raid on Room of AD Watts Reveals Negress under Bed," *N&O*, January 29, 1923.
45. George B. Autry and Ferrel Guillory, *The Carolinas, Yesterday, Today, Tomorrow: An Exploration of Social and Economic Trends, 1924–1999* (Charlotte, N.C.: Duke Endowment, MDC Inc., 1999), p. 5.
46. Rippy, *F. M. Simmons*, pp. 216–17.
47. Thad Eure, interview with author, 1985.
48. Richard L. Watson Jr., "A Political Leader Bolts—F. M. Simmons in the Presidential Election of 1928," *North Carolina Historical Review* 37 (October 1960): 536; and "Tamany Demands Raise Negro Issue," *N&O*, October 27, 1928.
49. Tindall, *The Emergence of the New South*, p. 252.
50. Elmer L. Puryer, *Democratic Dissension in North Carolina, 1928–1936* (Chapel Hill: University of North Carolina Press, 1962), p. 37.
51. Richard L. Watson Jr., "A Southern Democratic Primary: Simmons vs. Bailey in 1930," *North Carolina Historical Review* 42 (January 1965): 21–46.
52. U.S. Bureau of the Census, *Urban and Rural Population: 1900 to 1990* (October 1995).
53. Tindall, *The Emergence of the New South*, p. 576.
54. Watson, "A Southern Democratic Primary," p. 186.
55. Jonathan Daniels, *The End of Innocence* (Philadelphia and New York: J. B. Lippincott Company, 1954); Daniels, *Tar Heels*, p. 321.
56. Rippy, *F. M. Simmons*.

CHAPTER 2

1. Jonathan Daniels, *Tar Heels: A Portrait of North Carolina* (New York: Dodd, Mead and Company, 1941), p. 324.
2. Grace Rutledge, *Miss Fay: A Biography of Fay Webb Gardner* (Charlotte, N.C.: Heritage Printers Inc., 1978), p. 23.
3. USDA Agriculture Statistics Service.
4. Rutledge, *Miss Fay*.
5. John L. Bell, *Hard Times: Beginnings of the Great Depression in North Carolina, 1929–1933* (Raleigh: N.C. Department of Cultural Resources, Office of Archives and History, 1982), p. 42.
6. Joseph L. Morrison, *Governor O. Max Gardner: A Power in North Carolina and New Deal Washington* (Chapel Hill: University of North Carolina Press, 1971), p. 102.
7. Edwin Gill, oral history interview by Archie Davis, 1973, Southern Historical Collection, University of North Carolina at Chapel Hill.
8. Edwin Gill, address at the dedication of Gardner Hall, North Carolina State University, May 6, 1953, Edwin Gill Papers, Southern Historical Collection, University of North Carolina at Chapel Hill.
9. Morrison, *Governor O. Max Gardner*, p. 85.
10. Lindley S. Butler and Alan D. Watson, *The North Carolina Experience: An Interpretive and Documentary History* (Chapel Hill: University of North Carolina Press, 1984), p. 84.

11. Morrison, *Governor O. Max Gardner*, p. 103.
12. U.S. Bureau of the Census, *Statistical Abstract of the United States* (2003).
13. U.S. Census Geospatial and Statistical Data Center, University of Virginia, Charlottesville, Virginia, <http://www2.lib.virginia.edu/geostat/index.html>.
14. Daniels, *Tar Heels*, p. 212.
15. George B. Tindall, *The Emergence of the New South, 1913–1945* (Baton Rouge: Louisiana State University Press, 1967), p. 318.
16. W. J. Cash, *The Mind of the South* (New York: Alfred A. Knopf, 1941), p. 204.
17. Tindall, *The Emergence of the New South*, p. 344.
18. Butler and Watson, *The North Carolina Experience*, p. 440.
19. Tindall, *The Emergence of the New South*, p. 349.
20. Cash, *The Mind of the South*, p. 362.
21. Warren Ashby, *Frank Porter Graham: A Southern Liberal* (Winston-Salem, N.C.: John F. Blair, Publisher, 1980), p. 77.
22. "Incidentally by Nell Battle Lewis," *N&O*, August 25, 1929; and "Incidentally by Nell Battle Lewis," *N&O*, September 8, 1929.
23. "Incidentally by Nell Battle Lewis," *N&O*, August 7, 1932.
24. Anthony J. Badger, *North Carolina and the New Deal* (Raleigh: N.C. Department of Cultural Resources, Office of Archives and History, 1981), p. 39.
25. U.S. Department of Labor, Bureau of Labor Statistics, table 5, "Union Affiliation of Employed Wage and Salary Workers," <http://www.bls.gov>.
26. Gill, address at the dedication of Gardner Hall.
27. Thad Eure, interview with author, 1985.
28. Daniels, *Tar Heels*, p. 65.
29. Ibid.
30. Morrison, *Governor O. Max Gardner*, p. 112.
31. Ibid., p. 72.
32. Ibid., p. 73.
33. Julian M. Pleasants, *Buncombe Bob: The Life and Times of Robert Rice Reynolds* (Chapel Hill: University of North Carolina Press, 2000), p. 27.
34. Ibid., p. 14.
35. Julian M. Pleasants, "The Senatorial Career of Robert Rice Reynolds" (Ph.D. diss., University of North Carolina at Chapel Hill, 1971).
36. Burke Davis, "Senator Bob Reynolds: Retrospective View," *Harper's Magazine*, March 1944.
37. Pleasants, *Buncombe Bob*, p. 33.
38. Ibid.
39. "Reynolds Flays GOP Policies," *N&O*, April 26, 1932.
40. "Reynolds Heads Back for Coast," *N&O*, May 31, 1932.
41. Arthur L. Shelton, "Buncombe Bob," *American Mercury*, October 1932, p. 142.
42. "Says Opponents Slandering Him," *N&O*, March 16, 1932.
43. "Incidentally by Nell Battle Lewis," *N&O*, June 26, 1932.
44. Pleasants, "The Senatorial Career of Robert Rice Reynolds," p. 197.
45. W. J. Cash, "The Arch Paladin of the Dry South," *American Mercury*, October 1931.

46. Pleasants, "The Senatorial Career of Robert Rice Reynolds," p. 116.
47. "Morrison Calls Rival Showman," *N&O*, June 28, 1932.
48. Pleasants, "The Senatorial Career of Robert Rice Reynolds," p. 142.
49. Ibid., p. 134.
50. Ibid., p. 138.
51. Morrison, *Governor O. Max Gardner*, p. 226.
52. Badger, *North Carolina and the New Deal*, p. 61.
53. Morrison, *Governor O. Max Gardner*, p. 201.
54. Ibid., p. 4.
55. Ibid., p. 183.
56. David Kennedy, *Freedom from Fear: The American People in Depression and War, 1929–1945* (Oxford: Oxford University Press, 1999), p. 340.
57. Dewey W. Grantham, *The South in Modern America* (New York: Harper Collins Publishers, 1994), p. 120.
58. David Leroy Corbitt, ed., *Addresses, Letters, and Papers of Clyde Roark Hoey, Governor of North Carolina, 1937–1941* (Raleigh: Raleigh Council of State of North Carolina, 1944), p. xviii.
59. Morrison, *Governor O. Max Gardner*, p. 221.
60. "Charges O. Max Gardner Ruling State by Phone," *N&O*, May 9, 1936.
61. Badger, *North Carolina and the New Deal*, p. 64.
63. "McDonald Tears into Tax System," *N&O*, May 24, 1936.
63. Raymond Goodmon, oral history interview, June 14, 1989, Southern Historical Collection, University of North Carolina at Chapel Hill.
64. Hall and others, *Like a Family*, p. 320.
65. "Vast Hall Here Jammed for Speech by McDonald," *N&O*, May 27, 1936.
66. *N&O*, June 1, 1936.
67. "Hoey Declares He Is Winning," *N&O*, May 31, 1936.
68. W. T. Bost, "McDonald Makes Fiery Request for Runoff in Gubernatorial Race," *Greensboro Daily News*, June 12, 1936.
69. E. C. Daniel Jr., "Hoey Declares McDonald Only Bared Himself," *N&O*, June 19, 1936; "Attacks Lobby Record of Hoey," *N&O*, June 24, 1936; Robert Williams, "Hoey Forgoes Inferences to Brand Dr. McDonald as Public Enemy Number One," *N&O*, June 26, 1936; Charles Parker, "McDonald Says Hoey Put Campaign into Gutter and Kept It There," *N&O*, June 28, 1936.
70. Morrison, *Governor O. Max Gardner*, p. 67.
71. Ibid.
72. V. O. Key, *Southern Politics in State and Nation* (New York: Alfred A. Knopf, 1949), p. 95.
73. Ronald E. Marcello, "The Politics of Relief: The North Carolina WPA and the Tar Heel Elections of 1936," *North Carolina Historical Review* 68 (January 1991): 166.
74. Robert Williams, "Hoey Forgoes Inferences to Brand Dr. McDonald as Public Enemy," *N&O*, July 4, 1936.
75. Charles Parker, "McDonald Says Gardner Came to Shelby to Name Governor for People," *N&O*, July 4, 1936.

76. Letter from Clyde Hoey, September 10, 1936, Oliver Max Gardner Papers, Southern Historical Collection, University of North Carolina at Chapel Hill.

77. Letter from Sen. Harry Byrd, July 18, 1936, Oliver Max Gardner Papers, Southern Historical Collection, University of North Carolina at Chapel Hill.

78. Francis Butler Simkins and Charles Pierce Roland, *A History of the South* (New York: Alfred A. Knopf, 1972), p. 540.

79. Elmer L. Puryer, *Democratic Dissension in North Carolina, 1928–1936* (Chapel Hill: University of North Carolina Press, 1962), p. 229.

80. Key, *Southern Politics*, p. 456.

81. Morrison, *Governor O. Max Gardner*, p. 220.

82. O. Max Gardner, letter to Clayton Moore, Williamston, N.C., November 10, 1936, Oliver Max Gardner Papers, Southern Historical Collection, University of North Carolina at Chapel Hill.

83. Morrison, *Governor O. Max Gardner*, p. 220.

84. Lauch Faircloth, interview with author, September 26, 2001, Clinton, N.C.

85. Pleasants, *Buncombe Bob*, p. 63.

86. Ibid., p. 65.

87. "Under the Dome," *N&O*, April 14, 1937.

88. Jonathan Daniels, "Interlude for an Isolationist," *N&O*, September 4, 1941.

89. Pleasants, *Buncombe Bob*, p. 332.

90. John Roy Carlson, *Under Cover* (New York: Dutton, 1943).

91. Pleasants, "The Senatorial Career of Robert Rice Reynolds," p. 407.

92. Pleasants, *Buncombe Bob*, p. 166.

93. Ibid., p. 457.

94. Pleasants, "The Senatorial Career of Robert Rice Reynolds," p. 505.

95. Pleasants, *Buncombe Bob*, p. 183.

96. Ibid., p. 585.

97. Ibid., p. 219.

98. Pleasants, "The Senatorial Career of Robert Rice Reynolds," p. 669.

99. Ibid.

100. Julian M. Pleasants, "The Last Hurrah: Bob Reynolds and the U.S. Senate Race in 1950," *North Carolina Historical Review* 65 (January 1988): 59.

101. Pleasants, "The Senatorial Career of Robert Rice Reynolds," p. 725.

102. Key, *Southern Politics*, p. 214.

CHAPTER 3

1. Jim Chaney, "Scott in Surprise Action Names Graham to Senate," *N&O*, March 23, 1949.

2. Julian M. Pleasants and Augustus M. Burns III, *Frank Porter Graham and the 1950 Senate Race in North Carolina* (Chapel Hill: University of North Carolina Press, 1990), p. 35.

3. Ibid., p. 36.

4. Robert W. Scott, interview with author, December 1999, Haw River, N.C.

5. Samuel Huntington Hobbs Jr., *North Carolina Economic and Social Profile* (Chapel Hill: University of North Carolina Press, 1930), p. 114.

6. William E. Leuchtenburg, *Franklin D. Roosevelt and the New Deal, 1932–1940* (New York: Harper and Row, 1963), p. 157.

7. Thomas C. Parramore, *Express Lanes and Country Roads: The Way We Lived in North Carolina, 1920–1970* (Chapel Hill: University of North Carolina Press, 1983), p. 21; and Samuel Huntington Hobbs Jr., *North Carolina: Economic and Social* (Chapel Hill: University of North Carolina Press, 1930), p. 85.

8. Anthony J. Badger, *North Carolina and the New Deal* (Raleigh: N.C. Department of Cultural Resources, Office of Archives and History, 1981), p. 2.

9. David Leroy Corbitt, ed., *Public Addresses, Letters, and Papers of William Kerr Scott* (Raleigh: Division of Publications, N.C. Office of Archives and History, 1957), p. xvi.

10. V. O. Key Jr., *Southern Politics in State and Nation* (New York: Alfred A. Knopf, 1949), p. 205.

11. Robert W. Scott, interview with author.

12. USDA National Agriculture Statistics Services, *U.S. & All States Data—Farm Numbers—Total Farms, Land in Farms, Average Farm Size*, <http://www.nass.usda.gov/index.asp>.

13. Terry Sanford, interview with author, February 1998, Durham, N.C.

14. "Scott Answers Johnson Attack," *N&O*, May 2, 1948.

15. "Johnson Raps Scott Record," *N&O*, June 19, 1948.

16. Jeffrey J. Crow, Paul D. Escott, and Flora J. Hatley, *A History of African Americans in North Carolina* (Raleigh: Office of Archives and History, N.C. Department of Cultural Resources, 1992), p. 149.

17. John William Coon, "Kerr Scott, the Go-Forward Governor: His Origins, His Program, and the North Carolina General Assembly" (master's thesis, University of North Carolina at Chapel Hill, 1968).

18. Simmons Fentress, "Kerr Scott," *N&O*, January 9, 1953.

19. Corbitt, *Public Addresses, Letters, and Papers of William Kerr Scott*, p. 4.

20. Parramore, *Express Lanes and Country Roads*, p. 74.

21. Raymond Massey, interview with author, November 12, 2003.

22. Fentress, "Kerr Scott."

23. Ibid.

24. Corbitt, *Public Addresses, Letters, and Papers of William Kerr Scott*, p. 98.

25. "Scott Pledges Negro Program," *N&O*, January 15, 1949.

26. Howard E. Covington Jr. and Marion A. Ellis, *Terry Sanford: Politics, Progress, and Outrageous Ambitions* (Durham: Duke University Press, 1999), p. 112.

27. "Scott Pledges Negro Program."

28. Jesse Helms, letter to Kerr Scott, September 16, 1949, Kerr Scott Papers, N.C. Office of Archives and History, Raleigh.

29. James Clotfelter, *Frank Porter Graham: Service to North Carolina and the Nation* (Greensboro, N.C.: North Carolina Service Project at the University of North Carolina at Greensboro, 1993), p. 126.

30. Julian M. Pleasants, "Frank Graham and the Politics of the New South," in *The Adaptable South: Essays in Honor of George Brown Tindall*, ed. Elizabeth Jaco-

way, Dan T. Carter, Lester C. Lamon, and Robert C. McMath Jr. (Baton Rouge: Louisiana State University Press, 1991), p. 183.

31. Warren Ashby, *Frank Porter Graham: A Southern Liberal* (Winston-Salem, N.C.: John F. Blair, Publisher, 1980), p. 93.

32. Ibid., p. 156.

33. Ibid., p. 235.

34. Frank Porter Graham, interview by Warren Ashby, June 12, 1962, Southern Oral History Program, University of North Carolina at Chapel Hill.

35. Pleasants and Burns, *Frank Porter Graham and the 1950 Senate Race in North Carolina*, p. 24.

36. Samuel Lubell, *The Future of American Politics* (New York: Harper and Brothers, 1951), p. 107.

37. Ashby, *Frank Porter Graham*, p. 233.

38. Gerald Johnson, "Gerald Johnson Graham of Carolina: Portrait of a Citizen at Large," *Survey Graphic*, April 1942, p. 188.

39. Corbitt, *Public Addresses, Letters, and Papers of William Kerr Scott*, p. 174.

40. "Graham Selection Praised by State, National Leaders," *N&O*, March 24, 1949.

41. Bryan Haislip, "UNC Students Say Good-bye to President Frank Graham," *N&O*, March 28, 1949.

42. Letter from Hill Scoggin to Kerr Scott, 1949, Kerr Scott Papers, N.C. Office of Archives and History, Raleigh.

43. Crow, Escott, and Hatley, *A History of African Americans in North Carolina*, p. 151.

44. David Cecelski and Timothy B. Tyson, *Democracy Betrayed: The Wilmington Race Riot of 1898 and Its Legacy* (Chapel Hill: University of North Carolina Press, 1998), p. 266.

45. Margaret Kernodle, "Southern Group Organizes Drive," *N&O*, March 6, 1948.

46. Covington and Ellis, *Terry Sanford*, p. 96.

47. H. C. Dale, letter to the editor, *N&O*, March 15, 1948.

48. Hubert Ellis, letter to the editor, *N&O*, March 24, 1948.

49. Marjorie Hunter, "Democrats Given Free Reign at Democratic Convention," *N&O*, May 21, 1948.

50. Nadine Cohodas, *Strom Thurmond and the Politics of Southern Change* (New York: Simon & Shuster, 1993), p. 184.

51. R. S. Hood, letter to the editor, *N&O*, August 8, 1948.

52. Sayoko Uesugi, "Gender, Race, and the Cold War: Mary Price and the Progressive Party in North Carolina, 1945–1948," *North Carolina Historical Review* 77 (July 2000): 305.

53. John Earl Haynes and Harvey Klehr, *Venona: Decoding Soviet Espionage in America* (New Haven: Yale University Press, 1999); and Herbert Romerstein and Eric Breindel, *The Venona Secrets: Exposing Soviet Espionage and America's Traitors* (Washington, D.C.: Regnery Publishing, 2000), p. 165.

54. Simmons Fentress, "Wallace Appearances Bring Showers of Tomatoes, Eggs," *N&O*, August 31, 1948.

55. John N. Popham, "President Assails Wallace Egging, Missiles Thrown Again in the South," *New York Times*, September 1, 1948.
56. Ibid.
57. James A. Hagerty, "48,000 Hear Wallace Assert Prejudice Will Fail in the South," *New York Times*, September 11, 1948.
58. Pleasants, "Frank Graham and the Politics of the New South," p. 197.
59. Key, *Southern Politics in State and Nation*, p. 206.
60. Pleasants and Burns, *Frank Porter Graham and the 1950 Senate Race in North Carolina*, p. 121.
61. Ibid., p. 125.
62. Ibid., pp. 133, 171.
63. Ibid., p. 100.
64. Ibid., pp. 174, 176.
65. Charles Broadwell, "Record Keeper," *Fayetteville Observer-Times*, April 4, 1999.
66. Pleasants and Burns, *Frank Porter Graham and the 1950 Senate Race in North Carolina*, p. 172.
67. Ibid., p. 115.
68. Lauch Faircloth, interview with author, September 26, 2001, Clinton, N.C.
69. Ashby, *Frank Porter Graham*, p. 261.
70. Pleasants and Burns, *Frank Porter Graham and the 1950 Senate Race in North Carolina*, pp. 162, 165.
71. L. J. Moore, letter to Gov. Kerr Scott, June 21, 1950, Kerr Scott Papers, N.C. Office of Archives and History, Raleigh.
72. Pleasants and Burns, *Frank Porter Graham and the 1950 Senate Race in North Carolina*, p. 117.
73. "Smith Advertisement: Compare Your Vote," *N&O*, June 23, 1950.
74. Pleasants and Burns, *Frank Porter Graham and the 1950 Senate Race in North Carolina*, p. 223.
75. Jonathan Daniels, "Sound the Tocsin," *N&O*, June 18, 1950.
76. Simmons Fentress, "Willis Smith Tours Home County," *N&O*, June 18, 1950.
77. Woodrow Price, "Graham Meets the Folks in Wake," *N&O*, June 18, 1950.
78. Ibid.
79. Lubell, *The Future of American Politics*, p. 110.
80. Ashby, *Frank Porter Graham*, p. 270.
81. Pleasants and Burns, *Frank Porter Graham and the 1950 Senate Race in North Carolina*, p. 263.
82. Ibid., p. 250.
83. Fanny Knight Thomas, letter to Gov. Kerr Scott, June 30, 1950, Kerr Scott Papers, N.C. Office of Archives and History, Raleigh.
84. Pleasants and Burns, *Frank Porter Graham and the 1950 Senate Race in North Carolina*, p. 273.
85. Lubell, *The Future of American Politics*, p. 120.
86. John Ehle, *Dr. Frank: Life with Frank Porter Graham* (Chapel Hill: Franklin Street Books, 1993), p. 191.

87. "Incidentally by Nell Battle Lewis," *N&O*, June 25, 1950.
88. William A. Link, *William Friday: Power, Purpose, and American Higher Education* (Chapel Hill: University of North Carolina Press, 1995), p. 73.
89. Jesse Helms, interview with John Bason, UNC-TV, August 31, 1999.
90. Ernest B. Furgurson, *Hard Right: The Rise of Jesse Helms* (New York and London: W. W. Norton & Company, 1986), pp. 53–54.
91. Ibid., p. 54.
92. Edwin H. Powell, letter to Kerr Scott, May 21, 1949, Kerr Scott Papers, N.C. Office of Archives and History, Raleigh.
93. Pleasants, "Frank Graham and the Politics of the New South," p. 248.
94. Ralph Scott, interview by Jacquelyn Hall and Bill Finger, April 22, 1974, Southern Oral History Program, University of North Carolina at Chapel Hill.
95. Fentress, "Kerr Scott."
96. Harry Golden, *The Right Time* (New York: G. P. Putnam's Sons, 1969), p. 273.
97. Lauch Faircloth, interview with author.
98. "Scott Gives Views on Court Decision," *N&O*, May 18, 1956.
99. Terry Sanford, interview with Brent Glass, May 14, 1976, Southern Oral History Program, University of North Carolina at Chapel Hill, p. 50.
100. Ibid., p. 63.
101. Ehle, *Dr. Frank*, p. 194.
102. Tom Wicker, *Facing the Lions* (New York: Viking Press, 1973), p. 49.
103. William D. Snider, "The Scotts of Haw River," in *The North Carolina Century: Tar Heels Who Made a Difference, 1900–2000*, ed. Howard E. Covington Jr. and Marion A. Ellis (Charlotte: Levine Museum of the New South, 2002), p. 521.
104. Jim Hunt, interview with author, April 1, 2003.

CHAPTER 4

1. Matt Schudel, "I. Beverly Lake: A Portrait at 80," *N&O*, September 12, 1986.
2. John Drescher, *Triumph of Good Will: How Terry Sanford Beat a Champion of Segregation and Reshaped the South* (Jackson: University Press of Mississippi, 2000), p. 41.
3. Louis Kraar, "Must Use Courts to Get Compliance, Negroes Told," *N&O*, May 14, 1956.
4. Carson McCoy, letter to the editor, *N&O*, May 20, 1954.
5. Woodrow Price, "Party Leaders Demand Voice in Appointments," *N&O*, March 17, 1957.
6. *N&O*, November 22, 1959.
7. S. Huntington Hobbs Jr., *North Carolina: An Economic and Social Profile* (Chapel Hill: University of North Carolina Press, 1958).
8. Ibid., p. 98.
9. Ibid., p. 158.
10. Luther H. Hodges, *Businessman in the State House: Six Years as Governor of North Carolina* (Chapel Hill: University of North Carolina Press, 1962), p. 203.

11. Timothy B. Tyson, *Radio Free Dixie: Robert F. Williams and the Roots of Black Power* (Chapel Hill: University of North Carolina Press, 1999), p. 75.

12. Hodges, *Businessman*, p. 97.

13. William H. Chafe, *Civilities and Civil Rights: Greensboro, North Carolina, and the Black Struggle for Freedom* (New York and Oxford: Oxford University Press, 1980), p. 75.

14. Roy Brantley, "Platform Cites Racial Problem," *N&O*, May 18, 1956.

15. R. Hargus Taylor, "Charles Bennett Deane," in *Dictionary of North Carolina Biography*, vol. 2, ed. William S. Powell (Chapel Hill: University of North Carolina Press, 1986), p. 47.

16. Associated Press, "Mississippi Interpretation," *N&O*, May 28, 1956.

17. Drescher, *Triumph of Good Will*, p. 42.

18. Tyson, *Radio Free Dixie*, p. 106.

19. Hodges, *Businessman*, p. 91.

20. Ibid.

21. Tyson, *Radio Free Dixie*, p. 107.

22. Ibid., p. 137.

23. Ibid., p. 138.

24. Ibid., p. 125.

25. Numan V. Bartley, *The New South, 1945–1980* (Baton Rouge: Louisiana State University Press, 1995), p. 222.

26. Howard E. Covington Jr. and Marion A. Ellis, *Terry Sanford: Politics, Progress, and Outrageous Ambitions* (Durham: Duke University Press, 1999), p. 137.

27. Henry S. Stroupe, "Irving Edward Carlyle," in *Dictionary of North Carolina Biography*, vol. 1, ed. William S. Powell (Chapel Hill: University of North Carolina Press, 1979), p. 325.

28. Edward Rankin, interview by Jay Jenkins, August 29, 1987, Southern Oral History Program, University of North Carolina at Chapel Hill.

29. Paul R. Clancy, *Just a Country Lawyer: A Biography of Senator Sam Ervin* (Bloomington: Indiana University Press, 1974), p. 72.

30. Ibid., p. 160.

31. Ibid., p. 172.

32. Ibid., p. 170.

33. Ibid., p. 223.

34. Ibid., p. 267.

35. Ibid., p. 269.

36. Ibid., p. 7.

37. Ibid., p. 291.

38. Ibid., p. 300.

CHAPTER 5

1. William H. Chafe, *Civilities and Civil Rights: Greensboro, North Carolina, and the Black Struggle for Freedom* (New York: Oxford University Press, 1980), p. 115.

2. John Drescher, *Triumph of Good Will: How Terry Sanford Beat a Champion of*

Segregation and Reshaped the South (Jackson: University Press of Mississippi, 2000), p. 71.
3. Ibid., p. 25.
4. Ibid., p. 131.
5. Ibid., p. 143.
6. Terry Sanford, interview with Joe B. Frantz, May 15, 1971, Lyndon B. Johnson Presidential Library, Austin, Texas, p. 2.
7. Howard E. Covington Jr. and Marion A. Ellis, *Terry Sanford: Politics, Progress, and Outrageous Ambitions* (Durham: Duke University Press, 1999), p. 216.
8. Drescher, *Triumph of Good Will*, p. 208.
9. David Cooper, "Sanford Lashes Lake Who Raps Labor," *N&O*, June 15, 1960.
10. Woodrow Price, "Sanford Slaps Back at Racist Campaign of Candidate Lake," *N&O*, June 1, 1960.
11. Biographical conversations with Terry Sanford, UNC-TV, 1997, p. 24.
12. Drescher, *Triumph of Good Will*, p. 170.
13. David Cooper, "Lake's Campaign Sang 'Dixie' in Defeat," *N&O*, June 26, 1960.
14. Drescher, *Triumph of Good Will*, p. 222.
15. Ibid., p. 232.
16. Ibid., p. 237.
17. Barbara Rohrman, interview with author, August 2000.
18. Mike Easley, interview with author, August 2000.
19. Terry Sanford, interview with Brent Glass, 1976, Southern Oral History Program, University of North Carolina at Chapel Hill, p. 52.
20. Numan Bartley and Hugh D. Graham, *Southern Politics and the Second Reconstruction* (Baltimore and London: The Johns Hopkins University Press, 1978), p. 93.
21. Memory F. Mitchell, *Messages, Addresses, and Public Papers of Terry Sanford, Governor of North Carolina, 1961–65* (Raleigh: State Office of Archives and History, 1966), p. 6.
22. U.S. Bureau of the Census, *Statistical Abstract of the U.S., 1962*, "Public School Expenditures by States" and other charts (chart nos. 141, 149, 163, 166).
23. Mitchell, *Messages, Addresses, and Public Papers of Terry Sanford*, p. 118.
24. Covington and Ellis, *Terry Sanford*, p. 257.
25. Ibid., p. 260.
26. Terry Sanford, interview with author, February 1998, Durham, N.C.
27. Covington and Ellis, *Terry Sanford*, p. 308.
28. U.S. Bureau of the Census, *Statistical Abstract 1960, No. 449*, "Money Income of Families—Percent Distribution by Income Level, 1959," "Personal Income Changes in Total and Per Capita Personal Income by States, 1929–60" (chart no. 433).
29. Thomas C. Parramore, *Express Lanes and Country Roads: The Way We Lived in North Carolina, 1920–1970* (Chapel Hill: University of North Carolina Press, 1983), p. 2.
30. Editorial, *Viewpoint*, WRAL-TV, September 14, 1961, Southern Historical Collection, University of North Carolina at Chapel Hill.

31. Terry Sanford, interview with author.

32. Ibid., p. 25.

33. David S. Cecelski, *Along Freedom Road: Hyde County, North Carolina, and the Fate of Black Schools in the South* (Chapel Hill: University of North Carolina Press, 1994), p. 39.

34. "North Carolina Labeled Most Active for Klan," *N&O*, October 20, 1965.

35. Roy Parker, "Klan Chiefs Termed Backers of Violence," *N&O*, October 22, 1965.

36. Cecelski, *Along Freedom Road*, p. 38.

37. Kate Erwin, "New Bern Working for Racial Harmony," *N&O*, October 3, 1965.

38. Timothy B. Tyson, *Blood Done Sign My Name* (New York: Crown Publishers, 2004), p. 53.

39. "Was Cross and Weiner Roast, Too," *N&O*, November 3, 1965.

40. Mitchell, *Messages, Addresses, and Public Papers of Terry Sanford*, p. 598.

41. Roy Peter Clark, *The Changing South of Gene Patterson: Journalism and Civil Rights, 1960–1968* (Gainesville: University of Florida Press, 2002), p. 131.

42. Mitchell, *Messages, Addresses, and Public Papers of Terry Sanford*, p. 579.

43. Chafe, *Civilities and Civil Rights*, p. 149.

44. Mitchell, *Messages, Addresses, and Public Papers of Terry Sanford*, p. 598.

45. William J. Billingsley, *Communists on Campus: Race, Politics, and the Public University in Sixties North Carolina* (Athens: University of Georgia Press, 1999), p. 68.

46. Editorial, *Viewpoint*, WRAL-TV, June 27, 1963, Southern Historical Collection, University of North Carolina at Chapel Hill.

47. Ibid., June 29, 1964.

48. Russell Clay, "Justice Denies His Papers to ECU," *N&O*, April 10, 1969.

49. Drescher, *Triumph of Good Will*, p. 269.

50. Ibid., p. 257.

51. Covington and Ellis, *Terry Sanford*, p. 350.

52. Terry Sanford, interview with Brent Glass.

53. Paul Popple to Walter Jenkins, August 20, 1964, Presidential Papers, Lyndon B. Johnson Presidential Library, Austin, Texas; Marvin Watson to Lyndon B. Johnson, July 16, 1966, Presidential Papers, Lyndon B. Johnson Presidential Library, Austin, Texas.

54. Biographical conversations with Terry Sanford, UNC-TV, p. 81.

55. Jules Witcover, *Marathon: The Pursuit of the Presidency, 1972–1976* (New York: Viking Press, 1977), p. 148.

CHAPTER 6

1. Earl Black and Merle Black, *The Rise of Southern Republicans* (Cambridge, Mass.: Harvard University Press, 2002), p. 32.

2. Editorial, *Viewpoint*, WRAL-TV, September 11, 1964, Southern Historical Collection, University of North Carolina at Chapel Hill.

3. Frank Rouse, interview, November 14, 1996, Southern Oral History Program, Southern Historical Collection, University of North Carolina at Chapel Hill.

4. Editorial, *Viewpoint*, WRAL-TV, December 18, 1964, Southern Historical Collection, University of North Carolina at Chapel Hill.

5. Wilton Duke, interview with author, October 15, 1995, Farmville, North Carolina.

6. Jane Pettis Wiseman, "The New Politics in North Carolina: James Gardner and the 1968 Governor's Race" (master's thesis, University of North Carolina at Chapel Hill, 1971), p. 14.

7. Ibid., p. 70.

8. Ibid., p. 73.

9. Editorial, *Viewpoint*, WRAL-TV, November 6, 1968, Southern Historical Collection, University of North Carolina at Chapel Hill.

10. Ibid., January 7, 1965.

11. Ernest B. Furgurson, *Hard Right: The Rise of Jesse Helms* (New York and London: W. W. Norton & Company, 1986), p. 31.

12. Timothy Tyson, *Radio Free Dixie: Robert F. Williams and the Roots of Black Power* (Chapel Hill: University of North Carolina Press, 1999), p. 113.

13. Howard E. Covington Jr., *Uncommon Giving: A. J. Fletcher and a North Carolina Legacy* (Raleigh: A. J. Fletcher Foundation, 1999), p. 92.

14. Furgurson, *Hard Right*, p. 23.

15. Rob Christensen, "Helms Spawns Passions among Supporters, Detractors," *N&O*, September 23, 1984.

16. Editorial, *Viewpoint*, WRAL-TV, April 26, 1968, Southern Historical Collection, University of North Carolina at Chapel Hill.

17. Covington, *Uncommon Giving*, p. 115.

18. Furgurson, *Hard Right*, p. 105.

19. Ibid., p. 111.

20. Connaught Marshner, interview with author, October 1984.

21. Furgurson, *Hard Right*, p. 110.

22. Ferrel Guillory, "Reagan Says Rocky Abused," *N&O*, July 26, 1975.

23. Jules Whitcover, *Marathon: The Pursuit of the Presidency, 1972–1976* (New York: Viking Press, 1977), p. 411.

24. Rob Christensen, "Jesse Helms' Race Politics," *N&O*, September 10, 1989.

25. Whitcover, *Marathon*, p. 415.

26. Lou Cannon, *Reagan* (New York: G. P. Putnam's Sons, 1982), p. 217.

27. Carter Wrenn, unpublished manuscript, 2006.

28. Alex Castellanos, interview with author, August 23, 2001, Washington, D.C.

29. Harvey Buckwalter, interview with author, March 1990.

30. Computer analysis by author, April 1991.

31. Alex Castellanos, interview with author.

32. Elizabeth Drew, "A Reporter at Large: Jesse Helms," *New Yorker*, July 20, 1981.

33. Furgurson, *Hard Right*, p. 161.

34. Carter Wrenn, interview with author, September 11, 2001.

35. *N&O*, February 25, 1990.

36. Jesse Helms, interview with author, October 16, 2003, Raleigh.

37. Carter Wrenn, interview with author.
38. Alexander P. Lamis, *Southern Politics in the 1990s* (Baton Rouge: Louisiana State University Press, 1999), p. 97.
39. U.S. Bureau of the Census, *Statistical Abstract of the U.S., 2003*.
40. Byron E. Shafer and Richard Johnston, *The End of Southern Exceptionalism: Class, Race, and Partisan Change in the Postwar South* (Cambridge, Mass.: Harvard University Press, 2006), p. 174.
41. Earl Black and Merle Black, *Politics and Society in the South* (Cambridge, Mass.: Harvard University Press, 1987), p. 297.
42. Carter Wrenn, interview with author.
43. "Text of Martin's Letter," *N&O*, February 25, 1990.

CHAPTER 7
1. Jim Gardner fund-raiser, Nashville, North Carolina, February 23, 1990.
2. Jim Hunt, interview with author, April 1, 2003.
3. Wayne Grimsley, *James B. Hunt, a North Carolina Progressive* (Jefferson, N.C.: McFarland & Company, 2003), p. 41.
4. Jim Hunt, interview with author.
5. Ibid.
6. Ibid.
7. Gary Orren and Pamela Varley, *The Helms-Hunt Senate Race*, Case Studies in Public Policy and Management, John F. Kennedy School of Government, Harvard University (1986), p. 29.
8. Ibid.
9. Jim Hunt, interview with author.
10. "Per-Pupil Expenditures as Percent of U.S. Average, 1890," in *The South in Modern America*, by Dewey Grantham (New York: Harper Collins Publishers, 1994), pp. 100, 205; "State Comparisons of Education Statistics, 1969–70, 1995–96," table 37, National Center for Education Statistics, U.S. Department of Education, October 15, 1998.
11. "Average Scale Score in Reading for 4th Graders in Public Schools by Race/ Ethnicity" (table 114), and "Math Proficiency of 8th Graders, Public Schools" (table 134), both in U.S. Department of Education, *Digest of Education Statistics, 2004*.
12. "Current Expenditures Per Pupil in Average Daily Attendance in Public Elementary and Secondary Schools" (table 171), U.S. Department of Education.
13. Jim Hunt, interview with author.
14. Zeno Ponder, interview by William Finger, March 22, 1974, Southern Oral History Program, University of North Carolina at Chapel Hill.
15. Ben Stocking, "Madison County Loses Political Legend," *N&O*, November 29, 1994.
16. *Congressional Record*, October 3, 1983.
17. Carter Wrenn, interview with author, September 11, 2001.
18. John Monk, "Helms' Secret Weapon," *Charlotte Observer*, May 1, 1994.
19. Orren and Varley, *Helms-Hunt Senate Race*.

20. Rob Christensen, "Helms Touts His Clout as Washington Insider," *N&O*, October 28, 1984.
21. Orren and Varley, *Helms-Hunt Senate Race*.
22. *National Right to Life News*, September 2001.
23. James Lucier, interview with author, November 15, 1993.
24. William D. Snider, *Helms and Hunt: The North Carolina Senate Race, 1984* (Chapel Hill: University of North Carolina Press, 1985), p. 200.
25. Jim Hunt, interview with author.
26. Rob Christensen and Van Denton, "Race Ends as It Started—Negatively," *N&O*, November 2, 1992.
27. Alexander P. Lamis, *Southern Politics in the 1990s* (Baton Rouge: Louisiana State University Press, 1999), p. 97.
28. Ferrel Guillory, interview with author, December 2000.

CHAPTER 8
1. Editorial, *Viewpoint*, WRAL-TV, January 29, 1963, Southern Historical Collection, University of North Carolina at Chapel Hill.
2. U.S. Bureau of the Census, *Urban and Rural Population, 1900 to 1990*; U.S. Bureau of the Census, *Persons by Poverty Status in 1969, 1979, and 1989 by State* (CPH-L-162); and "Household Income and Poverty Rates by State, 1990 and 1999–2001," table 20, *Digest of Education Statistics*, National Center for Education Statistics, U.S. Department of Education.
3. Donald R. Matthews and James W. Prothro, *Negroes and the New Southern Politics* (New York: Harcourt, Brace & World, 1966), p. 154.
4. Henry Frye, interview with author, March 1999.
5. *Equal Protection of the Laws in North Carolina*, Report of the North Carolina Advisory Committee to the U.S. Commission on Civil Rights, 1959–63, p. 16.
6. Editorial, *Viewpoint*, WRAL-TV, April 23, 1965, Southern Historical Collection, University of North Carolina at Chapel Hill.
7. Matthews and Prothro, *Negroes and the New Southern Politics*, p. 148.
8. Jeffrey J. Crow, Paul D. Escott, and Flora J. Hatley, *A History of African Americans in North Carolina* (Raleigh: N.C. Department of Cultural Resources, Office of Archives and History, 1992), p. 149.
9. Ernest B. Furgurson, *Hard Right: The Rise of Jesse Helms* (New York and London: W. W. Norton & Company, 1986), pp. 210, 217.
10. Rob Christensen, "Jesse Helms' Race Politics," *N&O*, September 10, 1989.
11. Jesse Helms campaign literature, in possession of the author.
12. Jesse Helms fund-raising letter, February 8, 1984, in possession of the author.
13. Rob Christensen, Carol Byrne Hall, and Jim Rosen, "To Mold a Nation," *N&O*, August 26, 2001.
14. Jesse Helms, letter to author, August 25, 1989.
15. Claude Sitton, "Helms Dusts Off His Old Campaign Standby," *N&O*, June 4, 1989.
16. Furgurson, *Hard Right*, p. 230.

17. Transcript of *Larry King Live*, CNN, September 12, 1995.
18. Jesse Helms, interview with John Bason, UNC-TV, August 1999.
19. Furgurson, *Hard Right*, p. 231.
20. Pamela Varley, *Jesse Helms vs. Harvey Gantt: Race, Culture, and Campaign Strategy in the 1990 Senate Battle* (Cambridge, Mass.: Kennedy School of Government Case Program, Harvard University, 1992), p. 19.
21. Harvey Gantt, speech to state Democratic convention, June 16, 1990, Raleigh.
22. President George H. W. Bush, speech at Helms fund-raiser, June 20, 1990, Charlotte.
23. Jesse Helms rally, May 19, 1990, Goldsboro, N.C.
24. Norrie Epstein, *The Friendly Shakespeare* (New York, London and Ontario: Viking, 1993), p. 123.
25. John Drescher, "Helms Says Campaign Not Racist," *Charlotte Observer*, August 27, 1990.
26. Christensen, Hall, and Rosen, "To Mold a Nation."
27. Rob Christensen, "Helms Targets Homosexuals' Donations to Gantt," *N&O*, October 24, 1990.
28. Harvey Gantt, interview with author, October 23, 1990.
29. Alex Castellanos, interview with author, July 20, 1996.
30. Ibid.
31. Tom Ellis, interview with author, September 13, 2001.
32. Jesse Helms campaign luncheon, October 30, 1990, Kinston, N.C.
33. C. W. Palmer, interview with author, October 30, 1990, Kinston, N.C.
34. Harvey Gantt news conference, state Democratic headquarters, October 31, 1990, Raleigh.
35. Jesse Helms rally, November 5, 1990, Raleigh-Durham Airport.
36. Thurston Quinn, interview with author, July 30, 1996, Wayne County.
37. Jesse Helms at state Republican Party convention, May 31, 1991, Wilmington.
38. Howard E. Covington Jr. and Marion A. Ellis, *Terry Sanford: Politics, Progress, and Outrageous Ambitions* (Durham: Duke University Press, 1999), p. 480.
39. Carter Wrenn, interview with author, September 11, 2001.
40. Editorial, *Viewpoint*, WRAL-TV, August 13, 1971, Southern Historical Collection, University of North Carolina at Chapel Hill.
41. Jesse Helms, interview with author, December 1993.
42. Jesse Helms, interview with John Bason, p. 82.
43. Tom Ellis, interview with author.
44. Ibid.
45. Carter Wrenn, interview with author.
46. Jesse Helms, interview with John Bason.

CHAPTER 9
1. Dedication of Jesse Helms Center, April 7, 1999, Wingate, N.C.
2. Elizabeth Dole campaign luncheon, September 16, 2002, Embassy Suites, Cary.

3. Elizabeth Dole, interview with author, September 2002, Salisbury, N.C.

4. Elizabeth Dole at Christian Coalition God and Country Banquet, September 18, 2002, New Bern, N.C.

5. Lloyd Neill Strickland, a convicted cocaine dealer, was sentenced to an additional nine years and five months in U.S. Federal District Court in Fayetteville in January 1990 on charges of attempting to put out a contract for the murder of Easley.

6. Mike Easley, speech at "New Strategies for Southern Progress" conference, February 25, 2005, Chapel Hill.

7. Alexander P. Lamis, *Southern Politics in the 1990s* (Baton Rouge: Louisiana State University Press, 1999), p. 97.

8. Rich Leonard (U.S. federal bankruptcy judge), interview with author, June 9, 2003, Raleigh.

9. Gary Pearce, interview with author, May 23, 2003, Raleigh.

10. Tony Coelho, telephone interview with author, August 2003.

11. Alan Lichtman, telephone interview with author, March 2, 2004.

EPILOGUE

1. U.S. Bureau of the Census, "Median Household Income by State: 1969, 1979, 1989, and 1999," table S1, <http://www.census.gov/hhes/www/income/histinc/state/state1.html>.

2. Gavin Wright, *Old South, New South: Revolutions in the Southern Economy since the Civil War* (New York: Basic Books, 1986), p. 80; and *Digest of Education Statistics*, table 171, National Center for Education Statistics, U.S. Department of Education.

3. U.S. Bureau of the Census, "Structural and Occupancy Characteristics of Housing," table 9, *United States Census of Population, 2000*.

4. Sorien K. Schmidt and Dan Gerlach, *Working Hard Is Not Enough* (Raleigh: N.C. Justice and Community Development Center and N.C. Equity, January 2001).

5. Rob Christensen and David Raynor, "Growth Transforms State GOP's Identity," *N&O*, November 5, 1996.

6. Election returns compiled from several editions of *The Almanac of American Politics* (Washington, D.C.: National Journal).

7. Exit polling data for North Carolina 2004 elections.

Index

influence at, 123–25, 157, 161, 220, 222; Graham's leadership of, 123–26; education institute at, 242, 294; poverty center at, 302
University of North Carolina Press, 121
UNC-TV, 196, 269

Valentine, Hazel, 126
Vance, Rupert B., 122
Veto, 246
Vietnam War, 153, 171, 205, 206, 210, 212
Viewpoint, 210
Viguerie, Richard, 220, 222
Vinroot, Richard, 294, 310
Vinson, Fred, 87
Voter fraud, 3, 50, 59–61, 99; secret ballot and, 58

Wachovia Bank, 52, 96, 114, 306
Waddell, Alfred, 21–23; role in race riot, 24–25
Wadesboro, 138
Wake County, 204–5
Wake County Chitlin Club, 118
Wake Forest University, 51, 56, 164, 208
Wallace, George, 3, 179, 197, 213, 265; 1972 presidential race and, 200–201, 206
Wallace, Henry, 129–33
Wall Street, 9, 38, 68, 82
Ward's Corner, 193
Warren, Fuller, 113
Warren County, 263, 279–80
Washington, N.C., 191
Washington Post, 178
Watergate, 175–78, 241
Watson, Richard L., 60
Watt, Mel, 277, 279
Watts, A. D., 48–50, 56–57
Watts, Virginia, 78
Wayne, John, 284
Wayne County, 43, 278
Webbley, 63, 100

Weld, William, 284
Weldon, 14
Webb, James L., 63
Webb, Yates, 49, 63
Weeksville, 193
Wendell, 141
Whitcover, Jules, 201
White, Cora, 19, 30
White, George, 253, 262, 308, 315; in Congress, 12–14, 19, 21; retires from Congress, 30–31
White Citizens Councils, 156
White Patriots of North Carolina, 163
Whiteville, 193
Wicker, Dennis, 293
Wicker, Tom, 152
Wiggins, Ella May, 72–73, 75
Wilder, Douglas, 262, 277
Williams, Kenneth R., 265
Williamston, 193
Wilmington, 9, 32, 92, 142, 244; race riot in, 23–27
Wilmington Daily Record, 17–18
Wilmington Ten, 244
Wilson, 14, 50, 239, 265
Wilson, Henry Hall, 207
Wilson, Woodrow, 15, 31, 41, 47, 52, 57, 199, 200
Wilson County, 236, 240, 256
Winborne, Pretlow, 194
Windsor, 14, 193
Windsor, Bob, 250
Windsor Ledger, 44
Winfield, Alvin, 208
Wingate College, 208, 284
Winston, Francis, 33
Winston, Robert, 33
Winston-Salem, 42, 51–52, 91, 97, 132, 162, 165, 168, 240, 265
Winston-Salem Journal, 151
Winston-Salem State University, 265
Winter, William, 199, 241
"Wisconsin of the South," 3
Wolfe, Thomas, 60
Women's rights, 4, 180; suffrage move-